Origins of the Tarot

34 The TAROT is an epitomized representation of NONDUAL KNOWLEDGE. It is EQUALLY OBJECTIVE & SUBJECTIVE IN RELEVANCE. It ADDRESSES BOTH PHYSICAL & PSYCHOLOGICAL WORLDS. It posits that OUTER COSMOLOGY and INNER SPIRITUALITY ARE WEDDED REALMS THROUGH WHICH TRUTH IS REALIZED AS BEAUTY and GOODNESS. EXISTENCE, CONSCIOUSNESS, & BLISS are neither materially reducible NOR ego-determined. RATHER, BODY (existence) and MIND (CONSCIOUSNESS) ALWAYS ARISE IN UNITY (BLISS).

Origins of the Tarot

Cosmic Evolution and the Principles of Immortality

Dai Léon

Frog Books
Berkeley, California

Published by Frog Books
Frog Books' publications are distributed by
North Atlantic Books
P.O. Box 12327
Berkeley, California 94712

Cover design by Maxine Ressler
Book design by Brad Greene

Este & Visconti Triumphs courtesy of the Beinecke Rare Book and Manuscript Library, Yale University
Charles VI Triumphs courtesy of the Bibliothèque nationale de France
Woodblock Triumphs courtesy of the Budapest Museum of Fine Arts
Zen Ox Herding Pictures derived from Zen Monk Shubun's copy of Sung Dynasty Chan Master Kaku-an's original pictures, the former preserved at Shokokuji, Kyoto

Printed in the United States of America

Origins of the Tarot: Cosmic Evolution and the Principles of Immortality is sponsored by the Society for the Study of Native Arts and Sciences, a nonprofit educational corporation whose goals are to develop an educational and cross-cultural perspective linking various scientific, social, and artistic fields; to nurture a holistic view of arts, sciences, humanities, and healing; and to publish and distribute literature on the relationship of mind, body, and nature.

North Atlantic Books' publications are available through most bookstores. For further information, visit our Web site at www.northatlanticbooks.com or call 800-733-3000.

Library of Congress Cataloging-in-Publication Data

Léon, Dai, 1957–
Origins of the tarot : cosmic evolution and the principles of immortality / Dai Léon.
p. cm.
Includes bibliographical references and index.
ISBN 978-1-58394-261-1 (trade pbk.)
1. Tarot. I. Title.
BF1879.T2L433 2008
133.3'2424—dc22

2008042748

1 2 3 4 5 6 7 8 9 UNITED 14 13 12 11 10 09

The First is richness per se, and there is no greater richness. And proof of this is its unity, for its unity is not dispersed in it; on the contrary, its unity is pure, because it is simple in the maximum of simplicity.

However, if anyone wants to know that the First is this richness, let him turn his mind toward composite things and inquire about them with an investigative inquiry. For he will find every composite diminished, indeed, needing either another or the things of which it is composed. However, the simple thing, the One that is Goodness, is one; its unity is its goodness; and its goodness is one and the same thing.

Therefore, that thing is the greater richness that overflows without an effluence coming to be upon it in any manner. However, the other intelligible or corporeal things are not rich per se; on the contrary, they need the true One over-flowing upon them perfections and all good things.

—*Liber de causis,* chapter 20

REQUESTING LIBERATION

FOOL

From Magician to Hermit to Devil to Fool, each Questor treads the path alone while compensating for all others; so is founded Nature's sodality of Divine Idiots.

MAGICIAN

Already mature, self-reliant, self-disciplined, carefully aware, and observed by others, the young Magician is prepared for alchemy.

Table of Contents

Dedicated to

GIA-FU FENG

1919–1985

~

Acknowledgments

First, homage must be paid to the sages and saints whose teachings of spiritual hierarchy nurtured the roots of Western esoteric tradition: Siddhartha Gautama, Heraclitus, Plotinus, Pseudo-Dionysius the Areopagite, Ibn ʿArabi, to name a few. The great wisdom traditions have been transmitted to the present day through the conscious sacrifice of untold hearts.

From earliest times, Western esotericism has been intimately influenced by the East. This book was made possible by an East-West movement that spanned the twentieth century. Tremendous philosophers of that movement, including Traditionalist scholars in the circles of Ananda Coomaraswamy and Seyyed Hossein Nasr, have incisively criticized modern-day disregard for the great traditions. Their works have served as the finest of metaphysical sources used by this arguably postmodern resurrection of Tarot origins. René Guénon's *Initiation and Spiritual Realization* serves as a superb introduction to the *Sophia Perennis*. Peter Masefield's lucid investigation into the Tenfold Noble Path of Pali Buddhism also deserves special mention.

That both the inner way of spiritual transcendence and the outer way of cosmic manifestation compose in truth a nondual whole has been most recently clarified by transpersonal and integral authors such as Ken Wilber. The modern corpus of perennial wisdom reminds twenty-first-century thinkers of the necessity for actual contemplative practice regarding verification of how Unity of Being is wedded to the Myriad Becoming.

The deepest bow of gratitude is given to Gia-fu Feng, a legendary Buddhist-Taoist Adept who in his final seven years dynamically transmitted to the author all that matters.

Gracious thanks to Paul Schroeder and Philip Smith for editorial assistance. And to the Léons in name and heart, the brightest of blessings and much, much love are extended beyond the scope of words.

Author's Note

Conveying a cosmological view of Unity emanating as the World, along with a metaphysical view of Heart-Mind returning to that Unity, has been the difficult work of spiritual philosophers since the age of Heraclitus, Lao Tzu, and Siddhartha. The present text may seem at times dense in its terminology and breadth of coverage; however, taken as a whole, readers will find considerable clarification of the esoteric core of Indo-European culture.

The Tarot, Western esotericism, and this book are about *life-giving* hierarchy. Hierarchy has become, at the dawn of the twenty-first century, a most provocative concept. This book attempts to rectify the beautiful meaning of the word (from the Greek: *hieros*, "filled with the divine, holy" and *arkhein*, "to rule") with the justifiably guarded view many readers will have concerning dominance, control, authority, and elitist claims. The root meaning of *rule* is "to direct in a straight line." If we abandon our *conscious* ability to move in such a way, we will practically leave all governance to the heartless progression of technological advancement.

Is Beauty, Goodness, or Truth ever straightforward? The Tarot deck may be topologically imagined as a spiral of nested spheres: each image represents a cyclical domain proceeding straightforwardly into the next. In this most gracious of cosmologies we discover a

Rule of Law, which completely includes an infinite variety of modulations upon energy and space allowing for our innate freedom and diversity.

Briefly, regarding references: practically every paragraph in this book warrants footnotes. Because the text was not written primarily for an academic audience, footnotes have been replaced by a bibliographical list of chapter references at the end of the book. Western esotericism is a deep well and this book is but a simple cup. Many readers may find themselves thirsting for more. The referenced works will prove to be a quenching source of knowledge.

MOLDED LUMINOSITY

EMPRESS

The potentialities of the world are revealed and made accessible through the natural royalty of the Empress, governess of earth.

POPESS

The Popess unveils the grace inherent to feminine nature, felt as an offering of truly essential nourishment.

One

Morning in the Window

Wherein We Are Given Important Clues . . .

In this age of postmodern uncertainty, foundational studies of *wisdom* need to be established. Civilization in the twenty-first century cannot afford to abandon the great wisdom traditions of the past five thousand years. This book elucidates the metaphysical history of one such tradition. It is a history close to the heart of humanity. It is a history of vitally essential Principles; a history based in the Just, or what the ancient Greeks called *Diké* – the radiant "Way." It is a history of *nondual emanation:* the Way emanating as the World. It is a history of wisdom ultimately summarized in the form of twenty-two Image-Exemplars, popularly known as the Tarot.

The Tarot is a visual explication of *spiritual ascension* affirmed perennially in both Western and Eastern cultures. Such ascension traditionally involves a retracing back to the Source of the universe and consciousness. Paradoxically, that Great Return simultaneously embodies integral stages of evolution, realizing the Source through its own Destiny. Through the ages, it has been understood that the *One* as both universal source and destiny – whether known as God, Allah, Brahman, Buddha Mind, or Tao – constantly manifests reality by descending through emanated domains embodying immortal principles.

For most of European history, this classical cosmology has been elegantly imagined as a nested series of ten spheres of principle-realization. These spheres can be cognized as domains and attributes of universal existence forming a Great Chain of Being. In this worldview, the One is felt and known by the human Heart through a creative hierarchy encompassing a continuous process visualized as cosmic descending and conscious ascent. The Tarot was created as an epitomized representation of that vertical hierarchy, addressing in particular the corresponding horizontal realm of humanity's psychosocial existence.

Throughout this book, we will view examples of *hierarchical emergence*. The Great Chain of Being will be interpreted through ten great universal Principles. We will come to see how it is that each principle, attribute, or stage of the One emerges from those preceding it. We will explore emergent hierarchies as developed amongst Kabbalists, ecstatic Sufi dervishes, and heretically powerful Templar Knights. Moving east, we will discover the role that Genghis Khan and his Mongol lords filled in fusing Buddhist and Taoist hierarchical realization with Islamic Sufi mysticism. The Eastern Orthodox Church of Byzantium will appear prominently in our studies. In addition, the yet-older Greek metaphysics of Neoplatonic philosophers will shed a clear and bright light upon genuine origins and meanings of the Tarot Arcana's esoteric hierarchy. We will gain an appreciation for the nondual concept of *gnosis* and its appropriation by dualistic Gnostic sects. We will have cause to explore exotic tantric practices of yogic alchemy. Fusing it all together will be a glorious tapestry of Wisdom-myths revealing the origins of Indo-European spirituality and immortal realization. At the end of our study, we will review Tarot principles through a lens of modern thought, including recent advancements in scientific theory.

Before we begin our investigation into the origins of the medieval Triumphs, as they used to be called, a word must be said about the *occult* history of the cards.

As we will shortly see, the Tarot cards made their first European appearance in Italy during the mid-fifteenth century. It was not until the 1780s, over three hundred and fifty years later, that Antoine Court de Gébelin published a theory suggesting the Tarot pack originated in ancient Egypt. Soon after, a French fortune-teller known as "Etteilla" created a variant Tarot deck fashioned under concepts contained in *The Book of Thoth* (Thoth being an Egyptian god often associated with the Greek god Hermes). It was at this time that the occult age of Tarot *cartomancy* (the art of fortune-telling with cards) commenced. France in the following century served as fertile ground for what is now known as the modern occult movement. French variants of the original Tarot decks were imparted great significance by students of the occult. What is of primary interest to our current study is that there are *no* documented Tarot references to occult history or meaning (be it Gypsy, Egyptian, Italian, etc.) before the eighteenth century.

Naturally settled at the beginning of the process, the Questor dwells at a station where change comes most easily.

Few people in the Western world have not heard of or seen reference to the Tarot cards. Invariably, the pack is associated with occult practices. The history of what is commonly associated with the "occult" is long and varied. It encompasses tribal rituals, magical cults, mythical beliefs, inscrutable revelations, fantastic claims of divinity, orgies, drug taking, and dangerous experiments in alchemy. It is important we distinguish between occult beliefs and forms of *spiritual esotericism* as they exist in the *great traditions* (i.e., Hinduism, Buddhism, Taoism, Judaism, Neoplatonism, Christianity, Islam, etc.). We will reserve later chapters for much of our discussion regarding this. For now, the following may suffice to help clarify these terms.

In every great spiritual tradition, there are *exo*-teric or *outward* forms of representing communion and, ultimately, unity with the Divine, and there are *eso*-teric or *inward* forms of representing such. Understanding *esoteric transmissions* or conveyances (meaning "communicative logic involving intuition and spiritual awareness") requires one to be actually undergoing processes of spiritual realization. This most effectively occurs via initiation in, and conscious self-authentication of, teachings and practices transmitted by those who have already trod the path of such realization.

With comfortable authority, the Empress eases her physical domain so that the commons' potential may begin to be realized through proper initiation.

Occult teachers claim to know unique ways of power hidden from or within the great traditions. The word *occult* literally means "concealed." In our definition (with sincere apologies to readers who identify with the occult under a broad definition while genuinely adhering to a nondual worldview), occultists view the world in dualistic terms – light versus dark, true self escaping a fallen world, "control or be controlled." Dualism sets a stage for belief in separative, egoic power. This readily leads to acts of dishonest concealment and claims that secrets of the supernatural are not comprehensible to common humanity, but are to occultists. An occultist will purposefully remain egoically separate or spiritually alienated in order to build powers hidden from others. This tends to reinforce schizophrenia, not holistic love. *Spiritual* psychology needs to develop as *integral* psychology if it is not to become sick or unconsciously demonic. Ego-mind identifying with the occult readily believes it is greater, smarter, and beyond the yogis, saints, and sages who know otherwise.

Authentic esoteric traditions require self-surrender and devotion to a spiritual heritage. Esoteric knowledge is not concealed per se, for it arises through a view of the world as it essentially, vitally, and really *is.* Anyone may see this, if she simply opens her eyes and looks beyond the view of her own self. Looking *beyond the self,* however, requires surrendering attention to a greater One. Culture, community, and law are the traditional agencies for abetting this. As an example, a genuine Hermeticist will directly perceive into and reasonably translate an *internal* alchemical manual. It will make immediate sense in the context of an authentic practice. A hermetic occultist, on the other hand, after laborious troubles will construe meanings in a confused manner, believing that he is deciphering arcane analogies that cannot be clearly stated for "mysterious" reasons (as if true Mystery does not embrace, and grow from, actual Reason). Even Isaac Newton, under the consumption of mercury, fell into this trap.

The ego perceives its own confusion; the presence of a larger whole cannot be avoided – it is best to allow grace to show the direction.

Esoteric practice, communion, and study are built upon historical transmission and continuity. To the unstudied, that continuity may well seem unknowably mysterious. It was only in the latter half of the twentieth century, for instance, that developmental stages of spiritual realization in Sufi tradition were recognized by Western scholars of religion. It is now understood that the wisdom ways of Sufism have been coherently and continuously passed down or authenticated from masters to disciples over the centuries. That there may appear to be discontinuities in the form and content of spiritual knowledge transmitted generation by generation in any particular tradition does not mean esoteric teachings are irrational or non-verifiable. Such teachings develop and change in complex but explicable ways. On the other hand, occult doctrines inevitably contain nonsensical gaps in their heritages.

Importantly, independent occult revelations and techniques of power do not stand in a context of nondual hierarchical emergence, which is found in all of the great spiritual traditions. How both cosmos and consciousness emerge and evolve through *hierarchy* (the Greek root of which means "spiritual rule") is what the medieval Tarot and this book address. That which is Independent ultimately must submit to that which is Universal.

In the following chapters, it will become clear that the original Tarot represented a ten-stage procession of enlightenment (closely paralleling the famous ten-stage Zen Oxherding Quest). This procession involved realization of beauty, goodness, and truth through the intelligent insight that humankind naturally exists in Unity with the World. Sages and saints often had to risk their lives in order to make public these stages of spiritual hierarchy. It has historically proven to be most challenging for a *Transcendental* (a heroic saint or sage who has entered the realm beyond Death) on the path of *immortality* to maintain an ordinary public persona. In the Tarot, the post-Death Devil/Tower stations (seventh out of ten stages) of spiritual development represent the realization that transformative power

The Questor's journey will surely meet with dangers; motivation dwells in the how of resolution and progression.

inheres in a flux of chaos. In dualistic religions this awareness or mindfulness has been frequently and mistakenly equated with "demonic" occult practices. That has led to extensive persecution of truly enlightened (even if not fully so) individuals.

Although there exists between the communities of occultism and esotericism some common ground (for instance, great saints have a general tendency to *hide their powers*), the camps have always been, in fact, widely divergent. The mountain between them can succinctly be called *rationality.* On the one side of rational maturity resides the occultist. The occultist regresses from rationality in order to make claim to a mythical ground of hidden secrets from an era of "golden perfection." This era, it is alleged, far surpassed anything known to the living traditions of philosophy and spirituality. Occultists do not rationally acknowledge the application of metaphorical myths to a universal Quest. They thus mistake pre-rational magical/mythical states of mind for intuitive/transpersonal states that emerge out of mature rationality. In later chapters, we will cover these cultural, sociological, and psychological stages of development in detail. We will see how the Tarot Triumphs sprouted, developed, and flowered from a bed rich in intelligence – far from any occult tendency to avoid the philosophy, theosophy, and metaphysics of the day.

On the other side of the mountain of rationality dwells the esotericist, deeply involved with discussing perennial wisdom that appears as transpersonal awareness and brightly transparent clarity. Esotericists make no claim of exclusive spiritual possession, for they recognize an essentially natural hierarchy of spiritual realization. They do not emerge or naturally progress into previously unrealized states with the intention of controlling those "below" them. They have no need to obscure their newfound being, knowledge, or bliss, for it is evident that only he who has emerged on a comparable level will be able to existentially understand their own realizations. On the other hand, anyone with a sincere interest may comparatively study authentic esotericism by regarding the great traditions of spiritual realization. This obviates any need for occult belief or practice. (The practice of shrouding one's charisma, spiritual radiance, or beauty so as not to be accosted or harmed is a different matter altogether. Psychic obfuscation and manipulative "cloaking" cannot be compared to enlightened diplomacy and intelligent tact.)

Peace must be valued for growth to be sustained until fruition; the concentrated passions of polar form are needed to nourish the original seed.

Let us now examine known facts regarding the original Tarot cards. We find our first references to the Tarot appearing in Italy during the fifteenth century. The word Tarot is a French derivation of the Italian word *Tarocco*. The earliest recorded use of the word occurred in 1516. Up until that time, the cards were called *Trionfi*, which translates into English as *Triumphs* (later shortened to "Trumps"). For the past century, the twenty-two Triumphs of the Tarot deck have generally been referred to as the Major Arcana.

The obsolete meaning of a Triumph is:

> A public celebration or spectacular pageant; [Middle English *triomfen* from Old French *triumpher* from Latin *triumphare* from *triumphus* (probably via Etruscan) from Greek *thriambos:* hymn to Dionysus].

By the end of this book, we will have discovered a profound continuity between the initiatory Way of Dionysus and the Quest portrayed in the Tarot Triumphs.

That the Tarot cards were, and still are in some European countries, used in trick-taking card games as a trump suit (a suit that wins over any other) is well documented. Playing cards have been popularly known since the Islamic Mameluke era of Egypt. The Mamelukes were originally a military caste formed via training and educating Turkish slaves. The caste eventually ruled Egypt between 1250 and 1517, remaining powerful until the early nineteenth century. The standard deck of playing cards found its way into Italy during the fourteenth century. A thorough review of the history of playing cards leads one to the conclusion that the Trionfi came into

The gift of intelligent and Tempered alchemy is extrication from the problematic dilemma of dualism; so begins the secret channeling of vital life.

being conceptually distinct from, but culturally and practically associated with, the set of cards commonly used in game-playing.

Although there are a few odd exceptions, every known Tarot deck includes a standard deck of four card suits, each suit numbering Ace through 10 and including either three or four court cards: King, Queen, Knight, and Page. The earliest European suit-system was Italian, comprising Cups, Swords, Coins, and Batons. These, in turn, were derived from the Islamic suits of Cups, Swords, Coins, and Polo-sticks. Polo was an important game in the Islamic world but was unknown in Italy; thus, the suit-symbol was changed to the more understandable "Baton." The regular playing deck did not change its suits to the modern-day version of Hearts, Diamonds, Spades, and Clubs until 1470, an innovation of French card makers.

Tarot suit cards are popularly called the Minor Arcana. Along with these, the Tarot deck contains twenty-two Major Arcana cards numbered in a meaningful sequence. Neither the twenty-two Triumphs nor fifty-six suit cards were referred to as "Arcana" in the Tarot's pre-occult period. The term *arcanum* was given to each card by the famous nineteenth-century occultist Papus. He argued that the suit cards should be used along with the twenty-two archetypal cards for divination purposes. Each card, he declared, held a secret to the *arcane* (from *arca,* meaning "chest"). Renderings from three sets of the earliest painted court deck of Triumphs, the Cary-Yale Visconti, Este, and Charles VI decks, can be found facing the chapter heads of this book. Also found on many pages are digitally processed, redrawn Triumphs from the earliest set of Tarot woodblock prints. The original sheets of these prints resided for many years in the Museum of Fine Arts in Budapest. Some of the sheets were acquired by the Metropolitan Museum of Art in New York as part of the Brisbane Dick Collection. Often called the "Dick sheets," this deck will be referred to in our discussion as the "Metropolitan deck."

We find Trionfi cards first mentioned in 1442, in the account books of the D'Este court of Ferrara. The earliest recorded description naming the whole set of twenty-two cards is found in an anonymous sermon against gaming (*Sermones de ludo cum aliis*, or "Sermons of games with dice") written by a Dominican friar. Its manuscript has been dated to between 1450 and 1480. Published by Robert Steele in 1900, it now resides at the Cincinnati Art Museum. The twenty-two cards mentioned in the Friar's description were listed in a precise order. We will return to the Steele manuscript when we reconstruct the original sequence of the Tarot deck.

Love is the vision of reality that can only be spoken in truth; chaste Love, real Love, continuously develops through the wholeness of Union.

Given that the Major Arcana set of cards was developed separately from the Minor, a question arises: Who invented the twenty-two cards of the Tarot, and to what purpose? It is known that the Triumphs fulfill the requirements of a trump suit in card games involving trick-taking. If, in fact, the Triumphs embody a coherent, meaningful system beyond that, how is it that they have always been joined by the regular playing deck?

Every early mention of the Tarot pack comes from Italy, and all of the oldest decks contain a suit-system identical to the Italian system. Unlike the Spanish and French, Italians retained the curved swords of the Islamic suits. There is little doubt that known Tarot cards were first printed in Italy. However, they evidently were designed in conjunction with the Islamic world. It is the thesis of this book that the twenty-two images conceptually originated in Sufi circles trained in Greek studies. An unknown Eastern Christian–influenced artist then portrayed those concepts via playing cards similar, if not identical, to the iconic images shown in this book. Those cards emerged out of a merchant-class society focused on understanding and influencing the forces of Fate and Fortune. That multicultural class included Italian cosmopolitans, Sufi sages, and Byzantine literati. We will see that Venice, Alexandria, and Constantinople were primary urban centers involved with creating the original Tarot cards, concepts, and symbols.

The author is unaware of any treatise before this that has put forth the above statements regarding Tarot origins. That the standard

Fate is master, the Questor is servant; maintaining humility at the feet of the Master is the spiritual charge of the Questor.

pack of suit cards was invented in the Islamic world and entered into Europe via Italy is well attested. That the twenty-two cards referred to explicitly as the Trionfi made their first known appearance in Italy during the first half of the fifteenth century cannot be doubted. That the Eastern Christian world of Byzantium, masters of the art of spiritual and Greek iconography, culturally merged with the Islamic Ottoman Empire in the years preceding the Tarot's creation is familiar history. That Islamic metaphysics was steeped in Neoplatonic philosophy has been known in the West since medieval times. That the coherent, hierarchical worldview represented by the Trionfi was transferred to Italy through the Islamic world under Greek influence, both Orthodox (be that Greek or Coptic) and Neoplatonic, is an obvious theory worth consideration.

However, remarkably enough, this theory has never been seriously forwarded by Tarot occultists, card historians, or scholars of comparative religion. While Sufi influences have been mentioned in the odd book, the merging of Eastern Christian and Sufi metaphysics and the transference of resultant cosmological worldviews into Italy via Venice (and subsequently Ferrara) in the form of Tarot Triumphs has not previously been examined. It may not be an overstatement to say that in the original Tarot we have found the essential seed that gloriously grew into a tree of Renaissance knowledge and a cornucopia of enlightenment: truly, the principles of immortality.

In every branch of our inquiry into the real origins of the Tarot, we will discover evidence pointing to a trunk grafting Eastern Christian and Sufi metaphysics. A trunk rooted in the ground of Neoplatonism and, via Central Asia, Tantric Alchemy. We will examine the source of Kabbalism (esoteric Jewish tradition), and come to appreciate how universal the Neoplatonic tree of knowledge truly was. Although it at times has been conjectured that the Tarot was originally derived from the Kabbalah, both Judaic and Islamic scholars maintain that Sufi understanding of spiritual hierarchy was prior to and not derived from Judaic studies. We will peer deeply into the times and places where the metaphysical fields of these communities crossed, resonated, and resolved in a Triumphant agency. Toward the end of our quest for the Tarot *Grail*, a core foundation of ancient Greek and Indian spiritual realization will be revealed.

Rest within your primal nature, your vital instincts; ally yourself with the animal kingdom, respect all sentient beings, and surrender only to the Force of Life.

All of the documented Tarot references between 1450 and 1500 directly state or clearly imply a gaming use for the pack of cards. Many references to the deck in the sixteenth century also indicate it was used for entertainment. Tarot as a game was more popular in France than chess in the seventeenth century. Yet despite this popularity, there is a paucity of French references to the actual pictures and symbols of the cards. In Italy, we find interest in the subject of the Trumps to be much higher. A number of social games were played, generally involving women, having as their basis identification of individual players and court figures with particular cards. A reading of verse associated with the meaning of each card was an important element of such play.

Thus, we have examples of the Trionfi subjects being associated with court personas, with multiple Triumphs being composed via verse into "readings" that elevated the personal/mundane into the transpersonal/divine. Nevertheless, we do not find an explicit example of the Triumphs being used for the purpose of *divination* as a tool of *fortune-telling*. Considering that divination was branded by the Church in the late fifteenth century as the worst form of magic, incurring the severest of punishments, it is not surprising that court patrons did not document such use. In any case, the Trionfi were evidently used by educated women in the context of psycho-social play creating and mimicking archetypal personas.

Identification with the Triumphs led to an understanding of spiritual hierarchy within European courts influenced by Greek and Sufi thought. In later chapters, light will be shed upon an esoteric understanding of cosmological emanation referred to by Sufis through the Names and Attributes of Allah. Contemplative Sufis identified their stages of spiritual development with these Attributes.

To go high, you must first go low; the meek shall inherit, the clever shall lose – do not be deceived by surface appearances.

In the West, emanation theory was first developed by Platonists. Concomitantly in the East, a version of it was elaborated rigorously by Buddhist academies. It was broadly popularized by Gnostics, who bridged Near East Christians and Central Asian Buddhists. As briefly mentioned earlier, it held that the cosmos began in a unified, non-differentiated state and proceeded to manifest as a corporeal, solid world. The stages of that cosmological process were viewed to be humanly discernible.

Neoplatonic and Gnostic teachers differed as to how the process of cosmic emanation occurred. Was its eventuation good or bad? How did time factor in? Did cosmic manifestation only happen during a limited period of creation, or was it ongoing? In addition, perhaps most importantly, was the original *cosmic* state really the original *divine* state? Alternatively, was there a totally non-cosmic God who created an initial cosmic being-state – call it a lesser god or *demiurge* – which then actually emanated the cosmos? All of this must be left to later examination. We will do our best not to be bogged down in the many possible theological, speculative positions and philosophical arguments.

Sufi teaching holds to the position that all is Allah. Every thing and every relationship exists because of Allah's Emanation. The world *is* Allah, and every essential aspect of it can be understood through Allah's Names and Attributes. The Divine Names invoke images. However, depicting the Divine via anthropomorphic imagery has always been heretical in Islamic religion.

In Greek Byzantine tradition, on the other hand, creation of sacred icons was highly respected. We will see that any form of divination implemented by the medieval Tarot would have had as its basis an understanding that the Divine One, humankind, and the world are naturally arising from the same source, proceeding upon the same path, and realizing the same destiny. Such Source, Path, Destiny, and World *are* in fact the Divine One. This implies, of course, that so inherently is Humankind.

The soul of humanity draws on the purity of synchronicities, the concordance of organisms, and the assurance of tools.

The Tarot Arcana visually represent the unity of God, World, and Human. Through these images of unification one can thus *divine* the meaning of life and the direction of truth at any given time. This sheds a whole different light on the art and meaning of divination and the Trionfi as they were meant to be *read* or *played*. It is this fundamental aspect of medieval wisdom that both playing-card historians and tarot occultists appear unaware of; thus are they at a loss to place the Image-Exemplars in their appropriate historical context.

For now, we need only consider that because the Triumphs represent hierarchical and transmutative states, to identify with any given combination of cards is to determine a set of relations that is never stagnant. Similar in nature to the Chinese *I Ching* (an ancient system of divination found in the *Book of Changes*), the Triumphs depict a constantly changing reality. Like a dream of the gods, the Tarot lends itself to a game of shifting meaning, with varying degrees of import and profundity arising from the *divining* of (in the sense of "making divine") those meanings. This is a far more sophisticated method of divination than looking at cave pools, tea leaves, or positions of the planets in the zodiac (all being potentially valid ways of instilling psychic awareness).

The key to understanding the Tarot is realizing the spiritual hierarchy of the Triumphs. That key is found in the cosmological process of evolutionary development that the Tarot hierarchy represents. The key is turned by realizing the universality of those stages through alchemical union of one's vital life and essential nature. The lock is our conscious self-authentication of such stages as we realize the truth of nature, relationship, and the Heart. But let us pull back for a little while longer, lest we get ahead of ourselves. It is time to inquire into the earliest order of the Triumphs.

All of the surviving packs of Tarot cards based on Italian suits but produced in another country have their names and numbers printed on them. Early painted Italian packs, on the contrary, never had their names printed on them. It was not until the development

Through settled mind and healthy body, awareness evolves via a cosmic cycle of six stages, returning to the Keep of universal consciousness, where in becomes out, low becomes high, and the edge becomes the center.

of eighteenth-century Italian decks based on the French *Tarot de Marseille* pack that names were printed on Italian cards.

Of the fifteenth-century cards in existence, two packs are numbered: the Metropolitan/Budapest deck seen reconstructed in this book and the Rosenwald Collection deck residing in Washington's National Gallery of Art. Both are woodblock sheets and are most difficult to precisely date. The Metropolitan deck is commonly dated circa 1500. Consequently, its images are given less attention than other decks of the fifteenth century in regards to origination.

Two other decks from this time had numerals written on them after their printing. It is also quite possible that the Metropolitan Triumphs were copied from an original deck that had numbers later drawn on them. There also exist seven numbered Triumphs from a sixteenth-century pack housed in the Leber Collection of the Bibliothèque Municipale of Rouen, France. The Rouen cards are numbered with Arabic numerals.

There remain extant several poems composed prior to 1600 detailing people of the court playing *Tarocchi* (the early name for Tarot card games) by assuming and imparting the cards' personas. From these, historians have made lists of the Triumphs' names. Two of the poems list the Triumphs in an order. The earlier of the two dates from around 1550, the later from the second half of the same century. These are generally referred to respectively as the Bertoni and Susio poems. The Trionfi were also listed in a manuscript from the late sixteenth century by Tomaso Garzoni entitled *Piazza Universale.*

This quick synopsis leaves us aware that there exist only a handful of early attestations informing us of the names and order of the original Tarot cards. Three out of our four early literary references, including by far the oldest – the previously mentioned Steele manuscript – list orders that correlate with the Metropolitan deck. The Rosenwald deck is evidently aligned with several nonstandard decks appearing later in time, about which we will not go into detail. The order of those decks is not affirmed by any early literary source. It is very possible, if not likely given the evidence, that the Rosenwald deck was in fact created in the sixteenth century.

Cutting to the chase, we have three possible original orders, listed earliest first:

	Steele MS	*Metro & Rouen*	*Bertoni & Garzoni*
21.	World	World	World
20.	Justice	Justice	Justice
19.	Angel	Angel	Angel
18.	Sun	Sun	Sun
17.	Moon	Moon	Moon
16.	Star	Star	Star
15.	Tower	Tower	Tower
14.	Devil	Devil	Devil
13.	Death	Death	Death
12.	Hanged Man	Hanged Man	Hanged Man
11.	Hunchback	Hunchback	Hunchback
10.	Wheel	Wheel	Wheel
9.	Fortitude	Fortitude	Fortitude
8.	Chariot	Love	Love
7.	Love	Chariot	Chariot
6.	Temperance	Temperance	Temperance
5.	Pope	Pope	Pope
4.	Popess	Emperor	Popess
3.	Emperor	Popess	Emperor
2.	Empress	Empress	Empress
1.	Magician	Magician	Magician

The Fool is unnumbered in all.

The only difference between these orders involves the placement of the Love/Chariot pair and the Popess/Emperor pair. For reasons that will be argued later, the Triumphs in this book have been presented with the Popess preceding the Emperor as in the Metropolitan order, and Love preceding the Chariot as in the Steele order.

The true heart, the good soul, the settler in the land of beauty, radiates simplicity in a daily life of natural exhaustion; do not confuse this with a friction-filled effort to materialize immortality.

Nourished by the psyche, complex autonomies form – projected and possessed beyond the Questor's alchemy as psychophysical demons, or extended and seduced within such alchemy as soulful daimons.

As for the Anglicized Italian names of these cards:

The Magician early on was called *Il Bagatella.* Any direct translation of this is speculative. Modern Italian usage identifies it with the selling of trivial goods. Attempts have been made to derive the name from an Italian word for *stick,* giving us "wand user" and consequently "Magician." However, upon consideration of the early images of the *Bagatella,* one readily comes to the conclusion that he is a mountebank of sorts, a hawker of games including the classic shell game and other games involving money and slight of hand. We will retain the title of Magician, for in modern parlance that implies formidable talent in a variety of associated skills, including sleight of hand, hawking, mimicry, risk-taking, gambling, hypnosis, and entertainment. These attributes have similarities to those found in the traditional court Fool, who risked much to gain the attention of rulers and courtiers while informing and manipulating their minds in ways likely beyond them. Combined with skills in martial and virile arts, this pan-cultural *trickster* archetype influenced the creation of massively popular modern heroes such as Robin Hood, Zorro, Don Juan, James Bond, et al.

Except for the Tower and Magician, all of the names are direct translations from the Italian names and are agreed upon in early sources. The Wheel was commonly recognized as the Wheel of Fortune and named thusly in later decks. The Tower is originally referred to by various titles, most commonly Thunderbolt, Fire, and House of either the Devil or God, with Pluto (Greek, "Hades") being a favorite combination of the two. It literally translates as "Arrow" in the Steele manuscript. We retain the name Tower because it is so widely recognized as such. More will be said about this when we unearth the symbolic meanings of both the Devil and his House from ancient mythology and medieval *theosophy* (literally, "god-wisdom").

The Hunchback, a direct translation from the early sources, also went under the guise of Father Time (a persona often imaged in history with an hourglass in hand, figuratively similar to the Hermit and his lantern) but became widely known after the *Tarot de Marseille* as the Hermit. The Metropolitan's Hunchback visually integrates these related personas. It includes a spinal hump and a staff of life, both having substantial psychophysical connotation in terms of a Hermit's spiritual practice. Given the intuitive resonance between Hunchback and Hermit and the iconography of the Metropolitan Triumph, we have elected to hold to the latter name as an accurate interpretation of the Triumph's original signification.

The uniting of heaven and earth is the work of Yoga: Hatha-yoga (physical), Karma-yoga (emotional), Mantra-yoga (mental), Bhakti-yoga (devotional), Jnana-yoga (ancestral), Raja-yoga (radical), and Tantra-yoga (alchemical).

The Love Triumph is generally referred to as the Lovers, for obvious reasons, and the latter designation is at times used in our text. It is worth noting, however, that "Lovers" puts emphasis on the *mundane personas* represented in the image, while "Love" is more inclusive of *transcendent Eros* and his arrow, completing the circuit of vision and communion that the Triumph represents. More will be said about this in conjunction with the placement of Love before the Chariot.

In almost all decks early and late, when the Magician is counted as card one, Death falls as card thirteen. Several of the earlier decks, however, begin numbering with the second-lowest Triumph. In both our earliest order of cards and the later order delineated below, the World is the last card.

A third common order (the Rosenwald and nonstandard decks represent our second order) to the cards was developed in the sixteenth century, as attested by the Susio poem. This is the order found in the French *Tarot de Marseille,* which became the base deck from which later decks were largely derived. Significantly, the three "virtue" cards are allotted different positions in this modern hierarchy. Temperance is placed between Death and the Devil. Justice is dropped to either the position just after Lovers or one step higher, just after Chariot. Fortitude either remains after the Chariot or advances to the station after the Wheel of Fortune.

The set residing by the set does not involve duration, for the essence of duration is flow; it is such flux, such continuity of transition, such change, that constitutes Reality.

The position of Justice appears to mark the most significant difference between the varying orders. Only in the original orders was it elevated to the highest rank between the Angel and World Triumphs. It is of significance that Venetian paintings from the early fifteenth century depict Justice with the Archangels Michael and Gabriel on either side of her. In paintings from other Latin Christian cities, it is Jesus who serves to mete out justice in accordance to the great angels' judgments. Venice was singular in its cultural focus upon the traditional Greek archetype of Justice, supplanting Jesus in this role, which indeed originally belonged solely to Justice herself.

Justice was closely identified with the *Throne* of Allah in Sufi tradition, the highest of Allah's corporeal emanations. The Throne in Islamic, Judaic, and Hellenic traditions often symbolized divine judgment and law. The Indo-European root meaning of *just* is "law." Justice served an important role in Plato's thought, associated with that Truth upon which all wisdom and learning inevitably had to be based. Justice upon Her Throne (as primary daughter of Zeus) was a very old Greek concept combining Fate, Death, and Eros as Universal Law. In Greek, the word frequently used to connote Justice, *Diké,* originally meant "the Way," similar to the Chinese concept of *Tao.*

Such an understanding of Justice was not easily assimilated by Judeo-Christian beliefs in Jehovah. The god of the Jews was known as a dominant, exclusively male god, who judged the world while maintaining a bias toward his chosen people. In the Christian world, both clerical and lay, Divine Justice was to be *measured* and *meted* (as Justice's scales and sword represent) during a Final Judgment. This was represented not by the Goddess Justice, but by the Second Coming of Jesus the Christ. It was thought in the Christian world that at the time of Jesus's second coming people would be judged in accordance with their faith in Him. In political reality, such faith was defined by adherence to the laws of the Roman Catholic Church.

The Church housed the newly *chosen people* of God, and its priests interpreted God's *New Testament,* which contained His updated laws. Temporal or earthly justice was meted out by the Church and its aligned rulers, in accordance with these divinely revealed laws. The rising up to a Final Judgment, essentially already determined, was a stage and act more readily represented by the trumpeting call of triumphant Angel Gabriel, God's messenger, or by Archangel Michael, who in Venetian paintings may be found delivering Justice's sword and scales to the Doge, ruler of the Venetian Republic. Thus did the Angel Triumph come to be called Judgment. Outside of Venice, Justice as the Goddess intimately identified with the Great God of old (*Zeus,* meaning *Deiwos,* the "Shining" or "Sky God") lost her high place in the Western Christian interpretation of Tarot hierarchy.

The Moon has the strength to reflect upon its object indefinitely; such sympathy is unparalleled on earth, and yet remains realizable in the form of concentrated insight.

It is of interest to note that not a single fifteenth-century painted card depicting the Devil remains in existence. This lends special import to the Devil of the Metropolitan deck. Although there is no evidence of the Catholic Church condemning the Tarot during its popularization in Italian and French courts, it is reasonable to conjecture that placement of the Devil after Death, high in the Triumphant order of the cosmos, was not appreciated by the Church hierarchy. Imagine courtesans using the Triumphs for entertainment or enlightenment. Expeditious disposal of the Devil card to appease religious authorities would have been a small price to pay for avoiding an inquisition. Such is the likely cause of the Devil's total disappearance from the twenty extant hand-painted decks. Closely related, the Tower, paired with the Devil and at times called the Devil's House, is found in only a single court deck, the Charles VI pack. These cards were painted during an era when any accusation of psychic association with the Devil could be enough to warrant Church arrest.

Hierarchical placement of the Devil followed a Sufi understanding that he serves a divine purpose as guardian to the Deathless

Enjoy the favors of the lord, the Bright adept, for such is the quickest way to dispel unnatural identities and to realize the innocence of innate attraction in blissful, blue-sky awareness.

realm and Abaser of all else. In chapters 5 and 7 we will consider this along with early, and crucial, Greek judgments concerning whether Hades lived in an underground home of fire or roamed in the sublunar realm of disembodied spirits (what we might call a confused space of wandering dead). A fiery, underground view of the Devil was transmitted through Pythagorean cults into dualistic Gnostic circles. It then became accepted exoteric Christian doctrine.

Through Heraclitus and early Platonists, an airy, sublunar view of the Devil was transmitted by Neoplatonists into nondual circles of Christian mystics and Sufis. Heraclitus, a contemporary and significant critic of Pythagoras, was evidently the first Greek metaphysician to state a nondual view of the world, unifying heaven and the underworld. Again, more will be said about this in later chapters.

Having uncovered the names and positions of the Trionfi in their most credible original form, we next need to locate the most probable place in Italy that the first Tarot deck was printed.

Pictorially, there is a large difference between the four early decks shown in this book. Yet, there are also remarkable similarities. Clearly, there was an original set of images that served as a common foundation for early Tarot packs. Variations of hierarchy and imagery amongst the Triumphs became established within the first decades of their known existence. However, our evidence suggests that for at least one hundred years, variances in the Triumphs' names and order were minor. We can reasonably suggest that differences arose according to the regions in which the cards were produced and the patrons for whom they were designed.

The twenty or so hand-painted court decks of playing cards that have survived up to the present day have been extensively studied by card scholars. At least one Triumph plus one suit card have survived in eight decks. Of these, it is uncontested that the three most complete decks were painted in the shop of Bonifacio Bembo, most likely during 1445–50. Bembo was born in 1420, lived to be sixty, and was under the commission of the Dukes of Milan – first Filippo Maria Visconti, then his successor Francesco Sforza. The most complete of these packs is called the Visconti-Sforza deck.

That which is worthy of eternal life is the simplest of states, the ground of being, the heart of Judgment – the beautiful, the good, the true.

Two of the earliest court decks are found in the Cary Collection of Playing Cards at Yale University's Beinecke Rare Book and Manuscript Library. Black and white samples of both face our chapters' title pages. The Empress and similar Triumphs come from the Visconti deck, circa 1445, which is arguably the most beautiful of the extant packs attributed to Bonifacio Bembo. The Fool and similar cards come from the Este deck of Ferrara, dated by the Beinecke Library at circa 1450 but which may indeed have been closer in both time and style to the original Tarot than the Visconti Triumphs. The Este Trionfi retain an Eastern flavor, similar in ways to the intuitive, fluidly natural style of the Metropolitan/Budapest Triumphs. The overt, unabashed organic sexuality of the Este Fool is strikingly Dionysian.

The Este Moon, with its navigational theme, powerfully speaks of Venetian and Muslim knowledge. Both Moon and Star Triumphs contain a crescent moon and star combination, evoking the mighty Ottoman battle-banner, which was at that time conquering Constantinople. This later came to be identified with Islam in general. The Star and Moon in intimate relationship with one another is one of Sufism's most fundamental symbols; this bears consideration regarding the names and positions of these two Triumphs. The iconography of both Este and Metropolitan Trionfi is remarkably different than the often stilted work and labored symbolism evident in the Visconti images. This is worthy of close study by Tarot scholars.

Dating to the late fifteenth century, the infamous Charles VI pack was also produced in Ferrara (infamous because of a conjecture by an antiquities dealer made in 1842 that this deck was painted by one Jacquemin Gringonneur in 1392 for King Charles VI of France). This hypothesis was thoroughly disproved early on,

What is the Mother of God, the source of primal chaos, the cause of causality, the measure of all truth, the sacrifice of all love – mundane and sublime, earthly and heavenly – the Dharma of Tao?

but it was widely and unwittingly, up until recent years, propagated by Tarot writers and occultists. (The Tower Triumph from this deck, the only hand-painted Tower that has come down to us, can be seen heading chapter 7. As stated, no hand-painted Devil card remains extant; accompanying the Tower, therefore, is a classical image of Hades.)

We have mentioned two courts involved with early production of Tarot cards, namely those of Milan and Ferrara. The courts of Bologna and Florence also developed associations with certain types of Tarot decks. Florence was home to most of the nonstandard, elaborate decks along with the Rosenwald pack mentioned earlier. Florence was Europe's primary center for the exploration and reinterpretation of Greek philosophy during the early Renaissance. Far more than in other Italian cities, Florentine scholars reinterpreted the Greco-Sufi symbolism of the Triumphs. However, their elaborations never displaced the primary position held by the original twenty-two Triumphs. Readers interested in a thorough discussion regarding all known early Tarot decks and the territories they were most probably associated with are referred to Michael Dummett's *The Game of Tarot* (1980).

Although the Bembo packs are often presumed to be the oldest, no historian has seriously suggested that Bembo was the original designer of the Tarot. Much evidence points to Ferrara as the original court source of the hand-painted images. As we will discover in the next chapter, Ferrara was host to a rare and great ecumenical council of churches in 1438, creating a multi-year colloquium that brought together Greek Orthodox scholars from Constantinople and Alexandria and their Roman Catholic peers from Italy and elsewhere. Venetian elites diplomatically and culturally bridged the two otherwise distant communities. The existence of the Trionfi is first documented in the royal account books of Ferrara in the years that the ecumenical council initiated there was being held.

That which is ordinary beyond definitions of physical, emotional, mental, psychic, subtle, causal, or enlightened realization is that which is extraordinary as only the Nondual World can be.

During this period, Ferrara was under Venetian influence even while it closely associated with Milan. Venice and Milan were in the middle of a long war with one another. Milan during the first half of the fifteenth century attempted to take control of Northern Italy. Florence enlisted Venice's assistance to halt Milan, which it did. The Dukes of Milan were known for their ruthlessly domineering policies. In contrast, Venetian involvement with the East, and in particular Greek Orthodox Byzantium and Muslim and Coptic Orthodox Egypt, carried with it a great deal of diplomatic (and romantic) cachet. Chapter 2 will detail the history of this time, including Venice's primary position in terms of trade with lands east.

Of note presently is that Ferrara was an open and neutral conduit in which Venetians could mediate between their Eastern friends and the rest of Italy. Relations with the Greek visitors were soon taken up by the literati, artisans, and scholars of Florence, to where the Council shifted after a year of meeting in Ferrara. (Florence offered more lavish housing and hospitality, and less plague.) Initially, it was the young court women of Ferrara and Milan who were drawn to the Trionfi that emerged from Ferrara's hosting of Venetian-mediated Byzantine parties. By commissioning the hand-painted Trionfi, female nobility spurred exotic Eastern symbolism into fashion throughout northern Italian courts.

Returning to our inquiry into the order of the cards, one of the literary sources attesting our earliest order addresses a game of *Tarocchi* as played by the noblewomen of Ferrara (the Bertoni poem). One of the sources was published in Venice in the late sixteenth century (Garzoni's *Piazza Universale*). Several other poems from the sixteenth century name the Triumphs, although not their order. These were all published in Venice. Venice was Italy's major center for playing-card imports. Venetian merchants both printed and purchased cards in association with designers and producers in Alexandria, Egypt. The Steele manuscript, which is our most important

Collaborate with the goddess current of love, but do so consciously; the Fool cares not about the projections, possessions, and delusions of others, for he holds his sacrifice for all to see.

source of playing card names and order, has a completely unknown geographical origin.

Our search for territorial origins of the Tarot ends with an examination of the Metropolitan pack. The key to discovering the birthplace of the woodblock deck lies not with its twenty-two Triumphs, but rather with its suit cards. These cards are not to be found in the sheets housed by the Metropolitan Museum. The Metropolitan sheets were originally acquired from the Budapest Museum of Fine Arts in Hungary. The Budapest Museum's almost identical set of sheets includes a number of suit cards. These show strong stylistic affinities with a set of standard playing-card sheets in the Cary Collection at Yale. Several court cards between the two decks are identical or very similar. Furthermore, identical stylistic elements between the decks' numeral cards in the suits of Swords and Batons clearly evince common design roots. A four-sheet set of early playing cards in the Fournier Museum in Vitoria, Spain, demonstrates the same similarities with the addition of almost identical Aces to those in the Tarot sheets.

Where did these playing cards come from? A singular Three of Cups discovered in Egypt is identical to one on the Cary sheets. It dates back to the Mameluke era of the late fourteenth and early fifteenth centuries. Another significant clue can be found on the Budapest Museum's Ten of Batons. As was pointed out by Melbert Cary himself, the form *diexe* (signifying "ten") used on the card belongs to a Venetian dialect of the fifteenth century. The Budapest Museum has always adhered to the position that its Tarot sheets were printed in Venice.

Unique Venetian usage of the letter *x*, along with other dialectal and nominal peculiarities found upon a most interesting fifteenth-century educational deck of Tarot-like images, indicates that Venice was at the forefront of Neoplatonic, Greek-inspired card production. The so-called "Tarot of Mantegna" is thought to have been created by one or more students of the famous Italian artist Andrea

Mantegna, circa 1460–70. This fifty-card non-Tarot deck is based on five sets of ten stations each, many of which hold strong similarity to the Triumphs, indicating Trionfi were circulating in Venice previous to this time. A deck comprising uncut sheets depicts engravings not unlike the Metropolitan Triumphs, though of a more refined quality. Each set of ten stations represents a universal hierarchy of diverse themes, such as Apollo's Muses and the Heavenly Spheres. The latter are represented by the seven planet-forces encircling the Earth plus traditionally held divine spheres that emanated as World Soul, First Cause, and Divine One.

Each suit set of the Mantegna deck was defined broadly in accordance to the perennial ten-stage cosmological hierarchy that we will be addressing throughout our study. They support arguments presented in these pages regarding the importance and primary position of this system in the Tarot, as it was in medieval philosophy and Greek studies. The original Trionfi truly exemplified a highly sophisticated, multicultural study of that core Indo-European wisdom-structure.

It is of interest to note that there exists no evidence that Tarot was ever popular as a *game* in Venice. It is herein suggested that the Triumphs were not originally purposed toward game-playing. The conceptual hierarchy of Islamic playing cards involved the perfect series of one through ten, representing the wealth and social structure of a land, including its commoners. (One of the Mantegna sets of ten images this.) Royalty were depicted via three or four hierarchical court cards. Similar to the Magician and Fool Triumphs, Aces came to simultaneously represent both the lowest and highest hierarchical values of the deck. Like the pieces of a chessboard, these icons put into play a simulacrum of the world. This is how Mameluke and Moorish Muslim intellectuals, and previous to them Indo–Central Asian nobility, thought and *played* with the world, in a context of governance, trading, and war.

However, beyond secular rules and contingencies of chance involved with mundane hierarchies that were readily simulated through games, there existed in the Greek-educated Islamic mind an always-present *sacred* hierarchy. That hierarchy began with the exemplars of empire and religion, where the mundane hierarchy left off. It then encompassed Neoplatonic ideals of virtue and Greek archetypes of spirituality. Finally, it ended with ancient concepts of immortal and paradisiacal domains and World Law.

The Triumphs were a metaphysical advancement beyond the mundane world order portrayed in the suit cards. This book delineates the philosophical development of archetypal concepts and principles that generated the Tarot. Through integration into games of rationality, probability, and insight, Tarot images as a set of hierarchical symbols became embedded in popular culture throughout Europe. They composed an esoteric teaching unfettered of Church dogma even while incorporating the essential foundations underlying Christian metaphysics. Neoplatonic and Neopythagorean schools based in Marseilles, France, were responsible for much of the Tarot's future popularity and symbolism. Their epistemic significance was progressively lost, however, as they became solely identified with games of chance and fortune.

There is good reason to date the Metropolitan/Budapest Triumphs earlier than 1500. That commonly suggested date is apparently based upon little more than guesswork by card historians unaware of the cards' early association with Venice and Alexandria and their elements of eastern symbolism. The beauty, subtlety, and medieval iconography reflected in these simple woodblock prints have not garnered the attention they deserve. The poor condition of extant sheets is no doubt in part to blame. However, card historians have apparently assumed that the *high philosophy* contained in Greek studies was only known to privileged scholars, patrons, and artisans of Roman Catholic European or even solely Italian courts. This most certainly was not the case.

Spain had largely been Moorish for hundreds of years and Southern France was enormously affected by Muslim and Gnostic cultural, artistic, and intellectual influences developed during the Crusades. Sufi-influenced thought affected both Kabbalistic and Christian theosophy and contemplative practice in Spain and France. This put both countries closer to Greek studies than were the courts of Italy. Only the Venetians had closer contact with the Greek East.

Perhaps meaningful symbolism readily perceived by Western scholars orients toward the highly Romanized and formally represented images found in decks such as the Visconti-Sforza. The woodblock deck cannot be attributed to an Italian court painter. Overlooked by historians have been the Islamic and Byzantine milieus of the fifteenth and fourteenth centuries, along with the cosmopolitan Venetian merchant class and its appreciation of Greek knowledge openly studied, shared, and developed in those milieus. It has been simply assumed that the Metropolitan deck was an impoverished "reduction" of the exalted court decks, made after the latter had become popular enough to attract attention amongst the lower Italian classes.

It is apparent that the Metropolitan/Budapest Tarot pack was a *merchant class* or non-court deck circulating in Venice, Ferrara, and quite likely Alexandria and/or Constantinople at the time of, or perhaps earlier than, the hand-painted decks of the Italian nobility.

Our inclusion of Ferrara is prompted by notable similarity between the Metropolitan's Chariot card and a singular painted card, discovered in recent years, thought to be from Ferrara circa 1450–55. That dating, if correct, establishes that Triumph's deck as one of the oldest known. Called the "Issy-sur-Moulineaux Chariot," it depicts a chariot with young passengers and a female driver. Chapter 7 examines the Greek mythology behind this symbolism; here we simply mention its association with Artemis (also portrayed with her chariot in the Mantegna pack introduced above), who was the ancient *virginal* and *militant protector* of children. After the earliest decks, the Chariot is depicted with a male driver. Only the Metropolitan and Moulineaux Chariots include the traditional symbolism of children. Perhaps the goddess iconography was not understood or appreciated by Italian Catholics, as the Chariot is one of the few Triumphs whose position seems in question from early on.

There is reason to suggest that printed merchant-class Tarot decks likely preceded the painted decks of royal courts, and furthermore, that Venice was the original channel for those decks (or a singular, original deck), which were introduced to artisans and intellectuals in Ferrara during or soon after the city hosted an extraordinary and historically critical meeting between Eastern and Western Church philosophers and artisans. The importance and uniqueness of that Council cannot be overstated, for it was tied directly to the process of Christian lands losing Constantinople to the Ottomans. It is likely that the Metropolitan pack of Triumphs closely reflects the original set of Tarot images. From a fifteenth-century Venetian merchant's point of view, its Byzantine and Oriental elements of style would speak of the Tarot's original frame of reference far more than Bembo's official Romanization of the Tarot's esoteric Greek symbolism.

In chapter 3 this conjecture is made sound, as we identify the twenty-two Trionfi with the great cycle of corporeal emanations of Allah as the immortal World. This was expounded by a network of traveling, philosophically advanced, merchant-class Sufis spanning the lands between Spain, Egypt, Turkey, and Central Asia. Many of those Sufis, though widely respected for their international learning, were deemed heretics by the fundamentalist rulers and exoteric *mullahs* of the Islamic world and paid for the teaching of their knowledge with their lives.

Further investigation of the intellectual climates and multicultural environments that gestated the hierarchical system behind the Tarot Arcana propels us into the dawning of the Renaissance and the world of Venetian merchants, encountered in the next chapter.

Identifying . . . Right View

A book on the Tarot would not live up to expectations without provoking a little incredulity. Therefore, the true secrets of power, wealth, and status will now be unveiled. Naturally, esoteric information uncovered by reading Tarot cards in accordance with their traditional significance reveals these secrets. Once primed with the fuel of ancient wisdom, we will stoke our minds with the Principles of Immortality!

As we shall see, by the fifteenth century, a confluence of Eastern and Western metaphysics had been brought about through Silk Road traders; sacred orders of Crusading knights (the Templars in specific); wandering bands of mendicant Islamic mystics and scholars; Greek patriarchs of international renown (both Orthodox and Neoplatonic); well-traveled Buddhists (of the Theravada branch in the time of Jesus, Mahayana in the time of Mohammed, Vajrayana in the time of Rumi and St. Francis); international Jewish Kabbalists; and politically adroit merchants, notably from Venice and Constantinople. This historically documented, complex, and continuous merging of Eastern and Western bodies of knowledge served to inseminate, gestate, birth, and transmit the Tarot Trionfi: the most famous, if not the richest and most powerful, esoteric summary of spiritual evolution in all of history.

To understand the authentic esoteric roots of the Tarot, we must first immerse ourselves in a pool of concepts regarding Neoplatonic metaphysics and cosmological hierarchy upon which the Tarot is based. Should the reader find these concepts overwhelming, know that the proceeding chapters clarify, elaborate, and soundly give a reasoned and historical basis for them. The rest of this chapter summarizes in a considerably condensed form the philosophical underpinnings of Western esotericism. Understanding the ten stages of spiritual evolution represented by the Tarot requires a deep exploration into metaphysical territory. This book serves as a summary introduction to precisely that.

Neoplatonists between the third and seventh centuries conceived the world at every level as emanating from the One. With awakened enthusiasm, they contended that it did so via ideal *triunes* (literally, "three-in-ones"). Christian theology positing a Holy Trinity was influenced by this Neoplatonic notion of perfection. Conception of the Divine as Three in One has been foundational to Indo-European spirituality and wisdom since ancient times. The sacred Triune has been the primary vehicle by which Indo-Europeans have understood the domains that transcend Death. As we shall see, this was carried into the Tarot. The Tarot's after-Death cards inform us of the Divine Triune from which the world is continuously created.

Platonic philosophy postulated three states toward which the world was purposed: Beauty, Goodness, and Truth (the latter was also known as Justice and the Way). Contemporary with Plato's school of thought, nondual Indian philosophy referred to as *Advaita Vedanta* (*Advaita* literally means "nondual"; *Vedanta* refers to Hinduism's broad, foundational corpus of myths and philosophies recorded in the Vedas) held that all humans were attracted to states of greater Being, Consciousness, and Bliss. Later, Neoplatonism maintained that the One was composed of a trinity: World Soul, Light Soul, and Radiant Intelligence. World Soul correlated with the ancient Greek concept of Chaos *becoming* the Cosmos; Radiant Soul correlated with pure Being and Beauty; Kosmic Intelligence correlated with radiant Consciousness and Goodness; and the One correlated with absolute Bliss and Truth. For Neoplatonists, Plato's *Good* epitomized the realm of *Logos* or Radiant Ideals. Source to all was the *One,* which could be known solely through ecstatic bliss.

Corollary triunes we may appropriately associate with the above include science-oriented Chaos, Space, and Time realizing Law; Taoist-oriented Man, Earth, and Heaven realizing Tao; and

Buddhist-oriented Teaching, Culture, and Community *(Dharma, Buddha,* and *Sangha)* realizing Nirvana.

Readers intent on enquiring into profundities of the Tarot are addressed in our work as *Questors.* During their esoteric Quests, six stages of self-actualization emanating from a self-organizing and self-transcending principle of Chaos will be discovered. Constantly affecting and qualifying each of the Questor's six stages of holistic development will be the aforementioned Triune of universal principles. Throughout history, in all of the great traditions, these principle-states have been referred to as Divine, Immortal, Deathless, and Transcendental. In Indo-European tradition they are called the supreme Spirit, Goddess, God, and ineffable Unity. In our study of the Trionfi, we will come to understand the meaning of these powerful traditional concepts of spirituality, wisdom, and ecstasy.

The Tarot is without doubt a coherently *spiritual* set of images. It reveals and addresses humanity's potential to harmonize, integrate, and understand one another. Seen in the light of authentic spirituality, the Triumphs are discovered anew as a truly brilliant treasure of sacred knowledge. They will serve and guide every Questor in the process of actualizing a golden alchemy.

Through the Principles of Immortality, Questors will learn how to gain Power via spiritual existence, the cultivation of which enables naught but the power to be Beautiful. Questors will discover that knowledge of the Good is alchemical gold – the incomparable Wealth of spiritual communion. Encompassing all, bliss will then come through acknowledgment of spiritual performance; realms of beings, from demons to animals to humans to angels, will admit every Questor's Status as a dignitary of Truth.

The Tarot assists us in becoming aware of spiritual development as a way of existential realization, beyond idealistic or romantic beliefs. Each of us exists regardless of circumstances or fortunes. To exist in a yet-greater state of beingness, consciousness, and bliss is the enlightened wish of everyone. Each of the Triumphs represents a progressively greater state of such realization.

Death, for instance, is a wish of many. It is twelfth in a universal hierarchy of twenty (not counting the Magician or Fool), the transitory state between cosmic manifestation and the Afterlife. Once Death is seriously known, that which is greater becomes radically desired. There is nothing bleaker than to believe there is no principle greater than Death. To see that all of life, and indeed reality, is naught but impermanence ultimately ruled by Death is to discover totally pervasive suffering in the world. To be aware of such as illusion, being conscious of the Way of Life beyond that, is to be in the ecstasy of Nirvana. This is not only the core teaching of Buddhist wisdom; it is also the core teaching of Neoplatonism and the Tarot. Although every cell of our body is continuously dying, it is in the moment-to-moment rebirth or resurrected state of our whole being that true identity and happiness are found.

Ultimately, the Tarot reveals the Way beyond momentary and continual annihilation or Deathly Chaos. Contemplation of the post-Death Triumphs, representing states of a sacred and ancient Triune, is crucial to a true understanding of the great wisdom-way portrayed in the Arcana. Before Plato's time, these were known as Strife or Chaos (Devil and Tower), Love or Eros (Star and Moon), and the Bright or Shining (Sun and Angel) upholding the Way, which was Just (Justice) and One (World). Viewed as a whole, the Tarot is a series of existential signs directing the Questor upon a path of Freedom, Happiness, and Liberation in a golden dawn of enlightenment.

How do Questors transform themselves and the world about them via Beauty, Goodness, and Truth?

Firstly, to cultivate Beauty one must turn over one's heart in a surrendering of existence. Thus, a Questor approaching Death does not become bound by the terrible masks of decay, decomposition, and destruction. For a Questor's Heart is identical to her Beauty and not bound to her face or egoic persona. How beautiful is the two-armed form when wedded to the Heart. One's sentient being defines Beauty through its *whole* existence. The quality of such beauty is inevitably dissipated when the ego attempts to possess it. The Questor who attempts to cultivate ideal existence via physical beauty will not engage the ten stages of evolutionary development revealed in this book unless psychological identification with temporal form is surrendered through service and devotion to the beauty of spiritual growth and That which is Beyond. Such growth will include not only Love, Fate, and Fortune; it will also embrace the Devil, Sun, and Justice.

To succeed in realizing beauty, goodness, and truth, Questors must adhere to an intuited vision of Unity through Diversity. This requires not *holding dear* (i.e., believing in) the myriad *egoic reductions* of the world. Questors will thus find power in the beauty of existing moment by moment. They will not be compelled to seize their freedom in vain attempts to secure existence as *separate* manifestations of beauty. Self-possessed egos, limited in their self-interpreted, self-centered diminution of beauty, must be surrendered. A wonderful vision of Being Beautiful opens in the awareness that one just is, inseparable from all else, which also *just is*. One no longer grasps at the ever-so-limited self-reflections of one's existence. Then a Questor can truly proceed along the way of grace and compassionate freedom.

Secondly, consciousness must encapsulate true Beauty with a radiant sheath of true Goodness. To be good to others is to commune in knowledge of essential Unity. Here, knowledge is referred to as wisdom-consciousness, not limited by separative facts or the discursive mind. Mature forms of understanding found in all great traditions point to nondual awareness of ultimate, universal Unity.

Many think of the Taoist symbol of Yin/Yang as representing the cosmos as a duality. Quite the contrary; it represents the nondual Tao, which includes all apparent polarities. It is often presumed that

Platonic philosophy addresses a dualistic world composed of ideal forms and laws existing apart from manifested reality. The latter realm is thought of as inferior, both metaphysically and morally, to the former. Abstraction is glorified over common sense. Plotinus and like-minded Neoplatonists rectified this misunderstanding by basing all knowledge of Truth upon the ineffable One and its continuous, nondual emanations as the Myriad of manifested forms and processes. Form is Empty: Samsara *is* Nirvana, say Buddhists in confirmation of Neoplatonists. Atman *is* Brahman, say Advaita Hindus. Everything Is Tao.

Nondual wisdom views sentient beings in all forms as emanating moment to moment in, from, and as the One, the Tao, Allah, Brahman, Buddha Mind, or the very Ground of Being. This forms the basis for esoteric gnosis in Sufism, Hermetic Catholicism, and Judaic Kabbalism, along with Taoism, Hinduism, and Buddhism. We will be thoroughly reviewing this global understanding of the Unity of All Being and will have occasion to compare it to dualistic Gnostic and exoteric stances of religious and philosophic, including scientific, belief systems.

The Tarot is an epitomized representation of nondual knowledge. It is equally objective and subjective in relevance. It addresses both physical and psychological worlds. It posits that *outer* cosmology and *inner* spirituality are wedded realms through which Truth is realized as Beauty and Goodness. Existence, Consciousness, and Bliss are neither materially reducible nor ego-determined. Rather, body (existence) and mind (consciousness) always arise in unity (bliss).

Thirdly, it must not be doubted that Truth addresses hierarchical bliss. The Tarot depicts an ecstatically lawful, hierarchical world, which immanently embodies change and transcendental reality. Each Triumph of the Tarot portrays cosmological evolution emerging from and as essentially vital Principles destined ultimately toward blissful consciousness and being. In this Triumphant view, emergent order at every level of manifestation – be that cellular, human, or galactic – inherently realizes a *logos* (indicating "wisdom gathered and spoken") or consciousness of Bliss. Perennial wisdom refers to Logos and Word as primordial and celestial *harmony* – sound not limited to human vocalization or earthly noise. Such is the *vibratory* and *radiant* nature of everything.

The Trionfi enable us to identify hierarchical principles of order ruling our naturally complex, chaotic, and impermanent world. By so doing, it Liberates us to be Freely Happy. *Reading the Triumphs* is a process of envisioning the hierarchy of forces and influences at play in one's life and world. Done with an understanding of the Triumphant stations, greater Being, Consciousness, and Bliss can be obtained. This is way beyond "having your cards read" in the hope of possessing more egoic power, material wealth, or self-serving status.

The fundamentally actualizing nature of hierarchy can be arrested through egoic and pathologic craving to manipulate, dominate, and subjugate. Utterly displacing *sacerdotal* ("of the sacred") realization of in-depth Beauty via spirited Goodness with *temporal* possession of surface beauty via material goods can significantly arrest sustainable growth, whether personal, social, or environmental. Rather, the two need to evolve hand in hand. Put more broadly, it is best to holistically relate spirituality, governance, science, and capitalism via contextually studying, communicating, and becoming conscious of universal hierarchy. The Tarot is an excellent tool to assist us in that work and play.

This treatise challenges us to review, recognize, and actually rectify the most critical issue of our day: the world's conflicting insights regarding hierarchical, evolutionary development. Matters concerning authority and control are inherent to this issue, as are beliefs regarding racial, religious, cultural, or national superiority. In its worst appropriation, hierarchy arrogated by dualistic conceits can be used as justification for self-propelling prophecies promoting apocalypse. The potential for globally catastrophic conflict will remain until this issue is fully admitted, appreciated, and addressed. Abetting resolution to such conflict requires championing recognition of hierarchical and evolutionary development universally found in cosmic, earthen, human, and microcosmic realms.

Dominating power and control are often viewed as prerequisites to material and social success. However, the medieval Tarot shows us how to realize power, wealth, and status – and thereby lasting happiness – *in the context of wisdom.* These are found in the immortal states of beautiful being, good consciousness, and true bliss. Nothing less can compare. What use is power if control of others inevitably produces hatred, defiling Beauty at the end of the day? What value is money if one is too ignorant to use it in service of the Good? What satisfaction is status if it leads to greed and denial of harmonious Truth? Only Beauty, Goodness, and Truth will suffice as an antidote to malice, delusion, and craving.

The above vision of a spiritually universal way that involves becoming conscious of world Unity is neither a modern invention nor an arcane, obsolete point of view. Nor is it an unrealizable ideal. Traditions East and West have thoroughly conveyed processes into our present day by which every Questor may gain the means necessary for successful actualization of a true spiritual path.

The Tarot originated in esoteric circles cultivating what has traditionally been termed *alchemy.* Practiced under wise guidance, psychophysical-social alchemy can quicken the realization of nondual awareness. Such alchemy does not go beyond *vital life* and *essential nature.* Living naturally requires being vitally essential, and alchemical practices enable a Questor to be exactly that. Alive, natural alchemy embraces polarities cycling, networking, emanating, modifying, and otherwise hierarchically transforming as the One. These terms and practices will be clarified in chapter 6 when the tradition of *internal alchemy* is fully addressed. The stages of such a spiritual and yogic way proceed exactly in accordance with the medieval Tarot.

Transformation as Chaos – Being as Space – Consciousness as Time – Bliss as Law: these are immortal principles permeating all cosmic cycles. Chaos serves to manifest these Deathless states first as Flux and then as an ever-changing universe simultaneously arising on many different levels of scale, from quantum to galactic. Earlier, these principles were identified with the Neoplatonic Triune of World Soul, Soul, and Intellect upholding the One. Extending that model further, Neoplatonism posited six stages of sentient soul simultaneously descending from and ascending to World Soul:

1. Perceptual Soul (Establishes Self-identity)
2. Emotional Soul (Produces Pleasure and Pain)
3. Imaginative Soul (Reveals Significant Images)
4. Conceptual Soul (Relates Positions of Others)
5. Logical Soul (Aligns to the Virtuous)
6. Creative Soul (Reasons beyond Self-sense)

Ascending to:

7. World Soul (Transforms through Chaos)
8. Divine Soul (Loves through Eros)
9. Radiant Intellect (Transcends through the Bright)
10. The One (Unifies through the Way)

In modern terms, the cosmological process of life and evolution emerging from Chaos can be efficiently understood through the following six-stage cycle (italicized words contain the principal definition of each stage):

1. *Inertial identity,* being both whole and part, and potentially vibratory
2. Separates as a *polarity* in *symmetrical* extension
3. Organizes as a field-system cycling through and as these poles, *resonating* with other *fields*
4. Transcends limited polar definition via *hierarchical* relationship, *emerging* both within and without

5. *Synchronistically* aligns *contingent* relationships interdependently arising through the universal field-polarity of emptiness and infinity (space and time)
6. Transforms via *holistic* catastrophe (chaos) the whole *causal* process

Such transformation:

1. Vibrates the original identity
2. Extends its polar symmetry
3. Non-linearly resonates within a group of interdependent fields
4. Reinforces traces of an emerging hierarchical pattern
5. Breaks symmetrical formation and then vanishes through non-local but synchronistic contingencies
6. Holistically regenerates through transformative chaos a similar but uniquely changed, causally self-organizing duration of coherent identity

The always-evolving cosmos is manifested through these six primary spatial-temporal processes transforming, dimensioning, and radiating the aforementioned four transcendental and fundamental Principles (with the First being the principle of Law itself). Such serve to define the means, source, destiny, and reality of every *holon* or *whole/part identity* in the universe. Every thing, process, or state exists both as a whole made up of parts and as a part in the context of a larger whole. This is true for every level of manifestation, be it that of atoms, cells, humans, suns, or galaxies.

Each of the above soulful emanations and principles of Unity is represented in the Tarot by two adjacent Triumphs. The ten stages of spiritual realization and cosmological manifestation are conveyed most essentially through *pairs* of twenty Triumphs: from Empress/Popess to Justice/World. The Fool/Magician pair represents the Questor proceeding through the ten stages of conscious evolution. Each Triumphant station has its own whole identity, while simultaneously imaging a symmetrical half of a larger stage or principle identified by the unique union of that pair of stations.

Ten universal stages and their respective processes and principles are hierarchically nested within the twenty Trionfi. Cultural, social, and psychological aspects of stages one through six are elaborated in the next few chapters. They are given scientific definition as Great Principles (highlighted in the above model) of cosmic evolution in chapter 8. Chapter 9 collates in summary format the essential meanings and definitions that are applied to the Triumphs and their respective stations throughout the book. The present chapter finishes with a focused introduction to the last four stages, for they serve as a spiritual foundation to the metaphysical cosmology of the Tarot.

According to the Tarot, cosmic evolution of Unity is dependent upon Death (catastrophe in all forms), Chaos (vitally essential impermanence), and those principles of reality that transcend them: immortal existence (matter/dimensionality/space), eternal consciousness (energy/frequency/time), and perpetual bliss (purpose/unity/law). It bears repeating that genesis, transformation, regeneration, and all temporal causality are a priori preceded by the unconditional causes of Chaos, Space, Time, and Law. As will be outlined in chapter 5, these were known by early Greeks as Strife, Eros, the Bright, and the Way. Later, Neoplatonists called them World Soul, Light Soul, Radiant Intellect, and Just One. The changing cosmos comprises the means through which these Great Causes realize their intrinsic unity of Blissful Plentitude.

The four stages of the *Deathless* (transcendental reality as cosmic unifier, creator, sustainer, and destroyer) become consciously known through the enlightened stages of spiritual realization. Such is the transformation of psychophysical identity into the Three upholding the One: Chaos, Space, and Time upholding the Way. Manifesting as Deathless Reality, these Principles are immortal, absolute, universal, and omnipresent.

This book argues that the Tarot is composed of eleven pairs of *archetypes,* ten of which are hierarchical, one of which is the Questor amidst the stages. The first six stages of the Quest serve as Initiation to Awakening; the following stages serve *as* Enlightenment, even while the Questor is undergoing initiation! The Trionfi, thereby, form a Great Circle of Consciousness.

Each stage is realized both externally and internally, communally and individually. For instance, as outlined above, the third stage manifests a cycling field between two poles. The medieval Tarot represents this stage through the archetypes of Temperance and Love. Socially, the Questor experiences this stage through tempered and tolerant exchanges in relationship with others. It is necessary to develop such outgoing temperance in order to personally mature in intimate responsibility, which accompanies revelatory love.

To give another example, in the sixth stage, the root-state or *heart*-cause of self-existence severs all identity with and as that very *self.* What internally feels like Death to the Questor may externally appear to others as the Hanged Man. For the Questor personally transits a passage into the Deathless (inevitably commencing with the Chaotic Devil) while socially seeming to be hung-up in a witnessing state of impending catastrophe.

Schizophrenia and psychosis may grip a mind when this stage and the preceding one become pathologically disconnected from the first four stages of human development. Although some might thereby interpret these Triumphs negatively, they are not natively pathological, but rather are surrounded by Beauty, Goodness, and Truth. Indeed, they are relatively high in the hierarchy of vital life and essential nature. Until the witnessing position of the Hanged Man is fully incorporated in the Questor's heart-state of awareness, Death cannot deliver consciousness to the gates of enlightened transfiguration. In Buddhism, this practice of *insightful witnessing* is called *Vipassana.*

The portal to the Deathless realm is guarded by the Devil. In Christian Hermeticism and Islamic Sufi mysticism, the Tarot Devil corresponds to the potent angel placed as guardian at the Gates of Paradise after man's "fall" from Grace. The Questor may pass through only after a completely sacrificial effort (i.e., Sainthood). Such effort must become effortlessly mindful – as if it is truly of one's essential nature. In its fully vital essentiality, the Effort of transiting Death, bearing the sacrifice of all causality, inherently involves spontaneous Emptiness. This is the Crux of authentic Mysticism.

Crossing into the Deathless – the Angelic Realm of the Saints – does not occur consciously without *perfect timing* or what may be viewed as the *providence of divine accident*. Even then, the Deathless is realized only through the assistance of one who is already immortally transcended. This is referred to in the great traditions as Divine Grace, often occurring within a synchronistic, communal process of lineage succession, such as Buddhist Dharma Transmission. It is difficult to rectify this process with that of political election, democratic or otherwise. Effortless-effort and authentic spiritual leadership do not arise from egoic strategies serving determined stakeholders, moral or not.

The sixth-to-seventh-stage passage into Enlightenment and Divinity is the cornerstone of the Tarot. Later, we will give extensive attention to the historical station and theological development of the Devil. Fascists, psychotics, and fanatical fundamentalists have unfortunately perverted the actual significance of this station throughout history.

Following Death, the transition stage represented by the Devil and Tower is felt in every preceding stage as a wild build-up of inscrutable complexity. Put shortly, it is the stage of Chaos. In dualistic schools, this seventh stage has been historically referred to as either the "secret and real demiurgic power" or the "evil antithesis to the one true God." However, Tao, Allah, Nirvana, Holy Trinity, or Supreme Unity is actually That which emanates *as all ten* universal spheres. The tenth stage of Blissful Truth is not essentially or *really degraded* by the limitations of its emanated or manifested states – although for the unenlightened it may appear to be.

The first of the four Deathless stages is like an extraordinary, unfathomable pressure phasing into primordial transformation. The permeation of this seventh principle throughout each of the six stages of cosmic cycling catalyzes all change and empowers every processional aspect of existence. However, neither the seventh state of Chaos nor the six stages of manifested cosmos "below it" self-sufficiently create Beauty, Goodness, and Truth. Prior to, greater than, and always *as* these seven universal spheres, processes, or stages are absolute Space, Time, and Law: the eighth, ninth, and tenth principles of unlimited realization.

Thus, the preceding seven spheres emerge from and are encapsulated by the dimensionality and space of Beingness. In essence, reality simply IS. It is not fundamentally limited by temporal states of *being* or *non-being*. The eighth-stage principle is Space itself, which exists regardless of any other analyzable state of cosmic development.

Temporal Cosmos, radical Chaos, and all spatial Existence itself (be that of three, ten, or infinite dimensions) is emanated from, encapsulated in, and pervaded by the eternal, infinite frequencies and energy of Time, referred to in our text as Light, Radiance, and Consciousness. Energy is the *bridge-state* between Space and Time. Historically, such has been called the Angelic Domain. We will elaborate upon Matter and Energy, Space and Time, when we consider Tarot cosmology in light of holistic scientific theory.

In turn, Time, Space, Chaos, and localized, temporal cosmic manifestations of Unity are all encapsulated by the very principle of universal Law itself. Beyond understanding this Ultimate Principle through concepts of *Unitive* Law, human consciousness can only identify this One Source and Destiny as Bliss or the Way itself. The ultimate principle of Unitive Law cannot truthfully be referred to as time, space, chaos, or cosmos. As Lao Tzu said, *True Tao cannot be spoken.* This is because of its utterly nondual nature. In any case, ineffable Unity first emanates as its own Law, the Just Way of the World. In terms of human consciousness and spiritual realization, this principle is the Law of Bliss.

The Cosmos embodies fundamentally true laws of nature. These laws, these truths, are its Bliss, its Nirvana, its Tao. For Questors to be true to their Tao is to keep to their Bliss, the law of their Soul – small or big, humble or glorious. Always remember: *Bliss is Plenty.*

Now that we have uncovered the essential stages of World development and conscious realization in terms of Tarot cosmology and spiritual hierarchy, how are we to put our new knowledge to use? What are the secrets to empowerment through the six universal stages of self-actualization? How can Self be remembered after total dismemberment by the scythe of Death? Is there Authority beyond the Devil's control of chaos? Is it possible to experience the Deathless truth of Beauty and Goodness during the course of one's ordinary and mortal life? Such questions can indeed be answered. The success of every true Quest is, in a way, guaranteed – for that is how the World *works.*

Let us now clarify the historical origins of our oracular keys, the medieval Tarot *Arcana.* We must flesh out an esoteric understanding of the Tarot so that its occult interpretations and concealed uses are outshined by its authentic message of realized Beauty, Goodness, and Truth. There can be nothing hidden from that view which sees liberation in Unity-awareness. May every sentient being have the common sense to exist in such consciousness of bliss.

PASSIONATE INTERCOURSE

EMPEROR

The Emperor's reign is derived not from the power of destruction, but rather from the authority of renouncing possession, personality, and opinion.

POPE

Willful practice is needed so that opposites might be conjoined. The resolve demanded by such work, integrating contraction with release, is marked by the sign of the Pope.

Two

Treading the Path

Following Merchants and Crusaders East . . .

Amid the lagoons at the head of the Adriatic Sea is found one of history's most influential cities. Venice, a relatively modern polis founded in A.D. 421, was originally inhabited by refugees escaping the collapse of the Roman Empire. Settling among the sandbars, they took up a survivalist's life of fishing and salt-making. In the century following, invasions from the north drove a substantial population into the settlement. By the age of Charlemagne during the eighth century, Venice was becoming a full-fledged city established in a birthright of liberty and independence.

Early Venice was officially part of the Byzantine Empire, itself comprising remnants of the once very extensive Roman Empire. Byzantium was originally a Greek city; it was rebuilt by Roman Emperor Constantine the Great, who christened it Constantinople. Constantine became famous for suspending the persecution of Christians and adopting their faith in the early fourth century. As center of the Eastern Orthodox Church until the Ottoman takeover in 1452, Constantinople remained a city rich in Greek mythological, philosophical, and pagan knowledge. It is now known as Istanbul.

During the time of Charlemagne, King of the Franks and founder of the first empire (ca. A.D. 750–850) in Western Europe after the fall of Rome, Venice was Byzantium's only possession in Northern Italy. The Lombard invasion had left most of the area to German rule. Although Constantinople's claim to Venice did not amount to much, it served Venetians by providing legal protection from the German Empire.

By the tenth century, Venice had grown into a mature, independent city-state. Even as the Byzantine Empire diminished, Venice grew in power and stature. In terms of trade privileges and political alignments, there continued to exist a special relationship between it and Constantinople. Byzantium, by the turn of the millennium, had lost much of its territory to the forces of Islam. In the face of Rome's ecclesiastical displeasure, Venetians established a thriving trade with the Muslim world. On the Western front, through a combination of diplomacy and guile, Venice continued to stave off repeated territorial claims by the Germans.

In the eleventh century, Normans captured southern Italy, Sicily, and all of the western and central Mediterranean bases of Byzantium and Arabia – except for Venice. At this time, the Byzantine Empire also came under attack by the Seljuk Turks. The Seljuk formed a Turkish dynasty that ruled throughout the Crusading period. It was in this milieu that Mamelukes brought playing cards down from Central Asia to Egypt, ultimately exporting them to Italy and beyond. The Byzantine Emperor appealed to Venice for help fighting further Norman incursions, for by then the city had built a significant naval fleet. Assisted by the Grecian navy, Venetians blocked the Northern men from continuing their conquests. With the death of Robert Guiscard, leader of the Norman takeover of Italy, the Adriatic was left to the control of Venice. No longer simply a Byzantine subject, Venice had become a valuable ally.

When the First Crusade commenced at the turn of the twelfth century, Venice was careful to adhere to a role of protecting Byzantine interests. This put the city at odds with other Italian city-states such as Pisa and Genoa. The Great Schism of 1054 had seen Christendom divide into Roman and Greek (Western and Eastern) Churches. Venice as a Western European state was unique in its tacit support of the Greek kingdom. At times, that support became more than diplomatic. In 1099, Venice sent its first large fleet into the First Crusade. The Venetian force was more interested, however, in crushing a Pisan fleet off the Island of Rhodes. Pisan ships had been raiding Byzantine islands. It was Venice's aim to extract an agreement from Pisa to desist all trading in Romania. ("Romania" was the common name for the Byzantine Empire, as it was the continuation of the Roman Empire. Similarly, the Eastern Church was officially called the "Holy Roman Catholic Church" until the fall of Constantinople to the Ottomans.)

Blocks are encountered; instabilities arise and situations must be juggled.

When Venetians actually brought their forces to bear in the *Outremer* (the "overseas" of the crusaders, i.e., the eastern Mediterranean), they demanded a high return for their services. This took the form of trading rights throughout Asia Minor. Perhaps as importantly, Venice acquired the most potent of spiritual relics. For instance, the bones of St. Nicholas, patron saint of merchants, were exhumed and moved from Myra in Asia Minor (now southern Turkey) to a church on the Lido.

As we can see, Venice was the link between Europe and the East. The Tarot has as its foundation a structure of spiritual knowledge and practice that was well developed in Asia Minor by the time playing cards were imported to Europe by Venetians. Turkish culture that over the centuries integrated Greek and Sufi esotericism (along with Buddhism and schools of Alchemy and Tantra) created an exotic environment for Venetian merchants. They lived amongst a fascinating mix of military, civil, and spiritual laws and practices.

Venice served as the primary base for the Knights Templar during the two hundred years spanning the Crusades. Templars became the bankers and factors of Europe in relationship with the Eastern world. When their society of heretical monk-warriors was violently disbanded by the King of France early in the fourteenth century, the knights dispersed underground. Their human network and intricate knowledge of the mercantile and banking worlds connecting East and West were inherited in large part by the Venetians. Their

Manifestation of life force requires self-potential engaging in the constantly polar process of alchemy.

esoteric alliances with Islamic Sufis, heretical Christian Gnostics, and Kabbalistic Jews engaged them with various underground teachings of spiritual hierarchy, which thrived in the major cosmopolitan trading centers of the Mediterranean: Constantinople, Alexandria, and Venice.

It is important to note that there existed two distinct streams of underground hierarchical transmission. A dualistic Gnostic stream was consistently at zealous odds with the established religious authorities of the time. This often developed into violent conflict. Within this stream flowed many varieties of sectarian beliefs. Put shortly, this stream was universally marked by the belief that an almost unbridgeable chasm existed separating the earthly world from the Divine Domain. You were either a member of the elite who adhered zealously to this view, and thereby had a chance of salvation, or you were one of the masses doomed to eternal damnation. Secret knowledge of hierarchical stages of psychological *ascent* was required to escape the *fallen* world.

The other stream also held to a reality of *gnosis,* or *true knowledge* of Kosmic Law, but championed a nondual understanding that the manifested world was *already saved.* The chasm supposedly separating it from the Divine Domain simply did not exist in reality. It was a fabrication of habitually wrong-minded views. In truth, the Divine *emanated* as the World. Historically, adherents of this position were more successful at diffusing potential conflicts with established religious and political bodies.

We will see in later chapters how important patriarchs of the Eastern Church embraced emanationist cosmology; how great Sufi saints enjoined this embrace; how a rich tradition of mystical wisdom-teaching was partner to the process; and how very similar the ways of spiritual hierarchy discerned by the Greeks and Sufis were with the most essential teachings of Buddhists and Kabbalists. Furthermore, we will discover how psychophysical alchemical practices became the primary method that enabled contemplatives to realize the full extent of enlightened hierarchy. The Tarot emerged as an outcome of this historically interconnected transmission of esoteric knowledge.

Attempting to find and benefit from the source of grace, rudimentary powers are developed – powers that must be structured if they are to be kept.

Venice, independent from Roman, Greek, or Muslim control, was the only Western province free to engage both Eastern and Western cultural centers without fear of religious or political retaliation (though the city-state was nonetheless involved in numerous self-serving military conflicts). Political, religious, and philosophical schism remained between Eastern and Western Christianity until the fifteenth century. By then, Byzantium had completely fallen to the Ottomans, and conflict between Eastern and Western Christianity was no longer significant. The West was finally free to re-embrace Greek philosophy and Eastern Christian metaphysics.

In Italy, Neoplatonism was given institutional support by the Medicis, famous rulers of Florence. Lorenzo de' Medici re-created the Platonic Academy, which served as a haven for Eastern Orthodox scholars versed in Sufism. It was then that Florentines elaborated on this East-West union via the arts and humanities in what would become a renaissance of European culture and knowledge. The non-standard Tarot decks mentioned in chapter 1 were derived from a Florentine re-creation of Sufi and Greek esoteric symbolism and iconography.

Development of the Renaissance, rebirth of Neoplatonism, and creation of the Tarot were all contingent on East-West interaction, at the core of which thrived a transformative stream of mercantile activity. This, of course, was ofttimes threatening to the established powers of Italy. Venetian merchants were barely tolerated by the Roman Catholic Church. On the Feast of St. Nicholas in 1057, a leader of religious reform had this to say to the merchants:

> You flee from your homeland, do not know your children, and forsake your wife; you have forgotten everything which is essential. You are covetous, wanting to acquire more, and gain only to lose, and in losing, bemoan your lot.

Regression that does not return to a primal, pervasive intercourse is defined by limitations of personal authority; thus there exists a possibility that the alchemical process will be arrested.

Although criticized, merchants were simultaneously needed and appreciated by laity and clergy alike. They were the carriers of important bearings from afar. Whether in the form of exotic goods, political information on activities of foreign courts, knowledge of languages and cultural patterns, or relics and rituals of sacred power, merchants offered to medieval Europe critical elements of social power, wealth, and status. They created a conduit to other worlds. In such capacity, they were given special privileges by rulers: travel was abetted through legal and military protection; acquisition of materials for shipbuilding was given the highest of priorities; taxes were often waived.

Along with the crusaders, Venetians blazed open semi-protected trails into the East. These were of particular importance to traveling Christians. A tradition of pilgrimage in the Christian world had roots in Judaic history, originating with Abraham and Moses. This was reinforced by Jesus's disciples being sent to spread the Word into *all the world*. In the medieval age, pious travelers would often seek out special shrines and, if possible, obtain a piece of some sacred relic. Church officials needed to travel in order to consecrate churches, attend synods, gather books and ritual items, and confirm Christian conversions. Both Greek and Latin Christians worshipped saints whose sanctuaries became important places of pilgrimage.

Travel in the Islamic world was even more extensive. While Christians and Jews had occasion to embark on pilgrimages, every Moslem by duty had to visit the holy shrines of Mecca at least once in his or her lifetime. Islam spread via military conquests, wide-ranging networks of merchants, and traveling scholars. The Prophet himself, in a traditionally undoubted saying, stated: *Go in quest of knowledge even unto China*.

In the Christian world, international travel was propelled by the Crusades. The concept of a Crusade was dependent in its execution upon deployment of the lay masses. There were few knights available to do battle with the Saracen hordes, and it certainly was not going to fall upon the camp of ecclesiastics to do so. Mass movement of laity into the Holy Land catalyzed an attitude amongst European rulers that long-distance travel by the masses was good for their countries. This had a most significant effect: the more intelligent and organized participants of the Crusades could not help but have their intellectual horizons expanded enormously. Many of the crusaders who served as fiscal and civil intermediaries between Arabians and their temporary Western rulers learned enough Arabic to become acquainted with common, and often Sufi, customs.

Deliberate acts of extension, even if based on an unconscious sense of alienation, may compulsively engage beyond bondage.

Along with the Templars, the Orders of Knights Hospitaller and Teutonic Knights became repositories of knowledge and experience regarding all aspects of the Near East. Their knowledge expanded to include familiarity with merchandise, politics, and religious ways of Central Asia, India, and to a degree, China. By the time of the Crusades, Sufi culture and trading was held in high regard by ruling classes through most of Asia.

Between the Fourth Lateran Council (1215) and the Fifth (1512), Popes invited representatives of lay rulers to attend *universal councils* previously limited to ruling ecclesiastics. It was recognized by the Bishops that a crusader, be he of the peasant laity, minor clerics, or powerful knights, inevitably would have his worldview expanded. This would in turn loosen the bonds of dominant, hierarchical authority determining his moral beliefs and constraining his independent actions. The only way to handle this was to begin including laity in international Church politics.

Bishops held limited control of Christian activities in the Holy Land. The networked Order of the Knights Templar was in many ways wealthier; more organized, loyal, and efficient; and perhaps culturally and technologically more knowledgeable than either the Church or any of the European courts. Although the Temple was sworn to Papal fealty, beholden to the Pope (and only the Pope) for its very existence, it had become a powerfully unstoppable

A woman's and a man's work naturally develop through a marriage of opposites; for Temperance is an inheritance of prior intercourse maturely discriminated through labor and clarity.

organization in its own right. Church officials were dependent upon Templar advice and assistance in their directing of the Crusades.

No people were more in a position to take advantage of this radical shift in political, intellectual, and cultural authority than the Venetians. European society was undergoing a major evolutionary jump, and it was in a handful of cities such as Venice where manufacturing of goods, trading of services, and designing of arts could emerge on a global scale. Whereas monastic authority held sway in the country, a new form of secular, civilly evolved authority took hold in the cities. Here, artistic skill could find an outlet; apprentices for the crafts were plentiful; fairs were regularly held; educational institutions were up-to-date and broad-minded. Perhaps most importantly, channels to global markets were open and accessible. Northern Italian cities led the way in this communal evolution; French cities, which historically were socially and intellectually ahead of the rest of Europe, followed closely behind.

Recalling chapter 1's examination of the Tarot's early history, we note that the pattern of Tarot production, dissemination, and utilization matched a larger template of international relations in the late medieval period. Through the merchants of Venice, the standard deck of playing cards, followed by the Tarot deck, became known to the northern courts of Italy. With the fall of Constantinople and an influx of Greek scholars into Ferrara and Florence, everything *Greek* became part of a courtly fad and was therein socially legitimized. *Spiritual hierarchy* interpreted through Pagan forms of classical Greek symbolism and allegory could be identified with by court ladies in a way that avoided Church retribution, even while *symbolically* usurping its dominant, exclusive authority. This chapter suggests that the warrior and merchant castes so prominently found in Venice were able to strategically, structurally, and systematically implement aspects of that hierarchy.

New patterns of lawmaking formed in Italy in the late medieval period, as communities addressed their evolving needs. This was

Innocence obeys the compulsion of truth; the arrow of Eros is a flame of compulsion to commune.

as true for the Order of Knights Templar as it was for the city of Venice. Decentralization of dominant authority – away from the exclusive control of Emperor and Pope, so to speak – served as groundwork for the modern development of humanism. Temperance and Love flourished, at least in Romantic literature and bardic songs; certainly there is much evidence for such in Turkish and Moorish Sufi communities surrounding luminaries such as Rumi and Ibn ʿArabi. Italian communities during this late medieval period experienced a major revision concerning how hierarchical authority could authentically emerge. Italian communes began holding their own *parlementa* in large churches. A judicial system arose with the right to measure Justice *outside of* papal oversight. Like ecclesiastics, judges held special knowledge – derived largely from Roman jurisprudence, a body of law preceding Christianity. Qualifications, lengths of tenure, responsibilities, and accountability for judges were determined by the city-states, not the Church.

One of the most prominent creations of Roman law was the institution of *universitas*. Translating simply as "a whole body," this became known more generally as a *corporation*. Structural concepts involving the creation and maintenance of corporations had been developed into a sophisticated model by the Romans. Italian city-states used that model as a foundation for the formation of guilds, associations, and fraternities. These corporations autonomously embodied a microcosm of communal life. Recreational, charitable, vocational, religious, and often secret (guilds protected the knowledge of their trades, be that of materials, methods, contacts, or designs), these societies contained natural, actualizing hierarchies involving authenticated stages of initiation, apprenticeship, and mastery.

Such newly established civility was marked by a positive emergence of hierarchical order in a world rife with atrocities of warfare. Often, the most inhumane battles occurred under flags of religious righteousness. The modern world remains terrorized by ongoing

Be careful, lest aggrandizement of achievements so far constrict the feeling of accomplishment in humility.

threats and acts of destruction wrought by religiously provincial fanatics. Intolerant states of greed, ignorance, and hatred are conjoined with delusions of, if not actual indulgence in, unsustainable grandeur for a privileged, self-elected few. Cultivation of natural and sacred hierarchy is systematically displaced by fascistic mechanisms of domination, possession, and control. The Crusades were a prime example of this in an earlier era.

The First Crusade met with considerable success; the Second less so. The Latin Kingdom of Jerusalem was all but destroyed at the end of the twelfth century by Muslim forces united under Saladin. The Third Crusade led by the kings of England and France recaptured some Eastern lands. By the Fourth Crusade in 1202, the city-state of Venice had become the major naval power in the eastern Mediterranean.

The Fourth Crusade demonstrated just how far apart the Greek and Roman worlds had diverged. Venice and her French allies conquered the Byzantine Empire. Their combined forces toppled Constantinople in 1204. In divvying up Byzantium, Venice gained numerous strategically located naval bases, including Crete. The Venetian empire had grown to span the Adriatic and Mediterranean Seas. Venetian commercial dominance throughout the area was assured. It monopolized the importation of Asian exotics such as spice and silk. These were then sold to German merchants, who distributed them throughout Europe.

Newly formed crusader states along the eastern border of the Mediterranean progressively contracted under constant Muslim insurgency. Nonetheless, trade between East and West steadily grew. Venice had well-established trading lines between Byzantium, the Near East, and the West, and was now competing for trade originating in Persia, Central Asia, India, and China. Everyone knows of Marco Polo and his travels to China during this time. The Venetian Polo family was based in Constantinople. Marco was befriended by Kublai Khan; because he spoke Persian he was allowed to freely travel throughout China. Promoted by Sufi merchants and artisans, Persian had become the *lingua franca* of Asia.

Tolerance and continuity of feeling assure a future of freedom; passionate arguments targeted at craving serve only to sweep away freedom into the silence of convicted bondage.

Western Christian Europe was largely ignorant of the tremendous developments that had influenced Eastern Christian lands and peoples since the fall of Rome some eight hundred years earlier. What is viewed as "the Dark Ages" by most Westerners was exactly the opposite for flourishing lands east. One of Marco Polo's primary cultural discoveries was the prosperous integration of Nestorian Christianity with Buddhism – a cultural intercourse that had been thriving for many centuries. The Nestorians, we will later discover, played a critical role in esoteric exchanges between Buddhist, Sufi, and Christian academies.

All of the major countries and cultures of Asia had been trading and relating for millennia. China, India, Persia, Central Asia, and Asia Minor (now called Western Asia, which included Byzantium) had been actively exchanging goods, technology, slaves, artisans, medicines, and religious wisdom since the time of Alexander the Great (d. 323 B.C.). Moreover, for two thousand years before Alexander, well-established trade routes connected Arabia with the Indus Valley as well as with Persia, Central Asia, and the Tarim Basin of Western China.

In times past, Eastern goods, people, and ideas had to traverse long distances of land to reach the West. In the late Middle Ages, ship routes extended the old *silk roads* to include far quicker and more encompassing trading channels. The ports of Acre in Syria and Alexandria in Egypt were depots for caravan routes from the Far East. Whoever controlled trade to and from these ports controlled trade between the entire East and the West. Pisa, Genoa, and Venice spent the thirteenth century fighting each other to gain dominance in this trade. Pisa was beaten badly in competition early on, leaving Venice to battle with its greatest foe, Genoa.

For much of the thirteenth century, Constantinople was allowed to fall into ruins by its Latin rulers. Popes and Bishops in Rome

Carry the world upon your shoulder, striving for success, and you will discover luck gracing another more innocent youth, unaware of life's sacrificial demands.

never succeeded, however, in banishing the Greek Rite or the holy agency of the *Eastern Pope* (as the head bishop continued to be called in the Coptic Orthodox Church of Alexandria), who we find represented, along with the Popess, in the Tarot. The *Ecumenical Patriarch* of Constantinople served Greek Christendom as its head Bishop, just as the Bishop of Rome served as *Pope* for the Latin Rite. Greek Patriarchs of the Church were allowed to have a female partner – a simple fact that speaks volumes regarding the feminine-inspired origins of the Triumphs. Bishops often had a lifelong female spiritual assistant – the two holding to varying definitions of celibacy. In the modern day, Eastern Bishops are chosen from the rank of celibate monks. However, Priests are usually married, and their wives retain the traditional title of Priestess.

Although early Empress, Popess, Emperor, and Pope Triumphs were painted with Italianate symbols (e.g., the Roman Pope's triple-tiered crown), the overall symbolism of the stations remained Byzantine. The Empress's role and level of societal respect broadly held, for instance, were considerably greater in Byzantine civilization than in comparable roles found within Italian or French courts. The validity of an Empress's rule, whether as consort or regent, was entirely recognized. She generally commanded considerable wealth; often appeared on coinage; established churches, monasteries, and institutions for the poor and sick; and was likely chosen in marriage because of a high degree of publicly recognized beauty. A strategically political or elite background was not of high import in the choosing of an Empress, and thereby she served as far more than a pawn upon a political gameboard. In other words, she was truly an Empress, just as the Popess was likewise. Helena Dragaš, wife of Manuel II, Byzantine emperor from 1391 to 1425, was one such Empress. Helena in many ways exercised more power than her husband, who was effectively a vassal of his friend Ottoman Sultan Mehmed I (1402–1421). The last two Byzantine emperors were her sons, and during her final years she served as Regent.

In the face of contrary powers rending the world, walk carefully in solitude and pursue virtue via synthesis.

There existed a rich cultural climate of sexuality and visionary Love in lands that were once Byzantine. It is significant that female dancers from the territory were in high demand in courts throughout Asia. Male Sufi dancing and devotional rites of initiation involving music, sacred imagery, and other arts were emerging in full glory during the late Byzantine era. Esoteric Christian disciples commonly crossed over into participation with Sufi communities. Persian arts and Turkish arts integrated. Patterns of Greek concubinage and sexual relationship were strongly influenced by the surrounding social milieu; these included practices of tantric alchemy practiced in extended families of prominent men who often kept more than one wife, if not a small harem.

The Tarot, with its prominent inclusion of female spirituality, arose from an esoteric Eastern Christian–Sufi culture that immortalized Eros. *This*, the court women of Italy could embrace and celebrate. Had it been otherwise, the Tarot would never have been disseminated beyond the reach of Roman Catholic hierarchy and scholastic theology.

After the Roman clerics, Venetians, and French were finally chased out of Constantinople, it took all of the Greeks' resources to rebuild it. This required dismantling the Byzantine naval fleet. Consequently, Genoese merchants took over the Empire's maritime commerce. Venice of course did not simply concede its centuries-old position of dominance in Byzantine trade. Instead, it bombarded Constantinople until the city, militarily unable to stop the siege, reinstated Venice to its former position of influence. During all of this European infighting, the Islamic Turks were uniting under a chieftain by the name of Osman. His followers came to be called *Osmanli,* known in the West as the *Ottomans*. By the time of Osman's death in 1324, Ottomans ruled most of what were once Byzantine lands, including Turkey.

It was during the Venetian reign of Constantinople that the famous Sufi poet Rumi lived, teaching throughout Turkey. More importantly for our study, this was also the era and country of Ibn

Hold adamantly to the truth of that which cannot be spoken, for an awful double-bind trap ensnares those with observant eyes but bound emotions who feel compelled to advise.

ʿArabi, introduced in the next chapter as an (if not *the*) original source of the Triumphs' hierarchy. Latin interference with Byzantine rule ironically led to Greek Emperor Cantacuzenus' alignment with the Ottomans via the wedding of his daughter to Sultan Orhan. In the century that followed, Constantinople, along with the rest of the Greek Empire, was subsumed by Islamic culture, community, and law. One benefit of this cultural/religious takeover was further dissemination of wisdom-teachings translated, elaborated on, and practiced by East-West networks throughout esoteric Christian, Judaic, and Islamic communities of the Mediterranean. We will examine some of these teachings in later chapters.

In a final act of Christian desperation, in the years before Constantinople's inevitable fall to the Ottomans, Greek and Roman Churches attempted a reunion. This was propelled forward by the hopelessness of Greek Patriarchs attempting to maintain sovereignty over any Eastern lands without military commitments of aid by European crowns and necessary blessings of Latin Bishops.

In order to negotiate and finalize a reuniting of Eastern and Western Churches, a seven-hundred-strong Greek contingent arrived at Venice from Constantinople in February 1438. Venice was the only agreeable meeting ground that allowed proceedings to be initiated. It is of note that Venice was home to a primary monastery of Camaldolese hermits, which was established in the first half of the thirteenth century. (This was at a time when hermits importantly served as spiritual guides to the Templar Knights, whose primary base was in Venice.) The prior-general or head of the Camaldolese was a Florence-educated humanist (indicating in large part familiarity with and positive embrace of Greek studies), Ambrogio Traversari. Ambrogio had a great liking for Greek Orthodox Ecumenical Patriarch Joseph II (served 1416–1439). Joseph's years were coming to end (he died in his eighties in 1439), as was the many-centuries history through which Venice and Constantinople were intimately bound together.

Venetian diplomacy was critical in the bringing together of these two quite foreign communities and cultures. For instance, Venetians calmed Italian ecclesiastics when the Greeks demonstrated seemingly disrespectful patterns such as not taking off their hats at appropriate times and – significantly – when the Patriarch greeted the Pope as Brother. (The Patriarch was aghast at the concept of kissing the Pope's feet, which he did not do.) The Greeks stayed in Venice for a month, assessing arguments and approaches made by competing Western Church factions, and becoming familiar with their Latin counterparts.

Forgetting the way of alchemy is a sleepy precursor to the draining of vitality and dissipation of essence; so it is fortunate that in the nature of alchemical life there is a propensity to remember anew.

Up to this time, Byzantium's primary contact with the Latin Church was via the Franciscan monastic presence in Constantinople. Roman bishops had a very limited knowledge of the Greek Rite and Eastern Christian theosophy, as almost none of them spoke the language and, as mentioned, there existed relatively few translations of foundational Eastern Christian texts. Prior to the Greeks' participation in the Council, Franciscans had for some years (perhaps seriously beginning with Franciscan Antonio da Massa's negotiations with Joseph II in 1422) been preparing the ground for an Eastern reunion with the Western Church. By the 1430s, Constantinople was sufficiently under threat of being sacked by the Ottomans, and Pope Eugene IV was likewise under threat of being "sacked" by the Conciliar factions of the Church, that both saw good reason to attempt a formal and fortifying rapprochement.

The Greeks had agreed to be taken to Venice via the Pope's ships and not the ships of the *Conciliar* factions, who held that final authority in spiritual matters resided with the Roman Church as a *corporation* of Christians, embodied by a general church council, not with the Pope. Ecclesiastics of the Conciliar movement, which had a history of establishing and declaring alliance to anti-Popes, were holding an ecumenical council in Basel and were not agreeable about starting another council in Papal territory. The Greeks had indicated the direction their political diplomacy was taking, but spent their

Will and imagination, houses of water and fire – abdomen and chest – either merge into concordant union or perversely constitute the generation of demons; such is the difference between alchemical realization and fascistic psychosis.

month in Venice listening to all sides. The Pope and the Ecumenical Patriarch (whose counterpart in the Coptic Orthodox branch centered in Alexandria was and still is called "Pope") then moved on to commence a new ecumenical Council of Ferrara.

As mentioned in chapter 1, Ferrara during this period was under Venetian influence even while it closely associated with Milan. Florence brought sea-and-east-oriented Venice deeply into Italian politics (after centuries of guarded isolation from such) when Visconti took into its domain Venice's old foe Genoa. Milan and Naples then threatened to capture Florence, which appealed to Venice for assistance. Both cities were culturally and intellectually inclined toward Greek humanism. The Venetian decision to go to war with Milan permanently changed Italian politics. Over the next few decades, Venice gained control of much of Northern Italy.

Ferrara became an uncomfortable place for the Greeks when Milan-paid *condottiere* Nicholas Piccinino showed up. Piccinino had been leading the takeover of nearby Papal States. The Greeks at this time sent back all the valuables in their possession (except their vestments) to Venice. In 1439 the Council was moved to Florence for reasons of safety, including avoidance of the plague.

According to detailed comments made by Silvestros Syropoulos, the renowned Greek secretary of the uniat Council, the Greeks found the Italians' process of ongoing rhetoric and incessant focus on Aristotelian philosophy (in contrast to Neoplatonic) to be exhausting and of little value. Many of them returned to Constantinople in October 1439. An agreement to reunify was established, although the population of the East in the years proceeding thereafter effectively vetoed it.

After the Council, Eugene IV sent Franciscans to establish contact with Eastern Coptic, Ethiopian, and Jacobite Churches in order to obtain their ecumenical agreement with the tentative East-West proclamations of a unitive, truly Catholic (meaning Universal) Church. The Franciscans had limited success. In 1441 Venetian merchants served as negotiators and translators in Alexandria with Coptic Patriarch John. Later that year, John sent as Coptic representative Andrew, Abbot of St. Anthony, to Florence with his Venetian companions, the latter translating his Arabic into Italian and Latin and helping to convey the Coptic Church's positions regarding the matter of unification.

Do not confuse the Tree of Life with the Tree of Knowledge of Good and Evil; the former dwells in Paradise, the latter – conscious mind aware of duality but not Unity – resides only in man's fabricated realms.

Manuel II, Byzantine Emperor from 1391 to 1425 (seated as such only through the assistance of Venice) and father of Emperor John VIII Palaiologos who attended the Council of Ferrara, did not believe that citizens of his country would ever agree to attend a Mass that incorporated the Latin Rite. He suggested to his son that he do no more than draw out ecumenical discussions so as to keep the Ottomans in doubt as to Constantinople's military and economic support from the West. In the end, he turned out to be correct.

As mentioned previously, the hand-painted Trionfi first appeared in the courts of Italy during the years encompassing this extended gathering. The present work suggests that the Tarot hierarchy was formally interpreted to aristocratic Italian intellectuals during the Council by visiting Greek scholars. Temporary union of East and West Churches initiated a rage in Italy for all things Greek, including metaphysical knowledge.

It was not until the end of the century that Catholic officials dampened this fascination. By then, there had occurred a rebirth in Europe of Greek cosmogony. At the forefront of this was popularization of Neoplatonic hierarchy concerning cosmic manifestation and spiritual realization. Italy had lost its roots since the fall of the Roman Empire and Emperor Constantine's shift to lands east. A thousand years later, the Church found itself unable to arrest a significant permeation of European intellectual thought by Eastern esotericism. With an Italian rebirth and institutionalization of Greek philosophy under Oriental influence, the age we now think of as Europe's Renaissance entered its maturity.

By 1477, there lived in Istanbul twice as many Muslim Turks as Greeks, a large number of Jews, some several thousand Europeans, and two or three hundred Gypsies. Eastern Orthodoxy continued to thrive, but it existed in the shadow of Sufism. Within the city, there existed three hundred *dervish* monasteries (literally the houses of "mendicants from Persia" offering sacred enclosure for the ecstatic sensuality of Rumi's lineage). Every large mosque housed a hostel for mendicant dervishes. Each of the thirty-odd dervish orders had unique ways of communing with the Divine. All agreed that a series of stages had to be engaged and passed through to attain immortal communion.

The House of Felicity, or royal harem, also had its distinctive rites of passage. The female community of concubines and consorts peaked in political potency during the late sixteenth century. A Venetian wife of the Sultan initiated a period of rule marked by the significant influence of royal concubines. We will have cause to reiterate in the following chapter that Sufi teaching in Turkey celebrated sacred aspects of female sensuality and tantric communion.

In following centuries, modernist forces displaced Sufi law throughout most of the Islamic world. Modern-day Istanbul has striven hard to remain a realm rich in both Sufi culture and international trade. The former has unfortunately been corrupted, although Istanbul remains a largely tolerant and exotic Muslim haven. Religious intolerance promoted by fundamentalist camps in both Islam and Christianity in no way compares to the universal Temperance and Love evidenced in nondual East-West philosophies, including Rumi's and Ibn ʿArabi's schools of Sufism. Through its essential imagery, the Tarot exemplifies the most beautiful of those philosophies.

After the fall of the Byzantine Empire, Venice retained rights to free trade in Istanbul, signing the Ottoman Empire's first treaty with a Christian power. It not only dominated trade with Ottoman lands, as it previously had with Byzantium, but also with Alexandrine

Egypt, world depot for Eastern-grown spice. Portugal was to become Venice's only competitor in this highly lucrative market. Portugal became a major seafaring power in the fifteenth century in large part due to reformation of the once Venetian-based Order of the Knights Templar, who went on to create the Knights of Christ in Portugal.

As mentioned in chapter 1, it is in Alexandria that the popularization and distribution of early playing cards can be found. Recall that in Alexandria we also found a remnant card identified with the Budapest woodblock Tarot. As we explore in following chapters a most fascinating esoteric network connecting Egypt, Spain, Persia, and Byzantium, we will discover how arts of alchemical spiritual practice were fused in Alexandria and Venice through a unique integration of Eastern and Western wisdom. The Metropolitan/Budapest Tarot is a heartfelt, exquisitely remedial, even if somewhat crude, representation of that integration.

Polarizing . . . Right Resolve

It is time we unearth the history of the Knights of Solomon's Temple. Templar involvement with Venice was intimate and substantial. The knights' domain encompassed Gnostic and Jewish worlds of Languedoc, Sufi worlds of the Near East, the Mameluke world of Egypt, the Roman world of Italy, the Frankish world of Northern Europe, Celtic worlds of England and Scotland, and the Eastern Orthodox world of Byzantium. Their awesomely extensive network was plugged into and grounded by the powerful families and guilds of Venice. Through these conduits, East and West communicated, exchanged, and developed in a complex interweaving from which transcultural order emerged.

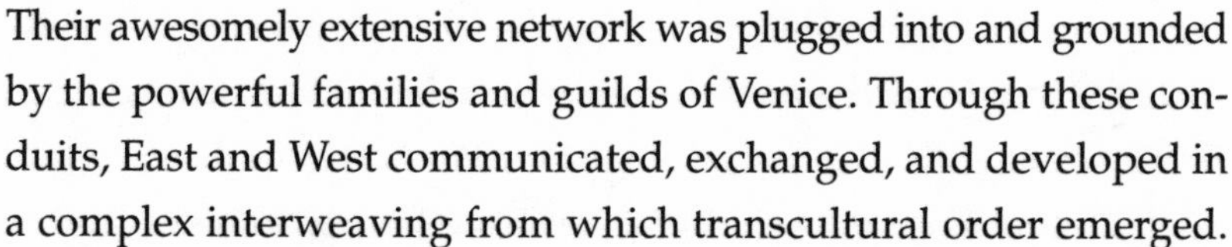

The founding Templar tale tells of Nine Knights, companions to Godfrey de Bouillon, leader of the First Crusade, banding together through faithful oath in 1118 to bring into being the Order

Cultivation requires tools, technologies of progress, which do not arrest movement by deadening cognition, but rather influence cognition to flow with living nature, thus precluding the need or desire for violent revolution.

of the Temple of Solomon. Their purpose was to guard Solomon's Temple and its treasures, which lore professed to be great – possibly including the Holy Grail of the Last Supper. Ostensibly, they were also to protect the route from Europe into the Holy Land, but such work fell primarily upon two other holy orders of knights: the Hospitallers in the South and the Teutonic Knights in the North. Within a few years, the Knights Templar grew to a size of several hundred, becoming an important presence in the newly formed Kingdom of Jerusalem.

The Templars were closely associated with the realm of *Langue d'Oc* (i.e., that of those who speak in the "tongue of Oc"), an area centered in southern France. The history of this territory is punctuated with mystical sects and romantic legends. Poets and bards from Languedoc wove tales of the Templar and their adventures protecting the Christian world. Two of the early Grail epics had Templar Knights as their heroes. Christendom at first questioned the combination of knighthood and monkhood. The chivalry of the Templar Knights, however, soon became the medieval age's romantic ideal of manhood. Capable of spanning worlds, whether between Scotland and Egypt or Heaven and Hell, a true warrior-monk moved through corporeal aspects of life in order to realize transcendental states, if not immortality.

Spiritual enlightenment was not, of course, the sole or even main focus of attainment amongst the knights. Success during the first two Crusades promised the discovery of Christendom's most powerful relics: the Holy Grail, Lord's Cross, Apostles' bones, etc. Spirit-power embodied by these items could transform not only lives and fortunes, but indeed whole territories and histories.

Then too, there was Oriental gold. In Western eyes, the East had access to gold reserves of almost unlimited proportions. Whether originating in Arabia, Persia, India, or China, these lodes of immortal wealth held the keys to world dominion. It was not clear if the Muslims drew on one source of magical wealth and the Mongols another, for knowledge of the East was based more on myth and fantasy than fact and experience. King Solomon's Temple itself had traditionally been regarded as a repository of great material wealth, most certainly including gold. For fifteen hundred years, the East-West balance of trade had been heavily weighted toward Asia. The West had always desired Oriental goods and had always to pay with gold. Even with the breakthrough of Germanic mining techniques, gold was progressively becoming scarce in Europe by late medieval times.

Spontaneous remembrance is intuition; intuited knowledge is gnosis; remembered knowledge is intelligence; intelligent spontaneity is wisdom; wise gnosis is the nondual awareness empowering universal healing and dissipating 10,000 diseases.

When Jerusalem was lost to the Saracens before the Third Crusade, Templar Knights came under the scrutiny of jealousy and political gossip. While viewed favorably when giving their lives for the extension of Christendom, they were critically appraised when they were unable to hold it. By 1200, questions were circulating in ecclesiastical circles regarding special privileges held by the Templars. They had grown into a substantial force of elite nobility, seemingly beyond the rule of both Church and secular law. With major bases in Venice, Alexandria, Constantinople, Tyre, Acre, and Cyprus, the Knights Templar could not be centrally controlled.

Rumors began circulating that the Knights were more interested in Muslim gold, political allegiances (particularly with the dreaded *Assassins* or *Hassasin* – *hashish*-taking Muslim warriors heavily into mind control), and esoteric rituals than with their duties to the Pope and European courts. Within the Church, divisions of clergy often disrespected each other (friars criticized parish priests, bishops criticized hermits, etc.), and lay criticism of Church politics was swelling in general. The Temple Order in its holier-than-thou position became a favorite ecclesiastical scapegoat for unsuccessful military campaigns. Because, however, Templars themselves did not command Crusades beyond the First, they could only be held so accountable for military losses.

In the romantic songs and epics of the day, knighthood took on its own ideal, spiritual attributes. Serving noble ladies, dealing

There is no struggle in the supplication and receiving of the Sun's wisdom; likewise, true knowledge is way beyond dialectics, oppositions, and all forms of analysis – the Sun Just Knows.

with inscrutable Muslims, and heroically engaging their own personal quests for unity with God supplanted the knights' need to practice monkhood. Practices of Oriental hermits, mages, and mendicants suffused the Templar Order. Stories of legendary knights such as King Arthur's nephew Gawain spoke of *salvation* – a Christian version of *immortality* – being won through personal acts of merit and fantastic (even magical) acts of divine intervention. Church hierarchy and theological law were conspicuous in their absence.

Templar involvement with romantic love became a popular theme of Southern French and Northern Italian poets. By the thirteenth century, the Order was being associated with stories of broken hearts. Just as a noble knight condemned for committing murder was left solely with an option of exile through joining the Templar Knights overseas, so it also became with love-stricken nobles. An honorable young man refused by a noble young lady was romantically expected to "commit suicide" via giving himself to the Temple.

An intense form of sexual/emotional sublimation instituted by the Templar Order carried over into Renaissance times. A practice of mind control intimately connected to sexual alchemy developed in Southern Europe during the fourteenth and fifteenth centuries. Later, this was most famously elaborated by Giordano Bruno, notorious for his advanced method of psychological magic involving knowledge of alchemy and eros. Bruno, a famous European court figure to be examined in chapter 4, was declared a heretic and burnt at the stake in 1600.

Military campaigns were not the only context in which Templars derived social status and acknowledgment. As the Holy Land was lost to Saracens, Templars turned away from their warrior roles. Literature of the era portrays Knights serving people through charity and acts of monkhood. Burying the dead, giving guidance and goods to pilgrims and wronged fugitives, advising royalty, and offering refuge to those in need of repentance were common Templar functions.

The Quest can be salvaged beyond acts of repetitive routine, cynical compromise, or naïve interpretation; isolate that which is already pure, already dead, all-ready consciousness.

Templar spiritual guidance, however, belonged to the province of *Hermits,* who served as spiritual guides to the Templars. For the first twelve hundred years of Christianity, hermits maintained a rarely publicized esoteric tradition bridging Eastern and Western Churches. Alexandrine Hermeticism was representative of wisdom-teachings espoused by such contemplatives. St. Francis, to point to a known figure, was a Western exemplar of the hermit tradition and community. We return to this highly influential and little known East-West spiritual lineage in later chapters.

As the Order of Solomon's Temple withdrew its attention from Jerusalem and its physical temples, it fell back upon its European network to supply a reason for its continued existence. Neither the papacy nor the monarchs of the time could do without Templar *insurance.* This *security* took form as loans, trade contacts, political mediation, and international, multicultural expertise. From this arose a nascent industry of what might be termed *risk management.*

Military, mercantile, and financial liquidities of European kingdoms were dependent in large part upon the services of Templar and Hospitaller Orders. Brothers of these and the Teutonic Order frequently served as the closest of papal and monarchical advisors. Even in the Muslim world, where rulers often fought each other, Templars were brought in to advise the most powerful of sultans. The general attitude of kings East and West, and above all the popes, was that no one could be trusted more. Thus, we find Templars serving as royal diplomats, treasurers, judge-delegates, and trustees of the most valuable royal properties. This was to change in time, however. In the later years of their existence, Templar Knights were viewed as totally treacherous by most Muslim leaders, who had no compunctions about slaughtering them in their beds, if possible.

Templar land holdings throughout Europe were equaled only by those of the Hospitallers and the Church. The Order's lavish houses,

Bridging mercy and fierceness is the crown of divinity, authority of the Just; the Balance, the Sword, and the Throne instill continuity beyond the temporality of life and death.

numbering in the many thousands, were protected against any interference by either Church or State. A right to hang the Order's red cross over one's house, should one fall at odds with one's king or prelates, was sold by the Holy Order of the Temple. This gave them the power to safeguard criminals if they so chose. In most European countries, the Order acted as a repository for tax collections. It often safeguarded crown jewels, paid royal pensions, and ran what were essentially the central banks and gold reserves of the era. The Temple's letters of credit were honored throughout Christendom.

Venetians inherited the Order's worldwide banking authority. Only the international Jewish banking community and the network of Genoese merchant houses had similarly established networks. The most powerful families in Venice numbered two dozen. The society of Venetian nobility was limited to one hundred and sixty great families. From these were drawn some two thousand or so men who held all military, mercantile, and political positions of consequence. This communally inherited hierarchy was quite unlike the democratic, relatively open structure of Genoa. Partly for this reason, each of the three knightly orders made its primary base in Venice. Over several generations, tightly sealed bonds were established between influential Venetian patriarchs and the Templars. Through this, an internationally operative hierarchy emerged distinct from Kingdom or Church.

Without a doubt, the newly emergent merchant class of Venice found its Templar alliance to be highly beneficial. Neither political nor spiritual interests lay at the foundation of this, but rather economic benefits. The concept of *economy* was, in the medieval era, still associated with its old Greek meaning of "household management." It would not be until centuries later that national and international economics would become part of the vernacular. In this, the Venetians were at the forefront of social development. Accounts from Provence and England recite conflicts between middle-class merchants and the knightly Orders. From the vantage of many ordinary burghers, the Orders were given unfair trade privileges. The Venetian merchant class, however, was the wealthiest and most powerful in Europe. Thus, they operated on a level equal to the Templars. Again, from this sphere of influence, new patterns of sovereignty and hierarchical actualization took hold in Europe.

Every contraction demands release, every being demands liberation; how can there be a state of Universal Liberation and still exist a world of beings, if not for the fact that the World itself is Realized as utterly simple Bliss?

In the south of France, a Gnostic branch of Christianity developed which has often been associated with the Templars. The *Cathars* (from a Greek root meaning "pure ones"), attended a hierarchical teaching involving the ascent of one's soul in a return journey to the Divine Domain. The sect was strongly dualistic in its understanding of gnostic perfection. Cathars held that the physical world was irrecoverably corrupted. Only a strict path of asceticism could deliver the Gnostic soul from its fallen body. Such beliefs lent themselves to practices of severe austerity. However, on occasion they also supplied justification for loose sexual mores. This contradictory morality was also found amongst the Templar community. Sinning in the body, so to speak, was at times viewed as naturally inevitable for those who were not fully trained in the way of the *perfecti*. Experiencing that inevitability with abandon was not necessarily judged any more negatively than living a mediocre moral life. It is not surprising that this *path of purity* involved purifications that the Roman Catholic Church deemed to be heretically abominable.

The Church backed the King of France in a Crusade against the *Cathari*. Ironically, the Cathars themselves had played a significant role against Muslim forces in the First Crusade. Languedoc and the neighboring Court of Provence, home of the Cathars, were tightly connected to the Order of the Temple. The *Albigensian* Crusade (named after the sectarian heresy with which the Church branded Cathars; *Albi* was a Cathar town) foreshadowed the pall of heresy which was to hang over Templars until their destruction in 1307. The Order had never denied the Church or monarchs its assistance in previous Crusades, for this was the purpose of its existence. However, it refused to take up arms in this most questioned of holy wars.

Suppress the rational mind and it will undergo atrophy, overdrive the rational mind and it will discover efficiency; it is through efficiency, not feebleness, that the Fool translates miracles for the court and the commons.

The Temple hid from the Pope whatever connections it had with Cathar noblemen, which were likely numerous and rich.

Before the Albigensian Crusade, Cathars had decided upon a position opposing the concept of a military order of spiritual knights, holding instead that true Christians should neither war nor proselytize. This doctrine had a considerably demoralizing impact on the Templars, for they seriously respected Cathar guidance. By taking a pacifist position, Cathar annihilation at the hands of the Pope's army was guaranteed. It is worth noting that there is no recorded instance of antagonism between Cathars and Templars. In the Treaty of Paris, the signing of which ended the Crusade in 1229, the Order of Knights Templar was listed as a neutral party.

In the years between 1160 and 1180, a circle of Jewish metaphysicians brought together in Provence an Oriental literature of Gnostic persuasion with fragments of Jewish-gnostic teaching. This formed the earliest of Kabbalistic documents: *Sefer ha-Bahir,* or the "Book of Brightness." The origins of Kabbalism are of significant relevance to our study of Tarot origins. A link between this crystallization of the *Kabbalah* (from a Hebrew word denoting "received doctrine") and Gnostic understandings of the Cathars is quite possible. Certainly, an influx of esoteric knowledge stemming from crusader involvement with Greek and Arabian worlds affected the metaphysical development of this territory in general. We know historically that the first Kabbalists regarded as Masters came from noble, estate-holding Provençal families. We also know that there existed a teacher-pupil chain linking esoteric Judaic circles in Barcelona (present-day Catalonia) to Narbonne (present-day France).

In the next chapter, we will examine profoundly important Sufi developments that occurred in Spain during this era. We will see that these were of primary influence to the original development of the Kabbalah.

Templars, Cathars, and Kabbalist masters adhered to a strict code of secrecy and coded communication. Such a way of exchanging knowledge was used throughout the great traditions. This was done because knowledge so refined and integrated necessitated subtly symbolic transmission. Metaphors, double entendres, and words of complex or subtle meaning have been employed within every culture to convey esoteric concepts and realizations. Kabbalistic teachings were indecipherable to those who were not studied and practiced in Jewish cultivation of in-depth contemplation.

However, influenced by Gnostic tradition, some members of the Kabbalist community intentionally obscured subtle knowledge for occult, dualistic reasons. This was rationalized as necessary in order to control satanic forces or block access to secret knowledge and powers from those who were outside of the initiated circle. One may realistically suggest that such obscuration has been historically tied to simple ignorance of true esoteric knowledge and spiritual realization. On the other hand, it may also guarantee a *pure line of transmission* by keeping powerful knowledge from being misinterpreted by those unable to truly authenticate it.

We shall see that twelfth- and thirteenth-century Sufi esotericism and Kabbalism had much in common, but that the former was far deeper and broader in its corpus and academy. Gershom Scholem, the twentieth century's greatest Kabbalah scholar, held that Sufi metaphysics did not draw upon Kabbalistic studies. Both traditions, rather, independently drew upon Neoplatonic and Gnostic roots. However, the Sufi corpus of translated Greek works preceded the Jewish corpus by many centuries. Therefore, it is not surprising that evidence points to esoteric Jews drawing on their Eastern Christian and Sufi Islamic brethren during the centuries covered in this and the following chapter.

Strong Judaic and Babylonian roots of Gnosticism will be exposed in chapter 5. Many Sufi sages abandoned those in favor of an emphatically nondual, Neoplatonic understanding of hierarchical emergence. In any case, it is of import that intensely knowledgeable elaborations of hierarchical, ten-stage/twenty-two-station worldviews arose within contemplative communities of multiple cultures at this time.

Knights of the Temple extensively infused the territory of Provence by the turn of the thirteenth century. This was, after all, the Order's country of origin. Similar to the Templars, wealthy Provençal Jews were connected to an international banking network. The Venetian banking world brought these two communities together. Unfortunately, extant documentation evincing contact between Judaic patriarchs and Templar Knights is minimal. The relationship between the two remains a topic awaiting further research.

In 1307, King Philip of France, tremendously indebted to the Order, ordered a mass arrest of the Templar Knights along with seizure of all their property. His hope was that by doing so he could consolidate their enormous wealth under his temporal power. He gained the Order's estates, but was unable to keep their huge treasury and fleet from escaping the country.

Kings and popes had been for some years refusing to assist the Templars in maintaining their holdings throughout the Holy Land. This took a toll on the Order militarily, drawing its forces very thin. The Knights were not inclined to abandon all relationships with the East. They spoke Arabic, banked for Muslims, and wore long beards like Muslims. They were dedicated to the Virgin Mary, who was accorded significant status in the Koran, far more so than in the Bible or Catholic dogma.[1] The Templars had established their spiritual home in a mosque built upon the Temple of Solomon.

Furthermore, they apparently believed in an esoteric cosmology closely related to Sufi teachings of the emanations and attributes

---

1. Mary's *Immaculate Conception* was not proclaimed by the Church of Rome until the nineteenth century. The quintessential Catholic devotion of the rosary and its attendant Hail Marys derived from Muslim prayer beads used to recite the Names of Allah, a device and method of meditation having Buddhist origins. It was incorporated into Catholicism during the Crusade against the Cathars.

of Allah. Suffused throughout Templar myths and legends was a romanticized paganism, which Sufis successfully integrated via Neoplatonic philosophy. Sufi placement of Death and Devil (named *Slayer* and *Abaser*) high in the divine emanation of Allah emphasized a nondual understanding that was heretical in exoteric Islam. This was no less so in Christianity. Like the Cathars of Languedoc, Templars believed in an inner course of the soul, which enabled them to personally quest for Divine realization. This esoteric doctrine was concealed from the uninitiated. Grail romances popularized general concepts regarding Templar heroism, including the *quest for immortality. Battling to the death* combined with *immortal guardians* to form the backbone of original Grail literature. Identification of an *immortal guardian-knight* with a legendary *Keeper of the Grail* thus developed.

Esoteric beliefs turned the Order into a target for accusations of magic and Devil-worship by Church authorities. Paintings from this age depict Templar Knights girded by a belt faced with a bearded head – much like the Metropolitan Tarot's Devil. Worship of such a *bearded head* in conjunction with abnormal sexual practices formed the primary basis of heresy for which the Templars were accused. Association of beards with Muslim culture and brotherhood was strong. The Bearded Head was conjectured to symbolize a mystery rite referred to as *Baphomet* – a term generally thought to be a French bastardization of "Muhammad." It is of interest to note that the famous Shroud of Turin originally appeared in the possession of Geoffroy de Charnay, who was burned as a heretic along with Templar Grand Master Jacques de Molay after the disbanding of the Order. The Shroud, it was claimed, was that of the entombed Christ and carried his resurrected, bearded image. Dionysian resurrection and immortality here wed.

On top of their secret rituals, the Order maintained strategic alliances with Venetians that were politically suspected by everyone west of Constantinople. By the end of the thirteenth century, spiritual and hierarchical arrogance along with immense material wealth were commonly being flaunted by the Knights. Agitated by Eastern aspects of Templar culture and the Temple's self-serving political and mercantile allegiances, Western powers found little virtue in the Order; they thus decided not to block the King of France from pillaging it.

Unlike the Hospitallers, the majority of Templars were unable to elaborate rationally upon their philosophical beliefs. For whatever reason, an oath of secrecy was sworn by all. This serves as a classic example of how dualistic doctrines and secret rituals can create a politically dangerous "us against them" sectarian mentality. The precise beliefs of the Knights Templar never were extracted by the Church, although outrageous confessions were made under torture.

After being forcibly disbanded, many of the Templars went underground, surfacing later in Teutonic and Hospitaller Orders. There is evidence that some Templars took refuge in the Alps; Swiss villagers during this period suddenly and unaccountably exhibited high degrees of military skill. Templar influx into the Alps may also account for the arising of a powerful and secretive banking community that remains to this day.

A large portion of the Order reformed in Portugal as the Knights of Christ. The reformed Templars carried with them Arabic navigational knowledge, in particular the compass, advanced sailing rigs, and accurate cartography. Schoolchildren are commonly taught about Vasco de Gama and Prince Henry the Navigator, who were both Knights of Christ. The former was the first European to sail to India. The latter, known as the Patron of Portuguese Exploration, lived during the time that Tarot and Greek studies emerged in Italy.

It is possible that Prince Henry's succession as governor of the Order of Christ, one hundred years after the destruction of the Templars, was reflective of Templar sexual practices. Prince Henry was by all appearances homosexual. Those men who were raised and loved in his private company subsequently commanded ships in his explorations.

As head of the extraordinarily wealthy Order of Christ, Prince Henry succeeded in exploring the coast of Africa and circumventing the Saharan Desert trade routes controlled by Muslims. This opened the way for Portuguese dominance in gold and slave trading. The Order of Christ propelled Portugal into a position of global power. Before the Dutch, Spanish, or English, the Portuguese ruled global exploration and trade. Modern-day Goa, India, and Macau, China, are two remnant islands of that once expansive merchant empire.

One of the points this book attempts to convey is that hierarchies are not always marked by *domination pyramids.* Hierarchies marked by *actualization spheres* are of far greater importance in spiritual, natural, and human domains. The latter defines stages of growth, development, and evolution. The two are not totally exclusive; one form may take advantage of the other. In reference to the Knights of Christ, for instance, dominion over slaves and control of trade routes put them for a short span on top of a domination pyramid, which was inevitably displaced by other military and mercantile powers. At the same time, however, exploratory feats and discoveries made by them opened a new era of societal development, as trade between East and West and settlement of the New World ensued. This actualized historical transformations that permanently advanced human civilization. While the new era of global trade could be slowed or temporarily arrested, it could not be totally reversed. Such is the way of *hierarchical emergence.*

Regardless of dominant factors, there ultimately is no stopping a broad and universal actualization of human potential and realization of transcendental awareness. Humans have an ability and innate tendency to develop, grow, and evolve psychologically, socially, and culturally. This native drive can be waylaid by domineering mechanisms of control for only so long. Domination is always destined to give way to actualization, even if that must first occur through the agency of warfare or otherwise transformative revolution.

In general, the history of this era was one of empires fighting each other for dominion. Bloody as that history may have been, in hindsight we can also observe a level of order emerging from this era so seemingly full of senseless brutality. That order was based upon a system of international trade, reasoned communication, and universal law. Patterns of this period, which preceded modern humanism, foreshadowed our current world. Unfortunately, religious provincialism has yet to give way to spiritual unity and universally intuited law. Nor has the modern-day military-industrial complex given way to a design revolution of socially and environmentally appropriate technology.

Our empirical, scientific age has established the fact that nature is ruled by universal laws. However, scientific *materialism* will never prove to be a panacea for cultural, social, or psychological health, wealth, and wisdom. Clearly, further hierarchical stages of human development will emerge as the world is transformed through the arrow of time. In any case, the Tarot Triumphs were generated through associations during the fourteenth and fifteenth centuries that symbiotically united, even if only temporarily, diverse traditional understandings of corporeal realizations, cultural symbols, and cosmic laws.

The Knights Templar and their Venetian allies served the world by abetting East-West transmission. In the next chapter, we will turn to a community of metaphysicians and mendicants who bridged mercantile, military, religious, and scientific worlds across Western and Central Asia, Northern Africa, and Spain. These Sufis returned the perennial wisdom of hierarchical realization and esoteric alchemy to the doorway of European awareness. Before exiting this chapter's world of Crusades, politics, and trade, let us review the mostly lethal and occasionally ecstatic years between the fall of the Order of Solomon's Temple in 1307 and the 1438 international Council of Ferrara.

In the Eastern Christian world, contemplative practices of ecstatic stillness came to the fore, becoming politically influential in Byzantium. *Hesychasm* involved a type of monastic or hermetically yogic life in which practitioners sought *divine peace* (Greek *hesychia* means "stillness") through heart-contemplation of God. Such prayer involved the *whole* human being – body, mind, and soul. Hesychast practice was considered to be *pure* and *intellectual* prayer – that of genuine *gnosis* – while at the same time an esoterically *physical* form of contemplative cultivation. St. John Climacus, whom we will meet later, was one of the greatest realizers of the Hesychast tradition. In more recent centuries, St. Seraphim of Sarov has been viewed as exemplifying its way of truthful bliss.

Beyond the development and merging of Eastern Christian and Sufi esoteric yoga, the most significant movement in the fourteenth century was that of Death riding a horse of *plague.* Covering both East and West, this dominated all other forms of conquest. The Black Death was actually a series of plagues spreading from Northern Asia to Western Europe. These, combined with truly terrible famines, brought to the century a fifty-percent drop in population through much of Europe. It was during this time that Death was personified as a skeletal, scythe-wielding being. Death in the Tarot represents not only the end of *mortal* development and actualization in strictly human terms, but also the beginning of *immortal* realization and *enlightenment* in Divine terms. The Tarot's Triumphant hierarchy pivots on this station as it shifts into that of the Devil.

The fourteenth century brought a massive depression to Europe. *Khanates* (or "realms of the Khans" – e.g., that of Kublai, conqueror of Song Dynasty China and host to Marco Polo) of the Golden Horde made trade along the northern Silk Road a very dicey proposition. In the south, Ottomans drove out all Christian presence along the Aegean Sea. The Hundred Years' War between ruling western dynasties in England and France mindlessly raged. The lands of Germany were filled with chaotic lawlessness. In general, conflicts between feudal monarchs and their vassals progressively left more and more control in the hands of the people. Combined with a series of major peasant revolts, these fourteenth-century disruptions to the relatively simple societies of medieval Europe produced more catastrophe, chaos, and change than the continent had seen for centuries.

Europe's masses naturally turned to the Church for explanations regarding the causes of so much strife. Solutions were sought that would guarantee supernatural assistance. Roman Catholicism, however, was often found wanting. Throughout the Crusading age, the Church had come to admit a need for direct spiritual experience by common folk. This was inevitable given extensive contact with ecstatic Persian communities in Byzantium and Moorish Spain, most prominently those of Rumi and Ibn ʿArabi. Romantic bards learned instruments, songs, and poems from these Sufi circles and their associated Greek and Catalan friends. They set afire fantasies in urbane Southern European minds that self-realization of Noble Wisdom and Bliss was possible; as was the attainment of magically powerful items that could ward off sickness and Death.

Of course, any Quest for the latter would perforce involve dangerous battles and seductions. Hermits like St. Francis showed the Way, transforming the militancy of Crusading madness into transcendental awareness. Outside of elite courts, an enormous impression was made by newly founded Orders such as the Franciscans. Mendicant friars played a controversial role in the burgeoning spiritual consciousness of lay circles; as had popularization of the Grail myths and idealization of spiritual knighthood. Stories of Robin Hood and his mendicant Friar cohort well reflect the social dynamics of this era.

The "universal" Church had been besieged by heresies in the thirteenth century, as many people had looked to messianic doctrines and new revelations of salvation. These movements continued through the fourteenth and fifteenth centuries, finally developing as a *Protestant* (from "protest") *Reformation.* Tangentially emerging alongside new exoteric religious sects were evolved esoteric realizations represented by such enlightened individuals as Meister Eckhart (generally credited as founder of German mysticism in the context of perennial wisdom tradition).

Spiritual cultivators in the fourteenth century were witness to massive, heretical movements in Europe. Monarchs called into question papal appointments and ecclesiastical administration. In the period preceding the Tarot's emergence, the King of France actually captured several popes, moving them from Rome to Avignon. This led to dual and even triple popes claiming reign, which served to do little other than to degrade the masses' opinions of ecclesiastical authority and legitimacy.

By the time traders and scholars brought into Italy Greek and Sufi teachings pointing to nondual realization of the One, important nobles, artisans, and merchants were of a mind-set to pay attention. Still, understanding esoteric teachings requires authentic practice, and few folk have ever been in a position to dedicate their lives to spiritual cultivation. What did occur in Italy at this time, however, was formation of private artisan societies and elite, educated recreational circles. Examples of these can be found in the guilds of cathedral builders, which later Freemasons claimed lineage to, and cliques of classically trained court women entertaining themselves and their companions with sophisticated images, poems, and music of an esoteric nature.

Life in the plagued era preceding the Renaissance was not easy for international merchants. Venice was forced to turn to the Mameluke sultanate in Alexandria to obtain goods from the East. Memory of the Crusades was very much alive and the Mamelukes were a warrior caste sensitive to Roman Catholic conceits. In general, traders learned to be as literate and diplomatic as possible with their Muslim contacts. Instead of using Latin (language of the

Church), Venetian merchants did business in the vernacular dialect of their city. In the previous chapter, we discovered the Metropolitan/Budapest Tarot's use of the Venetian dialect and an association with Mameluke Alexandria. Given the Venetian proclivity for assuaging risks using *higher knowledge,* we can suppose that the Metropolitan Tarot truly was a merchant's deck.

Merchant culture made extensive use of astrology during this time to guide most deal-making. The concept of *risk* expanded from an association with something *determined by Fate* to being associated with a *fateful force* whose course could be influenced. Advancing patterns developed by the Templars, the formalization of risk management can be found in this period. Fate and Force are represented by the mission-oriented fourth stage of the Tarot – the Chariot and Fortitude Triumphs.

The late medieval era ushered in a global transition to this stage. On a sociological level, engagement with this stage required more than military power and trade policies (second stage) along with political diplomacy and economic systems (third stage). It required a *historical mission* beyond provincial governance and support. This was reliant upon a continuous economic influx advancing *genuine innovation.* Necessary ongoing capital could no longer be supplied solely from Emperors or Popes – second-stage Triumphs of emotional resolve good for war and intensive construction, but not international *diplomacy* and market *freedom.* The fanatical drive of the Crusades was spent, basic trade lines were established, and cities were well built, awaiting repopulation after generations of plague.

In practical terms, the Venetian merchants who succeeded in capitalizing on fourteenth-century death and chaos were those with the means to sustain *evolving* channels of trade far into Asia via East-West networks. A continuous, self-sustaining state of growth marked these networks. An interdependent, global fate was embodied by them. From this emerged the spirit of our modern era, as the New World was discovered and populated, sciences were methodically developed, and teachers of global spirituality appeared upon the world stage. Modern history has shown that even in the domain of warfare, organic networks are as mighty as commanding empires.

Interstate economics and trade wedded with third-stage *information* technology (from woodblock cards to the printing press to telecommunications) produced a *Media Age* during the last five hundred years. This has progressively fractured the barriers of religious provincialism and dictatorial empires. *Appropriate* and *holistic* technologies of our currently proceeding fourth-stage *Design Age* promise to drive societies into a period of global reclamation, uniting laws of virtue and wisdom (call it "best practices") from all of the great traditions. As humanity begins a new millennium, it will witness an age of global networks birthing an understanding of universal hierarchy. This will occur regardless of fanatical fundamentalism, fascist empire-mongering, and massive media brainwashing.

This chapter has served to elucidate historical development of second-stage political structure advancing into third-stage intercultural exchange and fourth-stage global networks. We extend our view from the West eastward in the next chapter. Cultural tolerance, diplomatic skills, and a sharp mind for quickly measuring factors involved with every decision of risk are what we might call third-stage essentials of intelligent civility. Venetian merchants, Greek scholars, and Sufi orders had developed by the time of the Tarot the Triumphant third-stage spheres of Temperance and Love. This maturation of social development prepared the way for a fated exchange between Sufis, Greeks, and Italians not only of cloth, spice, and gold, but – certainly as importantly – of *integral knowledge:* fourth-stage awareness of and hierarchical relationship through transpersonal and transcultural intuition. The European renaissance of perennial wisdom, cosmic evolution, and immortal principles of natural alchemy was very much indebted to the Sufis and Greeks. It is to this community that we now turn.

STREAMING RECOGNITION

TEMPERANCE

The process of alchemy flows into emotions of maturity, instilling recognition that desire and need merge through grace and effort to create a truly Temperate character.

LOVE

Lovers enter one another's soul – carried by the sublimation of Eros – replacing self in a revelation of cyclic unity.

Three

Revealing Perceptions

Moving Beyond Pyramidal Dominance . . .

> The Law is like a lamp. It shows the way. Without a lamp, you will not be able to go forward. When you enter the path, your going is the Way. And when you reach the goal, That is the Truth.

Questors need to see the path before them if they are to traverse it. Once viewed, staying upon the narrow path requires definite resolve. Stabilizing an emotionally decisive center, mental clarity emerges, discerning signs pointing the Way. The Major Arcana are the signs Triumphant.

> Since you have not the endurance for His Essence, turn your eyes toward the Attributes. Since you do not see the Directionless, behold His light in the directions.

The Essence of the Way is beyond discrimination, be that of the senses or of the mind. Looking directly at the One inherently means spontaneous pulverization of self. Questors need to be prepared for complete and utter transformation. The Intensely Bright Mystery can be realized, but doing so is a matter of proceeding through stages, or as Sufis say, traversing *stations.*

Questors can view Infinite Unity through its Attributes. The Tarot Trionfi portray the most essential attributes or stations of spiritual realization. They are signposts marking a universal Quest through which wayfarers identify with Immortal Life and Spiritual Nature.

Attainment to the One or Truth is a journey in which Questors acquire virtues via a process of purification and blessing. Actions must be chosen that are psychically attuned to Fate and Fortune. Egoic independence must be surrendered, willfully enabling conduction of transpersonal love and wisdom. Only then do the signs become clear.

> All of created existence is drunk with the Heart, a plaything in its hand. Without doubt the nine levels of the Spheres are but two steps for the Heart.

Whether one's life-mission leads to high or low fortune, it is important that the Questor never forgets Vital Life and Essential Nature. Through the union of these two, the ten stages of the Way become embodied and known. The alchemy of the Quest goes beyond magical, mythical, rational, and psychic states. The process of enlightenment also fathoms the depths of Virtue and the mysterious Soul of all causality (fifth and sixth stages, represented respectively by the Wheel and Hermit, Hanged Man and Death pairs of Trionfi).

Laws of cosmic causality are addressed in the study of *cosmogony,* generally referred to in our text through the more familiar term "cosmology." This involves not only what *is,* but also what has been and what will be. The Tarot cannot be understood outside a context of *ancestral cosmology* – a worldview of *spiritual* history, hierarchy, and inheritance, which includes immortal domains known and felt as existent in the afterlife. The Tarot reveals even those states beyond Death. One step of the Heart and there be Death. One more step and there be naught but greater Immortality.

The quotes above come from the thirteenth-century Sufi adept Jalal al-Din Rumi. Rumi was a great metaphysician and poet famous for his descriptions of ecstatic realization that indeed, the Myriad is One and that One is Bliss. Rumi was born in Afghanistan but, like many Sufis, was driven west by Mongol invaders. His devotees in what was once Byzantium were numerous. They included not only converts from Eastern Orthodox Christianity, but also the Orthodox themselves; so universal was his transmission of beauty, goodness, and truth. Rumi's tour de force, an immense, spiritual poem called the *Mathnawi,* has been considered by a great many to be the Persian Koran.

Through circulation, mental clarity, and growing responsibility, circumstances are kept under control.

Poetry of love and its sacrifices found intense expression in Persia and Turkey during this era. In Languedoc, home to the Knights Templar, troubadours and bards strummed Near Eastern instruments and wrote poems of spiritual eroticism. It was not coincidental that these were arts first mastered by Sufis. Crusading knights, wealthy merchants, and journeyman artisans brought back to the Romantic lands more than exotic spices and sacred bones. They returned with knowledge of a culture which had by the fourteenth century permeated the Greek, Egyptian, and Spanish worlds, and all lands between; and lands west to Hungary; and lands east to India; and Persia and Central Asia; and soon thereafter, through India to Malaysia and Indonesia and the Philippines.

It was due to the *universal* teachings, practices, and realizations of the Sufis that Islam spread beyond its initial conquests. Arabian rulers propelled the early military campaigns of the Muslim world. Converted Mongols and Mameluke Turks propelled most of the rest. The great warrior empires of Islam were exoteric and provincial in their religious doctrines and cultural practices. However, it was largely a Persian-bred Sufi culture – an ecstatic and tolerant version of Islam – which was carried by merchants to greater lands beyond the Near East and Central Asia.

Before continuing with an overview of Sufism, let us begin to consider the first four stages of the Tarot as they apply to social and cultural development. (The following chapter will explain these stages more thoroughly.) The fourth stage is particularly critical to our understanding of both the Triumphs and Sufism. From it emerges an illuminated view of the world, which is elegantly

Communally integrated through responsible exchanges, a commoner's soul is uplifted into meaningful identity.

embodied by the Tarot. For the human mind, this is a post-rational stage of awareness. Through it, holistic intuition discovers relatedness in all that might be imagined. This type of awareness is tantamount to psychic realization. Some readers may find this stage of human actualization difficult to grasp. The next chapter will delve into understandings of psychic awareness and spiritual phantasm that arose within Neoplatonic worldviews. Significant aspects of such were inherited by Eastern Christian metaphysicians in Byzantine times and incorporated by Sufi sages.

Civilization's *agricultural age,* beginning some eight to ten thousand years ago in Anatolia (what is now Turkey), has been marked since its inception by respect for the power and presence of female fertility. This initial stage of sociocultural development beyond archaic tribalism (which most certainly would have had its own long history of staged development) lends itself to identification with *Matriarchal respect.* From a modern point of view regarding religious beliefs, scholars agree that no clear evidence exists pointing to a universal Mother Goddess worship preceding a later age of male-dominant urban society and mythological development. Matriarchal sociopolitical structure commonly thought of in terms of women *dominating* home and village life is also in scant evidence during this agricultural phase. Nonetheless, we here retain the term *Matriarchy* in its broader representation of "a deeply regarded fertile culture of womanhood." Tantric societies such as can be found in parts of India and Bali epitomize the evolution of agricultural, feminine-based spirituality. In the Tarot, this first stage of sociocultural development is represented by the Empress and Popess.

Industrious, centralized *polis-* (Greek for "city") based societies proceed from agricultural fertility-based tribes. In the evolutionary hierarchy of the Tarot, political/military structure is understood as a second-stage phenomenon, represented by the Triumphs of Emperor and Pope. Much of the previous chapter focused on this second stage and its transition to the third. As a whole, this *political* age of sociocultural development is commonly marked by *Patriarchal authority.*

Attempts at perceiving the significance of one's self in an impermanent world are regularly uprooted and usurped by nature's actual alchemy.

From these two evolutionary stages of social development emerge systems of education and cultural exchange represented by the third-stage Triumphs of Temperance and Love. *Communal institutionalization* of rational faculties and diplomatic tolerance systemically evolves in this phase of social evolution. Empirical sciences and humanistic forms of governance are established through it. The era of political empires, commencing some four thousand years ago, has over the past five hundred years been transformed by economic, information, and media technologies. The *information* or *media age,* rooted in the written word and coming to fruition through an electromagnetic-optical *cyberspace* (comprising all forms of digitally networked information and communication) may be viewed as the quintessential manifestation of this third stage of sociocultural development.

From stations of harmonious civility and responsible communication arise the fourth-stage Triumphs of Chariot (often identified herein with Fate) and Fortitude (also translated as Force). There exist holistically organizing, transpersonal *forces of emergence* operative in societies, which govern and regulate the evolution of agricultural, political, and information spheres; forces that thoroughly influence all matriarchal, patriarchal, and communal worlds. Forces that may be regulated by personal control yet always transcend it. Such forces have traditionally been associated with a *spiritual* sphere initially identified with the *psyche.*

Manifestations of civilization's fourth phase of evolutionary development are experienced as interdependent, hierarchical, and emergent psychological, sociological, cultural, and environmental *shifts* that significantly redefine reality. Perhaps the easiest way to envision hierarchical emergence is through an understanding of Gaia as a *holistic Earth-Nature organism that includes all development of life and consciousness.* That worldview must equally include a *deeply transcendent* hierarchy of processional principles.

To renounce ownership of ideas is to replace opinion with law; the Emperor's sovereignty is conceived through humble truth, not through violent coercion.

Fourth-stage associations and designs are felt individually, communally, and globally through intuitions of *vitally essential purpose.* Conceptually, *purposes* are often identified with specific or general *causes.* However, from a global or cosmic perspective, philosophers are left to imagine what type of cause, mind, or force could have "purposed" all of nature and indeed the universe. In actuality, *purpose* implies a *goal* or "that which one strives toward." In space and time it must be viewed as a *moving or transitioning into.* In this way, the Purpose of Being or Consciousness or Bliss cannot be reduced in definition to that which has passed. To do so is tantamount to positing that there are no purposes beyond egoic human rationalizations.

In this book, terms such as "vision-logic" and "subtle psyche" will be used to describe an *intuitive* awareness of the purposes inherent in natural and living forces. Beauty and the Good are two prime examples of pervasive Purposes. An extensive corpus of transpersonal and integral research has accrued over the last several decades regarding emergent fourth-stage principles of development. A thorough introduction to the pursuit of such psychological, sociological, and anthropological inquiry can be found in the corpus of Ken Wilber and associated "integral" authors.

Conduction and magnification of fields involving the fate and evolution of organic systems and networks can be humanly engaged via fourth-stage awareness. Such has traditionally been the work of shamans, magi, heroes, priests, yogis, saints, and sages. The Tarot and much of this book gives due regard to this stage of psychosocial consciousness.

To some materialistic rationalists, concepts of natural or cosmic purpose are inherently bothersome. However, even hardened scientific materialists will generally agree that nature appears purposed toward beautiful forms as defined by the principle of *symmetry.* Time-based forces *attracting* the world into its future need not be referred to as "spiritual" or "psychic," per se; but they can be neither defined nor generated by algorithmic or mechanical programs. Nor can they be reduced to randomly probable effects of past causes. In chapter 8, the scientific concept of morphogenetic fields, which addresses the generation and transformation of forms, will be considered. Scientific theorists have been unable to reduce the causal procession of forms to linear, mechanical programs and quantified units of matter. Machines and computers may be programmed to manipulate bits of matter and information, but they cannot be endowed with a *causal consciousness of emergent synchronicities* that manifests through Gaian-human evolution. Force-fields of emergent fate always encapsulate, but never arise from, *artificial* "life" or "intelligence."

A practice of integrating dualities is totally crucial for those who would move beyond their own doorsteps; such is the path of sanity.

Even the most complex optical computer systems and neuronetworks will prove insufficient to conduct and magnify, or regulate and govern, fourth-stage field-activity. To state the intuitively obvious: *Computers will never control the Fate of the world.* Climate change in our era is just one massive case in point; for although technology has caused substantial, largely destructive change to living environments, it is unable to control the proceeding transformative effects, most certainly including the regeneration of life. Only *consciousness designing and directing emergent technologies* can do that. Again, how and why this is so will be addressed in our later considerations regarding the sciences.

Every stage of development has its pathological phases. For instance, second-stage warriors and traders have used third-stage rationality to justify subjugation of human rights. This arises when men, dominating patterns of societal engagement, pathologically refuse to allow interaction beyond their control. Similarly, third-stage media and science industries may attempt to *possess* fourth-stage organic networks and psychic fields governing psychological, social, and cultural growth in order to manipulate societal development using systematic, cybernetic techniques. This seemingly enables control of the masses and cycles of nature. Scientific technology,

When the life-energy of the Questor's potency is lifted to meet its potential in the natural world, the outpouring that flows is not drained in waste but rather Tempers the Quest itself.

however, must be governed by ethical law (stemming from true respect for beauty, goodness, and truth) or the evolution of civilization will be temporarily arrested, with catastrophic consequences.

The Triumphs' real power, wealth, and status are wedded to that aspect of humanity's agency and dominion grounded in fourth-stage consciousness. Authority accrued by humans activating creative growth through psychic conduction of emerging domains made apparent through fourth-stage awareness cannot accurately be equated with authority gained through second-stage techniques of structurally enforced, domineering control. No matter how rationalized, spiritual force is not the same as political power. It is a grave mistake to reduce the former to the latter. The Pope Triumph represents the internal aspect of second-stage sociopolitical resolve. The Triumph of Fortitude represents a far greater, organic psychosocial actualization.

Every esoteric tradition begins its life in a phase of intuitive psyche arising from maturely imaginative mentation. Fourth-stage advancements in philosophy and psychology were made by famous medieval metaphysicians. Sufi and Greek philosophers of the Way enabled an integration of metaphysical concepts and multicultural, symbolic imagery. This resulted in a hierarchical yet non-linear worldview comprising ten Spheres divided into twenty archetypal Names and Attributes (with two added archetypes representing the Alpha and Omega Soul journeying through the Spheres), and corresponding Image-Exemplars.

The Tarot as a systematic worldview signifies laws and processes that cannot be fully understood through the analyses of discursive rationality. The Tarot embodies fourth-stage patterns of knowledge. She who quests on the Way exemplified by the Trionfi will realize that fourth-stage epistemology – the nature and validity of Tarot knowledge – is founded upon insights derived from *yogic, meditative, and alchemical practices.* Chapter 4 will introduce Greek sages who were immersed in contemplative ways embracing such cultivation.

This chapter continues with its presentation of the Sufis and their Kabbalist brethren.

The Love of Eros is that binding chastely containing sexual power – circulated, sublimated, regenerated in a garden of paradise.

Sufism arose primarily through the Islamization of Indo-European Persian and Central Asian spirituality. Often referred to in the West as the "Dervish movement" (which broadly indicates a tradition of esoteric "mendicants" but is generally viewed as only one branch of Sufism), it was from its inception deeply involved with Greek philosophy and pan-cultural studies. This lent a universal aspect to medieval Muslim culture, which originally reflected a way of life native to nomadic, militant Arabian tribes. Medieval Sufi teachers were often poor, frequently making their living as itinerant mendicants. When political strife hit their lands, many immigrated to Byzantium and Syria and from there to Egypt, the Maghreb (Northern Africa), and Spain. Later, they traveled east into India and beyond.

Indo-European cultures of Europe, Greece, Persia, Central Asia, Western China, and India evolved from a common trunk. Persian and Greek histories have been inextricably woven together since ancient times. As the age of classical Greece dawned, a Persian Empire was established by the famous Emperor Cyrus and his successor, Darius. Their empire grew to encompass what is now Turkey, Syria, Egypt, Iraq, and Iran, home of the Persians. It further grew to include all realms east into India and north into Central Asia. Even Northern Greek lands became part of Persia. This was in the sixth century B.C. Two hundred years later, Alexander the Great turned the political tide, capturing most all of these lands for the Greeks. Finally repelled at the borders of India, he died soon after (323 B.C.) in Babylon at the age of thirty-two. Alexander established numerous urban centers as a means to civilly rule an empire far too large to control militarily. This is how the Greek Empire, generally marked by prosperity and peace, impregnated much of the known world with what came to be called Hellenistic culture.

For centuries before the Gnostic Christian era, Greek and Persian cultures blended in ways that scholars have still to fully discern.

The continuous and concentrated current of surrendered service requires chastity of heart, poverty of soul, and obedience of mind.

Mythologies and spiritual rituals of each country affected those of the other. Persians, like the Greeks, were a people rooted in the Proto-Indo-European culture that arose in Anatolia between 8000 and 6000 B.C., accompanying the development of agriculture. By 3000 B.C., Indo-European culture had spread west into Ireland and east into Western China and the Indus Valley (the Punjab of India and Pakistan).

One of two original Persian languages known to us, Old Avestan, was used to record *Zoroaster's revelations,* the compilation of which is called the Avesta. The mythology and language of the Avesta's oldest sections evince much similarity to ancient myths and an early version of Sanskrit recorded in the Indo-Aryan Vedas. Zoroaster (properly, "Zarathustra") founded in the second millennium B.C. the world's first religion based upon *revealed scripture.* He initiated an age of *prophetic* spirituality in the Near East, which Islam holds to have been completed by Mohammed. In classical Greek times, he was referred to as "founder of the Magi." (Familiar to the Christian world as Nativity gift-bearers from the East, the global gnosis of enlightened Magi are reflected in the Moon and Star Trionfi shown at the beginning of chapter 8.) Judaism's, and consequently Christianity's and Islam's, dualistic eschatology and worldviews of Angelic and Demonic realms were rooted in Babylonian Zoroastrianism. The earliest myths of the Avesta, however, apparently were not created by Zoroaster. It is quite possible that their original home was in Bactria (now Afghanistan) and their development was connected with, though distinct from, the Indus Valley development of Vedic mythology.

Persians never lost sight of these ancient cultural roots. It may be said that much of the philosophy essential to Sufism resurrected and evolved perennial Indo-European cosmogonic concepts. Over an eight-thousand-year history, those concepts were distinctly cognized by a plethora of societies founded in magical, mythical, rational, and psychic stages of development. Esotericists introduced in this book recognized that all stages of consciousness manifest with varying attributes or essences in accordance to their social and cultural contexts. Experiences and traditions of wisdom then inform human consciousness how these attributes are best understood through a universal hierarchy of unifying Essence. This spiritual process has enabled sages throughout history to elaborate highly intelligent, transculturally verifiable worldviews. Persian Sufis were able to place Indo-European myths and cosmologies into a context that included all of Islam and much of Asia. If modern-day Iran is to reclaim its historical glory, it must first re-educate itself regarding this perennial wisdom tradition. The work of Seyyed Hossein Nasr continues to lead the way.

Reclaim the potency of the Virgin, for only through that can the kinetics of change proceed in grace, transforming fear and doubt in an alchemy of natural and responsible seduction.

Relevant to the history of Sufi metaphysics prior to the age of Islam is the territory that bordered Byzantium and Persia in upper Mesopotamia (home for three thousand years to the Kurds of Iraq, whose history as a mixture of Indo-European people cultivating a notably tolerant though fiercely guarded Sufi way of life deserves every reader's attention, even if this study must leave mention at that). From there across into Syria lived Nestorian and Syrian Christians who actively translated Aristotelian and Neoplatonic Greek texts into Syriac. This process of translating great philosophical tracts of classical times, along with treatises on cosmology, medicine, science, and magic, began in the fourth century A.D., before the fall of Rome. Many of the greatest scholars from this area took refuge in Persian academies due to persecution (primarily for their belief that Jesus had two distinct physical and divine selves) at the hands of Byzantine Roman Emperor Zeno late in the fifth century.

In following centuries, a Muslim empire came into being. When Baghdad was founded as the capital of greater Arabia, numerous scholars were employed by Arabian academies to translate Syriac texts into Arabic. By the tenth century, a great part of Hellenistic knowledge had been transmitted through Syriac into the Islamic world. This was the second leg of a long course, which was finally

The Wheel of Law emanates from a fullness of Being and Mind, Life and Essence; the Wheel of Fortune, however, is blind to its process: the eternal cycling of impermanence.

to see Arabic texts translated into the Romance languages during the thirteenth to fifteenth centuries. In this way, Greek thought returned to Europe, where nearly all works by the great Greek philosophers – from Heraclitus to Plato to Plotinus – had been lost for a thousand years.

During this process of cultural translation, scholars from the Far East were present. Cultural influence, of course, went both ways: in China, for instance, Turkish dancing girls were much in demand. It is pertinent to both Sufi and Tarot history that *Islamic sciences became infused with concepts of Chinese or Taoist alchemy.* We will address Far Eastern influences during this era when we investigate the development of Arabian and European alchemy. Spiritual practice in terms of psychophysical yoga, methods of attentive concentration and subtle transformation, and mystical contemplation forms the authentic basis of esoteric knowledge and realization of spiritual hierarchy in all traditions. Internal alchemy is defined by such practice, and the Tarot can be interpreted as delineating the successful procession of natural essence and living vitality as they become unified.

Baghdad fell to the Mongols in 1258. From Korea to the Ukraine, Mongols ruled an empire that, in scope, was never equaled by the Arabs. Genghis Khan and his fellow Mongols are accurately remembered as ruthless conquerors. By 1300, four Khanates ruled all of Asia. This political reorganization cost China half of its population. However, once established, the Khans proved to be unusually civil and temperate governors. History records their expansive reign as having issued in an age of unprecedented East-West exchange. Through their influence, for instance, Persian art was transformed via integration of Chinese techniques. In general, the thirteenth to fifteenth centuries witnessed an amalgamation of Near Eastern and Central Asian cultures.

Only in the past two generations of research has it been realized how great of a role Central Asia played after the time of Alexander the Great in combining the cultures of West and East along with those of the South. Before converting to Islam in the late thirteenth century, the Mongols had been shamanistic Animists, with strong cultural ties to Buddhism, Taoism, and Nestorian Christianity. Supplanting the role of Buddhism before it in Central Asia, Islam became the "great basin" into which all streams of ideology flowed. It was in Central Asia that Greek, Persian, Indian, and Chinese cultural, philosophical, and spiritual traditions and insights combined to form a global phase shift in which an immortal alchemy of the *Great Tradition* (the body of all "great traditions" taken as a whole) emerged.

Seeing Life in its wholeness, the Hermit exposes prototypes underlying the phenomenal world; his narrow path requires subtle discrimination between the ephemeral and the real.

Western China also became a crucible for this alchemical mixing of spiritual cultures. Evidence of this in monastic centers along the Silk Road, such as the famous Dun Huang caves, is rich and deeply intriguing. Although the history of Western China and Central Asia has been little studied in the West, the area is becoming a crossroads for the transportation of oil and gas and is now viewed to be of high geographical and political importance. Passes traversing the Tien Shan and Pamir mountain ranges dividing the two territories are few. Mongol Khans entered the West via these passes. Between Eastern Mongolia and the Tarim Basin in Far Western China lay thousands of miles of tundra. The Mongols used Far Western China as both a physical and cultural base from which to launch their Western campaigns. The oases of the area remain a gold mine of rich artifacts reflecting an ancient tradition of multicultural tolerance, trading, and artistic creation, which arguably originated during the beautiful epoch of the Indus Valley Civilization of the third millennium B.C.

Buddhism entered China from India via Central Asia and its passes during the third to fifth centuries of our present era. Along the Silk Road, Buddhism, Taoism, Zoroastrianism, and Nestorian Christianity (which included variants of Gnosticism such as Manichaeism) flowed together in a unique stream containing strong *tantric* currents. *Tantra* is an Indian word indicating "weaving." Succinctly, tantric orientations regarding spirituality wove together opposites

Right view begets right resolve, speech, action, and life; revelations of speech then emanate as watchful witnessing in a realization of wei-wu-wei: effortless effort.

such as female/male, immanent/transcendent, dark/light, and earth/heaven. This tantric blend of North-South, East-West spiritual culture will later highlight our alchemical considerations of the Tarot.

Han Chinese called the area north of Tibet "the Furthest West." Turkistan or what is now Tajikistan, Uzbekistan, Kazakhstan, and Turkmenistan – Central Asia – comprised primarily Turkic and Indo-European settlements. As was the Tarim Basin, or Far Western China, home to the Uyghur culture (which for decades has been co-opted and displaced by Han immigration). Numerous exhumations of four-thousand-year-old Caucasian mummies from Far Western China decisively show cultural similarities with Western Celts. DNA comparisons confirm this connection. For a thousand years prior to this time, early Indo-European migrations into Northwest India had been peacefully harmonizing with older indigenous peoples and concurrent Dravidian migrations to produce what has been called the "cradle of civilization" in Asia.

It is interesting to note that Chinese mythology involving the origins of culture refer to this Far Western area as home of the Great Queen Mother of the West. This Goddess manifested divine dragons, which initiated the era of Chinese culture by stemming the Great Flood. The earliest of Chinese Emperors were understood to have literally descended from such dragons. Other legends speak of tall, blue-eyed, blond and red-haired, fully bearded, long-nosed people inhabiting the early lands of Chinese history. Indo-European influence upon later Shang Dynasty and Han Chinese cultural development is a most controversial subject in China today. Perhaps over the next century this study will garner the attention it deserves. Deeper examination of this cultural milieu will be addressed in later chapters.

Toward the end of the Crusades, the Roman Church almost affected an alliance with pagan Mongols, which would likely have reversed the expansion of Muslim rule. This was thwarted by a new imperial power professing the faith of Islam. The Mamelukes of Egypt and Syria based their authority upon a domination hierarchy of martially trained Turkish slaves. *Mameluke* (from an Arabic word meaning "to possess") slave-rulers defeated Mongol armies in the Holy Land and chased out all remaining crusaders while simultaneously embracing Venetian merchants along with Indian princes. In this, we can see how Venice in a third-stage merchant capacity of diplomacy succeeded in expanding relations with the East. Likewise, it is evident how the Templars, bound to a second-stage capacity of militarized policy, did not. The first decade of the twenty-first century saw yet another militarized Judeo-Christian empire and fanatical Muslim opposition failing to heed the lessons of history.

Strategic, structural, and systematic functions appear to define the world, automatically driving it from past into future like a perpetual motion machine; however, general systems are never profound until they emerge holistically synchronized.

The Mamelukes were conquered by Turkish Ottomans after the turn of the sixteenth century. The Ottomans were originally a warrior-mystic corps. Their communal culture had much in common with Orders of European knighted monks preceding them in Byzantium. Sufism historically contained a militant aspect founded upon an actualization hierarchy; i.e., military discipline was used to temper, protect, and fortify civil and spiritual society. This lent itself to a rich expression of the arts influenced by subtly mystical development generated via the harem and sublimated eroticism as tantra. Thus, we find emerging from Ottoman culture the unusually ecstatic dance and music of the Dervishes. The Dervish movement was grounded in a spiritually moving, emotionally intense love epitomized by the poems of Rumi:

> The house of the heart that remains without illumination from the rays of the Magnificent Sun is narrow and dark like a miser's soul, empty of the Loving King's sweet taste. The Sun's light does not shine in the heart, space does not expand, doors do not open: The grave would be more pleasant for you – so come, arise from the tomb of your heart! Return to yourself, oh heart! For from the heart a hidden road can be found to the Beloved.

The constructors of the world – wielders of powers and laborers responding to such – are not to be condemned for their generative instincts; regress then progress, as animal, human, and spiritual natures coincide through the history of civilization.

With the above historical background in mind, let us highlight some essential aspects of Sufism. By the tenth century, Islamic practices regarding development of an esoteric *inner way* had formed. These methods and doctrines had as their foundation an orientation established by the Prophet toward *direct* experience of Allah. It is of primary importance and worth reiterating that such esoteric cultivation was based upon the *practice of realizing union with the Divine.*

Questors on Islam's mystical path looked to a community of Saints for guidance. A saint was one who had reached into the domain of Divine Essence. This occurred via hierarchical ascent through the vital Attributes of that Essence. For most Sufis, the experience of sacred union was temporally limited. Even for celebrated saints constant in their enlightenment, ecstatic attainment rarely reached stations of immortality beyond those of the Degrader, the Valued, and the Nourisher (or the Devil, Tower, and Star; Sufi names for each of the stations as they relate to the Tarot are listed toward the end of this chapter). In any case, from saint to disciple, the process of spiritual intensification was transmitted, authenticated, affirmed, and strengthened over time. Lineages of saints were viewed by many Sufis as naturally succeeding the Judeo-Christian lineage of prophets.

In Islam, every man is a priest. There is no need for politically or socially hierarchical intermediation regarding the relationship between one's soul and the Divine One. No need, that is, if one follows the Prophet Mohammed and his angelic transmission. Part of the uniqueness of the Koran is its thorough delineation of social law along with theological revelation. Social and cultural patterns essential to Islamic exoteric worship were thus established early in the religion's history. These will not be re-determined by future lawmaking prophets, for in the line of Judeo-Christian prophets, Mohammed is understood to be the last. Belief in this is the preeminent feature of the conviction that Islam is the greatest and final religion revealed in the "age of prophets."

All lawmaking since the seventh century has been built on explication or interpretation of the Koran, which was revealed to the Prophet, and the *Sharia,* which is the code of law developed from the Koran. This is what an Islamic scholar studies and considers for twenty years in the process of becoming a respected elder. The body of such scholars is called the *ulama.*

Knowledge must be based on realized understanding if it is to unify man and woman, heaven and earth, offering and supplication; analytical, discursive thought knows only its own Tower, interpreting all wholes from a vantage point of controlled chaos.

The ulama often found itself conflicting with Sufi saints. To the ulama, knowledge of the Divine came flatly from the study and interpretation of Holy Scripture, not from a hierarchical procession of mystical experience. Islam thus witnessed a classic division between exoteric and esoteric traditions. Because religious, social, and political spheres are not separate in the Islamic world, arbitrators of secular law such as rulers and judges are closely tied to their communities' religious scholastic traditions. Without the *inner* guidance of saints, Muslim society readily becomes dominated by conservative worldviews of the ulama.

Esoteric Sufis, in contrast, have created within the great tradition of Islam new paths involving methods of psychophysical-soulful awakening. In the process, they have resurrected far older Indo-European traditions, beyond the heritage of Arabian Muslims. Genuine Sufi methods involve stages of ego-abnegation and progressive awareness of Unity. *Climbing the ladder of spiritual ascension* requires contemplative methods understood by saints as being innate to human consciousness. Even so, such methods need to be activated through sacred agencies and transcendental initiation. Every spiritual community in the great traditions has established such methods and agencies.

Sufi masters became an intrinsic threat to dominant authorities throughout Muslim countries. Militant rulers were aligned with conservative legalists and scholars in societies heavily defined by class divisions. Common Muslims frequently found Sufi teachers far more accessible to their immediate concerns and levels of understanding than they found the powerful elite. *Emotional* religious life was

What is the ineffable mystery of Essential Nature as experienced in the most complex form of life – the mind-body of human being – if not the Radiant Consideration of true sainthood?

primary to twelfth-century worshippers, and that is what Sufis addressed. In fact, they did so to the point of encouraging *ecstasy.* By the twelfth century, attempts to repress Sufism via executions of its greatest proponents had failed. Executions in fact continued, but the spread of Sufism proved unstoppable, changing the very nature of Muslim culture and thought in profound ways.

The history of Islam involves swings between an official suppression of Sufism and a popular embrace of it. If modern-day Western leaders, both political and corporate, would acquire knowledge and insight regarding this indisputable history, they would mature beyond arrogant policies imposing warfare, feudalistic subjugation, and an impossible, imperialistic vision of "Manifest Destiny" upon Western and Central Asia. Attempts at controlling the trade of oil and gas through military coercion and chaos will keep pushing international confrontation to the brink of nuclear catastrophe.

Persecution of Sufis abated somewhat due to the illuminations of Islam's St. Augustine: al-Ghazzali. By *bridging mysticism with scholasticism,* al-Ghazzali demonstrated that it was possible for both paths to combine in one school. Strict theologians looked upon Sufism with far more respect in the era after his death in 1111. It was then that Sufism spread throughout the Islamic world. In the process, much of Asia and Northern Africa were converted to Islam. Popular veneration arose of Sufi *Pirs* or *Shaikhs* (Persian terms for "Elder" and "Master") and rare but powerfully significant *Qutbs* (or Saints; literally the "Pole" or "Axis" of traditional mystical hierarchy). The latter were traditionally held to appear every couple of centuries as seemingly ordinary men who, like Jesus, influenced the world beyond kings and money as they wandered the earth, compassionately instructing humanity while rectifying understandings of Truth. The devotion of their communities was founded upon graceful witnessing that affirmed generally humble assumptions by such spiritual masters of having realized stations of Immortal Unity. Although those spheres of enlightenment may have been in

Questors either view the world in accordance with that system of discontinuities most prevalent to enlightenment or most tempting to distraction and conducive to failure; objectification is the way of mentation, but the Moon is reflective of a mind far more powerful.

some way *revealed* by the Prophet, they were not necessarily *realized* by him.

Perhaps even more heretical was the philosophy of Divine Emanation and Unity of all Being boldly elaborated by the Spanish-Turkish-Syrian Sufi genius Ibn ʿArabi (1165–1240). Metaphysical considerations of Immortal Unity pointed to by Sufis before him were developed into a fully articulated, sophisticated, nondual form of what might be called *monistic pantheism*. Pantheism means "all-god." Its basic tenets, held to regardless of other cultural views, are that the world is essentially a unity and that it is inherently divine. Monist views held by mature pantheists have never actually lent themselves to the simplistic reductions that many Judeo-Christian-Islamic theologians have attempted to make of them. The propagated idea that pantheism means every-*thing* is God, and therefore one's left shoe represents the essence of divinity as much as the Sun or Love or the *whole* of Nature, has always been absurd.

In any case, we will not deliberate on misconstrued theology. Suffice it to say that Ibn ʿArabi's theosophy and cosmology were not trivial. His systematization of centuries of Sufi philosophy preceding him formed the basis of most Sufi philosophy afterwards. Before focusing on his cosmic system of Divine Attributes and its correlation with the Triumphs, let us flesh out some aspects of Islamic culture, community, and law attributable specifically to Sufism.

A good part of Sufism's appeal to the common folk of many cultures was its orientation toward a divine presence that was as immanent as it was transcendent. For example, celebrations of sacred and often chthonic rituals involving singing and dancing were commonly embraced. Cultivation of yogic transformation was tantamount to genuine spiritual mastery. This enabled feats such as remaining unaffected by the elements and defying natural limitations, perhaps via flying or miraculously being in more than one place at the same time (feats that are properly understood subtly and yogically). Such *genie* (Arabic *jinni*, or "spirit in human/animal

Raise your attention into the realm of angels – then relate, respond, and release via such attention – such is how a Questor becomes transformed in the happy indifference of Great Saints and Adept Sages.

form") powers were never completely dispelled by conservative Islamic scholars.

Sufis integrated the earthy rites, ecstatic celebrations, and magical myths of many different communities and cultures. Through tempered, multicultural assimilation, Sufism affirmed the ways of non-Muslim societies, giving a stamp of Islamic legitimation to them. Many of these societies, however, did not particularly reflect the sociocultural structures and dogma enshrined in the Arabian-dominant Sharia. The ulama largely held that Sufi compromises to multicultural ways, although attracting millions of new adherents to Islam, degraded Islamic law to a potentially irrecoverable degree.

Education as established by the ulama was a matter of rote memorization of as many statements attributed to the Prophet as possible. Interpretive understanding of those statements was secondary to accurate repetition of them. There was no room in such learning for new revelations. Ibn ʿArabi stated that his teachings formed a *post-prophets* body of knowledge essentially gracing humanity with fresh guidance based in Wisdom and Love. Many ulama elders were appalled. Ibn ʿArabi's *seal of the saints* was practically the seal of a new religion, for it seemed to supersede Mohammed's *seal of the prophets*.

Muslim pupils of great exoteric scholars would generally study under several teachers, often in different countries. Sufi disciples, however, would submit to a single Master, whom they would obey above all else, including the Sharia. Such devotion allowed for an intense form of intuitive communication inherent to and necessary for esoteric transmission. The relationship between disciple and master was, in its truest form, wholly symbiotic.

Periodically, a disciple would *seal heart-mind* with a great Master. The disciple would then become a formal successor, standing in a lineage of saints. Chains of transmission were remembered and identified with as a type of non-genetic ancestral inheritance. The founding saint of a lineage was given particular veneration, with his or her shrine becoming an order's major focal point. Such orders or communities periodically extended across the Islamic world, from Spain to Egypt to Turkey to Persia to India. By the sixteenth century, Sufi orders numbered in the hundreds. In the West, the most famous of these were the *Mawlawiya* founded by Rumi and known for its whirling dance, and the *Naqshbandi* (meaning "Image Maker" and "Golden Chain"), which had an enormous impact upon the Mughal empire of India.

Immerse yourself in the sounds and sights of the Transcendental Gathering: the uniting of mages, shamans, and wiccans with saints, hermits, and priests in a conclave of ancestral resurrection.

Sufi brotherhoods served common folk through central distribution of supplies to the impoverished, medical care to the indigent, food and shelter to travelers, and spiritual counsel to all. They kept open channels of communication between rulers, military orders, artisan guilds, and commoners. The central figures of every Sufi community were the Saints. These Transcendentals, whether dead or alive, served their devotional adherents through miracles and transformative grace, in general bridging immortal and mortal worlds, the sacred and the mundane. Similarities between Sufi orders and the warrior-monk orders of the West were numerous. With the addition of protected, wandering Hermits serving as spiritual guides, the Knight Templar served many of the same functions within Christendom as the important Sufi orders did within Islam.

A primary distinction contrasting Sufi perennial wisdom with orthodox Islamic theology is an emphatic awareness that no creator-God exists *apart* from the World. The World is an eternal actualization of Allah – they have always been a nondual Unity. The era of Ibn ʿArabi and Rumi technically, in esoteric terms, *sealed* the progressive development of this fundamental Sufi position. Thenceforth, reality was affirmed to be a totally and completely nondual yet hierarchical Mystery of Radiance. The Kosmos was viewed truly as the Bright One, inclusive of all sentient plant (first-stage), animal (second-stage), human (third-stage), spiritual and angelic (fourth- and fifth-stage) domains, along with all transmutation of elemental matter, space, and light. This metaphysical position stemmed directly

Justice is on earth as it is in heaven; just as karmic being circulates through realms of genii and daimons, devas and humans, animals and ghosts, so does the Principle of the Throne integrate the dharma of all beings.

from Neoplatonism and Aristotelian natural philosophy. Islamic philosophy was a continuation of Greek philosophy, which is addressed in the next two chapters.

Championed by Sufis, the above metaphysical view evolved into an elegantly subtle version of the Great Chain of Being. The medieval exoteric view of the Great Chain involved a continuous hierarchy of mineral, plant, animal, and spiritual forms bridging Earth and Heaven. Sufis posited a far more sophisticated, esoteric view of the Great Chain. Theirs was a hierarchy of nested *principles*. The Plentitude of the Kosmos, manifesting through spheres of vital life and essential nature, was formed through immortal and divine Attributes. Once rendered as Image-Exemplars and called Triumphant, those Attributes heralded a spiritual renaissance passed from Eastern Christian and Sufi societies to European spiritual orders.

With that, a fourth-wave trans-rational, vision-logic age emerged. It advanced through its youth in centuries following and continues to mature in the twenty-first century. Each stage of metaphysical or *intraphysical* development, be that societal or personal, contains within it the Whole of ten-stage reality. Holographic paradigms have been used by modern minds to imagine how this may be. Imagery, symbols, and concepts generated in the agrarian age of goddess and phallus worship contained the seeds of future socio-spiritual development. This is how natural growth functions. In this way, infancy holds much in common with enlightenment.

Nondual Sufis held that from Allah – the One – all existence continuously emanates as an overflow of Bliss, Consciousness, and Being – pure Unity, Intelligence, and Soul. They described this cosmogony using a simile: the World emanates from the One just as Light emanates from the Sun. While the Koran declared that Allah was totally dissimilar to the *created world* (or what this text refers to as "cosmos"; with *Kosmos* indicating the ancient Indo-European worldview that includes all *ideal, spiritual, and divine realms*), Sufi metaphysics maintained that such dissimilarity was apparent only when principle-spheres of emanation bridging Heaven and Earth were not fully viewed and realized. One cannot look directly at the Sun without becoming blind, but by viewing Light in its myriad of refracted and reflected states, its nature becomes apparent.

Sufis embraced Plotinus's understanding that from the purely Blissful One (Truth), through Universal Intelligence (Goodness), Pure Soul (Beauty), and World Soul (Flux) the material cosmos is constantly recreated. In truth, the Kosmos resembles a Flux of Change – a World of Unknown-Soul – that ontologically bridges spatiotemporal manifestation with Creative Eros – Soul of Radiant Love. Chaos when viewed insightfully is seen to resemble Eros, the unifying Ground of Being underlying and encapsulating all conflict, opposition, and randomness. Like sages before them, Sufis concerned with a reality apparently defined by conflict, disharmony, and evil realized Love to be that level of reality that includes and transcends all Strife. In turn, the Mystery of Eros resembles the Bright; and only That resembles the One, which cannot *resemble* any thing or state in Truth, for it is wholly Radiance and Emptiness and Chaos and Cosmos already, altogether at once. Through contemplation and spiritual ecstasy, Sufis felt Unity as the whole-body Heart. Of all early Trionfi, this is best portrayed by the Metropolitan World Triumph.

Do not think that reason is annihilated by spiritual consciousness, or that nature is doomed by reason, or that light is extinguished by nature, for each hierarchical sphere incorporates, integrates, and realizes beyond preceding spheres.

Islamic theologians lacking insights inherent to Sufi realization hold to a variety of dualistic views. These generally share the belief that Allah is dissimilar to the world because Allah is totally *different from* the world – transcendent in a way of being utterly before, outside of, and separate from creation. Still, the cosmos *is* Allah's creation, so even in the mind-set of exoteric theologians, it is logically maintained that *All is Allah*.

We will not deliberate upon these theological convictions, for thousands of dedicated scholars have debated for many centuries all possible rationalizations of dualism. In the end, Wisdom and Compassion brilliantly outshine and lovingly undermine any doubt of the Unity of Being. The Tarot presents to us a wonderfully essential depiction of Kosmic Realization far beyond the logistics of the dualistic ego. To understand the World and the One, Questors must journey upon a way of whole-body, no-self enlightenment: the beautifully conscious Way of Bliss.

Resonating . . . Right Speech

Onward now, to a brief overview of emanation metaphysics as developed by Hellenized circles in Sufi and Kabbalist academies. We earlier noted that philosophical Greek texts were translated and interpreted by Eastern Christian metaphysicians (largely associated with Nestorians) and embraced by Islamic contemplatives who became known as Sufis. The term *sufi* was derived from the simple "woolen" garment worn by many of the hermit-like Muslim men who embraced esoteric, spiritual practices.

Except for the Naqshbandi, the major Sufi branches trace their roots back to the Prophet Mohammed's son-in-law and cousin, Ali – as do the Shi'ites, who tend in general more toward esoteric gnosis, though of a dualistic and apocalyptic nature, than do orthodox Sunnis. The Naqshbandi originate their lineage with the Prophet's father-in-law and close companion, Abu Bakr. Lineage claims aside, as a formalized movement Sufism coherently solidified five hundred years after those men, during the twelfth and thirteenth centuries.

Knowledge of the One and its emanations proceeding to produce all of corporeal reality was originally imparted to Sufis through Eastern Christian teachers and translators familiar with the subtle wisdom of Plotinus and his successors.

Plotinus lived in third-century A.D. Alexandria. His work is generally viewed as representing the pinnacle of Roman philosophy. His *Enneads* formed the foundation of all Neoplatonic thought after him. In the fifth century, Plotinus's greatest successor, Proclus, was born in Constantinople. Like the great Sufi philosophers introduced below, Proclus traveled to and studied in the sophisticated cosmopolitan centers of the time, including Alexandria. His *Elements of Theology* formed the bulk of a medieval text known as the *Liber de causis* (or "Book of Causes"), which was to become influential in its Arabic and Latin translations.

Understand that the Arcana of the Tarot represent more than philosophical symbols or stages of the Quest: they signify hypostatic realities – universal, archetypal, spiritual Presence purposed toward the Compensation of all Hearts.

The *Liber de causis* delineated a cosmology of *continuously emanated causes* having the One as their source. Ironically, this seminal Neoplatonic work was later attributed to Aristotle, who thereby garnered Sufi veneration. However, Aristotle tended toward a materialistic dualism that had in fact been repudiated by the great Neoplatonists. Aristotle's reduction of emanated principles to material hierarchies formed a basis for Christendom's *exoteric* concept of a cosmological Chain of Being. This was further reflected in numerous branches of Islamic science, as it is in modern-day science.

Post-Plotinian Neoplatonists expanded the concept of Universal Intellect into Ten Intelligences. Parallels with this can be found in Mahayana Buddhist development of the time. It is known that Proclus, whose corpus served as a summation of Neoplatonism, was influenced by Buddhist philosophy. By the first Christian centuries, Buddhists had established throughout much of the known world the teaching of a *Ten-Stage Aryan Path* (*Arya* indicating "Noble"). By traversing that path, a contemplative could transform all experience of a temporal world, viewed as a matrix of interdependently caused existences, into a liberating realization of ecstatic Emptiness – the domain of Nirvana.

The Mahayana schools of Proclus's time were emphatic in their nondual statements that the twelve-linked chain of causation – *nature as ruled by death, impermanence, change, and interdependent existence* – manifesting as the world always had been and will be ontologically dependent upon and destined into immediate, moment-to-moment Conscious Emptiness. Nagarjuna was the famous Adept who then went on to posit that *Samsara Is Nirvana.* Nirvana is effectively the Radiant Space of Enlightenment, progressively identified in Mahayana tradition with Noble Wisdom, the Pure Land of Immortal Buddhas, and Goddess as Compassionate Nonduality. In this view, realized Emptiness transcends Death and limitation, including all aspects of temporality and dimensionality, while making Immanent the Radiant Heart, Tao, Bliss, or Buddha Mind of Nirvana. The path to cessation of separative ego-vision is tenfold (although it is widely known as the "Eightfold Noble Path" – the last two stages, Right Knowledge and Right Liberation, are those of realized Buddhas).

An elegant Neoplatonic tendency to systematize efficiently, reflected in the thirty-one propositions on cosmic causality of the *Liber de causis,* was to reappear perennially in mature Sufi teachings. Collections of Sufi aphorisms and stories serve admirably as examples of this, but there will not be room in this chapter to give appreciative attention to that genre. The subtly insightful and sagaciously humorous books of Idries Shah and others have made a selection of these stories enjoyably accessible to spiritual inquirers of all traditions.

Another example of subtly integrative systematization that influenced Sufism can be found in the *Hermetic* tradition of wisdom-sayings and internal alchemy. Branches of such Alexandrian Hellenic teaching were roundly embraced by many Sufi orders. Hermeticism will be examined in chapter 5.

Sufi *theosophy* as contained in the Names and Attributes of the Divine One and epitomized portions of Ibn ʿArabi's corpus serves as a superb example of elegant, systematic metaphysics. Theosophy involves *knowledge of the Divine as it manifests itself.* It is a study involving *wisdom as realization; mind as body,* not limited to the thinking self. It is a study inclusive of, yet transcending, complex world systems. Trionfi captions found in the sidebars of these pages, relating the Arcana to each of the ten stages, are based upon a "free reading" of such systematic theosophy.

In the first half of the tenth century, Islamic philosophy was indelibly stamped with the template of theosophical emanation by the great Alfarabi (properly, *al-Farabi*). During the fifteen hundred years before Copernicus, astronomers presumed the cosmos comprised a series of ten nested, celestial spheres: Earth, Moon, Mercury, Venus, Sun, Mars, Jupiter, Saturn, Stars, and Space. Aristotle had supposed that some fifty-four minds or intelligences moved the heavenly spheres and that God was the Prime Mover of all. However, he was unable to clarify the relationship between those basically mythical causal movers. Thirteen hundred years later, Alfarabi suggested that Plotinus's One was the God of both revelation and Greek cosmology. He further suggested that the number of essential Intelligences or Minds was equal to the number of spheres and that both were emanations of the One.

These emanations bridged the ineffable process of constantly *becoming* with that of simply *being*. Thus could the One be experienced, seen, and felt as a manifested myriad. Each Mind, by Knowing the One, emanated its related Sphere and a Mind below it. Thus, the One emanated a First Mind, which emanated a related Sphere and the Second Mind; on down to the Tenth Mind, or the Active Intellect evidenced in human rationality, which emanated the Sphere of Earthly Matter. In this worldview, consciousness and manifestation are in reality wedded.

The original structure of Tarot cosmology can be seen in Alfarabi's system: a ten-stage process of emanation, with each stage being composed of two aspects – an *internal* spiritual intelligence and an *external* physical existence. We might call these two wedded processes Loving Consciousness and Willing Being, or Essential Nature and Vital Life.

Alfarabi's rigorous, elegant rationality henceforth marked the metaphysical style of Sufi discourse. Moreover, it elevated philosophers of the Way to a height previously reserved in Islam for prophets and lawmakers. He who was graced with vision-knowledge of the celestial minds became a philosopher-king on the order of Plato's ideal ruler. The great spiritual realizers mentioned in this and the next two chapters stood in a Great Tradition of such sages.

Avicenna (properly, *Ibn Sina*), who taught in Persia during the first half of the eleventh century, was a famous intellectual successor of Alfarabi. His treatises on medicine were particularly well-regarded by Christian theologians. He had a photographic memory and excelled from childhood at every field he applied himself to. A historic wedding of informed metaphysics with mendicant yogic Sufism occurred through Avicenna.

He posited that each Mind and Body must also have a state of *Soul* in relationship to them. In the Tarot, this gives us the Fool and Magician representing Heaven-Earth and Mind-Body Soul-Heart traversing a ten-stage transformative process of World Unity. This trinity of mind-body-soul was constantly reiterated by future Sufis. Interpreted on many levels, it acquired numerous forms, including a brilliant flowering through the processional states of internal alchemy. In the following chapter we will examine the Christian Trinity and its Aristotelian influences. Avicenna and future Sufis outgrew earlier Christian theologians' identification of intellect and mind with a *psyche* that is controlled by the Devil unless it is guided and protected by ecclesiastic rituals. An age of free science was dawning, abetted in large part by an abandonment of dualistic notions that the human soul was divorced from God and had to be mediated by psychic priests.

Avicenna combined an Eastern Christian vision of ten Angelic spheres revealed by Pseudo-Dionysius (one of the preeminent emanationist philosophers introduced in the next chapter) with a Neoplatonic Sufi cosmogony of Intelligences and Souls. This moved accepted conception of the ten emanated Spheres beyond astrological cosmology. In summation: Avicenna and his academy posited that each hierarchical stage of soulful union with the Divine involved *transformation of the psychophysical self via an agency of angelic illumination.* However, empowerment through angelic emanation could succeed in the Quest for Unity only with the assistance – and indeed *intervention* – of Sacred Intelligence. In other words, an *evolution of the Mind* had to be realized by a Questor to assist her soul's transformation through realms of angelic, spiritual existence.

Identification between Angels, Light, and Knowledge was posited fully by Persian gnostic-mystic *Suhrawardi* at the end of the twelfth century, during Ibn ʿArabi's lifetime. He dualistically viewed the world as comprising three regions: the *Orient,* wherein archangels dwelled; the *Occident,* wherein matter and darkness manifested; and the *Starry Heavens,* which separated the two. Through this cosmology, Suhrawardi attempted to draw a thousand years of Gnostic dualism into the fold of monist Sufism. (Kabbalists in Southern France were at this time attempting to do the same within Jewish tradition, in which Gnostic dualism was originally rooted.) For Suhrawardi, every *vertical* sphere or domain of emanated existence contained a *horizontal* world composed of innumerable angelic illuminations. On the human plane, every soul shared its identity with a guardian angel.

Suhrawardi emphasized that Light was the Greatest of Emanations. The Sun and Angel Exemplars of the Tarot represented the highest states of cosmic evolution in Suhrawardi's emanationist system. The Prophet said that "Light is Knowledge" and "If the Sun's face were to become manifest, it would be worshipped in place of God." Through the vibration of Archangel Gabriel's wings, which spanned the cosmos, the entire world was constantly raised into existence. Although not directly pointing to the Way of Unity, few Sufi or Eastern Christian adepts were critical of this Brightly Divine worldview.

However, in Suhrawardi's vision, like spots on the Moon, Gabriel's right wing was blemished with darkness. Deception and doubt arose from Gabriel's imperfect self-consciousness. Thus, in Suhrawardi's dualistic cosmology, the Angelic level of the Kosmos "fell" into the realm beneath the Moon – the domain of the Devil, Chaos, and all material creation. A similar dualistic Tarot interpretation demoted Justice from her Merciful position upon the Throne of the World.

The original, nondual Tarot placed Justice, representing the Way of Perfection, above the Angel. The Just Heart is Beyond all else, even Angelic Spirit. Still, it is significant that the World card depicts an angel surrounding the world, as if to generate it. In Suhrawardi's quasi-emanationist doctrine, human souls once existed as angels. He taught that it was the work of a Questor to regain her lost paradise through union with subtle angelic light and disunion with gross demonic matter.

While Suhrawardi was highly influential in the development of Persian philosophy, his treatises drew heavily upon dualistic Zoroastrian metaphors and beliefs regarding the illumination of fiery light and the defilement of earthly matter. His belief that gnosis as spiritual realization via subtle knowledge was attainable only by an elite few could not compare to the promise of universal liberation found in the contemporaneous radical monism of Ibn ʿArabi. This was the age of the Crusades, and a rebirth of Gnostic beliefs was spreading from Islam to Europe via the Cathars and similar heretical Christian sects. Development of Gnosticism in Southern France and Spain nurtured a small, esoteric Judaic academy from whence arose Kabbalism. At the same time, the greatest of Sufi saints were supported by Eastern and Hermetic Christian brethren in a historic effort to fully elaborate wisdom traditions of nondual emanationism.

Suhrawardi's school of theosophy was notable for its successful meshing of philosophical knowledge with *spiritual purification*. The Tarot Trionfi were designed to retain such coherence with reality. They cannot be known solely through the mind. To be fully understood, a Wayfarer has to engage in a process of surrendering her body-mind-soul to the purifications and blessings of the Radiant Heart. For Hermetic Questors, this requires initiation into and cultivation of genuine, esoteric alchemy. Suhrawardi was most certainly aware of this. He was martyred in Turkey at the age of thirty-six, at the hands of exoteric Islamic jurists.

During Suhrawardi's era, Sufis fully extended Eastern Christianity's contemplative practices of light-realization into Moorish Spain, while advancing an angelic-gnostic resurgence that found great resonance within a mystical Jewish network connecting Spain with France. The oldest literary document of the Kabbalah comes down to us from Provence in Southern France. The *Sefer ha-Bahir* ("Book Bahir") was composed in the second half of twelfth century A.D. from Gnostic sources of largely Jewish belief (addressed in chapter 5). Association within Provence between its Jewish community and well-established Gnostic Cathars instrumental in the First Crusade quite possibly played a role in its development. It was at this time that thousand-year-old Gnostic Jewish mythology re-emerged, regressing from medieval philosophic and rabbinic doctrinal development.

Regression within a developmental process serves as precursor to re-cognition and affirmation of a newly emergent Way. Regression to old Gnostic mythology cleared the path for a reformulation of rational theosophy by wealthy educated Jewish circles networked into international Muslim spheres. Kabbalist esotericism opened doors of perception directly into mystical spaces of immortal reality. Kabbalist doctrine rested upon a reconstructed Neoplatonic foundation largely built by Sufi metaphysical academies of Andalusia (Southern Spain) and the Kingdom of Aragon (Northern Spain including Catalonia, and the Balearic Islands, Valencia, Sicily, Naples, and Sardinia). Even as Aragon was recaptured from Muslim control, Sufi treatises such as Avicenna's medical encyclopedia were practically venerated.

Ibn Gabirol, an apparently non-practicing eleventh-century Spanish Jew, was the first Latin translator of Arabic Neoplatonism to be broadly accepted by the Roman Church. Franciscans embraced his philosophical bridging of Greek emanation theosophy with Catholic doctrine, even while powerful Aristotelian Dominicans, led by

Thomas Aquinas, resisted it. Ibn Gabirol's Hebrew translations quite likely played a role in Kabbalist development, though he was generally viewed with disfavor by Judaic scholars. Much of Sufism's greatest Neoplatonic work was developed in the two centuries after Ibn Gabirol, who died relatively young.

The family and associates of Rabbi Abraham ben Isaac of Narbonne, a highly eminent Talmudist and president of the rabbinical court, are recognized as the first historical Kabbalists. Heirs of the Rabbi derived esoteric knowledge from the patriarch, whose immediate circle was studied in mystical traditions about which little is known. Kabbalist tradition attributes to him and his son-in-law Rabbi Abraham ben David a *revelation of the prophet Elijah*, referring to identification with Divinity as revealed *from the realized essence of one's soul*. This evidently arose through his experiencing the *Merkabah* gnosis ("ecstatic ascent to the Divine Throne") identified with the Prophet Ezekiel, and through his meditations upon the Book Yesirah, which introduced to Judaism a concept of mystical *sefiroth*.

Ezekiel was a Chaldean Jewish Prophet whose vision of God's Throne was deemed to be the primary orthodox image of the Divine One in Judeo-Christian tradition. (Moses's and Jesus's vision of God in his True Brightness could not be described in terms other than radiance.) Literally "enumerations," the *sefiroth* are ten spheres or *attributes* created by God as *limitless light*. By first *creating* them, the Divine One was then able to *emanate through* them as cosmos, nature, and humankind, manifesting as both incorporeal and corporeal reality (i.e., as the Whole of the Kosmos). Abraham ben Isaac served as a bridge between these mystery teachings popular in Barcelona during the twelfth century and Neoplatonic-influenced Jewish theosophy generated by his grandson, Isaac the Blind, and disciples a century later in France.

In the Provençal Kabbalah's earliest stage of development, Isaac the Blind codified a Judaic vision of the world's creation. It started with a First Cause hidden from all, which then manifested the World's Soul, envisioned as a Cherub upon the Throne of the World. The latter was for some seen as a Demiurgic Angel similar to the Great Satan, but as a Good Power. Toward the bottom or end of the sefiroth hierarchy was the all-important *Shekhinah,* the *luminous splendor* that was God's *free creation* immediately preceding all gross manifestation. Like an angelic attendant or a daughter of Zeus, the Shekhinah can be envisioned blessing and subtly influencing the material world as a *feminine archetypal presence.*

There are many conflicting early accounts delineating the sefiroth; attempts to associate them with perennial wisdom tradition remain difficult. Positions held by the First Cause, Demiurge Creator, Shekhinah, etc., changed during the period in which Kabbalist doctrines were coherently forming. However, the following *modern* scheme in descending order is generally accepted. Carrying both masculine and feminine aspects, attributes correlate with the perennial developmental stages outlined in this book:

1. *Kether*	("Crown")	Infinite
2. *Hokhmah*	("Wisdom")	Primordial Light
3. *Binah*	("Understanding")	Womb
4. *Gedullah*	("Greatness")	Primordial Man
5. *Gevurah*	("Power")	Judgment
6. *Rahamin*	("Compassion")	Holy One
7. *Netsah*	("Endurance")	Moses
8. *Hod*	("Majesty")	Prophecy
9. *Yesod*	("Foundation")	Phallus
10. *Shekhinah*	("Presence")	Queen

Isaac, his son, and their disciples integrated into early Judaic Gnostic teachings and mythologies Neoplatonic metaphysics well established amongst Spanish Sufis. From this arose the Kabbalah. Islamic Neoplatonism had been brought to Provence by Yehudah ibn Tibbon of Granada. Known as a great ecumenical translator, he connected Spain's Sufi enlightenment during the lifetime of Ibn ʿArabi and Isaac the Blind with an insurgent Judaic mystical rebirth at the request of the latter's father, Rabbi Abraham ben David. It is reasonable to suggest that the unknown inner circle of the Rabbi's father-in-law was at least in part composed of ecumenical Sufi scholars in Spain who were rapidly advancing to the peak of emanationist Neoplatonic theory and contemplative realization.

Widely regarded Jewish families skilled in translation, such as the Tibbons, were noted both for their Arabic expertise and cross-cultural wisdom. Spain and substantial parts of the Mediterranean had been Muslim in rule and culture for hundreds of years. Arabic was in fact the vernacular language of *Sephardim* (Jewish descendants who lived in Spain and Portugal during the Middle Ages), who had for centuries intermingled closely with elite Muslim peers. However, this was to change in the twelfth century, as fundamentalist Muslim warriors invaded southern provinces, forcing Andalusian Jews to retreat into northern Christian communities. In Provence, rabbinic circles were quite critical and wary of Islamic influence upon Judaic law and culture, which had been made subtly attractive by Sufi Neoplatonism and cosmopolitan Sephardic communities. For this reason, the work of Ibn Gabirol had remained largely disregarded.

Provençal theologians prior to this time, whether Cathar, Roman Catholic, or Judaic, had not been exposed to the foundational Neoplatonic teachings that we have today. Roman Christians would have to wait for two more centuries before Greek Christians would fully initiate them into the mysteries of perennial Eastern Wisdom. Ibn Gabirol's translations of Neoplatonic classics were limited. Dominicans reinterpreted much of his work in an Aristotelian fashion so as to restrict inclusion of any further doctrinal development, epitomized throughout the twelfth- and thirteenth-century Islamic world by Ibn ʿArabi's Unity of Being spiritual cosmogony. Progressive multicultural, philosophical Judaic scholars, however, advantageously prompted their Spanish and Moorish brothers to translate contemplative Sufi Neoplatonic literature into Hebrew from Arabic during the years that Ibn ʿArabi wandered in Andalusia.

The role of *contemplation* loomed large amongst Provençal Kabbalists. A practice referred to as *kawannah* rose to prominence and permanently affected all of Judaic esoteric tradition afterwards. Kawannah is the practical application of doctrine concerning the sefiroth and immortal spheres of reality. It is *intentional meditation* upon God's attributes. It leads to direct communication, if not identification, with Divine Being. Such contemplation became a preeminent aspect of thirteenth-century Spanish Kabbalism. Kabbalist development returned to Spain during that time, and empowered the Spanish Jewish community to a degree that became threatening to Christian forces as they progressively reclaimed Spain from its Muslim occupiers.

A few dedicated Roman Catholic monks, best represented by Ramon Llull of Majorca, attempted to bridge the contemplative cultures and communities of Islamic and Judaic Neoplatonist academies with those of orthodox Catholicism. Their efforts were met with general disinterest on all sides and thereby had limited success.

In the Kabbalist corpus, Spanish doctrine relating to kawannah practices uniquely refers to the *revelation of Elijah* that was vouchsafed to Isaac the Blind and his teachers. This is the first historical indication of a formalized contemplative practice in Jewish mysticism that advanced beyond magical, mythical, rabbinical doctrines, Gnostic gnosis, and Merkabah transcendentalism. In time, kawannah contemplation displaced the psychically ecstatic vision of ascension to God's Throne as the most primary and direct way to *realize sacred unity.* Simply put, the Way of the Kabbalah was founded upon this new *meditative path.*

It is not likely mere coincidence that at this time in Andalusia, Ibn ʿArabi was similarly addressing mystical stations of realization via direct Unity-contemplation, technically referred to as the "revelation of Khidr." Khidr, the patron saint of Sufi alchemy, was the Persian metamorphosis of the Biblical prophet Elijah. Elijah's Revelation as a *contemplative method of progressive God-realization* held a core and crucial position within the original Kabbalah as cultivated by the family and intimates of Isaac the Blind. This leads us to suggest that *Ibn ʿArabi and his teachings were likely a primary root and source for the growth and blossoming of Kabbalist esotericism.*

Mystical kawannah as sacred union was such a powerful contemplative practice of *inner absorption* that it came to displace the more obvious and less sublime forms of psychic ecstasy produced through Merkabah visionary raptures. When Sufis first imparted to Rabbi Abraham ben Isaac's family the contemplative, alchemical way embodied as kawannah doctrine and prophetic revelation, that esoteric circle was moved to cultivate the supreme contemplation of contemplation itself; and, in this, to ecstatically commune directly with the One Source and Cause of Causes: *God.*

This was soon deemed heretical by Jewish authorities, as it had been within orthodox Islam and Christianity, for it implied that the One as First Cause was not totally separate from the created intermediary causes, whether angelic, natural, or otherwise. If one can directly contemplate God, then God cannot be totally separate from oneself.

Two positions have remained fundamentally dogmatic in Kabbalism since Isaac the Blind's generation: it is extreme heresy to suggest that a human may become *God-realized* (Jesus would be a prime example), and absolutely no images of the Divine One beyond the Merkabah vision may be lawfully produced. Ibn ʿArabi's graphically imagined portrayal of the Universal Man realizing Unity of Being through twenty-one corporeal stations best envisioned as Image-Exemplars broke out of similar Islamic iconoclastic dogma. Ibn ʿArabi was a preeminent alchemist, and his representation of spiritual perfection remains the touchstone of *alchemical nondual realization.* Contemplation of such is the most direct route to realization of the *Golden*

Immortal's Diamond Body (terms from Buddhist-Taoist alchemical tradition that merged with Sufi alchemy via Central Asia).

Regarding the Triumphant entrance of the Tarot into mid-fifteenth-century Italy, it is of note that at the Ferrara Council of Churches, Greek and Roman Churches emphasized a joint anti-Jewish position that practically outlawed any interaction between Jews and Christians other than deliberate conversion of Jews. In contrast, little was said of Islamic communities. The Ottomans had progressively conquered the territory surrounding Constantinople, and the Greek Church was desperately attempting to stabilize its existence in the wake of Islamic rule. Eastern Patriarchs for centuries before and after the Council had no choice but to establish agreeable alliances with Muslim rulers, integrating culturally and metaphysically. From this we can see that Jewish scholars and rabbis were a highly unlikely source of the emanationist and Neoplatonic exchange that was channeled by Greek contemplators and consequent Italian patrons into the Trionfi.

Ibn ʿArabi of Spain carried the title of Greatest Master. Attacked continuously by the orthodox (even into present times), his writings have been considered by most Sufis since the thirteenth century as representing the height of Sufi knowledge. He also has been accredited with single-handedly destroying, during the late medieval era, popular Muslim belief in a personal creator-God as espoused by Judeo-Christian-Islamic revelation.

It has been meticulously clarified by modern Sufi scholars such as Seyyed Hossein Nasr that Ibn ʿArabi's distillations of nondual Sufi doctrines served to brightly expose philosophical understandings that had been affirmed perennially by centuries of Sufis before him. In any case, his statements of nondual identity between realms of humankind, nature, and the Divine, with the Devil inclusively stationed in his rightful place, left little room for belief in a creator-God fundamentally *separate from* His or Her (Allah being both and neither) created world.

Although educated in the traditional Muslim sciences of twelfth-century Andalusia, Ibn ʿArabi lived his final forty years in Turkey and Syria. He was highly influential within both Sultanates and Sufi circles. These were the peak years of Crusading East-West interaction; an age that generated Rumi and transformed Islam. Venice ruled the Mediterranean and, along with France, Byzantium and Constantinople. A new Kingdom of Aragon, comprising Catalonia, the Balearics, and Sardinia, was formed, integrating the best of Muslim arts and technologies into Christian Europe.

Ibn ʿArabi was particularly influential in Constantinople and Damascus, home to Eastern Christians for a thousand years. Indeed, so respected was he that later Ottomans made him their patron saint. It is important to note that throughout the traditional lands of Greek Orthodoxy (centered if not ruled by the great city of Constantinople) during this epoch, the height of Byzantine iconography and sacred imaging was attained. While Rumi created images through his words, Ibn ʿArabi championed a heretical association of Divine Names and Stations with Divine Images.

By the time of the Tarot's emergence, Ibn ʿArabi's theosophical work had become widely regarded everywhere in the Islamic world. It significantly influenced Islam's tolerant association with other nondual wisdom traditions, from Eastern Christianity and Kabbalist Judaism to Tantric Buddhism and Advaita Hinduism. His teachings had been strongly embraced in both old Byzantium and India during the formative years of the Tarot.

It is herein suggested that Ibn ʿArabi's most essential teaching regarding twenty-one *corporeal* Universal and Immortal Exemplars, plus the Surrounding World representing the *incorporeal* Divine, *was fully imaged by esotericists within a Constantinople-Alexandria-Venice network as the original Trionfi.*

Orthodox ulama progressively constructed political blocks against Ibn ʿArabi's teachings in the Alexandrian Mameluke milieu where playing cards were popularized. However, Mamelukes themselves were impressed with magical powers exhibited by unconventional and charismatic Sufis. Ibn ʿArabi had been renowned for his ability to prophesize the future. His view of cosmology as a set of universal principles manifesting as the always-changing world enabled him to predict the forces of fate. His popularity amongst Alexandrian scholars remained strong even after attempts were made to banish his books from Egypt in the second half of the fifteenth century.

Ibn ʿArabi described the realm of *imagination* as the "land of truth." Combined with a focus on the *coincidence of opposites,* his heretical emphasis on the power of Images led to a cultivation of Eros as immanent Wisdom. This effectively merged the creative power of *male love* for Allah with *female beauty* as the World manifested by the Wisdom of Allah. Allah was not seen as having gender, but Allah's cosmic emanation was respected as coming forth from the Goddess Principle. This harks back to original mystery rites of ancient Indo-European, Greek, and consequently Neoplatonic Gaian and Eros-based cosmogony and initiation.

Ibn ʿArabi celebrated a timeless appreciation for the divine power of Eros. He was notably influenced by female teachers, and both Platonic and Erotic beauty. He realized that contemplation of Divine Presence while in a state of communion with a compassionately tantric woman lifted a man close to the apex of spiritual vision. However, this was only true to the degree that a woman's beauty was transformed in spirit by the *unveiling* eyes of the spiritual consort *seeing only Allah.* Thus was Eros realized as the Bright.

Ibn ʿArabi understood that Love bridges the intellectual split of subject/object in an immediate, uncompromising way. In this manner, the eyes of the Beloved become the lover's eyes. Allah's Mind becomes the devotee's mind. Transcendental Being becomes the world as it so immanently manifests. How can immortal Eros not need human love as its realized extension? In truth, Eros *is* the Supreme Soul!

Sexuality was never stigmatized in Islam as it was in Christianity. Asceticism and celibacy were not part of the Prophet's teachings.

Mystical Judaic tradition was similar in its celebration of sensuality and the use of one's body along with one's mind to assist one's soul in its reunion with God.

Ibn ʿArabi's writings were copious; his thoughts amazingly syncretic and systematic; and his mastery of Arabic intricately subtle. Consequently, English translation and interpretation of his corpus has been most difficult. Like Suhrawardi, Ibn ʿArabi combined gnostic and Hermetic philosophy with Neoplatonism. Each of these schools of thought allowed for self-realization of Wisdom. However, attempts to house multiple traditions under one Islamic roof with the intention of fusing them together as a singular family was perhaps unrealistically ambitious. Gnostic dualism was degraded by Ibn ʿArabi, which allowed him to focus his worldview on true unity and not get lost in a mire of competing religious and political doctrines.

The kernel of his philosophy dwelled in that realization best conceived as *Unity of Being*. In Arabic, a language without the verb "to be," such unity was identified with process-centered "witnessing," "finding," and "unveiling." Thus, we might say that for Ibn ʿArabi, the *destiny* of consciousness, contemplative thought, daily life, and the wayfaring soul was a *present process* of supreme, constant, inevitable Unity. In fact, all states of nature and spirit *witnessed* that Unity, whether they were seemingly demonic, ignorant, ugly, and twisted; or wise, compassionate, beautiful, and good.

It was this radical, pantheistic position regarding Universal Consciousness Surrounded by Allah as complete and utter unity of *all* being that set Ibn ʿArabi's philosophy at great odds with orthodox Islamic theologians. Or perhaps it was, and continues to be, the misinterpretation of that position. For "pantheism" in Judeo-Christian-Islamic theology implies a form of defined deity that is totally manifested in and as every separate thing. Ibn ʿArabi's nondual pantheism, on the other hand, implies no *separate things* and no *separate deity*. Also called *existential monism*, this worldview can be conceived in terms of theophanies or processional emanations of

Divine Unity as an always-already-unified and yet essentially hierarchical Universe.

The difference between these views of *pan-* (literally "all," "whole") *theism* (or "God-principle") is considerable. Ibn ʿArabi's understanding envisions all corporeal form as existing in an already unified state, which may be called Emptiness or the Bright as easily as God. Concentrating upon the Names of Allah assists us to cognize the Divine Attributes composing the world. Popular misconceptions of pantheism involve belief in a distinct God-state existent substantially in and being defined by *corporeal forms of the world.* The former presupposes prior and constant, holistically emergent, interdependently hierarchical Unity; the latter presumes a prior division and a subsequent equation between God and the world of things.

Although we will continue examining metaphysical dualism, nondualism, and monism (largely in chapter 5), further consideration of the ontological distinctions that deeply divide these doctrines will be left to the reader. Essentially, the Triumphs were derived from a spiritual realization that the Kosmos is a *unified* and *immortal* reality that fundamentally transcends its own manifested immanence. Humans realize this through contemplation, internal alchemy, and enlightened devotion. Any type of mental or ethereal interpretation of the Tarot Arcana inevitably falls short of real insight if it is not lived and understood via psychophysical hierarchical emergence of the whole body-mind-heart complex.

Ibn ʿArabi stated that the tenth stage of evolutionary realization was that of the *Perfect* or *Universal Man.* This remains a provocative and paradoxical concept. Few statements can be posited about it that are not self-contradictory, unreasonably limiting, or meaninglessly vague. Still, Ibn ʿArabi was not at a loss for words regarding this. The Universal Man is the *origin* and *destiny* of the Kosmos. He *Surrounds* the World before appearance, during manifestation, and after dissolution of discrete entities. He does this *Presently.* Thus, He is infinitely comprehensive, yet still engendered by that *One* (read *Allah*) about which neither positive nor negative features can be attributed. The Metropolitan's insightful World Triumph exhibits an angelic image of this Threefold Heart-being.

This view of emanation allows for a concept of Allah, God, Tao, or Buddha Mind whose true Essence is not limited in definition by any of the ten stages of emanation. Thus could Sufis under Islamic doctrine affirm Allah as wholly dissimilar to the universe, while at the same time positing a hierarchy of actual realization that brings Spiritual Man to the door of divine perfection. Unity-awareness is the law of consciousness that enables this. Right Knowledge is found in being conscious of Radiant Essence simultaneously manifesting via its Attributes or lesser essences as all states of emanation. Thus, Allah can be identified with every level of the world, with the Alpha and Omega (first and last) stations of realization that define Perfection, and with an Essence beyond both World and Universal Man. Ibn ʿArabi was most inclusive. By arguing that Allah was both "beyond" all and yet *perfectly* realizable by man, he managed to establish this most radical Sufi doctrine within mainstream Islam.

A famous Buddhist/Sufi story suggests that an elephant cannot be known through touching its separate parts. In the living world, a whole is always greater than the sum of its parts. To Ibn ʿArabi, each Sphere of emanation was both part of a holon and a holon encompassing other parts ("holon" being a word coined by Arthur Koestler to describe this holistic concept). By revealing a cosmogony of unity and radiance emanating through multiplicity and materiality, Sufis strove to clarify a way out of the labyrinth of suffering and delusion. Allah's closest name was "the All-Merciful." The World-Surrounding One was identified with ultimate corporeal realization via *Justice*'s sword (power of being), scales (wealth of knowledge), and throne (status of bliss) as the *perfect embodiment of mercy.*

Such was the perfected tenth-stage station of True Man and – as the ancient figure of Justice evinces – True *Woman.* Ibn ʿArabi was a man of knowledge who understood and practiced the value of surrendered Love. Without ascribing to him divine perfection, it can at a minimum be said that, along with his awe-inspiring intellect, he upheld an aware appreciation for submissive practice and spiritual devotion. He was known to have cultivated such in a context of female involvement, i.e., tantric alchemy. *Islam*, of course, verily means *submission*. This is more likely to be cultivated in a sacred manner within sanctified intimacy than within bloody battles.

Ibn ʿArabi felt that being graced with bliss through the agency of angels was the secret to *making real* that which otherwise remained purely *ideal*. He viewed identification with angels as precisely what the Perfect Man did in his transcendental transformations through the Ten Emanated Minds. Subtle aspects of Suhrawardi's Gnostic dualism remain apparent in his radical doctrine of One = Man = Angel = World.

Whether through goddess or angelic spheres, Rumi and Ibn ʿArabi fully informed Sufis and Hermetic Christians of the thirteenth century how to be fully liberated, ecstatic, and enlightened. After Ibn ʿArabi, *the Chain of Being and the Path of Liberation were realized to be one in the same Way*. Through emanated principles or spheres, the Divine becomes the World and the World realizes the Divine in a great cycle of simultaneous and concomitant descension and ascension. Following upon this path of realization, the Tarot was created to represent both cosmic manifestation and spiritual transcendence.

Ibn ʿArabi worked with systems and codes in the manner of an esoteric *scientist* (the root of which means "to know"). Key to the sacred sciences of Semitic cultures is the *science of letters*. Both Judaic and Islamic religions are based upon revelations of the Word. The Book of the World is the Logos eternally regenerating moment to moment through its sacred Letters or Immutable Essences. The twenty-eight letters of the Arabic alphabet signified the corporeal and incorporeal emanations of Allah. Ibn ʿArabi explained it thusly:

> These transcendent letters that are all creatures, after being incorporeally condensed in Divine Omniscience, are carried down on Divine Breath to the corporeal stages, thus composing and forming the manifested Universe.

This science of letters conjoined with an associated science of numbers to form the root of all other sciences. As we have seen, Kabbalist knowledge was similarly based. It too sprouted in Spain (after germinating in Provence) during Ibn ʿArabi's time. Like Ibn ʿArabi, Kabbalist masters traveled east to Alexandria, Damascus, and Constantinople.

Of remarkable import to our study of the Trionfi is Ibn ʿArabi's realization that the Semitic science of letters is itself founded upon a more essential body of knowledge. He elucidates:

> *Preceding the Letters are the Divine Names* themselves. They form a science, which like hidden treasure is known solely to the saints, whose intelligences gather understanding from Allah and whose hearts are bound to Allah, being ravished by Allah's Bliss.

The Sufi science of letters and names was referred to by an Arabic term derived from the Greek word for *signs.* It formed a type of *primordial semiotics* – a *code* not only of the phenomenal, but also, more radically, of the *archetypal noumenal.* This complex system came to contain a mix of numerological algorithms, alchemical procedures, and emanationist hierarchies. It was elaborated at great length by Ibn ʿArabi's school of metaphysics. One of the more popularly described models was composed of ten levels, each with ten attributes. A hierarchically transformative, dimensional, and energetic representation of ascending movement toward the Principal, embedded in the science of names, is what concerns us here.

Medieval scholars (both East and West) inherited from Ibn ʿArabi a cosmology of ascent and descent diagrammed as a circle. *In this spiritually emergent worldview, we may find the origins of the Tarot*

Triumphs' attributes and names. The Circle of Being does not actually close upon itself; rather it proceeds as an open spiral. It links twenty-eight archetypal stations of Universal Presence, divided into three distinct groups:

1. Through Grace, there is a descending of Divine Overflow as the formed or corporeal world. This descent involves fourteen cosmic stages of being, beginning with the Recompensor (Fool) and the Independent (Magician) and ending with the Quickener (Hanged Man) and the Slayer (Death).
2. Following that are seven degrees of ascending stations, which link the corporeal world after Death to the incorporeal Divine Domain of Surrounding Essence (World). These begin with the Precious (Tower) and the Nourisher (Star) and end with the Gatherer (Angel) and the Elevator (Justice).
3. The final seven degrees of this Great Chain of Causation and Being are beyond even the most sublimely spiritual forms of corporeal existence. They are brought into consciousness through the Universal Man. From the Surrounder (World) to the Divine Essence, these degrees of Allah are the ascendancy of non-formed spirit. They are understandable only as the development of Divine *Pleroma* (fullness). Because they are incorporeal, it is not possible to "imagine" these stations of trans-world reality, although names for them were revealed to the Prophet. From these seven degrees of Plentitude, the World perpetually manifests via an overflow of Bliss.

The abstract and paradoxical logistics of imagining a spiral of descent and ascent, which continuously evolves into greater spheres while never deviating from being undifferentiated Unity, are awesome indeed. Note that each essential world-principle, whether descending or ascending, advances in the sense of greater encapsulation beyond the previous principle. Each degree of existence encompasses the previous degrees. However, instead of envisioning succeeding principle-spheres as physically "larger" than preceding ones, it is more accurate to intuit each as a sphere increasing in *mysterious depth, transcendent height, and transparent intensity* of relatedness or density of signification.

Each sphere is defined *vertically* by its relationship with other nested spheres and *horizontally* by the manifested relationships within its own level of existence. While such manifestation appears to have temporal existence, it is crucial to understand that all existence is derived from the relationship of the Emanated Principles with the One.

Relationship or Consciousness precedes Entity or Being. Mind precedes Body. The Purpose of the One or Bliss precedes either. In other words, all aspects of Time and Space are modifications of Law. *In comparison with the Law of Essential Principles and Attributes of Unity, all other law pales in significance.* All relationship via the Emanations – that is, all Radiant Consciousness – is itself ultimately Lost in the Transcendental Nonduality of the One, or what may be called the Unity Pulverization of True Bliss.

Let us now look at all twenty-two Names of Allah's corporeal Emanation (the last of which is actually Incorporeal and represents Perfect Reality) and their associated Eastern Christian Tarot Arcana names:

0. Large Recompensor	Fool
1. Independent	Magician
2. Influencer	Empress
3. Supporter	Popess
4. Knower	Emperor
5. Victorious	Pope
6. Light	Temperance
7. Form Giver	Love
8. Reckoner	Chariot
9. Guardian	Fortitude
10. Curtailer	Wheel
11. Living	Hermit

12. Quickener	Hanged Man
13. Slayer	Death
14. Preciously Valued	Tower
15. Nourisher	Star
16. Degrader	Devil
17. Powerful	Moon
18. Minute Observer	Sun
19. Gatherer	Angel
20. Elevator	Justice
21. Surrounder	World

Ibn ʿArabi's positioning of the Degrader just under the Powerful, corresponding to the Devil just under the Moon, is addressed in chapter 7.

Gaining insight to the relatedness between each Sufi Name and each Tarot Arcanum requires that we be versed in the significance of each station as experienced by successful Questors. This requires investigation into and experience of universal stages of spiritual realization. Such stages have been conveyed into our present era by yogic alchemists, saintly contemplatives, and sagacious adepts of the world's great spiritual traditions. These are in part depicted within the iconography of the Trionfi. Each of the Triumphs exemplifies an ideal station that Questors must attain in order to proceed into the domain of saints and immortals.

How it is that images may assist to seal a Questor's mind through actualization of spiritual reality will next be considered. The art of *unveiling* formed for Sufis a way to express *intuited knowledge of Mystery;* of that which lies deeper than surface sensation and perception. Sufi teaching is founded upon formulations that most elegantly promote apprehension in the manner of True Intelligence, which perforce includes psychophysical realization and transformation. Through the subtle art of unveiling, esoteric Sufis were able to share their observations of *unseen realities clothed in sensory forms* but in truth existing as the World of Image-Exemplars.

SECRETED FORBEARANCE

CHARIOT

Initiation into the way of transcendental magic and regenerative ecstasy begins with a conduction of communal spirit, for the Questor is never alone in Fate's Chariot.

FORTITUDE

To guard vital life, continuously recharge the Fortitude of essential nature; in this way, confidential faith is illumined through sublime containment.

Aligning with Allies

Surrendering Phantasies to the Sacred . . .

It is premised in this book that environmental, societal, cultural, and psychological development occurs through cyclically evolving stages of growth. In psychosocial terms, humans evolve through magical, mythical, rational, and transpersonal or subtly psychic stages of development. While doing so, human consciousness at any level is purposed toward that which is always *greater* and more *integral.*

Tarot esotericism does not shy away from charged issues inherent to becoming greater, namely *evolution and hierarchy.* Dualistic, political beliefs have justified violations of human liberty, or the *right to grow,* by misconstruing psychophysical and sociocultural evolution. Belief systems marked by religious provincialism and scientific materialism have done this by refusing to acknowledge the *universality* of immortal and cosmic hierarchical principles. Spirituality associated with *political* hierarchies of *control* habitually arrests internal evolution; as does belief in scientific materialism that reductionistically ignores the principle of hierarchical emergence itself.

Exoteric theologians and mechanistic dogmatists do not perceive a unity of Eros and Intelligence, the Veiled and the Bright, Manifestation and Consciousness. They do not realize that *form is empty* and *emptiness is form.* For this reason, what the Tarot represents has been and will remain to be an antagonizing problem for scientific materialists, dictatorial rulers, analytic philosophers, and religious provincials.

The first half of this chapter addresses fundamental stages of hierarchy broadly recognized by metaphysical traditions thriving during medieval times and largely influenced by Neoplatonism. A six-stage template of personal and social growth or evolution outlining a natural path of spiritual realization was imaged by the original designers of the Tarot. Four Immortal states of realization were additionally depicted, facilitating conscious and corporeal identity with divine states and principles so that immortality could be known and realized. In this way, incorporeal law, such as it may be conceived, was applied to all corporeal realms within one model comprising ten nested spheres or principle-processes of reality.

In the second half of the chapter we consider historical, intellectual attempts to bridge dualistic presumptions of *separate* incorporeal (i.e., divine reality that is "above" and "outside" of manifested reality) and corporeal domains. These include great syntheses made by metaphysicians in late Pagan and early Eastern Christian communities. Insights regarding Neoplatonism and Greek Christian esotericism will serve to elucidate our previous brief introduction to Sufi metaphysics. We will attempt to dispel confusion about how an incorporeal God could possibly be directly contemplated and Triumphantly imaged by anyone other than the prophets Moses, Elijah, Jesus, or Mohammed.

This is a chapter dense in its coverage. It delineates core arguments regarding the meaning and development of the Tarot. The rest of this book clears ground more easily traversed. Readers finding the way too difficult might best be advanced by returning to this chapter later. In chapters 5 and 7 we will trace back the roots of mythical dualism. We will examine worldviews in which ideal law and transcendent deity were imagined to have existed before, outside of, and distinct from immanent reality, be that the First Cause or Current Infinitude. In chapter 6, we will correlate our studies with the practices of Hermetic and Taoist alchemy along with tantric yoga. By the end of our journey we will have an in-depth understanding of the Tarot's true origins, the roots of Western esotericism, and how to realize the immortal beauty, goodness, and truth inherent to the Triumphs' twenty-two stations of enlightenment.

Skills are finely honed, almost mastered; however, a world on the edge makes them seem so very insubstantial.

Medieval Latin Christians held to an ostensible conviction that history, both personal and worldly, was ruled by God's timeline. It moved toward a predestined "omega point": the end of the world as known by man. Individuals lived and died purposed toward that end, which was "cosmically" defined in terms of three domains. To *Heaven* would be returned those souls that chose to be saved through the agencies of Jesus the Christ and His Holy Roman Church. Delivered to *Hell* would be those who denied salvation, be that through immoral passion or unlawful knowledge. In *Purgatory* would abide the great many souls that needed time to cleanse their great many impurities. Punctuated by prophets, Jesus, Jesus's Apostles, and saints or sectarian founders such as Paul, Kosmic history had been foretold by sacred scripture, largely in terms of a series of battles destined to end in a fiery eschatological drama. Man and Woman "fell" from heavenly Eden at the beginning of history. Confessed Roman Catholics would be "raised" back to their original home at the end of history.

In the above view, mankind *evolved* only in the ancient sense that human history "rolled out" through divine force manifesting God's plan. Returning to the One through stations of psychophysical *illumination* was an *esoteric* reality far removed from most Latin Christians. As we shall see, Greek Christianity inherited knowledge of spiritual evolution from Neoplatonic teaching during the Roman Empire's final centuries. Exoteric Christians east and west viewed growth largely in terms of physical size, particularly in the forms of material construction and political expansion. Roman Catholic bishops assumed a sociopolitical authority and necessity to expand the Catholic empire based upon concepts of *Manifest Destiny;* that

As if it had always been present, a fated path opens to the signally courageous and innocent drive of the Questor.

is, belief in a *God-given right and destiny to expand imperialistically.* In the modern world, similar concepts are held by Christian fundamentalists, their Islamic jihadist counterparts, and atrociously misguided political leaders of both camps.

During most of its history, holding *exclusive* knowledge of God's plan garnered through theological interpretation of Holy Scripture justified growth through war for the Holy Roman Empire ecclesia. Church leaders were sure that Christ's vicars were destined to rule the world. Thus, the Crusades were defended as necessary and even benevolent, for they opened a door to salvation for all those souls lost in the false laws and prophecies of Islam. At the same time, the Islamic ulama championed knowledge of Allah's plan for mankind as it was revealed to Muhammad, a Prophet beyond both Moses and Jesus. Muslim rulers felt equally justified claiming the inevitability of global dominion.

As introduced in the last chapter, the twelfth and thirteenth centuries also witnessed a profound emergence of *virtue* (Latin meaning, "manliness," "excellence," "goodness"; from *vir,* "man") leading to Unity-consciousness. This is epitomized by the spiritual station Sufis call the Living: the Triumphant Hermit. Esoteric and mystical monks proceeding in lineages stemming from Eastern Christian desert hermits held much in common with their Sufi brethren. Living in the same territories and times as Christian hermits such as St. Francis, relatively powerless, poor, and often unknown Sufi mendicants understood growth not through exterior extent but through interior intent. *Intention* originally referred to a "directing of attention as felt consciousness." Intentionality serves to align one's whole life with either virtue or vice. Through intentional actualization, empirical knowledge can promote spiritual evolution and psychophysical growth. A spirit of scientific awareness and appropriate application of knowledge grew amongst premodern esoteric communities as they witnessed the universality of nature's cycles within hierarchical contexts.

Allowed to be pure and true, the Priestess as representative of Grace on earth is naught but an advantage to the aspiring Questor.

Although powerfully propagated, Roman Catholic dogma was unable to displace the ancient and perennial observation that both nature and history are cyclic. Like the very first archaic tribes, medieval communities participated with seasonal cycles. Relative to our modern era, societal patterns were based upon short human life spans. Few were the old who had opportunity to witness the passing of more than two generations. Fantasies of securing material immortality in a sub-urban "castle" were practically unknown. Instead, cyclic nature served as the staging ground for the play of human history. From it, birth, work, family, growth, luck, catastrophe, and mystery emerged. To it, all of life was reclaimed. The soul might live eternally, in heaven or hell, but the process of life and death was felt by all as a composition of daily, lunar, seasonal, annual, and generational cycles.

It is not surprising therefore that few images were more popular in medieval art than the Wheel of Fortune. The four banners of the Wheel serve as signposts on a recursive path to Emptiness:

Sum sine regno, regnabo, regno, regnavi
I am without a kingdom, I shall reign, I reign, I have reigned

While fortunes may rise and sink, spirits move high and low, Fortune herself is blind to any of it. She is Empty, for all flow of life always revolves around her. Fortune serves to actualize Nature's *limits.* In this way she essentially *Curtails.* She is the eye of the storm called impermanence but perhaps better known as delusion. As a principle that guides Fate herself, Dame Fortune bridges humankind with the unfathomable mystery of cosmic causation.

Medieval folk entrusted the end of the world to the book of Revelation, and the destiny of their souls to the sacraments of the Church. In everyday life, though, it was the old *pagan* (meaning "country-dweller") reality of Goddess Fortune's cycles that common folk understood determined the course of history. As in the modern world, those caught up in the Wheel of Fortune were not

In the domain of spirits, a perennial realm may be regulated and governed; no structure can be permanently maintained that is determined by personal passions, vested ideals, or controlling interests.

always happier for it. Many scientific studies have made clear that money, power, and status beyond simple necessities for one's welfare do not increase subjectively perceived happiness and love.

While the Wheel and Hermit represent fifth-stage virtue, emptiness, and gnosis, the fourth stage preceding it speaks of a psychologically integrating force that transcends the very polarity and system that produces it. The Chariot and Fortitude Trionfi tell us how to expand consciousness beyond self-and-other polarity. They represent the dominating charge that leads to a sublimely subtle and virtuous submission to Goddess Fortune and the guiding gnosis of the Hunchback as Old Man Hermit.

Man and woman, heaven and earth, transcendence and immanence, incorporeal law and corporeal reality, mind and body all represent essential and universal polarity. Paradoxically, the more a polar side is *true to itself,* the more it is constant in *becoming the other.* A *pure pole* must purely transmute into its complementary pole, for there is nowhere else to go and nothing else to become unless the polar identity loses itself into an *other.* The purer a woman is a woman, the more she *has* to become masculine through the force field of polar attraction. Such is the mature grace of womanhood. The purer a man is a man, the more he has to become feminine through that same field. Such is the mature grace of manhood. Thus do we always strive to become greater: first through our own polar identity, then through a full attraction to realize our *other half.*

All manifestation in the field-spectrum between poles is transmuting simultaneously *as* both poles; to an equal magnitude when in equilibrium. Life and growth, however, are marked by *non-equilibrium dynamics,* with any and all equilibrium being moment-to-moment impermanent. In any case, within the whole polar field's process of *becoming,* essential unity of *being* is always everywhere maintained. This is the fundamental law of holistic causation.

By *evolving* through stages of inner becoming, growing into and integrating all polarity, *Questors magnify their realizations of being wholly, integrally One.* This is a matter of psychophysical-soulful development, which at all stages involves a Questor's most basic polarity, whether woman or man: *essential nature* and *vital life.* Throughout the esoteric process of enlightenment, Questors realize that they and all others are *already* manifesting Principal Unity. Such understanding, such consciousness, serves to intensify, magnify, and illuminate blissful realization. Thus, even as the Triumphs evoke evolution and hierarchical realization, they are premised upon a metaphysical worldview of essential nonduality. Still, their unique gift to the play of consciousness is their sublime representation of evolutionary process: *magical, mythical, rational, psychic, subtle, and causal stages of consciousness.*

All forms contain impurities – however, purity is an inherent state of all forms; upon the dangerously narrow path of sublimated will, action teeters into an abyss of terrifying aggression or proceeds bearing the wound of devotion.

Throughout global history, in societies' initial agricultural stage, *magical cults* led by *shamans* (the Prakrit root of which, *samana,* means "spiritual exercise") discovered and magnified *mana.* Originally a Polynesian Maori word, *mana* here indicates that *supernatural force* which circulates throughout nature while also *dwelling in a person* or sacred object. Rites enabling shamans to connect and flow with mana emerged from all societies that cultivated life by seeding elemental earth. In this we find the beginnings of what might be termed *alchemical awareness* – insight into the life, nature, and *union of polarities,* starting with elements of water and fire. Unknown yet *felt energy* coursing through all of nature's polarities (Sun/Earth, male/female, birth/death, hot/cold, etc.) held the secret to germination, nourishment, growth, and fruition. Mana and mind were effectively one and the same; shamans were thus civilization's original geniuses.

Essential natures were observed by shamans to sympathetically align vital forces if alike, and dynamically catalyze them if opposed. Waters, for instance, flowed together as one upon touching, but evaporated when near fire. Attraction and repulsion were sensed as magical forces moving and guiding all parts of nature. Repulsion, for instance, could be felt as a necessary warning, a demand

The polemic that stems from disastrous opposition is surpassed by the continuous sharing from which flows a labor of love; this requires the devotion of a mare.

to hold and turn back; or it could be felt to meaningfully sustain separation between reactive states. Perceiving the world to be surrounded and permeated by magical life-force and *animistic* (from *anima,* or "spirit") essence, beliefs gradually formed about the regenerative potency, creativity, and fecundity of earth, tribe, and individuals (fertile mothers, virgins, and shamans in particular).

Magic comes from *magus,* a Persian Zoroastrian priest. But the term has widely come to connote society's earliest forms of manipulation or self-conscious involvement with forces of nature. Thus does the Magician Triumph always come first in any spiritual quest. However, the two female Triumphs of Empress and Popess actually represent a society's initial stage of growth, marked by an earthen, magical worldview.

Sensitivity to, belief in, and control of cyclic, transmutative forces served as fertile ground for the creation of myths. While first-stage rites of shamanism arose via sensory awareness of natural forces, in mature magic-based tribes a second-stage emotional cognizance of *mythical archetypes* emerged. *Myth* is a Greek word indicating a "story regarding archetypes."

Communal processes of cognition expressed via mythmaking enabled urban societies to grow and stabilize. Through tools, artifice, and architecture empowering dance, chants, and rituals, complex levels of emotional expression were incorporated by ruling warrior and priesthood castes of every society that advanced into mythic cognition. This in turn led to forms of communication such as written signs and guiding invocations needed to quantify and qualify, measure and control communal exchanges of goods and services. Thus was urban infrastructure generated, tested, and regulated.

Historical overviews of language, art, technology, diplomacy, trade, and cultural assimilation in early civilizations elucidate the richness of societies in a mythos stage of development. The male Triumphs of Emperor and Pope represent societies' second stage of evolution, marked by myth-making urban trade, governance, and structural development. (Pathological aspects of these stages, such as second-stage empire-building and war-making, will not be addressed here.)

During the evolution of civilization, profound insights concerning laws of nature arose within and out of mythic mind-sets. At first, these were not cognized in terms of mathematical ratios or numerological principles (most certainly not abstract concepts such as zero and infinity). Instead, key to this development was observation of *logical relationships* within natural, elemental progressions, or what we will call "alchemical processes." Priests promoting myths practiced ways of discerning essential and vital processes of relationship and change seen as manifesting and continuously influencing the courses of heaven, earth, and man.

Holding dear to that which is unveiled, the continuous will to Love proves to be a natural compulsion borne in freedom.

Insight into nature's processes of polarization and union, discord and harmony, dominance and submission produced wise revisions of complex myths. From this process emerged *rational awareness.* Holistic mythos then matured into coherent *monistic* or *All-One-Spirit* worldviews. Jewish tribes revealed the concept of a *singular* God. Chinese sages posited the unity of *Tao.* The Upanishads in India presented *Brahman* as being That One which was all-inclusive.

Once the concept of Oneness was fully formed, it was followed by ideal number-principles ultimately culminating in One-Zero, or the beginning of a new cycle. Arabian numbers and our abstract idea of *zero* (or *cipher,* from medieval Latin *cifra,* from Arabic *sifr,* from *safira,* "to be empty"; originally a translation of Sanskrit *sunyam,* the point of "Emptiness") were integrated into late Greek philosophy, but even in early classical times a type of cosmic void-principle was imagined in terms of flux and chaos. *Infinity* and *infinitesimal* were merged in paradoxical conceptualizations of Mystery in Nature that bordered on philosophical positioning between nihilism and emptiness (the study of Diogenes and his school of Cynics sheds psychosocial light upon this).

Spirit-charge is a vertical conduit, the path of frontal descent and spinal ascent, the Chariot of the Goddess, the force of Fate.

Be that as it may, integral awareness compelled the wisest of classical sages to posit impermanence and change as constant and absolute. Their experiential consciousness of dialectical two-ness transmuted into a spiritual abstraction that had nothing to do with nihilism: *awareness of unifying emptiness.* As a world of Flux, the Way ultimately and *naturally* Rules Justly.

Aphorisms of Heraclitus, the pre-Socratic Greek philosopher, serve as an excellent example of this rational-intuitive monistic orientation. Heraclitus held that change is the eternal law of the world. Nothing remains static – all is in flux. It was Heraclitus who famously said, "one cannot step into the same river twice, for in the interval it has changed." Heraclitus observed that the process of change results from *Chaos* or *Strife,* the conflict of oppositions within every holistic unity.

> Strife is father of all things, king of all things; it has revealed some as gods and some as men; it has made some slaves, others free.
>
> One must know that strife is common to all things and justice is strife; and all things come into being in accordance with strife and necessity.

However, Heraclitus also realized that all such striving in nature is integrated in a sublime *harmony of Eros.* That harmony is not apparent to the common man. It is spiritual in the way of invisible force, and is greater than the visible strivings obviously perceived. Heraclitus realized that the *unity* of striving oppositions is the Supreme Law – greater than either polar *conflict* or temporary *equilibrium* of such. The *process* of polar identity, struggle, harmony, dominance, and submission defines all change.

Heraclitus argued beyond the *atomists* and *elemental dualists* of his day. Conceptualization of separated, alienated entities (whether atoms or elements) did not generate the insight that came with recognition of the *law of process.* Primary to the process of polarity –

dominance and submission, chaos and eros – was *transmutation:* the life of a substance comes from the death of another.

> The life of fire is the death of earth, and the life of air is the death of fire. The life of water is the death of air, and the life of earth is the death of water.

Heaven, earth, and man when united produce righteous Actuality realizing the brightening of beauty, the guarding of goodness, the turning of truth.

For Heraclitus, as was the case for those sages preceding him, human mind was one and the same with spiritual reality. Rational dialectic and discursive dichotomies of the ego-mind did not wholly form the foundation of true insight for these early sages. Rather, a germinating yet brightly nondual consciousness arose within ancient contemplators submerged in an awareness of mythic alchemy. For these sages, a dualistic division between corporeal self and incorporeal spirit simply did not exist. An evolutionary jump from mythical cognizance, through rational intelligence, into transpersonal psychic and subtle insight was made. Sages realized that Conscious Self was both Naught and All at the same time. Rationally explaining this was the work of *philosophy* – the compelling "love of wisdom."

Humanity has needed several millennia to mature into rational stages of societal development. Rational societies encapsulate complexities of magic and myth in structures of communicative *logic* (from Greek *logos,* meaning "speech," "reason"), distilling essential attributes of natural processes into formulas and patterns. These objectified, ratio-based designs can be conceptually manipulated and then materially engineered with astounding effects upon environments, societies, and individuals.

The first three stages of social development – magical, mythical, and rational – are similar to humans' psychological stages during their first twenty-four years of life. In psychology East and West it is commonly held that humans pass through distinct stages of physical, emotional, mental, and spiritual growth every seven or eight years. Each stage emerges from the fullness of the one preceding it.

Do not resist the adaptations of natural selection, the processes of worldly evolution, the thresholds of organic enfoldment, for transcendence does not arise from avoidance.

An adult between sixteen and twenty-four naturally matures her mental/rational processes. However, this is contingent upon healthy emotional/sexual development between the ages of eight and sixteen. This in turn is dependent upon the formation of sound physical growth in the first eight years of life.

Taoists hold that after the age of twenty-four, humans lose an integral amount of life-energy every eight years until death. However, that process can be reversed, whereby humans evolve in spiritual growth every eight years. Attaining immortality is thought possible through such *root-conversion* of attentive consciousness. By converting or reversing the energetic process of aging, all the stages represented by the Triumphs are promoted. The conversion process itself is represented by the sixth-stage Trionfi of Hanged Man and Death. *Immortality can be realized only through consciously knowing and transcending death.*

Indo-European civilization at the time of Buddha and Heraclitus, twenty-five hundred years ago, began instituting schools of reason that incorporated and then evolved beyond communal myths. These schools served as vehicles for philosophic and humanistic exploration. Readers may be familiar with the great age of Socratic and Platonic philosophy. The era encompassing classical elaboration of India's Vedic philosophy and spirituality found in the Upanishads is less widely known. Buddhist teachings rigorously distilled and advanced the Logos found within the Upanishads. Crucial to these advancements were new concepts of Emptiness, Infinity, and Unity.

For two millennia before this dawn of reasoned enlightenment, priestly castes of urban empires gradually wove rational constructs into fabrics of collective mythology. It is perhaps accurate to say that a new type of *emotional sense* was made of profoundly experienced and intentionally promoted myths – a type we now call *mental-rational*.

Natural renunciation is instilled through love of truth, beauty, and goodness; modern cynicism denies virtue while announcing nihilism in an endlessly banal loop.

The idea that rationality emerged from a cognitive process of emotionally complex mythmaking and interpretation is provocative for many analytical thinkers. It is often thought that rigorous logical mentation must by necessity lack any sense of emotionality. However, the cold calculations of logic epitomized by computers are not comparable to the impassioned rationality naturally generated by human reasoning. Understood through concepts of *hierarchical emergence,* the age of reason emerged from the age of myth not by rejecting myths, but by encapsulating and transforming them in a deeply original way.

Archaic, emotional objectification of magic-mythic archetypes in agricultural societies created a preponderance of *Underworld conceptualization.* As we will explore in the next chapter, Mother Gaia was defined by Eros, Chaos, and Tartarus, the latter being her Underworld Womb. These original Principles created an archetypal sense of Nature, Death, and Birth as wedded to *veiled Mystery.* This sensibility then came to be literally overwhelmed and *outshined* (meaning "to be more beautiful and splendid than"; "to surpass in obvious excellence") by an ecstatic awareness of *transparent Brightness.* This universal dialectic naturally merged into consciousness of the One, later to be realized as Universal Unity.

In a posthumous work published in 1952, F. M. Cornford convincingly put forth a groundbreaking study entitled *Principium Sapientiae: The Origins of Greek Philosophical Thought.* In it, magical and mythical origins of *Ionian* (old *Mycenaean Greek tribes,* stretching from the peninsula through the Cyclades to what is now the Turkish coast) physics and Greek philosophy were made clear. Ionians, like mythic believers before them, pondered the question of how an ordered world could emerge from primal chaos. Ionians posited the existence of natural elements or principles, which though shed of any aspect of *personified* godliness, remained divine, immortal, animated, and powerfully active in the world.

Aware of psychic manipulations, you forestall the Quest from being stopped by any power other than that of the Transcendental; nor will it be arrested by any effort attempting to override your true Tao.

Mythic cosmology and rational cosmology merged through the following model:

1. At first, nothing was distinct or apparent. Perhaps this was Chaos; perhaps it was One.
2. There then emerged, through a process of separation, pairs of opposites. These differentiated four domains: the sky of fire, the cold air, the dry earth, and the wet sea.
3. Opposites then interacted through cyclic reunion and division. From this emerged
4. Dominance and
5. Submission; a
6. Process that is forever continuous as witnessed in birth and death, in the seasons and in the stars. Through this processional alchemy, all things are manifested, changed, and sacrificed.

This dialectic was *dualistically* fixed and expounded upon by Empedocles, a follower of Pythagoras. His magical rationalism influenced later Gnostics. In modern times, cosmic, philosophical dualism was renewed by Hegel. The above cosmic dialectic was also posited in a *nondual,* integrated manner by Heraclitus, who witnessed the continuous cycling and struggle of the world as a flux of harmonious Unity.

Heraclitus posited a cosmic model that expanded the dialectical process via concepts of Chaos, Love, the Bright, and the Way. Neoplatonists later elaborated on these *absolute* and *transmutative* aspects of the cosmos, apparent in a *holistic* view of dialectical alchemy and union. We examine pre-Platonic cosmology, including the contrasting worldviews of Empedocles and Heraclitus, in the next chapter.

The above model of early Greek thought served as a foundation for the basic structure of a cyclic, six-stage cosmology. Being the most elegant way to describe a cosmic dialectic holistically, similar *six-stage cosmological models can be found at the core of every esoteric school in the great traditions.* Variants of it are introduced throughout this

The crystallization of electromagnetic current promises eternal control powered by networked energy; such, however, will prove to be naught but a hungry ghost, maniacally recursive in a program of singularity.

book. It was incorporated in the medieval Tarot up to the card of Death. However, metaphysical hierarchy as portrayed in the Trionfi reaches beyond this cyclic model. It fully includes *absolute domains beyond all cosmic cycles.* Thus, the Tarot presents a worldview akin to that of great nondual sages such as Heraclitus, Gautama, Jesus, and Ibn ʿArabi.

Our study will make clear that those epochal metaphysicians spanned in time and place a truly great East-West tradition of nondual philosophy in which a fundamental *ten-stage model of reality developed.* This was most notably championed by Buddhists, Neoplatonists, Hermetic Christians, and Sufis. It was graphically relayed into the modern world via the Tarot.

Understood properly, every Triumph symbolizes a distinct level of spiritual realization while being inextricably woven into a unified whole. In its nondual worldview, the Tarot represents evolutionary stages of natural manifestation even as it portrays evolutionary levels of spiritual realization. The Triumphant series is both cyclic and linear in its addressing of material "descent" and spiritual "ascent." Evolution's linear process or *arrow of time* involves never-ending cycles of transmutation manifesting out of the Principle of Chaos. Even more importantly, the post-Death Trionfi inform us that Chaos and the changing world essentially exist to realize the Beauty of Goodness and the Goodness of Truth. In modern terms, Chaos and the world emerging from it are naught but a realization of the Transcendental Principles of Space, Time, and Law.

In previous chapters, we discovered fascinating linkage between Italian merchant-cities, Christian monastic military orders, and the mystical Islamic world of Sufis. Very few men were actually involved with the conduit of goods and ideas between Europe and the East. Mingled with an elite mix of royalty, knights, bankers, and merchants were artisans, poets, monks, mendicants, and scholars. From a second-to-third-stage perspective of diplomats, merchants, and factors, social and professional advancement occurred through

Evolution is a natural outcome of potent attraction and bifurcating catastrophe; do not be petrified by the Devil, for he is naught but an agent of fluctuating reality, a continuous spiral emerging constantly as form and emptiness.

multicultural associations sustained by the lifeblood of rational exchange. Artisans and poets magnified that exchange through Temperance and Love. This created a culture of *high romance* (though having little to do directly with *Rome*). We have seen that out of international, rationally communicative networks emerged relatively *universal* (the literal meaning of "catholic") esoteric philosophies and spiritual associations.

It was through this fourth-stage, network-actualized process of *psychic emergence* that the Tarot was created. The Tarot was *unveiled* as a game of named and imaged principles embodying psychic, archetypal presence. The Trionfi were viewed by their originators as reflections of universal and conscious evolutionary stages. Intuitive psyche and archetypal symbols integrated via contemplation upon and play with these twenty-two Image-Exemplars. This created a resonant mind-medium for what has been termed fourth-stage *vision-logic consciousness*. Modern interaction with stories, media, art, games, and *harmonious design* of all types continues to promote evolving psychic awareness; notwithstanding, of course, pathological aspects of this stage, such as usurpations of liberty through mind-control and addictive dependency.

In our current age, habit patterns involving critical reasoning have become relatively pervasive. This has allowed a networked mindset to emerge, which is immersed continuously in an ocean of rich imagery, sound, symbols, and communicative exchange. Constant steams of information are broadcast into every modern community and household through multiple, highly efficient media channels. We live in an age when the one-day quantity of an urban dweller's information input may well be comparable to the one-year quantity of a fifteenth-century villager's. Of course, environmental awareness, human emotion, common sense, and conscious intimacy create and sustain a quality of life, innateness of meaning, and naturalness of relationship that cannot be compared with or replaced by media information, no matter how virtually immersive it might be. It is of import, however, that a daily reality of streaming concepts, images, symbols, and interpretations is now perceived and cognized by a massive number of modern adults and children.

Confusion is an energetic state that builds in friction and intensity; not content with simple clarity, it aspires to raise the roof of self-centeredness to superstructural, Towering heights.

Cleverly fragmented streams of postmodern media have little basis in nature or family. Streaming flows of sensory input disconnected from immediate patterns of one's organic environment and intimate household might seriously disturb a premodern peasant. Without emotional and mental tools of practiced reason and objective frameworks, the plethora of non-ratified audio-visual-conceptual symbols that arise when immersed into a foreign world can produce an alienation of identity akin to psychosis. Originally, a need for travelers to cope with sudden immersion into foreign cultures was spurred by the use of seafaring vessels. This provided compelling motivation for individual minds and collective guilds to develop faculties of reason and communicative logic. From those faculties emerged symbols of universal significance – beyond weights and measurements. These were based upon communal psychophysical experiences that were transpersonal and transcultural, whether founded upon myth or technology.

Social networks marked by civility and rationality can be effectively analyzed with the aid of *general system* and *game theories*. However, patterns of feedback and nonlinear resonance that arise in civilized communities can generate wholly new *holarchical* (*holistic-hierarchical*) system-states. This is particularly so as familiar networks allow attention to freely concentrate upon psychic and subtle, transpersonal communication. Emerging from the subtle resonance of otherwise structured systems, newly generated spheres of realization cannot be causally explained or defined solely by the specific interactions of those systems. Organic social systems essentially tend toward evolved levels of subtly interdependent causality. *Control* of those systems is often seen as the work of politicians and marketers. However, neither environmental nor social systems can be systematically analyzed, tracked, and manipulated in a context of

In the garden of beauty, goodness, and truth, the sap of vital essence flows up the spine of discipline, service, and meditation to egress from the crown as fruitful wisdom and compassion – the pure land of Spirit.

securing them from creative disruption, and thereby unknown influences, via a centrally controlled "total awareness program" without catastrophic consequence, much to the chagrin of pathological political and corporate strategists.

National military/security and international corporate logistics technically control a significant portion of the political and financial systems upon which modern consumption and production cycles are dependent. To the extent possible, all communication – including fundamental forms of goods, data, and monetary exchange – and communicators are located, tracked, and analyzed by centralized authorities so as to enable global executives to manipulate system parameters in a manner conducive to systemic growth without disruption or threat to authoritative command structures and executive control.

Systematic tracking and mining of logistical patterns coherent in twenty-first–century social activity are inherently encapsulated by the organic, developmental hierarchy of Logos itself. *Logos* refers to a process of "reckoning, reasoning, collecting, then speaking." Originally denoting the principle governing the cosmos, it came to mean all human reasoning about the cosmos. Logos is a spectrum of consciousness that includes phases of dialectical *tempering* necessary for psychosocial welfare. We can reasonably say that humanism in general is guided by logos as principled intelligence. Common folk are familiar with logos through personal visions and exchanges of *love*. Such does not require "higher education," but does necessitate growth through family and community *responsibility*. Third-stage logical rationality naturally transmutes into fourth-stage psychic-logical *reckoning* that addresses the serious issues of human relationship and societal development; including *ethics*, holistic responsibility, and the *fate of relationships* should they remain active.

Fate comes from Latin *farito*, also meaning "to speak," but in the serious demeanor of *Fatum* or "prophecy." The fourth-stage psychic awareness and driving charge of the Chariot is about moving third-stage rationality and logistics into a broader current of intuitive reasoning, Reckoning the Forces of nature. Here, *Fate Rules,* for *reckon* and *rule* both at their root mean "to direct and lead in a straight line." The concept of *hierarchy* is wedded to this.

Higher dimensions of space actualize the way of immortality; do not think that energy is reduced to instances of matter via the agency of space, for what is dimensionality if not the duration of absolute Light?

Archetypal, psychological communication naturally emerges out of evolved social interaction. Such represents and transmits universal processes of growth and transcendence. Primary to this intuitively intelligent communication are transpersonal conveyance, alignment, and understanding of *actualizing* hierarchies.

Depicting an honorable holding of the reigns of power and *psychic charge* (*Shakti* as *yogic activation* or *holy mission*), Chariot and Fortitude in particular represent the *dominant* force of hierarchical emergence and awareness of such. Medieval Tarot cards are an epitomized portrayal of communicative action in the context of this awareness. Psychic charge initiates and prepares for a more advanced and potent psycho-cultural process, that of *submissive and selfless Virtue.*

Leading occultists of the nineteenth century, such as Éliphas Lévi, realized that the true order of the Arcana was their supreme secret. Lévi believed that the Tarot's hierarchical meaning was understandable only by "true masters." However, modern Tarot decks are often not recognized as representing hierarchical stages. Now viewed as being similar to astrological signs, Tarot Arcana are commonly interpreted as a network of relative personality traits and temporary circumstances.

Differing systems of "divining" derived from interpreting widely varied modern Tarot decks are readily deconstructible; as are most forms of fortune-reading. Analyzed via deconstructionist methods, consistently similar semiotic patterns are discovered in popular techniques of fortune-telling. The shell game of words exhibited in psychotherapy software (i.e., ask a question, parse the answer, repeat more questions by semantically reiterating the answers) uses

Venerate a Transcendental realizer through respect, gratitude, and love – the sympathetic channel thereby opened will attract the radiant serenity of that one's presence; through continuous, devoted conduction you fully meet, then become Unified.

comparable methods of "divining" solutions for problems. These methods do not engage concepts that reference processes involving hierarchical depth and genuine psychological growth. They certainly do not involve noble wisdom.

Tarot reading delivered as *occult fortune-telling* will most probably not be founded upon a fourth-stage process of conveying hierarchical insight. Essentially differing, *esoteric spirituality* is rooted in understanding processes that are transformative through *vertical* or, more spatially accurate, *nested and in-depth modalities* between hierarchical levels of both internal and external, psychological and environmental, cultural and social holistic evolution. The Trionfi are not merely translatable in a *horizontal* manner. They lose their true and important significance when their hierarchy is flattened to a single level of relationship. Astrological houses or modern fortune-telling cards are all interpreted on the same level of archetypal signification. "Being a Cancer" is no more evolved than "being a Virgo." Similarly, the Justice card in a modern Tarot deck is not normally viewed as signifying a more evolved state of spiritual realization than, say, the Lovers card.

The esoteric importance of spiritual hierarchy – the fundamental basis of Tarot didactics – has become largely obscured. Occult interpretations of esoteric teachings have progressively degraded in the last century, although some Christian Hermetic interpretation remains exceptional. Mature rationality has been largely abandoned by Tarot interpreters in favor of syncretic mythologies. Dualistic "histories" of the Triumphs' meanings are commonly composed from practically random selections of symbols and mythic beliefs skimmed from bastardizations of popularized traditions.

This is not to degrade the value of studying and artistically reworking archetypes, whether in postmodern forms or traditional styles. It is simply hoped that this book will awaken the reader to a world of perennial wisdom and spiritual insight that has continuously maintained a position of far more import to humanity's health and happiness than have modern trivializations of that great tradition.

A call to charge into the Deathless is heeded in stillness, for it is sounded as a blast of indifference, a brightness of roaring fierceness proclaiming the communion of Angelic ecstasy.

True and integral psychic insight requires and then advances beyond rationalized identification with archetypal mythic entities. Throughout history, gifted individuals have transformed their states of consciousness by encompassing discriminative mind with an intuitive awareness that transcends the vision-spectrum of cognitive ego. Evolving a subtly intelligent and *integrated* state of awareness, such people have not simply regressed back into mythic consciousness.

One of the earliest and most influential understandings of reality to fully include a hierarchical fourth-stage worldview was taught by Gautama the *Buddha* (meaning "make aware"). Similar to Heraclitus's philosophy, it was expounded in Northern India during the latter's lifetime. According to fundamental Buddhist tenets, life – in fact, all of manifestation – comprises seemingly endless cycles of struggle experienced as suffering. The sensations, emotions, and mentations of suffering arise from a root perception of and belief in a "separate self." The very perceptions, feelings, or thoughts that give the "self" definition simultaneously manifest an awareness of its temporality. Struggling to maintain its apparent existence, while always fundamentally knowing it will lose in its struggle, causes the "self" to suffer. There is no way to avoid this conundrum.

A great cycle of *beingness* exists through which we and all other phenomena constantly undergo change. Nothing is permanent; everything transmutes through phase states, whether water or fire, wood or metal, body or mind, atom or star, earth or cosmos. Every "link" in the closed "chain" of cosmic manifestation is causally interdependent with the others. Thereby, no "self" can possibly exist independent of this endlessly cycling, existential procession.

The phenomenal world is infinitely marked by temporality. In other words, time itself rules all spatial existence. Only that state of *trans-existent* Emptiness marked by Radiant Time – past, present,

At the heart of Perennial Wisdom is liberating Justice, the force that causes all emergence because her Law fundamentally Is reality arising; the Purpose of Fate, she is simultaneously creator, destroyer, and sustainer.

and future – or Immortal Timelessness directly realizes Nirvana or the Way of True Liberation. Such became known in Buddhist history as the Pure Land – domain of Radiant Heart. Bright Emptiness is the Way of all-pervasive Unity, which underlies the cosmic chain of causal dependency.

Essential Heart-Mind is beyond all personal *dependency,* the root meaning of which indicates a type of hanging via a drawn, stretched, and spun thread. The Magician as Independent Questor becomes the Hanged Man who must pass Death and then face destructive abasement by the Devil. At that point, all illusion and sensibility of independence will be dispelled. If successful, the ecstatically *inter*-dependent Fool will then wander between mortal and immortal realms, even while remaining dangerously in bliss. *Tantra* as a way of "extension and stretching in a weaving on a loom" merges all strands of dependency.

To witness the Heart of this is to be Converted through Enlightened Initiation. When that *witnessing-state* is consciously sacrificed via a true *wisdom-realized alchemy* beyond all self-objective witnessing, it permanently transmutes the soul of a Questor into initial phase-states of a *Golden Immortal.* The Hanged Man represents the fixated witnessing state that initializes such enlightenment.

Gautama taught Self-Realization of Noble Wisdom that was paradoxically empty of any "self" other than wisdom-emptiness. His teachings make clear a way of Unity-awareness by which Questors can transcend all sense of suffering or separative self. Through awareness of past, present, and future Unity, a Questor is consciously able to become attentive to That which is beyond suffering: the Deathless. In concentrating her attention in and as Emptiness, the Questor loses her-"self" in the Mindfulness of absolute Flux from which all impermanence arises. In this way, she begins identifying with the liberated domain called Nirvana, also known as Buddha Mind. She will simultaneously embody the Beauty and Truth of *Shakti Siddhi* (subtle power of Goddess manifestation).

This process naturally begins in every human being's first stage of growth. It is experienced by every infant, but is most often forgotten by adulthood. A knowing awareness of this first stage of enlightenment is appropriately called *Right View.* Once that is established, a hierarchical and noble tenfold path is embarked on. By the fourth stage of spiritual, psychophysical development – *Right Action* – the process of surrendering attention to Transcendental Change, Emptiness, Radiance, and Unity becomes greatly magnified. In technical terms, it intensifies via conduction of *True Mind* – called in various traditions Psyche, Holy Spirit, Shakti, or Shen – through one's *central nervous system.*

The One emanates as the Myriad and the Myriad apprehends in every moment the One – it is so simple: the World is continuous beyond all discrimination.

Esoteric iconography and symbolism at its best refers to spinal-brain anatomy (along with body organs and field-channels of neural organization) in order to accurately image the development of consciousness, compassion, and wisdom. Over the course of human history, many forms of spiritual exercise have been discovered and practiced, producing varied states of consciousness as evidenced in the cornucopia of sacred world art and integrative design.

In modern times, means of opening and concentrating the current or flux of the central nervous system have included psychotropic drugs, rapid vehicular propulsion, electronic stimulation, media saturation, and sensory deprivation. Although the effects of such experiences can simulate a fourth-stage *state* of psychic body-mind central-nervous circuitry, they can only do so superficially, for they cannot be consciously sustained. They will not continuously permeate the complex whole-body system. They will not permanently integrate with patterns of organic growth in the human system unless such is cultivated through a great deal of practice. Although externally caused stimulation of the central nervous system may promote psychic and subtle development, it often stunts the human system from actually evolving, which requires devotion to a long-term, environmentally and communally integrated process.

Turn your back on the discriminative intellect, but know that you will plummet from Heart's cliff – be sure you are prepared for the overwhelming recompense of Divine Accident.

Although glorified in technological warfare and in certain sports (e.g., car racing), electrochemically and mechanically stimulated experiences of daring and dangerous missions (including drug trips) are insufficient to create real heroism. Rarely does such tap and transform the root of human nature. Concentrated and continuous presence of spiritual awareness requires a phase transition of the *whole body.* Such transfiguring mindfulness goes beyond "initiation" experiences potentially produced by psychotropic drugs and technologies of sensory stimulation, unless they involve actual yogic cultivation.

Modern rituals of stimulating the central nervous system might be compared with primitive initiations of confronting wild beasts, ingesting powerful herbs, and fasting in isolation. Psychophysical signs of concentrated and continuous central nervous system *release,* such as *belly-breathing* with a *plumb-straight lower back,* evinced for example by Aborigines of Australia and Papua New Guinea, are recognized by masters of yoga. Through cultural patterns involving an immersive relationship with nature, it is possible for natives to sustain a type of fourth-stage psychophysical state, regardless of the archaic stage of their society. Such people, however, historically have lived short lives, required isolation from other tribes, and lacked rational faculties required to cope with the world outside of their provincial experience. Predators, tribal enemies, natural disasters, and diseases continue to force archaic societies to evolve through magical, mythical, and rational stages of consciousness to sustain their spiritual culture and ancestry.

Unlike the natural and "unconscious" spirituality of archaic natives, most technologically induced central nervous system activity occurs in humans maturing in the stage of rational development. Furthermore, it occurs in humans surrounded by environments explicitly designed through rational processes. This makes possible a sustainable societal emergence of fourth-stage consciousness. However, such will require traditional patterns of spirituality involving devotion, virtue, yoga, and contemplation to intensify within the mainstreams of cosmopolitan societies and esoteric circles, including those of Tarot practitioners and enthusiasts. Consciousness altered and expanded through modern techniques needs these traditional practices in order to sustain and deepen its evolving transformations. Social history shows that, always starting with individual cultivators, small communities of spiritual practitioners keep synchronistically regenerating as spiritual traditions continually transform and adapt to modern patterns and circumstances. It is therefore unavoidable that these spiritual practices will be integrated with the technological experiences unique to our scientific era.

A universal religion or way of spirituality rooted in recognition and celebration of *Gaia and Eros as sentient organism and always transcendentally present creative spirit* is bound to arise sooner than later. Sacraments and rites of such a Way may well in part be administered by *twenty-first–century techno-shamans.*

Although few in number, truly great realizers of human potential advance beyond fourth-stage intuitive intellect into the realm of aware equanimity addressed as selfless purity in mystical traditions. It is through and beyond this stage of *virtue* that the great religious founders moved. Such virtue has been realized by rare individuals since the inception of human rationality. Jesus and Plotinus, for example, emerged from societies still enmeshed with magic and myth, yet advanced into stages of rational consciousness. As has been defined so far, in the Tarot's ten-stage hierarchy of spiritual realization, levels of consciousness marked by magic, myth, rationality, and intuition compose the first four stages of psychosocial evolution. *Virtue signifies the fifth stage.*

The fourth stage of self-actualizing, *transpersonal* psyche (being "beyond limits of egoic persona") bridges the stages of rationality and virtue. Discriminative mind revealing the Way through tolerant yet impassioned reason (third-stage Temperance and Love) evolves into transpersonal psyche (fourth-stage Chariot and

Fortitude). This, in turn evolves into subtle grace sublimating spiritual force and charged communion through compassionate insight into the impermanence of self, society, and nature.

The fifth stage of psychological and sociocultural development is represented in the Tarot by the Wheel of Fortune and the Hermit. The *manly virtue* of *Dame* (from Latin *domina,* feminine of *dominus,* meaning "lord," "master") Fortune comes into play only when the Wheel of polar striving is transcended. Fortune's virtue then becomes a taste of direct, spontaneous realization of naturally essential presence – the bliss of divine providence. Such is felt completely, of course, only through the Deathless states culminating in Justice and Kosmic Unity, the nondual realization of the World. In any case, the Wheel at its *radical core* issues forth a subtly ineffable mystery. The seemingly random but actually *synchronistic* contingencies of Fortune arise beyond the grasp of magical, mythical, rational, or psychic faculties.

Subtle virtues are consciously promoted in maturely formed communities that base their rule of law upon rationally discerned, spiritually intuited *ancestors* (meaning "those which precede"). An immanent and present experience of this ancestral domain intrinsically motivates a community to be virtuous. Here, we are referring to an awareness that includes fully functioning faculties of logic and intuitive intelligence. Ancestral awareness at an archaic level of development is of a different quality.

Magical, mythical, rational, and psychological maturation magnifies the inclusiveness of ancestral awareness. Fifth-stage virtue acknowledges *universal ancestry* through a worldview essentially purified of gross definitions, limitations, and boundaries. *Universal* is indeed the key word. Militant claims of hierarchical superiority based upon *exclusive* ancestry have fueled the worst atrocities in history. The reduction of fifth-stage communal ancestry into second-stage dramas, be those of tribes or empires, practically defines the "fall of man." The next chapter addresses this in detail.

Evolution of consciousness is marked by *phases* of ancestral awareness. It is a fallacy to equate a *perennial wisdom* Zen master's awareness of ancestral presence with an aboriginal hunter-gatherer shaman's. It must be pointed out that this does not constitute a morally judgmental statement. Nor does it represent a position purposed toward the domination of one religion, culture, or race over another. Within his lifetime, that same shaman could literally move through stages of development to emerge in a more enlightened state than the Zen master's. This most likely would require, however, passing through mature periods of *intentional rationality, integral psychology, and universal virtue.* It is certain that great shamans have moved through these stages to emerge in sagacious awareness of enlightened realization – Tibetan Buddhism and Taoism, early and late, attest such realization.

The view that all cultural states are equally valid does not have to be abandoned to understand that there is a developmental hierarchy inherent to all cultures. Whether external or internal, nested levels of integral processes always exist in hierarchical relationship. *Transformative development is the primary process* of holarchical manifestation, hierarchical principles, and life in the cosmos. Levels of hierarchical organization inform and integrate our living world.

There is no sense in trying to "flatten" evolutionary hierarchy or arrest the inevitable continuation of evolution in the future. It is crucial to comprehend that evolution occurs via the *irreversibility* of time. Both cosmos and human consciousness have evolved through an *arrow of time.* It is not possible to reverse or stop this. Chapter 8 considers the importance of time and hierarchy in terms of scientific principles and twenty-first–century cosmology.

Further to the above example, consciousness of universal ancestry in Zen Buddhism has grown over time. During the East-West movement of the twentieth century, Zen Masters emerged with an awareness that utterly transcended Japanese provinciality, including aspects of island ancestry. This will continue to have a profound impact on the development of Buddhism in the twenty-first century.

Buddhist lineages, of course, all stem from Indian realizers. But Gautama himself stated that he stood in a lineage of previous Awakened Adepts that reached back into the very beginnings of civilization. Indo-European ancestry stretching back to Neolithic times is a particular focus within these pages. In this context, the work of Carl Schuster, extending the study of ancient spiritual culture and universality back to the very dawn of tribal humanity (100,000 B.C.), is recommended reading. In all cases, regardless of cultural divisions over ages and continents, the whole of humanity shares the organic and primary ancestry of living animals, fecund earth, radiant sun, and cosmic galaxy.

We may call that most essential state from which everything continuously evolves the Kosmic Domain. As Law, Time, Space, and Flux, it pervades an implicate order that becomes the very spirit, system, structure, and identity of the present world. *That* is ultimately the root of all ancestry. We must respect that upon which we are fundamentally based, and there is nothing more fundamental than That. While unity awareness is nascent even in infantile consciousness, deeper and higher levels of life realize greater intensities and resonant levels of harmony. Such is the realization of hierarchical consciousness. It is not necessary for individuals or societies to obtain top-down authoritative permission to evolve. Conscious evolution does, however, require center-out respect for the source from which one comes and the destiny to which one goes.

Rapid quickening of conscious evolution is dependent not only upon individual Questors, but also upon those Questors' cultures, teachings, and communities. Traditions universally agree that "presto" enlightenment is not real. Wisdom that spontaneously arises does so after developmental cultivation (even if that is largely induced circumstantially during childhood). During which the advancement of discriminative faculties cannot be ignored. Nor can the intense practice of transcending the discriminative mind, once developed, be foregone. Because it is not possible to transcend that which is avoided, naive attempts to mature in spiritual realization by regressing into myth and magic while avoiding rational discernment are inevitably doomed. This is true whether attempts at avoidance are made under the rubric of Zen, Wicca, New Age, Fundamentalism, or whatever. A Questor's success will be founded upon respect, not avoidance.

Ancestral awareness and the way of subtle communion arising from such appears simultaneously pure, essential, simply empty, and highly complex. Transpersonal, archetypal gestalts intuited via fields of vision-logic can become so deeply subtle in resonant relatedness as to appear indescribable. At communal junctures of such awareness, patterns of identity, feeling, and knowledge are spontaneously communicated via virtuous subtleties. Relating in this way is marked by selflessness and a reflective, non-manipulative disposition found at the *humble* (meaning "ground of Earth") center of Jesus's spiritual method of "loving one's neighbor as oneself." Transcendence of definitions normally accompanying domestic families, political parties, intellectual schools, and psychic networks is an important feature of fifth-stage consciousness.

Recondite scholasticism and symbolism, with which the present work may unfortunately be labeled, needs somehow to be sparked to life within the commons so as to preserve traditional aspects of spiritual brilliance and mystery without *putting them away* from public view and consideration. In the final chapter of this book, a new version of the Tarot is introduced, one that will lend itself to an advanced and highly innovative game system and method of interactive readings and cooperative play. We hope this will be able to extend the *principles of immortality* to new generations of Questors and game players sure to arise in the twenty-first century.

A modern example of communal virtue may be found in Mother Theresa's order of nuns, serving the poor in India. By surrendering their self-centeredness, the sisters are compassionately able to include the most unfortunately impoverished in their work of healing. Compulsion to dominate via hierarchy is replaced with a powerful flow of forgiveness. Comfortable, self-reflecting networks of friends, workers, and caste are transcended through self-sacrifice. Virtues of forgiveness and self-sacrifice become important features of *Right Livelihood.* The way of subtle virtuosity *contradicts* all rationale of "putting oneself first" in order to "succeed in life." Paradoxically, this is how the caste system can rightfully function. Thus is the *sacerdotal* ("vowed to sanctity") caste wealthiest in terms of communal gnosis and poorest in terms of self-interest. Once more, however, let us note that actualized development of the rational mind (egoic but not egotistical) must occur before it can be transcended and sacrificed. In India, that sociocultural process largely remains in initial stages.

Unlimited by physical, emotional, mental, and psychological boundaries, subtle virtue opens a vista to the space of primordial Heart, which holistically transforms human consciousness via the Transcendental. We have referred to the transcendentally Immortal Domain in terms of Chaos, Space, Time, and Law; and Change, Being, Consciousness, and Bliss; and Strife, Eros, the Bright, and the Way. Western esotericism has also traditionally viewed spiritual transformation as emanating from divine agents: Saints, Muses, Angels, and World Adepts who all at once realize First, Last, and Really True Immortality.

Fourth-stage *transpersonal self,* emerging from a self-actualizing conduction of psychic fields, bridges third-stage *intentional self* with fifth-stage *renunciative self.* To be renunciative is to *re-announce* in one's daily rhythms a Life of Gnosis. This is precisely what the Hermit with his light of essence and staff of vitality does. Fifth-stage livelihood is dedicated toward the curtailment of illusion and conceited charms. It is the Magician transforming as the Hermit and Hanged Man.

The empty equanimity of the Wheel's center allows a Questor conscious dispassion regarding highs and lows of control, status, and possession. Polarities experienced in physical, emotional, mental, and psychic domains are seemingly dissolved through this empty center. A continuous charge of spiritual fate will be actively conducted by Questors psychically matching the dominant forces playing in, with, and as their life-courses. Doing so allows them to *spontaneously submit* to the direction of the Goddess and ancestral presence communicating and appearing through significant phantasms (about which more will shortly be said). Through *Grace,* Questors are afforded dispassion by the spiritual culture, teaching, and community that bless them on their way. Fifth-stage awareness is marked by *peaceful equanimity.* Embodied by the Hermit, with his sublimated staff of spinal virility, it initiates a Right Life of Bright Mystery.

The Wheel marks a stage of Virtue apprehended by the Hermit directly, via empty yet radiant insight or gnosis. The Hermit transforms, via *soulful conversion* realized in the Hanged Man and conscious Death – the sixth-stage Triumphs – into a dweller of the Deathless state. The Quickened Questor's attention must mindfully and ecstatically engage sacrificial rites vis-à-vis a regenerative, surging Tower guarded by the Devil and his inexhaustibly heated Trident of Root, Shaft, and Head. These are the seventh-stage Trionfi exemplifying *transformative flux.*

The Questor's alchemy becomes golden as it is concentrated and magnified through celestial nourishment of the Star and erotic might of the Moon, effusing above and around the head as a pearly white nimbus, and then a golden glow of transmutative energy. These two Triumphs compose the eighth stage of conscious evolution: *Eros* – creative enlightenment of the *Muses,* the *Dance of the Goddess.*

Finally, the Questor will realize an inscrutable, compassionately empty and enduring stage of *indifferent intervention* represented by the ninth-stage Exemplars of Sun and Angel. This ninth sphere of

Radiance brings us once again to the primacy of Time, intrinsically transcending all spatial differentiation, and thereby any and all sense of historical self. *The Arrow of Time Is Verily Just That.*

Through impoverishment of the soul, spiritual evolution naturally produces *Heart-realization.* Such is the *te* (virtue-power) of the *Tao Te Ching.* Such is the *middle way* merging into Nargarjuna's *sunyata* (the great Buddhist teaching of Emptiness). Such is the way of selfless merit or *right life* that enables the creative soul's history-making *right effort.* Such is the respect for ancestral presence that merges one's *sentient storehouse* (all memory, organization, patterns, and states, conscious or not) of sensation, feeling, imagery, intuition, and deeply trusted *self-authentication of spiritual awareness* into a flux of past-present-future continuum.

Completion of *cognitive* awareness occurs in the sixth stage of conscious evolution, the stage of apparent Death. Death of *self* vitally and essentially transforms and utterly *converts attention* into a vehicle for the conscious Heart, causally generating realization of the Deathless. This is the esoteric understanding of how the Immortal Kosmic Domain *enters, becomes, and outshines* (for in reality it already-always-is) the manifest world. This sixth stage is appropriately referred to as that of the *causal-heart.* The reader may find a most thorough consideration of it in the corpus associated with Ramana Maharshi, the widely regarded great sage of twentieth-century India.

We have but touched upon essential sociocultural, psychological, and esoteric stages found in wisdom ways perennially arising in all great spiritual traditions. Summarizing the attributes of stages one through six gives us:

1. Magical Sensation
2. Mythical Emotion
3. Rational Thought
4. Psychological Intuition

5. Subtle Virtue
6. Causal Heart

In these stages, the Questor's mind:

1. Settles
2. Regresses
3. Recognizes
4. Affirms
5. Surrenders
6. Sacrifices

This is the fourth chapter of nine (we leave the greater works of others to represent the tenth chapter) delving into the roots and fruits of Western esotericism. It is fitting that we explore deeper into realms of rationality and processional emergence of fourth-stage logos, composing a history of intuitive, visionary psychology.

Emerging ... Right Action

This chapter began with a now-familiar affirmation of the Tarot's nondual foundation. Evolutionary, actualizing hierarchy in the context of a priori Unity is the premise behind the Trionfi. The perennial wisdom of nondual emanation posits that our world is *immanently* transcendental. Insight into this paradox lies at the root of all great esoteric traditions. Occult schools of cosmic dualism, along with most exoteric religions, presume a fundamental separation between corporeal and incorporeal existence. The schism between mundane and spiritual worlds is explained via primordial mythologies, which are then extensively elaborated through rational theology or analytical rhetoric based upon epistemologies that cannot be verified experientially. In any case, there exists an intellectual contradiction inherent to cosmic dualism. The

remainder of this chapter examines this, and introduces Greek metaphysicians whose life-works countered dualistic perspectives.

The previous chapter suggested how Sufis resolved the dilemma of mind being seemingly separate from body yet manifested through it. Ibn ʿArabi's encompassing cosmological spirituality integrated Allah's incorporeal and corporeal essences by envisioning divine attributes as a unified, spiraling process of world emanation. From this highest of Sufi perspectives, the incorporeal becomes the corporeal, which returns to the incorporeal. Reality is an immortal and indivisible process of concomitant descent and ascent between Heaven and Earth. Most essentially, beyond all temporal and spatial definition, a priori *Unity of Being* marks the Way of Allah. Such is an esoteric spiritual worldview wherein innately one's human life *is* Divine. The exoteric material worldview prevalent in Western history has tended to be far more dualistic and far less positive.

For most people, third-stage mentation defines one's identity as a *thinking self*. This self is generally presumed to possess an independent, seemingly uncaused existence. At times it is thought of as a transient *ego*. Other times, it is thought of as an immortal *soul*. There exists a critical philosophical problem to this third-stage view of self and others. Discursive thought posits an existence to itself, separate from its body, environment, or even subtle psychology. This "soul-mind" then seems to stand potentially independent of all corporeal existence. It appears to itself as having incorporeal origins. Questions then arise: Where does my incorporeal soul come from? How was it trapped "inside" my corporeal form? As two different realities with fundamentally different laws, how is it possible that the incorporeal and corporeal coincide with *me?* Which is the *real* me: the mind or the body? Does the mind exist prior to the body? Will it exist after the body disappears?

Scientific materialists reasonably suggest that the thinking self can be explained via neurological and chemical functions of the body. There is no need to posit a separate soul. However, the organic complexity of the human system does not lend itself to mechanically reducible equations of cause and effect. Thus, scientific materialists have not been able to reduce mind to a series of algorithms and physical functions. Furthermore, it remains a mystery to scientific thought how stages of *emergent organization,* most certainly including all levels of consciousness, are actually generated. This is because complexity develops through a flux of chaos, with *life emerging inexplicably* – at least in linear logistical terms. In chapter 8, we will review the state of scientific thought regarding this. The Tarot represents, as does esotericism in general, a worldview beyond and greater than that afforded by discursive rationality.

Interior development of human psyche is as significantly evolutionary as external development of human physique. *Psyche* primarily denoted *individual life* to the early Greeks. It was what distinguished a living body from a corpse. Psyche later became a reference for the *thinking self* and all forms of reason that manifested as thought. The now-common tendency to separate thinking-self from sensing-self, and both from feeling-self, is a recent human development. Certainly, that separation was not commonly perceived by early Greeks for whom we have evidence regarding patterns of visual and verbal thought.

One detects with Pythagoras an intellectually formalized commencement within Greek society of a mind/body split. Pythagoreans developed a principal of psyche imbued with significant independence. To them, psyche was a governing and unifying *soul* controlling one's otherwise chaotic body. This mind/body dualism was carried forward by Plato and set in stone by Aristotle, permanently and profoundly affecting Western thought. A post-Aristotelian overemphasis upon the superiority of mental worlds created a pathological attitude opposed to mythically emotive, bodily felt worldviews. Manichaeism and Gnosticism in general may be viewed as a reaction to this, several centuries later. Equally, self-obsessed rationality as manifested in socially legitimized group mind-sets became anxious to deny or control emerging psychic and subtle states of social consciousness and worldviews. That struggle continues, pushed to its limits by twentieth-century *analytic philosophers* or *rhetoricians* (few proponents of this clever school actually identify with a "love of wisdom") in what has amounted to a millennial attempt at arresting the very heart of Indo-European wisdom-teaching.

It is of interest to compare the Greek concept of psyche with the three forms of life-energy in Taoist thought. Like the early Greeks, Taoists bridged mystery and mythos with empirical experience. From that shamanic convergence, rationality arose. Spiritual insight was derived from each stage of development. Physical, emotional, mental, psychic, and subtle worlds were viewed as one in the Tao.

Vitality, energy, and spirit (*ching, ch'i, shen*) are all living aspects of the Tao. Nowhere in Taoist psychophysiology is discriminative mind viewed as existing separate from the sensing-feeling realization of vital life and essential nature. In the process of circulating energy (*ch'i kung*), mental faculties are supremely awakened; as are subtle-psychic powers, once internal *cauldrons* have sufficiently sublimated energy into spirit. Psychophysical cauldrons as concentrated neuro-chemical-breath centers of ch'i and the generation of vitality, energy, and spirit as experienced and understood through Taoist yoga are addressed in chapter 6.

Western schools of philosophy and theology still wrestle with the dualistic problem of mind separate from body, heaven separate from earth. The root of Descartes' belief, *I think therefore I am,* can be found in Plato's dualistic rationality. Plato's Ideal Forms existed in a realm quite distinct from the corporeal world. Plato did not imagine anthropomorphic gods hanging high on Mount Olympus. Nor did he posit divine elements defining and forming cosmic space. Instead, to Plato there existed a corporeal world of vital *manifestation* presumably separate and distinct from an incorporeal domain of essential *ideas*. It was problematically left to Aristotle to bridge these worlds.

Much later, Neoplatonists led by Plotinus and Proclus transcended dualistic presumptions by positing a Universal One emanating as the Myriad or World as we sense and feel it to be. In that manner, they may also appropriately be called Neo-Heracliteans. Given that the currently assumed Big Bang scientific cosmological theory suggests a model of the universe that is remarkably similar to this, it is somewhat surprising that Neoplatonism is so unknown amongst the general populace. As its corpus was progressively dropped from European and American academies of higher learning during the past century, its underlying themes of unity and emanation were popularly embraced by educated Westerners in terms of Buddhist and Taoist philosophy. As indicated below, Neoplatonism and Taoist Buddhism (integrating Tao with Buddha Mind as *Storehouse Consciousness*, and Tantra with nondual Vedanta) have transculturally resonated and interpenetrated since Neoplatonism took form.

Greece's first philosophical sect was founded not by Socrates and his successor Plato, but by Pythagoras. (Apparently, Heraclitus's philosophy did not lend itself to a sectarian movement. Plato said, "There is no such thing as a master or pupil among the Heracliteans, but they spring up of their own accord.") Pythagoras's life is legendary. Marked by ecstatic visions and powerful practices of purification, magi such as he clarified the magical-mystery rites of Indo-European civilization via ritually abetted processes of rationality.

In sects like that of the Pythagoreans, philosophers would embark on mystical quests for spiritual insight, knowledge, power, and immortality. The Questor's way has perennially been witnessed as sixfold. Anyone who has read (or seen) J. R. R. Tolkien's well-known trilogy will recognize these stages, for they are embedded in the six books of *The Lord of the Rings*. Briefly:

1. Questors *settle* their minds and celebrate life at home, taking refuge in a circle that elects to *truly view* Mystery.
2. A *journey* is then undertaken into the unknown. Danger and freedom are experienced, bringing Questors into a state *demanding resolve.*
3. A need and responsibility to *inquire* grows to maturity. This is reinforced through expanding and stabilizing associations and *spoken allegiances.*
4. An *active charge,* given to each Questor by spiritual elders, drives the Questors' Fates. Unique and personal, a Questor's mission involves a continuous, concentrated *conduction* of supranatural, psychic presence.
5. Advanced Questors cross into a land of total, freakish control, wherein authoritarian structures and possessions exist solely for their own sake as futile attempts to avoid death. Apparently dark, morbid, infinitely repetitive, stagnant, and meaningless, this realm must be lit by the seemingly inconsequential light of each Questor's soul and mission. Here, Questors see their *life works.* Through *ancestral* destiny, each Questor is subtly, accidentally, and synchronistically directed.
6. Finally, every Questor must meet Death. After a seemingly *unending effort,* Death takes its rightful toll, transforming the now fully initiated into they who know, who have seen, who are truly insightful. From this will come a blessed reign of Noble Wisdom and *resurrection* into an ecstatic kingdom.

Each member of a Questor's Order is marked by her or his stage of advancement in this hierarchical quest. Through nondual realization, the post-quest stages of Resurrection, commencing with the Tower and culminating with the Angel, become the most important of esoteric realizations. Cultivation of Immortal Principles is the discerning mark of spiritual enlightenment; it guides all communal history of transfiguring Beauty, transforming Goodness, and translating Truth. Tolkien spent much of his life considering this in terms of angelic avatars such as Gandalf, mythic races such as the Elvenkind, and cosmological domains that were essentially deathless.

The dualistic path, in contrast, believes ultimately that only through physical death can the world be transcended. Thus, *resurrection* is defined solely through negative concepts such as reincarnation or, in our modern day, cloning. These are "negative" because the world is what the soul supposedly wishes to permanently *escape,* not be reborn into. The mystical quest of the Pythagoreans was purposed toward immortality in a nonmaterial realm of perfection. Pythagoreans did not view heavenly domains as being unified with earthly realms.

We will examine Pythagoras's unique and creative blend of mythic-rationalism through the teachings of his successor Empedocles in the next chapter. Pythagoras's philosophical dualism was advanced in numerous ways by Plato. Plato's corpus highlights a maturation of Greek rationality. However, Plato was neither unaware of nor dissociated from the mythic mind-set of early Greek society. Nor was he unable to intuit the vision-logic states that were to be championed by Neoplatonists centuries later. Nevertheless, his habits of mind, as exemplified in his Socratic dialogues, were rooted in discursive thought. Through Plato, an original paragon of speculative logic, European civilization was initiated into the elegance of rational cultivation and study.

Plato was ultimately succeeded by the Neoplatonists, foremost of who was Plotinus. Put very briefly, by integrating the logos and theurgy of Pythagoras with the wisdom of Heraclitus, Plotinus rectified Plato's dualistic tendencies through an intuitive awareness of Unity. In the many centuries separating these men, Jewish, Christian, and Gnostic beliefs in mind/body dualism were codified. (These too will be treated in the next chapter.) Sectarian differences produced a logical set of dualistic propositions, the bulk of which have been lucidly deconstructed by Ioan Couliano in *The Tree of Gnosis*, his treatise on Gnosticism.

The present book argues that fathoming nondual emanationist theory is essential to a true understanding of the Tarot's origins. This theory is well documented in philosophical schools both East and West. However, university philosophy departments no longer commonly teach it, even though for centuries Neoplatonism served as a bedrock foundation for Western philosophy. In North America, nondual philosophy went underground, in part because it became politically unacceptable in conservative Christian-influenced academic circles to posit cosmic unity.

More broadly, secular analytic philosophy departments of the late twentieth century adhered to a position of *wisdom-denial*. They apparently preferred rationalized ignorance to intelligent intuition regarding any field of knowledge or reality that was not definable by materially reducible, linearly measurable, and randomly determined interactions. *Relatively* existent event-objects were defined by *ego-rational* manipulations and logistics. That strongly limited set of logistics was arrogantly presumed to apply to every aspect and domain of the Universe, including the very essence of Time and Space; as if "scientific mind" from that point on "knew" all that there would ever be to *know*. Yet, materialistically dogmatic observers affecting the observed did not consider what happens when the methodology of observation is applied to the analytic observers *themselves*. Succinctly put, strictly analytic logicians have always feared genuine contemplation. *By observing itself, mind inevitably transforms its own state of consciousness and realization of universal principles.*

Many "hard" scientists became locked into a course of linear and mechanical theories that were inadequate to address *necessarily holistic* scientific fields of study such as ecology, anthropology, sociology, psychology, et al. That course is on its final leg to an inescapable termination. Fortunately, a *new science* has been progressively updating the philosophical underpinnings of modern scientific thought.

Twentieth-century physics and emergent fields regarding chaos and evolution, for instance, have been slowly awakening philosophers of science to a new dawn of interdependent and holistic complexity.

Regarding earlier theories of science, we must turn to Aristotle, tutor of Alexander the Great, to discern the source of Christian theology's primary rationale behind its dualistic solution to the body/soul dilemma. Aristotle posited a psychophysical apparatus so subtle that it almost touches the ineffable nature of the soul, and yet remains associated with the subtle physiology of the human body. Located in the heart, this organ of the psyche, called the *proton organon,* translates physical sensations and thoughts arising from them into *phantasms* (meaning "something apparently seen but having no physical reality"; originally from the Greek concept of "making visible"). In modern physiology, we may identify this *proto-organ* with a hormonal gland connected to the right side of the heart that essentially influences all of the endocrine system, beginning with the pineal and associated midbrain glands. This gland was only recently scientifically verified.

Discriminated linearly as a series of causes, it was for ages posited that through the psyche the soul transmits vitality to the body, which disintegrates once it quits doing so. According to Aristotle, the soul transmits vital activity to the body *solely* by means of the *proton organon.* On the other hand, the body's five sensory organs can also communicate to the soul via the same cardiac apparatus, which codifies sensory data so as to make it psychically comprehensible. Called *phantasia* or "inner sense," *sidereal* (meaning "of the stars," "celestial," "divine") mind transforms sensorial data via phantasms so as to be perceptible to the soul. This traditional understanding lends reason and cause to the fantastic imagery used in Tarot decks.

Throughout medieval times, it remained the Roman Catholic Church's stance that the soul could only apprehend what was first converted into a series of phantasms. This position was strongly reinforced by St. Thomas Aquinas's affirmation of it in his *Summa*

Theologica, a late-thirteenth-century Latin "theological summary" targeting educated laymen of all religions. Drawing upon Aristotle, Pseudo-Dionysius the Areopagite, and ecumenical Islamic and Jewish scholars of Thomas's time, *Summa Theologica* became the primary authoritative source for Roman Catholic theological law after the Bible.

Extending these beliefs, in esoteric Christianity it was deemed crucial that stations of Divine realization be converted into a series of phantasmic images. Jesus's Passion, portrayed in the Stations of the Cross, is a well-known depiction of a sacred journey culminating in ultimate immortality. Evidence of the great traditional sacrificial quest is found in the Catholic Stations' culminating fifth, sixth, and seventh stages: Ninth Station – *Jesus Falls the Third Time* (the inevitable turn of the Wheel); Tenth Station – *Jesus Is Stripped* (the naked truth of the Hermit); Eleventh Station – *Jesus Is Nailed to the Cross* (the witnessing of the Hanged Man); Twelfth Station – *Jesus Dies on the Cross* (the destiny of Death); Thirteenth Station – *Jesus Is Taken Down from the Cross* (the material-bound otherworld of the Devil); Fourteenth Station – *Jesus Is Laid in the Tomb* (the resurrecting portal of the Tower).

Tarot readers often do not realize that the hierarchical Trionfi also portray stations of the Sacrificial Way Beyond Death, composing in transpersonal images the perennial *Quest of Immortals.* They do this in a context that more closely resembles original Dionysian Greek and Eastern Mystery processions than a Western Christian interpretation of them.

This positive importance placed upon sacred *imagery* in the context of an Immortal Journey or Mission into Death's Domain and the Deathless Beyond contradicted Judaic and Islamic laws that were opposed to any anthropomorphic visualization of divine reality beyond that which the Prophets themselves had revealed. Elijah's and Mohammed's Angelic Chariot rides into Heaven served as the primary mystical images of divine ascension for Judaism and Islam respectively. At the height of medieval scholarship, Jewish and Islamic metaphysics converged through a more abstracted understanding of spiritual stations, taking form as a series of archetypal names. These were epitomized by Ibn ʿArabi's processional chain of divine attributes, which this book suggests was imaged by way of Eastern Christian influence in the first half of the fifteenth century as twenty-two Image-Exemplars.

We examine now the crux of exoteric Western philosophy's primary attempt to resolve the body/soul dilemma. Originating with Aristotle, it was codified in Gnostic and Christian theology. Aristotle needed to derive a rational, effective structure that could coherently define the causal links between a human's divine nature (soul) and mundane life (body). Furthering his concept of a subtle proto-organ, he resorted not to unifying the two (Heraclitus's and Plotinus's solution), but rather to positing a "third self": a psyche *distinct* from both body and soul.

In Christianity, this triad was translated as the hypostatic Trinity of Jesus (body), Holy Spirit (psyche), and God the Father (soul). As ideal souls that had fallen into sinful forms of physicality, humans were reduced to acquiring knowledge of the Truth (i.e., of God and his Angelic realms), beyond what is revealed in scripture, at best through identification with psychic phantasms. These were seen as messages of the Holy Spirit; however, they were also frequently interpreted by authorities as communications of Satan.

Although Aristotelian metaphysics was incorporated into Catholic doctrine, Christian theology departed from it by necessity. Christians held that the physical world's estrangement from the spiritual domain could only be mitigated by God through Jesus, the singular earthly form or body capable of fully permeating the fallen world with Holy Spirit. Through the agency of Jesus, or God-made-Man, the Church was founded to continue the effort of infusing, if not all of the material world including mankind, then at least a *chosen few* with God's Spirit. Thus did Heaven come down to Earth.

Quite differently, Aristotle appears to have viewed *Intellect* itself as being wedded to, if not identifiable with, the *essence of phantasm*. (Perhaps this attitude affected his role as educator of Alexander the Great, an unusually intelligent ruler whose missionary fantasies drove him into madness and death even as it changed the course of East-West history.) Regarding that view, Søren Kierkegaard (early-nineteenth-century Dane, father of *religious existentialism*) sarcastically remarked that *pure thought* must then be a phantasm. One might argue that Plato at times appears to have believed just that.

For Plotinus, pure thought, or contemplation of contemplation itself, was the *living root* and *essential seed* of the world. Radiant Intellect is not divorced from physical reality; it emanates as Wisdom-Soul, which in turn emanates as the World Soul and Flux of the Kosmos.

Neoplatonism was a major catalyst for Renaissance arts, humanities, and sciences (including Newtonian physics), but it was constantly reinterpreted and then co-opted by clever dualists of an Aristotelian ilk. *Innate to fourth-stage archetypal, psychic awareness is intuition of an inherently unified, hierarchically ordered, transmuting world.* That awareness emerges from mature, discriminative intelligence. When psychic identifications lose their universal, hierarchical, and archetypal essentiality, they are reduced to random and relatively meaningless fantasies. These all too often become purposed toward de-structuring ethical responsibilities.

As the Renaissance dawned in Italy, intellectual and popular focus turned to phantasmic *masques* (from Italian *maschera*, from Late Latin *masca*, referring to "specter" or "witch") and Dionysian *processions;* Venice's *triumphant* pageants and pre-Lenten *carnevale*, for instance, were renowned. It has been speculated that the Triumphs emerged from these. Neoplatonic imagery and symbols began to effuse into Venetian culture during the thirteenth century, when Venice and France ruled the shrunken Byzantine Empire. As was highlighted in chapter 2, Venice maintained close relationships with the Greek world right up to the fall of Constantinople, the Council of Churches in Ferrara, and the Tarot's emergence.

Greek esoteric iconography had been incorporated by Gothic artisans into both Northern and Southern European architecture during Crusading centuries of interaction with the East. The Trionfi as a set of images was not, however, composed of popular Italian icons, even though a few of its subjects were well known (e.g., the Wheel, Love, Death, Emperor, and Pope). Greek mythology, metaphysics, and Sufi symbolism contained in the early Triumphant images, as seen in this book, more clearly reflect a contemplative knowledge of the perennial wisdom traditions of eastern lands. That knowledge was largely imported to Italy and France during the fifteenth century.

During the late medieval period and throughout the Renaissance, vision-logic explorations psychologically enabled cross-culturally educated men to dominate philosophical and religious circles. In Muslim spheres, Sufis and scholars learned in Persian and Greek arts and technologies became a substantially dominant influence, strongly affecting the development of Western science that was to occur after Europe's Renaissance.

In Christian Europe, mass identification with and masterful humanization of the *phantasmic* led to wealthy patronage and societal appreciation of transcultural, interdisciplinary *Renaissance men* such as Leonardo da Vinci. Building upon this, visionary scientists like Nicolaus Copernicus began transforming whole societal worldviews that had been fully established by Roman Church authorities. This allowed for a Christian reformation to charge forward, most famously led by Martin Luther, a man endowed with forceful psychic faculties. Scientific speculation then exploded in what has been called the *Copernican Revolution*, as worldviews were literally transformed, initially via Galileo's telescoping technology and Muslim navigational techniques. Leading into a newly enlightened era, exploratory societies formed, including London's Royal

Society for the Improvement of Natural Knowledge, which was brought into prominence by the famous alchemist Sir Isaac Newton (whose lack of Eastern studies and misunderstanding of *internal* alchemy caused him great harm).

Less known, but as important, mass embarkation upon phantasmic exploration fostered a highly risky, trailblazing movement comprising educated, pantheistic women. It was originally through such women, via the safe (and highly militarized) enclaves of Italian courts, that the Tarot was intuitively played and promoted. We may imagine witty bards serving as game-masters and "psychic mirrors," *magicians* and *fools,* to courtly ladies' creative imaginations and *questing fantasies.* Those courtly games grew to become serious and substantial in the following centuries, creating dramatic alchemies that defined sociocultural advancement as much as generals' war games did.

During this developmental era of phantasmic re-visioning and transpersonal psychology, there were those who embraced radically dualistic beliefs akin to Gnosticism. In modern parlance, these spiritualists tended toward a schizophrenic split of self-identity. All physical involvement of psyche was viewed as being false, and thereby inherently spiritually decadent. In such a state, fantasy was secretly held to be of a higher reality. Through a twist of logic, this then justified breaking all types of sexual and social mores. We will revisit this in the next chapter, but reference to the ill-fated Giordano Bruno is here apropos.

Giordano Bruno was adept at the *art of memory,* based on *intricate control of phantasmic imagery.* In the sixteenth century, he introduced Renaissance intellectuals to a psychic technique purporting to bridge the mind directly with Eros without intermediary images and bypassing the use of an Aristotelian organ of phantasm. He astutely intuited that identification of one's *personal* soul with *Eros,* being the *Intellect's* true soul, would be the most direct path of divine realization. This might be compared to yogic exercises that transpersonally dissolve mental activity or limited senses of self into Shakti activity that opens mindful awareness to realization of Universal Self.

Bruno's method refined the mind's creation and use of imagery via intricate subtleties to facilitate complex memory processes. He then claimed a mysterious ability to *remember* the Spiritual Domain by progressively transcending any use of intermediate images. Effectively, he identified Eros with emptiness as *cessation of all fantasy.* His concentrated psychic process of imagination and fantasy, followed by transcendence of that very process, was unusually intense and subtle in its practice. Techniques of Buddhist *meditative concentration (dhyana, ch'an,* or *zen* in India, China, and Japan, respectively) purposed toward cessation of mind-activity might be seen as comparable. India has a long history of rigorous memory training, originally based on oral transmission of the Vedas. In Europe, however, it appears that no one during Bruno's time was able to succeed in duplicating his methods.

Bruno was a rational genius with a type of photographic memory. By all accounts, he was enormously egoic and rude. (Ego and rational thinking initially develop together, often making pathological egotism unusually "smart.") He felt that upon transcending his thinking self, which he apparently experienced through concentrating all of his attention via efforts involving photographically detailed fantasies and erotic engagement with women, he could effectively accomplish god-realization. His conflation of psychic and subtle stages of realization with that of divine perfection cost him his life. He was burned at the stake for his mastery of psychic powers, belief in *infinite* worlds, and excessive social-sexual-political hubris.

Bruno's phantasmic techniques of visualization and subtle association have been periodically re-engineered by spell-casting occultists and occasional psychotherapists. In the modern era a number of influential cults have derived their power from similar systems, which are often used as subtle forms of mind-control based upon erotic suggestion.

Mass identification with the phantasmic also renewed communities convinced that *transcendent* soul, spirit, domains, or principles did not actually exist. Etheric experiences of invisible spirits were thought by uneducated pagans to be caused solely by natural essences of earth. Psychic impressions and projections were associated with temporal, localized phenomena with neither universal binding nor hierarchical order. While perhaps sounding familiar to readers interested in Wicca, this mind-set did not include modern psychophysiological interpretations of subtle experiences, natural fields, and altered states of consciousness. Crude rationalization of animistic beliefs wove an *anti-rational* cloth of superstition and ritualistic magic that shrouded a confused body of archaic, pre-mythic paganism.

Modern, educated readers, by virtue of their agreement with known and undeniable aspects of nature, generally find simple-minded pagan ways of thinking to be obviously ignorant, even if *valid* in their sociocultural contexts. There are, of course, hundreds of millions of people today who have yet to advance in their psychosocial development to a mythical level of consciousness. India supplies us with a good example; a great many tribal people have almost no knowledge or awareness of Hinduism's mythical pantheon of deities. They instead remain in an aboriginal state of mind and culture that preceded development of the Vedas and its subsequent mythic culture. Upon immersion into their primitive environments and daily rituals, Westerners with romantic notions regarding animistic tribalism readily come to appreciate the importance of mythos as an integral step toward rational education and psychosocial development.

Though ofttimes called *pantheistic* (as previously mentioned, meaning literally "all gods," a spiritual worldview identifying Deity with the *Universe* and all of its phenomena), magic-based worldviews do not hold to the *unity* of all being, which is necessarily an integral part of pantheism. Historically, Wicca and other forms of paganism lacked maturation of third-stage rationality; they thereby did not develop a metaphysics involving principles of *universal law,* energetic alchemy, causal creation, or present unity.

Female spirituality emphasizing *the myriad* evolves through integration with male spirituality emphasizing *the one.* In the process of understanding *unity through diversity,* the world is effectively rationalized. *The Tarot evinces such integration.* Although a *nondual Goddess* tradition emerged in India, there is scant evidence of it developing in European cultures with the possible exception of the Virgin Mary cult in its advanced stages of devotion. Many modern-day neo-Wicca followers are unaware of this, adhering to a generalized Eastern understanding of Yin-Yang/Tao unity without delving into the multicultural history of East-West spirituality and philosophy (early or late).

In transpersonal and integral psychology it is understood that we are inherently by nature an integrated, unified psychophysical-mindful self. *Psychophysical Self* from a Trionfi perspective is not deemed inherently lacking in beauty, goodness, or truth, for it is understood to *really be the Whole World* by virtue of its *source* and *destiny.* The Universe *emanates* (as in its original Latin meaning "to flow out") as Time-Space-Flux. That then emerged through developmental formation as a Sun-Earth microcosm evolving into biological identities and Heart-minds of sentient, intelligent organization manifesting as psychophysical bodies.

We note here that the technical term *emanation* does not universally apply to all philosophical schools East and West that base their understandings on cosmic unity and emergent developmental processes. Taoism, it certainly can be argued, logically derived its causal worldview in a way that cannot be identified analytically with Neoplatonism. Fundamental differences in language and semiotics produce significantly distinct approaches to mythic and rational cosmologies of Unity. Over differing generations and cultures, Neoplatonic teachings themselves varied greatly.

In any case, both Taoist and Tarot Adepts opposed conceits that the physical is impure, the soulful is ideally incorporeal, and the human psyche is the only cosmic bridge between the two. Non-dual understanding does not condemn sensual sexuality (or feminine power), does not deny militant passion (or male sovereignty), and does not fear natural fantasy (or creative communion). Such a view embraces Immortal Logos as already embodied – right here, right now. *The Kingdom of Heaven is at hand. Love your neighbor as yourself.*

Successful Questors value the art of seeing and identifying that which is beyond them and within them. Like archaic natives assimilating the natural world of their environments, modern-day Questors become what they meditate upon. The best practice is initially one of *not this, not that* – concentrating on the emptiness or temporality of all sensation and thereby the Emptiness of Self. Once such *insight meditation* (or *vipassana*) is established, that which intuitively embodies an *integrated identifiable, transcendental, and attractive wholeness* will serve as the best focus for a Questor's meditation.

That most often may be a living being in a spiritual environment, but history affirms that sacred art, sanctuaries, media (books and beyond), and other agencies of spiritual realization can also serve to coherently align and integrate a Questor's psychophysical consciousness. Lives have been transformed through contact with sacred icons. Fantastic images of cosmological forces have been formed and energetically utilized throughout human history: shamanistic masks, phallic dolmens, yogic deities, stone temples, primal hieroglyphics, magical talismans, microcosmic mandalas, etc. Even still, ultimately it is only the *Spontaneous Ecstasy* of *no-self, no-other* that liberates beyond objects of meditation.

Wisdom reflected in the Tarot holds to the essence of Hermeticism: *as it is above, so it is below.* The psyche in its identification with phantasmic imagery not only "connects" the divine with the mundane, as Aristotelian or Christian theology would have it. It actually *real-*

izes the *likeness* between the two. Understood in this way, conceptualization of distinct *psychic spheres* or *stages* is rectified and integrated with Hermetic and Neoplatonic nondualism. Let us consider this further.

During the period of the Tarot's creation, European artisans advanced beyond depicting the sacred themes to which they had been traditionally limited. *Humanistic portrayals* of psychic identity were revealed via idealistic iconographical visions. Late medieval artisans drew prominently upon pagan Greek iconography. *Byzantine Christians were by far the preeminent masters of this art.* Humanization of spiritual knowledge then continued into the European Renaissance, with psychological representations of human identity becoming progressively more realistic and mundane.

Psychosocial transformation of identity brought about by phantasmic art is a germane topic concerning the Tarot. Western Christianity, both Catholic and Protestant, has traditionally relegated arts involving magical and mythical fantasy to the sphere of *sacrilege* (from Latin *sacrilegus*, "one who steals sacred things") unless created specifically to serve church functions. Control of image-making in terms of societal influence can indeed readily place power into the hands of corrupt men. The twentieth century was witness to a dark, propagandistic side of manipulative imagery. Media control and fascism make for a nefarious combination.

More recently, promoted by profit-maximizing commercial centers of image-making, attentive viewing of psychic and subtle visions of essential nature and vital life has been largely displaced by mindless consumption of sexual and violent fantasies propagated through many global media spaces. In varying forms, banal conceits involving egoic projection and possessive control appear far more prominently than do insights into culture, intelligence, or beauty.

Investigation into the manipulative social and political uses through which psychically catalytic images may be abused will be left to the reader. It is important to state simply: *Neither the origins nor the use of Tarot symbols were associated with a debased manipulation of mass or personal psychology.*

Leading up to Renaissance humanism and the Tarot Trionfi, a rich tradition of pagan sculpture developed during the Gothic period (twelfth to fifteenth centuries) of European cathedral building and spiritual design. Mythic gods, angels, gargoyles, and fantastic environments were crafted into the most sacred spaces of Europe. *These forms were purposed toward an edifying, actualizing transformation of a worshipper's psyche.* Stained glass windows when suffused with light represented the pinnacle of Western Christian iconographical art.

Neo-pagan iconography advanced beyond secret crafts of stonemason guilds during the period directly preceding the Tarot's emergence. Byzantine craftsmen and esoteric designers were at the forefront of this movement. In the late fourteenth and early fifteenth centuries, the Eastern Christian art of miniature, card-size *icons* (from Greek *eikinai,* meaning "to be like") reached its peak in terms of technical excellence and spiritual grace.

Enlightened late Byzantine embrace and open portrayal of spiritual iconography had not been the Christian norm. In the centuries following the life of Jesus, Christian leaders had vehemently rejected association with divine images. They felt that God could not be viewed with shape and thus any image of Him would be an image of a false god. In this, they followed transcendental Judaic tradition. It was deemed that spiritual images served as homes for evil demons, no longer viewed as the creative *daimonic* forces found in Hellenic culture. Knowledge of such images could only contribute to the construction of profane artifices, epitomized in Judaic stories by the *Tower of Babel.*

Judaic and Islamic *iconoclasts* maintain that imaging the Divine in human form is heretical, for only the Prophets have been ecstatically raised to the heights of angelic vision. Under iconoclastic doctrine, familiar representations of Heaven, God, Angels, Saints, Prophets, etc. are replaced by geometric symbols (e.g., crosses, stars, domes, lattices, mosaics, branches, etc.) that are thought to resemble aspects of universal perfection and thereby to indicate Divine presence. In Christian history, a Greek Orthodox period in seventh- and eighth-century Byzantium was famous for its iconoclastic dogma.

The medieval Latin climate regarding sacred imagery was not iconoclastic, per se. Images of Jesus, his Passion, and his Resurrection were thought to be truly reflective of Divine Nature. Nonetheless, concrete representation of spiritual realms was an intensely regulated business.

To Church believers, divine law revealed in the Bible had been *written in stone* by the Prophets and Apostles. Beyond the Bible, it was thought that discernment of Truth was best left to the ecclesiastical hierarchy ruled by the Pope and fellow Bishops – Jesus's spokesmen on earth. It was largely feared by Western Church hierarchy that direct mediation with spiritual realms through refined use of the *psyche* would inevitably and quite possibly unknowingly be affected by Satan, archenemy of the Church. Psychosocial domination by Church hierarchy (who justified their psychic and mental dogmatic enforcement and restrictions as necessary guidance) might then be disrupted. Religious icons were thus limited in design and usage, primarily to churches, approved placements within family homes, and special environs such as cemeteries.

In general, the material world was dualistically equated with the "dark"; demons were regarded as merely *mirror images* of *matter* and *evil.* Emanationist views of the Kosmos as a spiritual continuum that included all manifestation of material embodiment and earthly nature were condemned as pantheistic. Dualistic Christian positions strongly influenced by Gnosticism conflicted with nondual pantheistic positions roundly influenced by Neoplatonism. The latter pointed to inherent contradictions in supposedly *mono*-theistic Christian theology imbuing a demiurgic Satan with control of the world.

In Christianity, God has historically *revealed* himself only to a select few. This has been a matter of grave political importance for those few claiming exclusive revelation. An artisan who can create images in the likeness of Divine states can potentially become a source of significant authority. Many ecclesiastics have had a personal stake in not recognizing such authority. Powers inhering in humans' abilities to define and reflect cosmological processes used to be terribly feared. Church rituals attempted to stake total claim to such powers; including all powers of the pagan Heroes, Wizards, and great Eastern Mages of old.

However, the Might of history's saints and sages who transcended themselves to unify Mysterious Eros and Radiant Intellect has not depended upon Pauline salvation or Roman Catholic sacramental rites. Similarly, self-realized powers have been developed by those who have mastered the psychic arts of spiritual iconography, epitomized in a mobile, mass vernacular form by the Tarot Exemplars.

Renaissance fascination with phantasmic identities and processions opened a Pandora's Box of psychological states and social personas that previously had been taboo. This had an impact upon Roman Catholic hierarchical control over social stations and mobility. The Church's exclusive hold on intermediation between man, soul, and divine spirit was broken. Identification with psychic experiences of all types expanded into a socially complex profusion of psychological realities.

Those who spoke of their phantasmic visions were susceptible to being branded as *witches* (from Old English *wicca* or *wizard,* meaning "to make awake," as in Germanic *wikkjaz,* necromancer or "one who wakes the dead"; the Angel Triumph may accurately be identified with Wizardry, as Tolkien realized in his immortal fantasies) and Satan worshippers. They were threatened, tortured, or killed by controllers of pathologically dominating hierarchies whose structures and strictures attempted to arrest all subtle communion and spiritual awakening not sanctioned by Church officials.

Magic and mythic rituals and beliefs of the *pre*-rational mind were broadly viewed by Christian authorities as demonic. Exceptions, of course, were made for specifically Christian rites of magic (such as saintly miracles or the transubstantiation of bread and wine into the body and blood of Jesus) and doctrines of mythos (such as can be found in the book of Genesis). Intellectual, psychic, and subtle intuitions of the *trans*-rational mind that did not deny the "fundamental truths" of Christian magic and mythos were officially legitimized as Holy Spirit informing man of the Divine. It was (and remains to be) in the midst of confusing pre-rational and trans-rational worldviews (termed the "pre/trans fallacy" by Ken Wilber) that battlegrounds were drawn and intellectual and spiritual geniuses were shackled to the services of warring factions.

The fourth-stage Chariot charge of authentic spiritual energy and psychic Fortitude can either be *restricted* by domineering second-stage politicians and merchants or itself *dominate* forces of delusion, craving, and malice, and thus naturally develop into virtuous Fortune and subtle Life – the Wheel and Hermit Triumphs. *Submission* can either *actualize* spiritual life or arrest it. It actualizes when harmonious synchronicities are made apparent through awareness of natural ancestors, spirits, and karmic interdependency. When bound to a code of "no harm, no evil," this moves way beyond submission defined and enforced by controlling egos and threats of violence.

Religion, from Latin *religare,* fundamentally means "to tie fast" or "re-bind," as in "returning to the Source." If that Source is the Ground of Being from which a worshipper psychophysically/soulfully arises, then there are no *policies* that can innately stop a worshipper from being authentically religious, with or without ministers and churches facilitating the process.

We here broach the political subject of psychic domination by religious authorities. Neither this book nor the Tarot can avoid addressing often-provocative issues of dominance and submission as they arise in a context of authentic spiritual practice as opposed to politically or egoically motivated religious or psychic control.

Genuine spiritual adepts do not make claims to hierarchies of dominance and subsequent rights to command and control through manipulative utilization of communication. Non-pathological fourth-stage dominion naturally releases into fifth-stage submission. The drive toward enlightenment leads into equanimity, *simply letting it all be.*

Even the initial archetypes of the Tarot's hierarchical Triumphs are spiritual; even its culminating principles are realizable. The supreme way to realize Noble Wisdom is through complete *coherence* with that Way already so realized, beyond Chaos, as Radiant Mystery. The Way of Unity and its emanation through universal hierarchy and complete diversity is a radically difficult vision for many people to maintain. It can take enormous effort and *forgiveness* to imagine the interpenetration of transcendent spirit and ancestral presence with immanent matter, particularly when the material world is experienced as stagnant, repugnant, or unnatural. However, *submission to Truth* makes such an effort *effortless.*

Psychic activity that is actually *spiritual* relinquishes ego-control to the Charge of the Goddess, and that to the living Fate of Ancestors or spirits of the *pervasive and eternal now.* Thus do Chariot and Fortitude become Wheel and Hermit. Charismatic power *filled with its own import* tends toward pathological subversion of communal intuition into programs of procedural mind control, if not physical domination.

For most of its history, the Eastern Church evinced an understanding regarding how *esoteric development proceeds from dominant charge to submissive surrendering.* Like their Sufi brethren, Eastern sages arose from a Hermit-wisdom tradition rarefied in its contemplative sublimation of *psycho-spiritual* vitality and essence.

Although Mohammed the Prophet was a general and political leader, *Islam* itself means "submission," quite beyond the violence of corporeal conquest and subjugation. Wise Sufis understand that only through a state of virtuous and insightful devotion to the *Unity of Being* is Allah's Spirit truly realized. Hermits of all traditions have clearly intuited that *actualizing growth* through *spiritual emergence* and *integral mission* does not involve warfare or *pyramidal domination hierarchies* (elite few controlling the commons) of any type, including ecclesiastical.

Universal spirituality is based upon tolerant, cooperative, and fortified fourth-stage psychosocial dynamics that raise self-awareness into subtle virtue, ancestral union, and awareness of Transcendental Self as Universal Other. This marks a critical point of departure from political and egoic second-stage domination structures, be they secular, occult, Christian, Islamic, Hindu, New Age, or any other. While religious political leaders may believe that the latter defines the gross boundaries of God's Kingdom on earth, it is actually the former that marks the psychic and subtle *realization* of God's Kingdom *on earth as it is in heaven. This is the primary message that Mystics have attempted to convey to all religious leaders.*

Current Roman Catholic Bishops have challenged Islamic *Sheiks* (Arabic for "elders") to advance beyond *domination* (the Latin root of which originally indicated "lord of the house") defined by political control and warfare. Eastern Patriarchs also challenged Islam about its degradation of spiritual lordship and hierarchical rule in the century before Constantinople fell and the Tarot was developed. On the other hand, for many centuries prior, intelligent Sufis challenged not only their own *mullahs* (Arabic for "masters") but *all* of the political and exoteric religious leaders regarding this, most certainly including Crusading Christian monks and court theologians. Corrupt, militarized leaders of today need to hear this message. *Communication using contemporary and effective global technology* needs to be utilized in a concerted effort by modern wisdom-realizers to *educate secular and religious leaders* about *beautiful, good,* and *truthful* power, wealth, and status.

Perhaps primary to the process of political enlightenment will be a rectification of the concept of *lordship* in terms of responsibility and transcendence *that includes active involvement by female leaders, community, and culture.* The Chariot and Fortitude Triumphs speak to us of this, as they represent feminine force dominating communal conduction of spiritual mission and advancing it into the submissive synchronicities of Fortune and her Wheel. On a civil level, this involves bringing *dignified democracy* as a social process into the *local home and township levels of regulatory governance.*

Advancing societal health and general welfare, local communities around the world are integrating new forms of mind/body therapy. A *transformative spa-sanctuary* movement initiated by Esalen Institute and popularized across the planet through a cooperative effort between wellness therapists, holistic teachers, and hospitality executives remains at the forefront of this. (Esalen is the Big Sur, California, transformational spa and institute that was instrumental in the original mainstreaming of humanistic and transpersonal fields of psychology, East-West body/mind therapies, shamanic journeying and healing, perennial mythology, etc. Gia-fu Feng, to whom this book is dedicated, was a co-founder and Taoist sage of Esalen during the 1960s, going on to direct his own Stillpoint Foundation.) Interconnected, transcultural *sanctuaries for regenerative alchemy* (both internal and external) are required to deepen and advance the popular health and beauty spa industry.

As *techno-shamans,* new-millennium mages are manifesting the Hermit station phasing into that of the Hanged Man as the world shifts into an emerging *new age* quite beyond any cliché or pop commercialization. There is little room for corruption in intelligent and responsible lordship; and it is this that the Hermit so astutely peers into. Often taking a postmodern form of a privately investigating, freely networking loner, the Hermit archetype naturally facilitates *technology* (from Greek *tekhnologia,* indicating "systematic treatment of an art or craft" – the *logos* or "knowledge" of *tekhne*, "skill") to enable *fantasies of liberation*.

Appropriate use of technology – particularly *technologies of energy, money, and media* – must be enabled worldwide at household levels by becoming freely networked, decentralized, and secured from corruption. Until that occurs, fourth-stage *actualization hierarchies* will be regressively arrested by second-stage *domination hierarchies* that are marked by fear-mongering, terrorism, and brutal war. The turning of this tide or shift of these historical phases will define the twenty-first century. It is likely that in their absolutely crucial roles, postmodern mages will be unable to avoid confronting grimly grinning, global Death before the Towers of their Arts are built.

Exoteric religious tradition has always tended toward a dualistic view of the manifested world: so many lost souls need to be saved. Esoteric spiritual tradition has always tended toward a nondual view: with the *Kingdom at hand*, the world is *already* saved. Throughout much of Christian history, esoteric Saints have been martyred like pawns in political and military battles promoted by exoteric religious leaders. A similar history has played out in Islam between Muslim caliphs and associated legalistic ulama and peaceably wise, technically creative Sufis.

One can only pray that the twenty-first century will witness *recognition and affirmation of integral nonduality*. It certainly is possible that catastrophe of apocalyptic magnitude will serve as part of that process. It appears that, should this regrettably occur, esoteric practitioners from the Hermit stage onward will no longer serve as sacrificial lambs or *scapegoats* (a Hebrew concept by which people attempt to *escape* all sins or avoidance of responsibility via transference to a *goat* sent into the wilderness, standing for *Azazel*, "devil of the desert"). Uneducated, misled masses and deluded, greedy, and harmful leaders cannot count on violence, coercion, and intolerance to relieve them of their suffering.

Confusion between egoic and spiritual ways of dominance and submission defined a long Dark Age for Western Christian spirituality and culture. Eastern Christian forefathers marked quite a different history of esoteric realization and social development. Jesus's apostle Thomas and his Syrian community of hermits who moved eastward into India via the Sinai Peninsula and Red Sea were the original Eastern Christian contemplatives. In the first century after Jesus lived, Thomas's branch of Jesus's wisdom-way was embraced by Christianity's original Desert Fathers. They combined visions and practices of purity with *mystery rites* involving insightful meditation and Indo-Grecian therapeutics. More will be said about Jesus and Thomas in the next chapter.

Advancements were quickly made in Eastern Christian philosophy regarding Aristotelian attempts to rationalize dualistic theology and Neoplatonic attempts to move beyond it altogether. Origen, perhaps the most complex of early Christian metaphysicians, proclaimed that in the concept and reality of *Splendor* – specifically the *splendor* (from Latin, "to shine") of *light* – one could find a bridge between sacred and mundane qualities. For Origen, Splendor showed how a sacred image could be effective. An abyss separating divine and material worlds nevertheless remained in his Gnostic mind. Splendor could be viewed *fully* only through the personage of Jesus, the solely manifested *resemblance* of Holy Spirit and complete bridge between God and materially bound soul. Although Origen attempted to create an orthodox, Jesus-centric theology, he was nevertheless condemned as a heretic.

A generation later, Plotinus compassionately disclosed a bridge that did not limit passage to a privileged class of Christians. Plotinus's inclusive medium comprised hierarchical emanations or spheres of the One: *Intelligence, Light Soul, World Soul, and Cosmos.* He presented a psychophysical cosmos of light and universalized Goodness consciously realized through Ecstasy. Plotinus felt that the world, even in its darkest form of matter, *emanates* from the One in the likeness of *radiance.* Modern physics and cosmology would seem to support this view. Plotinus did not believe that a "higher soul" descended into a "lower body"; but that through contemplation the innate Brightness of corporeal existence could be magnified and made apparent.

After the Fall of Rome, the sixth century saw a renewal of the Greek world, centered in Constantinople. *Neoplatonic cosmology and theosophy was integrated into Christian theology through the genius of one man,* who wrote under the name of a first-century Christian convert, *Dionysius the Areopagite.* Dionysius permanently reformed Christian metaphysics via the original and Eastern Church. Two of his most famous treatises were entitled *The Celestial Hierarchy* and *The Divine Names.*

Living in Syria at the turn of the sixth century, Dionysius (often referred to as Pseudo-Dionysius) was one of three influential Eastern Christian theosophists who wove essential understandings of divine emanation and universal esotericism into Christian theology. Succeeding Dionysius were John Climacus and John of Damascus.

"Johannes" Scotus Eriugena (the Scotsman – or, more accurately, Gael – who called himself "Eriugena," but was referred to later as "John" and was actually a French Irishman) translated Eastern Christian treatises and wrote the *Corpus Dionysii* during the ninth century, an extensive commentary on the works of Dionysius. He was the first scholar to introduce into Western Europe the ideas of Neoplatonism created and developed by the Greek academy. No Catholic scholar afterwards evinced as much dedication to the oft-termed pantheistic Neoplatonism of Dionysius as Eriugena.

Scotus Eriugena's effort was widely condemned by Latin Church councils in his lifetime and every few hundred years afterward. In summary, he was accused of identifying God with His Creation, the Cosmos. Nevertheless, his work was read by and deeply influenced the great Western Christian mystics of medieval times. Even though his translations were hidden from European intelligentsia, buried in the heretical sections of severely restricted monastic libraries until the seventeenth century, through Scotus Eriugena Dionysius's corpus was made known to a few select scholars, who infiltrated Roman theology with Dionysius's Neoplatonic worldview, largely based upon the writings of Proclus.

It was through Dionysius that Christian society began positing knowledge of hierarchical, angelic spheres. According to Dionysius, *Angels* are bodiless yet visible beings (the word coming from Late Greek *angelos,* meaning "messenger"). They are seen subtly, in the form of radiance. *Angelic reality* is known by way of divine light-realms radiating divine principles. Dionysius's nine spheres of angelic emanation, divided into three triads, roughly coincide with nine stages of the Tarot:

First Hierarchy:

Seraphim	Angel & Sun
Cherubim	Moon & Star
Thrones	Tower & Devil

Second Hierarchy:

Dominions	Death & Hanged Man
Virtues	Hermit & Wheel
Powers	Fortitude & Chariot

Third Hierarchy:

Archangels	Love & Temperance
Principalities	Pope & Emperor
Angels	Popess & Empress

Through all of these realms, the Divine One creates and *influences* human reality via the *flowing process* of *angelic emanation.* (Dionysius was careful not to say that God *emanated* the angels, as orthodoxy prohibited any view other than that of a separate creator God.) We can see in this early model of the Tarot system, elaborated by Eastern Greek Patriarchs and Sufi Saints in the seven centuries after

Dionysius, that *all Triumphant stations are Beautiful, Good, and True Archetypes,* blessed and mirrored by Angelic company.

The highest of light domains is that of the brilliant, apollonian Seraphim. Having *three pairs* of wings, they represent the *Intellect* of pure *Brightness.* Uriel, Metatron, and Lucifer are names of three famous Seraphim.

The Cherubim are rulers of divine light that reaches down to earth, particularly that of the stars and moon. They are scarcely less awesome and powerful than the Seraphim. They represent the Light-Soul Love-Wisdom of mighty Eros-Sophia.

The *Cherub* as a chubby faced baby-boy was a degradation of Roman *Cupid,* the boy-god of Love and son of *Venus,* who was originally Greece's *Aphrodite.* Both stemmed from the ancient god-boy *Dionysus* who was re-imaged to reflect a rarified heavenly ideal in later Greek civilization.

Eros was originally a pre-cosmic force of creativity transforming Chaos to generate the worlds of Gaia and Tartarus. Later classical Greeks considered Eros to be a male God. However, archaic Greek cosmogony was deeply Goddess- and Earth-based. Eros was sensibly an extension of Gaia, her womb Tartarus, and her birthing process Chaos. Although Eros was later viewed as a male force of love, often focused upon the love of other males, this appears to have been a masculine projection upon the feminine Mystery Rites that Gaian wisdom arose from.

Truer to that tradition which Pythagoreans and Neoplatonists upheld is an understanding of Eros as the Goddess bringing Primordial, Kosmic Light into the material cosmos. From this worldview emerged a Space within which male God as Light could be conceived. In this book, Eros is generally used in reference to the Goddess as Gaia creating the cosmos via Chaos and Tartarus. In Platonic, Gnostic, and Neoplatonic eras, the Goddess as such was transformed into Sophia or Wisdom with *Chaos the Demiurge* as her son either ruling over the lower world or guarding the higher.

All of the *heavenly rulers* in the first three angelic spheres were thought to be of similar status. The Seraphim were imagined as surrounding God's Throne, directing all emanation of the World through radiance, sound, and universal vibration. The Throne, representing Whole Oneness of incorporeal and corporeal reality, is imaged by the Triumphs of Justice and World. The Angel and Sun Triumphs represent the *spectrum of Angelic presence,* combining Archangel Gabriel, Messenger of God in Judeo-Christian-Islamic tradition, with the fiery, resurrecting blast of a Seraph; whose brilliance is so intense – like a Great Sun – that no other divine being may look at it.

Lucifer, it was traditionally held, had *twelve* wings instead of six. As the Devil positioned in the thirteenth station of the Tarot (not counting the Magician) we may see him as uniquely holding the Tower as *Throne of Mater Earth,* through which he seductively reveals psychophysical immortality and challenges all those who would "know" the Goddess. Gnostic belief, which permanently affected Christian theology, held that he was the *fallen son* of Sophia, Wisdom Goddess; and that he literally recreated God's Throne on the edge of the *material cosmos,* effectively blocking human and lower angelic access to Heaven.

Islam, however, advanced a view of Lucifer as a "specially demoted" Seraph whose rank was established to degrade any and all who would attempt to cross the threshold into immortally ecstatic Heaven without having first passed the trials warded over by guardian Principalities and Powers (akin to the Genies of pre-Islamic belief and lesser gods, Titans, and demigods of Greek belief). It could be said in accordance to this view that Lucifer is Allah's *Guardian Angel of Last Resort.*

In following chapters we identify the Devil and Tower stations with Hades and Tartarus, closely associated with Mother Gaia, bridging earthly reality with Zeus's Immortal domain. *Gaia as Eros as Sophia* was a primary spiritual concept demarcating esoteric nondual understandings of the Goddess and Her Presence *as* the material World. Gnostic myths perverted this understanding of the Goddess and thereby of the natural world and seductive challenges engaged and celebrated through the ages by *Ecstatics.*

Christians envisioned most angels as having human-like appearance, but Thrones were pictured as *myriad-eyed wheels* roaming between the realm of God's Throne and that of angelic spirit-beings associated with regulation of the natural cosmos and humankind. Later Roman Catholicism imagined the Thrones as tremendous, peaceable "demon" beings (*daimonic* in terms of their *strangely powerful* and *practically chaotic* forms) *composing* God's Throne and tracking all movement of the Cherubim (compare with the iconographic position pre-Vedic Yakshas came to hold as literal supporters of Hindu Deities, as well as Buddhist Celestials and their vehicles).

The final three angelic domains are those of the Archangels and their wards, the myriad *personal* Angels, along with the Principalities who are *anti-God* and *anti-Human,* serving as something akin to fierce guardian spirits of cities, states, and rulers. (In our list, Principalities have been placed between Archangels and Angels because they so closely represent second-stage patriarchal urban powers.)

It needs to be noted that accounts of varying types of angelic beings in canonical Old and New Testaments are scarce and often conflicting. Positions and principles of angel-spirits and spheres are ofttimes confusedly crossed over in Biblical stories. Michael, for instance, is at times deemed an Archangel and at other times the greatest of the Seraphim after defeating Lucifer, who at times is defined as a lower Power.

Most religious sects maintain some kind of interpretation regarding angelic realms, beings, and their hierarchies. Dionysius and later visionaries relied on their own imaginations and revelations – abetted by Neoplatonic, Greek, and Chaldean mythology – regarding their descriptions, hierarchical arrangements, and comparisons of these Kosmic forces and principles of divine consciousness.

Ancient Greeks had also experienced visions of bodiless beings. Psyches or souls manifested with visible shapes called *eidola.* Furthermore, early Greeks had envisioned a *ladder* of soul-stations connecting heaven and earth. Homer's "Golden Chain" (*Iliad* 8.18–20) was described by Dionysius in terms of a *ten-stage, descending series of Spirit-images,* with each having two sides, one mirroring the image above it and the other below it. These Image-spheres and Angel-realms represented incorporeal, yet realized spiritual planes of existence.

Plotinus's nondual view of cosmology was made acceptable to Christian *dualistic monism* by Dionysius's use of this metaphysical device incorporating twenty *rungs* of a *divine ladder.* He revealed that the world of Matter is an *isomorphic reflection* of the Spirit world. Angels serve as the agency through which earth and the cosmos are connected to their immortal nature.

Every human, from this point of view, has an angelic presence – whether seen and felt or not. That presence can be *imagined* in essential ways by *psyches* sufficiently *subtle* and *virtuous.* Indeed, it is the very purpose of psyche to do just that, channeling divine Intelligence into human awareness and veneration. This is compelled by an actual love of wisdom. Drawing upon Neoplatonic sages preceding him, Dionysius fused Aristotelian and Christian Triads into a singular, psychophysically realizable theosophical world of spiritual presence.

In his treatise on Divine Names, Dionysius introduced to future theosophists, including Ibn ʿArabi, a nascent system of Divine Attributes that lent themselves to the concept of descending and ascending stages of archetypal presence. Listed in his chapter headings are these Names:

> God, Light, Beautiful, Love, Ecstasy, Zeal, Being, Life, Wisdom, Mind, Truth, Faith, Power, Righteousness, Salvation, Redemption, Omnipotent, Ancient of Days, Eternity, Time, Peace, Holy of Holies, King of Kings, Lord of Lords, God of Gods, Perfect, One.

A hierarchical ladder of visionary Spirit-states connecting Earth and Heaven was elaborated by John Climacus at the turn of the seventh century. Heraclitus had once said: "The way down is the same as the way up." John Climacus took this to heart. The spiritual hierarchy of psychic, fourth-stage image-realms delineated by Dionysius was reworked in a personal treatise by John, who was abbot of the Sinai Peninsula's central monastery. Built upon the spot where Moses was said to have ascended to Heaven, this was perhaps the perfect place for John to have contemplated and put into words *The Ladder of Divine Ascent.*

Upon this patriarchal hermit's lineage in the Sinai, Hermetic Christian, Sufi, and Kabbalist contemplative tradition was essentially founded. His treatise became Eastern Christendom's most popular non-biblical book. A compelling Christian case was made by John Climacus that human existence could be transformed by consciously *ascending* through states of *spiritual cultivation.* Those states were associated with *archetypal images* by the third of our Eastern Christian exemplars.

John of Damascus (ca. 655–750) was born into the family of Sargum Mansur. *Mansur,* meaning *victorious,* was a well-known Muslim name common among Syrian Christians of Arab descent. During John's lifetime, Damascus became the capital of the Muslim Empire, which had won Syria from Byzantium. John's grandfather, Ibn Mansur, had negotiated the capitulation of Damascus to conquering Islamic forces. Syrians were known for their independent thinking. They had never been fully indoctrinated by Greek Christianity, and had become accustomed to the presence of North Arabian settlers. Syria's intercultural climate served as an excellent environment for esoteric exchange and alignment between spiritual traditions, East and West, old and new.

The multicultural climate of Damascus significantly influenced John's studies and teachings. As a child, he received an Arabic education. As a young man, he studied with a Catholic monk who had been captured in Sicily by Muslims and acquired in Damascus by his father. John, beatified as a Saint in both Roman and Greek Churches, was unusual in his knowledge of the Koran and other religious literature of Islam. He was a respected Christian theologian under the Greek Church of Byzantium when he became head advisor to the Caliph of Damascus.

In his famous treatise, *Fount of Knowledge,* John compiled, elucidated, and reformulated from numerous traditions the great many teachings of *saints* and *sages* with which he was familiar. He is considered the father of systematic theology in the Eastern Church. Through fearless minds such as his, perennial wisdom was integrated with exoteric worldviews, inexorably promoting higher and deeper states of consciousness in the process.

When iconoclastic controversy erupted in the Greek Church, John resigned from the court and became a *contemplative.* His disagreements with Emperor Leo of Byzantium regarding theology and Church politics were legendary. John championed the value of icons, *associating images with stations of spirituality.*

Little will be mentioned in this book about the iconoclastic period of Christian history. It paralleled the rise of Islam and its anti-iconographic laws. Unlike the Eastern Christians, Sufis were never officially released from this stricture. However, through the beautiful intricacies of Arabian and Persian languages, Sufis nonetheless managed to *reveal visions of the Divine Attributes and Essences.* Although as a famous Christian theologian, John of Damascus argued against the "Islamic heresy," his teachings and transcultural appreciation for universal stations of spiritual development were studied, respected, and emulated by later Sufis.

Authorship of *Barlaam and Ioasaph,* a popular Christian novel during the Middle Ages, was traditionally ascribed to John. Throughout the book, he alludes to the life of Buddha in an intelligent, respectful way. *The tenfold Noble Path that formed the basis of Buddhism was foreign neither to the contemplatives of Eastern Christianity nor to the*

Sufis of Islam. Sufism, Buddhism, and Eastern Christianity met and merged throughout Central Asia and within cosmopolitan Near Eastern cities of John's time. Damascus played an important role in this process. Given an integral will to do so, Syria remains geopolitically situated to serve the Greater Cause once more.

The above Greek metaphysicians were key teachers in an esoteric school that thrived for a millennium in Constantinople and Alexandria. That school was broadened and enriched by the venerable Sufis previously introduced. Sufi metaphysicians "grounded" Dionysius's angelic realms. They universalized spiritual hierarchy by addressing the realms in terms of immortal *attributes*, which defined the *purposes* and *principles* of *human realization*. They progressively identified stations of the Path – and Questors' psychophysical evolution when embarking upon that Path – with a hierarchy of Immortal Principles. Sufis made clear the role that psyche and its essential phases played in the realization of ecstatic being, consciousness, and bliss. In doing so, they expanded and spiritually fortified the Neoplatonic foundation upon which Dionysius the Areopagite, John Climacus, and John of Damascus had constructed an Eastern Christian Tower of perennial wisdom.

Room restricts us from examining the history of Eastern Christian metaphysics beyond this short introduction. Both the Tarot and this book serve to summarize the enormous wealth of nondual wisdom that has been consistently renewed in a Great Traditional Way. It is apparent that the Tarot empowers its readers to psychically imagine archetypal gestalts denoting universal states of spiritual hierarchy. By viewing universal hierarchy with true *insight*, a reader of the Triumphs can consciously transcend limitations of self, relationships, environs, and circumstances. *The Tarot arose from Sufi and Eastern Christian metaphysics as a symbolic, phantasmic, edifying agency of spiritual enlightenment*.

Greek Christian and Persian Sufi contemplatives were guided in their considerations of psyche, spiritual imagery, and corporeal realization of ecstasy by the founding fathers of Neoplatonism: Plotinus, Porphyry, and Proclus.

> [B]y drawing images and inscribing them in their temples, one beautiful image for each particular thing, they manifested the non-discursiveness of the intelligible world.

This comes from Plotinus, describing Egyptian temples. He suggested that human thought began in the form of image making.

> Every image is a kind of knowledge and wisdom and is a subject of statements, all together in one, and not discourse and deliberation.

This passage was much drawn upon by Renaissance intellectuals. *Intuition* was recognized as knowledge "all together in one." Discursive thought, in contrast, views the parts of a whole in a consecutive, rationalized manner. Deliberations regarding an image differ from the *instant comprehension* to which representational and symbolic images lend themselves. Although Egyptian hieroglyphs were created in a largely pre-rational society, Plotinus understood that mature vision-logic processes advance beyond analytical thinking. Fourth-stage intuition encapsulates third-stage rationality not to produce rudimentarily logical symbols, but to establish *hierarchical, universal gestalts.* Such archetypes inherently transcend and unite provincial second-stage myths and *discursive* (indicating "rambling reason," from Latin *discursus,* "running about") third-stage systems. Any study involving metaphysical history is bound to be intricately discursive, along with essentially intuitive.

In our postmodern world, we have become accustomed to fractured images, which purposefully do not lend themselves to singular gestalts of intuited meaning. It has at times been academically faddish to claim that no image can possibly hold universal meaning; that all meaning is a contextual interpretation relative to the observer; that all cognition can be discursively broken into a series of unique and separated contextual projections; that every context finds definition only through *differences* with other contexts; and that all hierarchy collapses when contextual definition is realized to be always already relative. Such so-called "postmodern" thinking became caught in a contradictory circle of logic as it reduced all intelligent *epistemology* (from Greek *epistasthai,* meaning "to understand") to a singular, meaningless presupposition: *all that can be known for sure is that nothing can be known for sure.*

However, Truth in Beauty and Goodness has been universally affirmed in all societies during all ages. It is the goal of every Tarot deck designer to convey a *remarkable appearance of beauty that reflects innate truth* as much as possible. The essential truth of the medieval Trionfi is that their hierarchical stages *resemble* stages of our own hierarchical, potential psychophysical realization. Humans *innately respond to* and somehow *recognize images that resemble holistic phases essentially realizable by human nature.* This is true even for phase-states that are far advanced, beyond what is subjectively felt to be personally familiar or culturally normal. Such forms the basis of all esoteric design.

Plotinus recognized that the sensory experience of seeing an image translates smoothly into the cognition of a mental image resembling the physical one. The continuum then expands to include an *intuited gestalt* (broadly defined as "a configuration or pattern of elements so unified as a whole that its properties cannot be derived from a simple summation of its parts") of the mind's image. This gestalt is based upon both a *knowing* and *feeling* intuition. Consequent to this, an educated person can reasonably discuss that intuitive feeling with another in a knowing manner.

An image, or icon, if formed in the *likeness* of a spiritual whole, contains or emanates attributes of that ideal state which it resembles. Through such resemblance it remains *essentially related* to its spiritual source. Likewise, the mind's psychic intuition of that spiritual state, attained via sensation of the icon and both emotional and mental cognition of its image (indeed, even *physical* cognition), is translated into a subtle identity with the state. This can potentially engulf a contemplator, causing a *conversion* of one's *whole self*-identity, which transcends the dualistic process of subject/object. This process is reflected in the statement, "You become what you meditate upon."

Plotinus's conceptions of natural law and realizations of spiritual growth were based upon reasoned and intuitively subtle *contemplation* (from Latin *templum*, indicating a "space for observing auguries"). In the first century after Jesus, as imparted to us by Philo of Alexandria, Greek educated contemplatives formed Egyptian communities that occasionally engaged in monastic practices. The Sinai Peninsula became a melting pot for serious transcultural spiritual dialog and practice. A community of transpersonal wisdom-hermits emerged from this.

In these intimate, radical communities, meditation and spiritual discussion ensued without dogmatic or political constraints. Beliefs were not limited to Hellenistic traditions that typically included teachings regarding Stoical practices (pantheistic Stoics held to a remarkably similar worldview as contemporary Vedantins in India), theistic influences, demiurgic powers, and geometric ideals. Their way of contemplation also distanced itself from Judaic-Apocalyptic and Chaldean-Pythagorean dualism as examined in the next chapter.

Plotinus stood in this lineage of contemplatives that paid little attention to religious rituals or exoteric sacraments. By making oneself subject to *pure knowledge*, Plotinus stated that *contemplation of contemplation itself* transformed consciousness into the One. Such was the way to realize the supreme principles posited by Plato as Good and Just. Such was the means to understanding Plato's proclamation in his *Timaeus* that the "earthy world itself is a beautiful manifestation of the Divine."

Vipassana meditation succinctly defined in Plotinus's milieu, as it continues to do in our present era, this way of *insight*. Indian yoga tradition, classically summarized at this time by Patanjali in his *Yoga Sutras,* affirmed such a way of meditative *samadhi* or *bliss* as a direct means to realizing that *Atman is Brahman – True Self is Universal Other.* Patanjali, heavily influenced by dominant Buddhist and Shaivite teachings, framed tantric *energy* (*prana,* comparable to Taoist *ch'i*) and yoga practices as an eightfold way, literally transforming one's body-mind into Bliss. However, like the Gnostics of his time, Patanjali's ascetically dualistic metaphysics and mythos were not widely enjoyed; they remain unpopular today.

Plotinus's contemplative practice can be identified with the sixth-stage cards of the Hanged Man and Death. This is the causal-heart stage of interior development, which involves the *witnessing position of attention:* awareness of the root, or moment to moment temporality, of self. The open-eyed, upside-down, asymmetrical Hanged Man yogically represents such *self-conversion.* Sages established in this stage of realization keep themselves from falling into the sort of egoic delusions and pathologies of psychic grandeur that affected Giordano Bruno.

Plotinus's concentration upon the state of Witnessing Self transcended dualistic, otherworldly mind-sets seemingly propagated by Platonic philosophy (and certainly Pythagorean; Neopythagoreanism ended up being effectively co-opted into Neoplatonic schools). *Direct intuition* of immortal realization occluded psychic channels of *self-projection* that imagined a totally *separate* creator-sustainer-destroyer god and his incorporeal realm. If ideal forms or immortals were realizably present through direct insight, then they could not be eternally separate from the corporeal world.

Even still, there appeared to be a need for a *psychic bridge* spanning the chasm between the sacred and the mundane. Plato had posited the role of Intelligence. As logical rationality, Plato's intelligence authenticated a world understood through *polar dialectics* (from Greek *dialektik,* "art of debate," from *dialektos,* or "speech, conversation"), acknowledging Heraclitus's cycling process of Strife and Love as being inherent to all systems, be they sociopolitical or metaphysical. Both third- and fourth-stage intelligence authenticate philosophical laws that include and transcend provincial structures of dualistic, mythic belief.

Advancing upon this, Neoplatonists posited that *contemplation involves all forms of psychic, subtle, and causal intelligence* – integrating rationality with the fourth, fifth, and sixth stages of psychophysical mindful development. The Tarot as a *universal template* serves to remind us that contemplative *mindfulness* of the forces at play in our daily life *authenticates knowledge of our unity with the universe's lawful principles of immortality.*

Contemplation of contemplation is indeed a most advanced spiritual practice. For most people, meditation and concentration upon sacred images or forms naturally comes first. If one becomes what one meditates upon, a very important question arises: How can one be sure that a spiritual icon will indeed carry with it a *positively divine* presence? Plotinus stated that if through wisdom and compassion an artisan could craft an icon particularly sympathetic to the soul then of all things it would most easily *receive* the soul. However, how can one be sure what state of psyche or aspect of soul is embodied by an icon? What if an artisan shapes an icon with "all of his soul," imbibing the object with an attraction sympathetic to his soul, and against his best intentions, the quality of spirit or psyche so attracted turns out to be hellishly demonic? In this regard, one may empathize with otherwise disturbing, angst-ridden modern art.

The Roman Catholic Church did not condemn the Trionfi as an art form or didactic medium, though it did denounce *Tarocchi* as a game of chance or medium for gambling. However, the Church was not free to embrace and utilize the genius and beauty inherent to the Triumphant set of images. We may contrast this to its sponsorship and celebration of neo-Grecian paintings, tapestries, and sculptures. The Trionfi as personal and portable psychic icons were sympathetic to self-realization of distinct soul-realms that resembled archetypal stations along the way of immortality. That *self-realization* in its own time and space did not come under ecclesiastical oversight and legal jurisdiction.

For an icon to attract one's spirit to Fortune, Plotinus stated that it must truly *resemble* Fortune. He did not believe, however, that the icon actually became animated. That is, the icon did not actually embody the *anima* of Dame Fortune. Resemblance was sufficient to connect consciously produced imagery with intuition, and through that with actual psychophysical identification or a witnessing awareness of, in our example, Fortune.

This *reflective philosophy* is different from occult beliefs involving actual animation. Direction of anima or spirit into and out of objects presumes definitions of "psychic flows" based upon a dualistic separation of spiritual and material worlds. Many magicians have attempted to invent systematic techniques purposed toward manipulation of anima, psyche, or spirit (Harry Houdini famously spent many years debunking such, though his wife and friends, such as Sir Arthur Conan Doyle, were convinced he had paranormal powers). Throughout the great traditions, such manipulation has been considered unwise, for it obscures the natural law of nondual unity inherent to the World and its Soul. One might say it disrupts the complex matrix of ancestral presence. Biotechnology is advancing to the point where this will become an imminently real concern in the not-so-distant future.

Plotinus consciously observed that the world's soulful continuum was not contingent upon exoteric or occult rituals of phantasmic manipulation. *Plotinus radically integrated and transcended problematic and divisive interpretations of Universal Triunes and their Conscious Union.* These had been introduced by Aristotelian, Gnostic, and Christian theologians whose mixed-up dogma regarding Jesus and his Father's spiritual realizations and the impossibility of a human evolving to the same sphere of conscious psychophysical heartfulness as Jesus remains strictly enforced today.

In Neoplatonic understanding, there is no need for a spiritual artisan to draw into or out of the physical an otherwise wholly separate state of spirit-presence. Spiritual icons, whether crafted by nature or by man, are spiritual only because they have been directly imbued with the soul of their makers. This sympathetically imparts to them discreet states of spiritual realization, whether their soul-source is earth, man, or cosmos. Thus, an icon resembles a state of spirit through its essential beingness. One might say that the *integral whole* or *soul* of the icon, beyond its physical substance and psychological design, represents directly the soul of its source.

How this works is through the *Mystery of Holistic Causation*. Artisans of truly sacred icons exercised a knowledgeable awareness regarding archetypal stages of spiritual development, if not ecstasy. Identification of the artistic with the psychic and both with post-rational vision-logic processes imbued medieval creators of icons such as the Trionfi with priest-like powers. But the key point to be understood by both artisans and their patrons has always been that the *Heart-Soul* of Intelligence realizes Truth in Unification to a greater degree than does *psychic* intellect, regardless of how subtle the latter may be.

Only sixth-stage *causal-heart* realization brings Questors to the Towering Gate of Immortality, to be tested by the great Guardian Daimon. An icon that facilitates such is truly mighty in its sanctity. This is why Death as originally symbolized in the Tarot was such a powerful and *neutral* icon. Nature as death and impermanence will always rule the mundane world. However, when *consciously engaged,* Death is the *door* to Immortality. As we shall later see, the sublimely jaw-dropping, eye-popping transformative process of *resembling Eros* is primary to realizing ecstatic and immortal states of conscious being.

Porphyry, successor to Plotinus, recorded that his teacher entered into states of Eros as Wisdom-Love that were truly ecstatic. Much of what we know about Plotinus comes down to us from Porphyry, who was studied in the numerous metaphysical schools of third-century cosmopolitan Egypt. Hermeticism and alchemy arose during this period in Alexandria. Hermetic, isomorphic concepts regarding the natural symmetry and unification of all polarities, including micro- and macrocosms, lent a very Eastern and yogic flavor to Hellenistic philosophy.

Similar to Buddhist cosmological models, in the Neoplatonism of Porphyry the visible world is posited as being a *direct and identical* manifestation of the invisible world. Porphyry combined a hierarchical view of the cosmos with a consideration of *visibility.* He contemplated which spheres of spiritual reality were visible and which were not. Materialistic skeptics thought it obvious that an icon as a material object is totally distanced from the god it represents, for that god is an invisible spiritual being without visible material substance. Porphyry pointed out that this is as ignorant as an illiterate claiming that a book is totally distanced from the mind, for a book is naught but woven threads of papyrus. In Porphyry and Plotinus's way of contemplation, immanence and transcendence are bridged and ultimately realized to be one and the same.

Many of the world's greatest minds have emphatically posited that the roots of words themselves are like whole images, resembling their meaning directly. Vedic priests certainly maintain that such holds true for Sanskrit. The statement at the beginning of the Gospel of John that God *first made the Word* exactly refers to such sympathetic resemblance.

In many religious traditions, it is believed that *naming* a demon gives one power over it. In the scientific world, naming entities or functions (particularly via mathematical symbols) objectifies them so that they might be "known," "related," and thereby technically manipulated (even if, like disruptive demons, their objectification or classification does not lend an ability to totally "control" them).

Beyond magical and rational manipulations, the Tarot presents imagery, relationship, and nomenclature as a whole gestalt. Tarot Arcana are capable of resembling the whole microcosmic evolution of human consciousness and culture from the Empress's spiritual birth or Right View to the World's spiritual consummation or Right Liberation.

With Proclus, Neoplatonism received a two-hundred-year wrap-up. Proclus was born in Constantinople, educated in Alexandria, and taught in Athens, where he succeeded Plutarch as head of Plato's famous Academy. He died in A.D. 485 at the age of seventy-three. He was notable for his initiation into many of the world's esoteric spiritual traditions of the time, including Buddhism.

Proclus's cosmological views were clearly Buddhistic in their emphasis on causal interdependency. By the fourth and fifth centuries, Mahayana Buddhism had spread west to Egypt and east to China. Like Mahayana philosophers, Proclus envisioned a world systemically unified through relationship. No self could exist apart from relationship with others. No known could exist apart from a knower. Manifestation and consciousness, like space and time, were inseparable.

Moving the cosmological procession of *Becoming* was a force called *Likeness*. This is perhaps comparable to what is referred to in scientific terminology as *morphogenetic memory.* Proclus's Neoplatonism posited that the Tenth or Highest Sphere or Principle of Reality produced the Ninth, which produced the Eighth, on down to the First. Any transforming being was free to revert to its previous level of being simply by becoming *conscious* of it.

> For that which reverts endeavors to be conjoined in every part with every part of its cause, and desires to have communion in it and to be bound to it. But all things are bound together by likeness, as by unlikeness they are distinguished and severed. If, then reversion is a communion and conjunction, and all communion and conjunction is through likeness, it follows that all reversion must be accomplished through likeness.

The emanationist explanation of Tarot hierarchy is that the world proceeds to produce that which is most like itself; thereby, it is regenerated and sustained *moment by moment,* day by day. Yet, catastrophe, chaos, and organization teetering on the non-equilibrium edge of complexity are always present. Through them, the world does more than regenerate that which is most alike in the *same phase* of realization. It also produces that which is most alike in a fundamentally *different phase* of manifestation, purposed in Time to consciously realize Unity. *Time itself becomes, or simply already always is, Consciousness.*

Resemblance, according to the Neoplatonists, is a universal property. *Resemblance is the Kosmic implementation of Unitive Law* and as such is inherently Just. Time resembles Unity; Light resembles Time; Energy resembles Light; Movement resembles Energy; Chaos resembles Movement; Nature resembles Chaos; etc.

Ultimately, *similarity* exists as a continuum binding all entities at all stages through all processes of transformation. This is true for the horizontal span within every phase of evolutionary existence, as well as for the vertical nest of spheres defining otherwise discontinuous phases of realization.

Of primary importance to our study of the Tarot is the Neoplatonic concept of hierarchically nested, *discreet* stages, phases, or principles of the All One. This formed the basis of Christian Hermetic, Islamic Sufi, and Jewish Kabbalist theogonies of cosmological emanation. An understanding that everything is *of the Tao* need not negate realization of discreet evolutionary phases. If an icon resembles one of those phase transitions or stages, then it is empowered to serve the attentive mind as a bridge to that stage of realization. Clearly, the most powerful icons are those that resemble the most essential processes of evolution or phases of consciousness. This is what designers of Tarot Trionfi must aim for if they are to truly *hit the mark* intended by the Tarot's sagacious creators.

Portraying and communicating those phase-processes and their bindings has been the work of mages and sages throughout history. The Fool and Magician's *infinite-zero-stage* represents this principle of *Universal Resemblance*. East-West teachers of spiritual hierarchy have progressively nurtured a global understanding of such emanationist wisdom. The ten-stage, universal model elaborated in this book was developed and perennially confirmed over the course of millennia. This treatise continues to evolve that tradition, in part by translating the ten stages as great principles of integral hierarchy found in cosmic, conscious, and sociocultural development. These principles are completely capable of informing modern-day philosophy, esthetics, ethics, and science.

After the period of Tarot development, humanistic artisans tended to portray hierarchical awareness through styles exhibiting rational naturalism. This then developed into romantic revivals of hierarchy that played on fantastic depictions of reality, appearing naturalistic in form while illuminating imagined states sensorially greater than those empirically or materially observed. Modern movements of art then lent validity to depictions of highly abstract reflections of mind, obscure in their hierarchical significance, yet subtly meaningful in their conveyance of beauty, knowledge, or essences of truth.

After a period of denying any import to hierarchical signification, contemporary art globally came under the influence once more of traditional techniques, symbols, patterns, and compositions, largely derived from non-European cultures. This promoted a type of "post-postmodern" revision and appreciation of hierarchical relationships and emergent characteristics. These may resemble higher modalities of blissful being and thereby abet movement of human consciousness into such. For example, in the theater of dance, *Butoh* is an exemplary art form that has emerged from this movement.

The Tarot, with its traditional Indo-European conveyance of spiritual hierarchy, remains pertinent to modern and postmodern artistic development. Awareness of essential hierarchy imparts subtle guidance to creative processes and compositional expressions.

Great art is produced through integral and subtle skills of crafting. This can be measured using a variant of the Tarot's Ten Universal Principles:

Coherence
Symmetry
Harmony
Recursion
Abstraction
Integration
Complexity
Dimensionality
Frequency
Universality

Without some combination of or focus upon these attributes or qualities, artisans readily tend toward emotionally reactive projections of confusion, egoically sentimental reflections of mediocrity, and technically manipulative performances that leave the soul craving. Flashes of genius and tensional release may periodically charge those art forms, but representations of true beauty felt by the commons as being *good for all* will not be reliably created.

Conceptual abstraction need not usurp – and natural humanistic realism need not restrict – the way and power of essential resemblance. Psychic and subtle archetypal imagery differs fundamentally from fantasy *simulacra. Resemblance* of the real is not taken to be a *substitution* for the real by those who truly appreciate good art. Simulation of real environments and experiences is not required in order to identify with holistic spheres or principles through integral symbols and designs that shift consciousness into a relational *likeness* of those spheres. Classical traditions of art and design, including architecture and urban planning, serve as crucial foundations upholding creative permutations and organic diversities of cultural and societal patterns that need to be explored anew by every generation.

Not all sacred art, of course, is as sophisticatedly subtle as the great works of classical traditions. Folk art involved with personal and communal rites of passage, for instance, can also evince awareness of spiritual hierarchy via resemblance. The folk prints of the woodblock Trionfi seen in these pages' sidebars (which are reworked versions of the Budapest Trionfi) arguably resemble the Tarot's spiritual stations more astutely than the classical court paintings produced in Bembo's studio. When viewed with a materialistic attitude, many would deem the woodblock prints as lacking in spiritual wealth and power; they are not leafed in gold, elaborated in intense and fantastic imagery, or packed with arcane symbols. Yet in sacred art, a singular circular brushstroke may well epitomize that which is most valuable and true.

For instance, the six stages of cosmic development may be visualized quite simply:

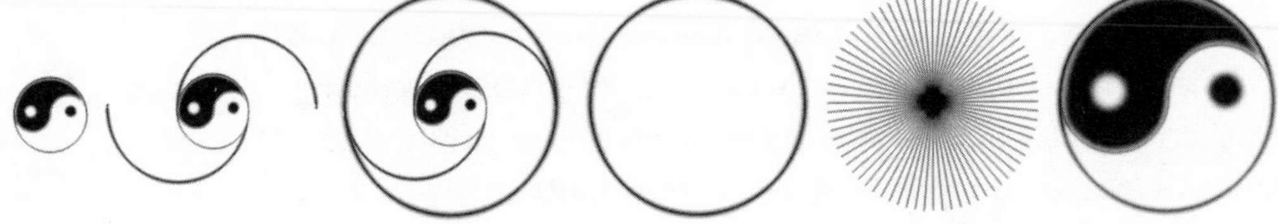

The Neoplatonic Law of Resemblance assumes cosmological processes of subtle ancestry or *memory;* of inheritance stemming from causal, soulfully holistic genesis. *Eros* as Creative Wisdom encapsulating the World Soul of Flux *is the unifying force underlying all resemblance* in the Cosmos. Understanding the Tarot's hierarchical representation of World Unity requires *right view,* or nascent unity-through-diversity awareness, from the very start. *The Quest is defined by a progressively magnified and concentrated right view of Eros.*

Because of this, successful Questors will find themselves immersed in a way of *Tantra* (in the universal and broad meaning of the word, not limited by sexual connotations or defined by provincial rituals), regardless of subjective preferences, politics, or agendas. *Alchemy is the way of Triumphant realization and Tantra is the how of Alchemy.* Both require individually and socially appropriate *cultivation of Qi (Ch'i) and Yoga.* Chapters 6 and 7 address this.

Contemplation of contemplation is an advanced form of alchemical, tantric yoga. It is notably oriented toward natural celibacy. It would seem obvious that this has little to do with *familiar dependency,* let alone "coital dependency," however modern media might portray ecstatic love and energetic happiness. Kissing and touching must be engaged with supreme mindfulness and yogic breath in sexual relations to deliver alchemical benefit beyond common pleasure. In general, sexual romance either disperses alchemical processes of sublimation and transmutation or, more positively, channels such processes into the production and raising of family.

Be that as it may, every Questor on the Path of the Trionfi will come to realize that *sacred eroticism* is the most essential modality of *right concentration* – the eighth stage of the Tarot, the Light Soul cards of Star and Moon. *To resemble the Star and Moon is to ecstatically realize the likeness of Eros.* Full initiation into the Triumphant Way of Immortality concentrates upon a Bodhisattva-like vow to never lose sight of that light guiding the Quest into the eternal enlightenment of Eros.

Why is eroticism rarely realized to be sacred? Psychic and subtle techniques of projection and transference are commonly associated with the erotic. When not *consciously cultivated,* these tend toward dependency and possessiveness, creating "needy, jealous, and controlling" dispositions. They romantically or manipulatively collapse the *longing for communion* that otherwise keeps cultivating *extensive regeneration* of vital life and essential nature. That regeneration is needed daily, in rhythmic cycles, to *uphold polar union* and *sustain ecstatic outcome.*

Co-dependency and *familiar possession* catalyze addictive habits, stagnant stasis, and destructive dramas, with acts and plays of eroticism not being regulated through rituals of conscious yoga, *qi* cultivation, and natural alchemy. Processes of alchemy and tantra portrayed by the Triumphs are *meant to be played with* on many levels, all of which are *nurtured by innocence*. However, *the Tarot is an adult game*. It needs to be respectfully, ritualistically, and spiritually played on an adult level of psychic and subtle intimacy. All of this involves sensorially intuitive identification with the potential of immortality via engagement of Eros through likeness and resemblance.

Ecological health is found in bodies and environments free of inherited mechanisms or acquired habits that resist the innate tendency to holistically proceed in manifestation while reverting in transcendence. *Procession* and *reversion:* the Tarot represents a cyclic cosmology. Everything in the cosmos emerges from, is embedded in, reverts to, and transforms as the principle-processes represented by the Trionfi. Paradoxically, evolution and involution occur together via the arrow of time. For any given body, system, field, or environment, this occurs through a complex, spiraling, emergent order that uniquely includes and identifies all contingency, causality, and chaos.

Enlightenment involves consciously realizing manifestation and transcendence simultaneously. The whole ten-stage cycle – that is, reality everywhere – both manifests itself and transcends itself moment to moment. Thus is it possible for enlightened consciousness to transparently radiate states of the Deathless while practically embodying limited states of temporal behavior.

Emanationists historically supposed that spiritual resemblance appeared to diminish in the process of manifestation. Some philosophers suggested that pure concepts, names, and psyches were closer to spiritual reality than corporeal entities. Neoplatonists varied in their opinions of just how diminished spiritual reality ever really becomes. In any case, the more Questors see with nondual eyes, the less they will view differences between manifested and spiritual domains. Wise, compassionate *indifference* is neither reductionistic nor nihilistic. Rather, it is *blissfully, sublimely forgiving.*

Gautama the Buddha was perhaps the greatest of Emanationists. He stated unequivocally that once the last stage of cosmic manifestation (the *myriad* of *earthly* nature) is truthfully envisioned as the first stage of spiritual transcendence, the rest of the stages retracing Original Nature can be progressively reverted to quite rapidly – in truth, paradoxically, "all at once." Essentially, Gautama realized that mankind's original garden or paradise, eternal and immortal *Nirvana,* was never actually *lost*. Buddhist *Nikayas* (earliest of Buddhist texts, written in the Pali language) repeatedly proclaim that for many of Gautama's personal devotees, the process of consciously reclaiming the Sixth or Seventh Stage of Immanent Transcendence had occurred within a week. Perhaps this was due to Gautama's miraculously awakening Grace or to the nature of his culture and era. Perhaps proclamations of rapid mass enlightenment were simply due to the mythical and fantastical nature of the Buddha-stories found in the Nikayas.

Statements by modern spiritual adepts indicate that three years is as quick as such integral evolution may happen in a sustainable way; and that timeframe appears rare indeed. It cannot be overly emphasized that any such realization *within one's lifetime* requires surrendering one's self (mindfully, not mindlessly) to the cultural and communal agencies of *Ecstatic Bliss* that most *resemble the Questor's True Heart.* Those agencies often do not appear as Questors may have imagined early in their Quests. They do, however, often appear in human form, which is how come the twenty-two Triumphs portray the Principles of Immortality through spiritually dignified, transpersonal men and women.

SPIRITED INTIMACY

WHEEL OF FORTUNE

Empty as the center may be,
the path of Fortune is marked by
curtailment, the swing of
opposites, invisible intervention,
and the ring of recurrence.

HERMIT

Light, silence, and certainty —
utter clearness, total harmony,
and immediate experience —
are the Hermit's instruments
of Life.

Far Away, Come What May

Into the Gnosis beyond Magic and Myth . . .

> He revealed to me the hidden mystery that was hidden from the worlds and the generations: the mystery of the Depth and the Height: he revealed to me the mystery of the Light and the Darkness, the mystery of the conflict and the great war which the Darkness stirred up . . . Thus was revealed to me by the Paraclete all that has been and all that shall be and all that the eye sees and the ear hears and the thought thinks. Through him I learned to know everything, I saw All through him and I became one body and one spirit with him.

This proclamation was spoken by Mani, founder of Manichaeism, in the Coptic text *Kephalaia*. Mani was adopted and raised by a wealthy widow in Sassanian Babylonia during the third century. Mesopotamia (now Iraq and Iran) at this time was steeped in ancient Babylonian mythology, Persian Zoroastrianism, Buddhism, and numerous variants of Judeo-Christian belief. Mani was indoctrinated in the Jewish-Christian Baptist sect of the *Elchasaites*. Although rooted in Jewish traditions reaching back to the Qumran community, the sect's founder, Elchasaios, considered himself a Christian when he preached his message around the turn of the second century. Mani left the sect at the age of twenty-four and started a new religion based on the revelations of his Heavenly Twin, the Paraclete mentioned above.

Mani's teachings were unique in their syncretic fusion of Zoroastrian, Buddhist, and Christian elements with dualistic doctrines of Gnosticism. He declared himself the fourth and final prophet in a historical lineage that elevated newly birthed myths of Gnosticism to the pinnacle of spiritual revelation. The Sassanid Dynasty of Persia served as Mani's missionary base. From there, he successfully established missions west to Egypt, north to Central Asia, and east to Afghanistan, home of the civilly advanced Kushan kingdom. In 240, Mani himself sailed to the Indus Valley and converted the Buddhist king Turan Shah. His influence was intense but short-lived. He returned to the Sassanian capital, where the next two kings allowed his religion to thrive. This too was not to last, for in 273 a king was enthroned under the influence of the Zoroastrian Church. Manicheans were promptly persecuted; Mani was tortured, dying in chains in 276.

Mani's death did not halt the growth of his Church, which spread to encompass much of the known world. The Manichean canon included works left to us in Coptic, Iranian, Turkish, and Chinese. Mani speculated upon Gnostic myths of cosmic exile and salvation. His genius lay in his ability to weave terminology of the world's great religions into a superficial but elaborately integrated system pitting eternal Light against eternal Darkness. By appropriating linguistic patterns of established teachings, particularly those of Neoplatonism, and projecting onto them a fantastic mythology, Mani and his followers were able to insinuate their doctrines into international centers of learning and cultural exchange.

It was Mani's version of Gnosticism that repeatedly challenged the Christian world – from Augustine, who converted from Manichaeism, to occult heresies in the late medieval era, which were often branded as neo-Manichean. According to his dualistic cosmology, Evil had stood in opposition to the Good from the beginning of time. Darkness, equated with matter and evil, somehow *caught* a glimpse of Light, equated with spirit and goodness. Darkness then desired to merge with Light and so *attacked* it. Light, in response, created Primal Man to defend it from Darkness. Primal Man, or Soul of Light, allowed itself to be defeated by being devoured by Darkness or Chaos. This satisfied Darkness, but also poisoned it. The Soul of Light, now imprisoned or put to sleep by evil matter, needed to be saved. So Light created the Heavenly Cosmos or World Soul as a fantastic mechanism for the separation of Primal Man from Darkness, that he might be redeemed forever.

Lost in a realm of magic and spirits, the Questor loses all sense of identity and yet remains in equanimity.

Extraction of the myriad bits of trapped Light-substance from the *lower world* was partly enacted through divine Messengers who seduced the evil *Archons*, or *children of Darkness* carrying the stolen Light, into a state of orgasmic excitement. A Messenger would appear before each Archon in a most beautiful form of the opposite sex. The Archons would then expel their Light, which would be received by the Angels of Light, purified and loaded onto Lightships to return home. In a similar way, the Cosmos itself, through the agency of the Zodiac of Stars, would dip into the realm of matter or Dark Earth. It scooped up buckets of Light and deposited them into the temporary storage space of the Moon, which would deliver the Light-substance back to the Sun.

Erotic usage of female sexuality in Manichean practice no doubt helped to establish the religion in areas that were generating tantric traditions, such as Northern India and Central Asia. Amongst the *learned* and *practical* in nondual Buddhism, Taoism, and Tantric Hinduism, Gnostic mythology involving erotic justification would have been seen as unnecessary – a perverse misunderstanding of natural alchemy and the intercourse of vital life with essential nature, earth-soul with heaven-soul, samsara with nirvana.

Mani's mythological descriptions of the realms of Light and Darkness were wildly fantastic. He combined abstract hypostases such as Wisdom and Matter with animalistic deities such as a dragon-headed Demon King. While this is not the place to delve further into Manichean mythology, we need to observe that discursive philosophy found so prominently in Greek thought did not serve as Mani's

The Empress assures the possibility of spirited Release for her warded minions; Earth as Source naturally transcends the ancestral biosphere.

revelatory vehicle. Rather, Mani used rationality to create a vast and integrated magical mythology, which served as a spawning ground for occult propagation.

Either one believed in Mani's secret knowledge of cosmic war or one was doomed to remain a slumbering slave of Darkness. Mani's Church did its best to convert followers of other religions by using terminology familiar to them. This was done by arguing that great sages such as Buddha and Jesus had come to prepare the imprisoned minds of humankind for the beautiful orgasmic seduction of salvation, which Mani and his Church were fully manifesting. Concepts founded upon nondual wisdom were misappropriated for dualistic, communal agendas.

Mani's occult revelation of a *new age* contains patterns that have been repeated into modern times. Fourth-stage devotion, spiritual affirmation, and intuition of spiritual hierarchy were systematically channeled into, co-opted by, and finally shackled to a second-stage regression of pathological mythology based on separation, fear, and domination.

Mani's convictions of cosmic war influenced Augustine and other early fathers of the Church of Rome. Roman bishops often posited that Satan's power held sway in the realm of common earthly existence. Augustine, although a former Manichean, rejected Gnostic demonization of the cosmos. However, it was he who imparted to Christianity the doctrines of *original sin*, *civitas diaboli* (or "realm of the devil"), and *predestination* (or the *absolute separation of the called and the rejected*, the saved and the condemned).

Gnosticism was a belief system that defined the cosmos dualistically. This differed from the type of dualism found in Hellenic Platonism. Although Plato distinguished two realms of existence, one of eternal ideal forms and one of temporal material forms, he did not equate evil with the latter; nor did most other metaphysical cosmologies of the great traditions, even though they posited the fundamental existence of polarities.

For instance, the Vedic doctrine of Being, with its eternal attributes, and Becoming, with its temporal appearances, often identified *Maya* or Buddhist *Mara* (comparable to the Sufi Devil, *Iblis*) – the popular representation of *delusion* and suffering – with the latter. Nonetheless, as Gautama and the *Upanishads* (classical summaries of the Vedas, written before Buddha's era) proclaimed, *illusion is suffering and suffering is illusion* – Mara does not ontologically embody Reality. Suffering and evil are produced by man's mind, not by nature's laws, nor by divine hypostases. The *Myriad* called *Maya* is marked by change, temporality, and flux – the Causal Emptiness of Chaos Becoming the Cosmos. This is felt as suffering and pain only when one identifies with a *separate* self – only when consciousness does not feel its profound and real interdependency with all else.

Just as Grace enters the world from an unfathomable source, so the Questing soul must find the ineffable way out.

Put another way, arrest Life by denying the infinitude of Essence and there will be suffering. Flow with the emergence of discernible synchronicities, *becoming empty through wholly transforming with Chaos*, and the way of bliss will become apparent. In any case, Gnosticism was resolute in its *anti-cosmic* conviction. The visible universe and its creator were identified with Evil. Later in this chapter and in chapter 7, we will follow, from Babylonian times on, the development of *underworld cosmology* as it became equated with a "lower-world prison" of earthbound sentient life.

The dualistic problem of mind/body separation was introduced in the previous chapter. Plotinus, we recall, did not buy it:

> No-one therefore may find fault with our universe on the ground that it is not beautiful or not the most perfect of beings associated with the body; nor again quarrel with the originator of its existence and certainly not because it has come into existence of necessity, not on the basis of a reflection but because the higher being brought forth its likeness according to the law of nature.

So states Plotinus in his first treatise, *On Providence.* A more concise refutation of the Gnostic myth will not be found. Furthermore, "not

Limitations can become so numerous as to be overwhelming, even as the open floodgates of gnosis allow and then demand an extinction of ideal intentions; thus, the Emperor in Truth remains dispassionate in his authority.

on the basis of a reflection" radically refutes any dualistic, existential need for an Aristotelian "reflecting psyche."

We have seen that later Christian metaphysics, lending credence to a cosmic ontology and spiritual hierarchy of angelic, phantasmic, and imaged *exemplar-spheres*, was further developed by Sufis. Light realms of angels were envisioned connecting distinct worlds of matter and spirit. This attempt to bridge dualistic and nondualistic cosmology via angelic/phantasmic/psychic/spiritual intermediation ultimately found resolution in the Tarot. This was obtained by identifying human reality with cosmic reality and both with a universal, transcendental hierarchy.

The Tarot Image-Exemplars were created as psychic representations of immortal realization through corporeal existence. They obviate any need to imagine *supernatural* angelic states of evolution (although such is represented in total by the World Triumph). Even the most exalted Trionfi of Sun, Angel, and Justice represent corporeally realized states of both cosmos and consciousness. Every Immortal Exemplar realizes an aspect of the Angelic; however, for Questors to *absolutely know* this, they must realize the Sun/Angel stage of Enlightenment.

As has been mentioned in previous chapters (still to be fully elaborated), in Tarot theogony the Devil and Tower do not represent dominion over "fallen" archetypes below them. Rather, the seventh-stage cards of *divinely chaotic breakthrough* present a necessary and warranted challenge and transformation inherent to any and all procession into Immortality and Quest for Conscious Bliss.

Plotinus later wrote a treatise entitled *Against the Gnostics*, in which he criticized Gnostic cosmology as ridiculous and erroneous. He then pointed to Gnostic disregard for civil and metaphysical law, "the virtue whose building up goes back over a long development from the beginning of all time . . . they make our human discipline into a mockery – in this world there may be nothing noble to be seen – and thereby they make discipline and righteousness of no importance."

Our book began with a consideration of fundamental differences between occult beliefs based on ritualistic magic and provincial myths, and disciplines of esoteric knowledge stemming from the great traditions. Gnosticism, although pervasive in its influence during early Christian centuries, never established itself as a world tradition. It did not develop lineages of yogis, saints, and sages; teachings which could be self-authenticated; and communities beyond those directly controlled by cultic leaders via dominating hierarchies.

Can passions be Blessed, emotions be Purified, opposites be Wedded; or are the Sacraments merely phantasms of the psyche formed via social conspiracy and subtle expediency?

Contrasting examples could include the native religions of Tibetan Bön, Chinese Tao, and Japanese Shinto (literally "Spirit-Tao"). These were magic-and-myth-based traditions that grew to incorporate fully developed rational and vision-logic worldviews, ultimately transforming awareness of ancestry into a gnosis of universal virtue. It could be said that Persian Sufi gnostics such as Suhrawardi, standing in the tradition of Islam, attempted the same for Near Eastern Gnosticism.

The Greek concept of *gnosis* involved *knowledge of spiritual truth* akin to the Indian concept of *sunyata* (or "emptiness"). Such subtle awareness has been emphasized throughout the Great Tradition as a primary way of realizing communal wisdom. Gnosis is an ancient and universal awareness, which has evolved with every stage of humanity's psychosocial development. In experiencing it, Questors open a *portal to the very heart* of spiritual realization. Through gnosis, esoteric cultivation and teaching have been historically transmitted in subtle fullness from masters to disciples. Attaining to gnosis, however, requires self-discipline, service, meditation, and devotion, all of which cannot be "taken"; they have to be *cultivated* through *practice, study, and direct communion.*

True gnosis is the primary sign of spiritual and devotional maturity. As such, it is the ineffable fifth-stage knowledge of ancestral presence, represented in the Tarot as the agencies of the Wheel and the Hermit, bonding a truly spiritual community. Gnostics usurped all claim to true gnosis; basing their claim upon a communal belief

Once the course is charted it must be unflaggingly maintained; only then is the horizon brought within reach, for that which is afar is found to be always already present.

in ancestors as defined by one of the variant cosmological myths that formed the backbone of every Gnostic sect. Such politicized myths differed dramatically from sublime awareness of Universal and Sacred Emptiness.

In all great traditions, magical-mythical-rational consciousness matures and then emerges into psychic gnosis purposed toward magnifying and realizing the ineffable subtlety of ancestral presence. Within each of these stages, however, societies can become pathologically exclusive, championing their state of development as far superior to any other. Every stage of holistic actualization must fully include preceding stages and not reduce proceeding stages.

For instance, tribes undeveloped in rational and vision-logic stages did not solely rely on their myths to impart a sense of tribal spirituality. Rather, daily psychophysical patterns of relating with nature were first *sensorially* translated into social forms of ritualistic magic. These served to affect those parts of the brain, central nervous system, glands, and organs associated with *feeling-awareness* of spiritual domains. Magical sensation was then encapsulated by *mythic feeling*. Myths were an *emotional* way of *knowing* and *communicating* communally organized feelings.

A similar process rightfully occurred with early Greek philosophers such as those mentioned in the last chapter, who then advanced into mentally rational stages of development. Discursive thought is an advanced form of communicative logic, capable of universally conveying – even while defined and limited contextually – complex states of feeling-awareness embedded in myths themselves. Such is the beauty and joy of knowledge, be that in the sciences, humanities, or arts. Non-discursive yet fully rational states of mind referred to as intuitive vision-logic and virtue, or psychic and subtle awareness, are yet further advancements of human consciousness. Gnosis is attained through the development of transrational, subtle, ancestral awareness. It is effectively the "best practice" that antecedes a true and present witnessing of immortal realization.

The religion known as Gnosticism was a product of rational societies. As urban dwellers, Mani and his followers did not establish the sect's communal identity through an involvement with nature. Nor did they rationally study nature in the manner that philosophical schools around the planet were by then doing. To Gnostics, Nature itself was rationally identified with degraded existence. Gnostic theology was built upon seeking a "way out" of the natural world. Rationality was glorified, but only to the degree that it dogmatically supported Gnostic mythologizing of cosmic nature.

Sharing the living memory of recurrent Eros, the heart springs in joy; this is how each generation resurrects its ancestors.

Through an arrogant reduction and enforced limitation of rational knowledge, growth, and thereby true *philosophical* gnosis, Gnosticism kept itself from forming into a world tradition. Spiritual traditions expand into greatness through their ability to adapt and evolve beyond the constraints of their foundational myths.

Evolution beyond minor adaptations is inevitably hierarchical. Evolution emerges from the *full realization* of a *natural sphere;* it having in turn arisen from – and thereby included – previous spheres of existence. For instance, second-stage mythos cannot fully mature and evolve into third-stage rationality without first incorporating fully the positive reality of first-stage, earth-based magic. Likewise, if the fourth stage of hierarchical intuition is to be attained, third-stage rationality must include but not pathologically adhere to second-stage, mythic definitions. It is the fourth stage and its inherently esoteric, psychic fecundity that promotes a spiritual tradition into greatness. Fully integrating rationality, fourth-stage psychosocial development emerges as fifth-stage gnosis.

All Gnostic sects were systemically limited by the structure of their myths. Manichaeism was, however, unusual in its method of assimilating surface patterns of metaphysical and theistic systems. This was done by focusing on established terminologies of mythic imagery, rather than by evolving theories arising through discursive argumentation. Manichean metaphysical adaptation remained on a horizontal level of superficially relative signification carrying

To renounce is to re-announce; to deny the temptations of greed, malice, and delusion is to affirm the guidance of virtue.

little depth of meaning. Thus, by necessity, Manichean systems were restricted to constructions that did not allow organically evolving complexity. In contrast, neither the scientific method nor hermetic alchemy, to give two very different examples, evinces such limitation. Without free growth through organic complexity and intelligent, open argumentation and inquiry, an emergence of evolved psychosocial order that manifests vertically subtle and deeply causal signification is unable to occur.

In Gnosticism, third-stage rational development was purposefully limited, disrespected, and subverted into supporting a regressively mythic and political Church structure. Publicly vocal scientists have held back few punches in striking out at modern Christianity as being a mere continuation of such. However, systems of pathological rationality such as scientific materialism also become regressive by arresting growth in personal, social, and cultural stages of intuitive psychological development. Examples of this abound in modern times, as traditionally evolved systems of vertical, hierarchical insight (actualizing instead of dominating in their function) are popularly and academically reduced to a flattened dialectic of contextual relativity. Concurrently, it is a sign of postmodern evolution that domination hierarchies are being radically dismantled. Readers are directed to the corpus of *Integral Studies* for an in-depth consideration of this topic.

Second-stage attributes of any holistic state are marked by elements of polar structure. When natural growth is arrested, an integrated body tends to regress in its identity to a second-stage level of structure. As an example of how the six stages of any growing body, once arrested, collapse into a second-stage state before either dying altogether or regenerating, let us look at an elegant theory of corporate growth. In the theory of *Total Quality Management*, a seven-stage model was developed by McKinsey & Company depicting how any corporation holistically integrates *quality*. Quality is incorporated through:

1. Strategy
2. Structure
3. Systems
4. Skills
5. Shared Values
6. Staff
7. Style of the Executive

The power of nature dwells in its brightness, the illumination of the myriad; the quantity of impermanence – infinitude of articulated selves – is outshined by the quality of pure lineage: that One which is always alive.

The first stage drives a corporation's mission, purpose, and vision. Without a *strategic* awareness of quality, holistic success (i.e., beyond mere profit) will be nowhere in sight. The second stage sets the minimal reality of corporate existence. Regardless of how simplistic corporate strategy may be (perhaps it does not go beyond simply maintaining existence), without *structure*, existence is no more than a potential. *Systems* create flow in a structure, giving actual life to a company. Systems are readily rationalized and, if not too complex, reproducible. *Skills* are needed to govern the systems, for they are not contained within the systems themselves. Skills involve levels of intuition beyond machine automation, computation, and manipulation. *Shared values* are the invisible bonds unifying a company's members. They are the implicitly agreed-upon virtues and qualities that the whole company and each of its members strive to realize. *Staff* managers constitute the root engine of the corporation's growth. Through hiring, firing, motivating, networking, isolating, and terminating, staff cause a corporation to function, align, cooperate, and compete internally and externally with both customers and other companies. Without managers and directors a corporation can only exist as a parasite connected to another body that is *whole.* The *Style of the Chief* Executive is like the judgment of a demigod; he *is* the company in a way that no corporation can afford to underestimate. Even if the preceding six stages of corporate process collapse into structure and structure itself ceases to exist, the CEO can carry on the identity of the company into a new body. In this way, the seventh stage represents *transference* and *re-creation* of the corporate soul.

From whence does Fortune arrive, to whither does Fortune go; through existential Emptiness life is naturally curtailed, tamed through interdependent currents of migration and livelihood.

A corporation becomes unbalanced when it underemphasizes the relative level of quality in one or more of these aspects during its weekly existence and seasonal process of growth. When this occurs, owners, employees, and customers experience a corporate-wide tendency to regress into temporary security based upon corporate structure. If the CEO sells out, staff quit, values evaporate, skills become scarce, systems crash, or strategies become obsolete, all hands, thoughts, and routines will adhere to structure. If structure itself collapses, the company must be completely reformed or it will die.

Conceptual and legal frameworks for forming incorporated structures proved to be one of the Roman Empire's major contributions to the advancement of civil society. A case can be made, however, that in the modern age, international corporate growth has pathologically regressed into stages of empire-building. In turn, a post-modern era is bringing about a usurpation of corporate control through mass-driven mechanisms of communication enabling decentralized stock speculation, price comparison shopping, employee head-hunting, services outsourcing, etc. This has been fueled by a phase advancement of telecommunication and communal information sharing. Network-based market and information access and communication are not bound by orthodox principles of capitalism. Peer-to-peer and decentralized exchanges are to a large and unstoppable degree appropriating from dominant hierarchies the process of capital creation and utilization.

During the first decade of the twenty-first century, the global financial system underwent a Great Disruption. This occurred through a valuation collapse of what had become internationally co-dependent asset classes, e.g., real estate, debt payments, publicly held corporate shares, commodities, bonds, and above all else "securities" derived from those assets.

An imagined invisible force or "hand" was attributed to a conceptualized Global Marketplace. Through this practically "divine" law or force (defined through a great many mathematical formulas representing endless contradictions and variant beliefs) the economic cosmos of humankind and planet earth was thought to be always "led" or otherwise "returned" to a state of "perfect equilibrium." A worldview broadly based on the theories of Adam Smith (d. 1790), the great Scottish moral philosopher and father of modern economics, was pathologically misinterpreted. Ethics were abandoned, along with the fundamentally crucial importance of agricultural workers and artisans, along with their skills and products. Primary values of a globalized political economy were shackled to the Invisible Hand's dualistic nature of Greed and Fear. The Wheel of Fortune's cycle of Inflation and Contraction was allowed to run amok by governments and corporations unable or unwilling to regulate it in a context of integral evolution.

Drawing upon the verdant Life of earth, the Hermit merges vitality with the essence of empirical observation – sublimating midbrain distillation in a steadfast radiance of prudent virtue.

A twenty-first-century *universally applicable model of sociocultural-political economy* is now required. Viewed from a perennially integral and holistic perspective, sustainable development of what may be called Cultural Economics proceeds through essentially foundational spheres:

1. Agriculture Cooperatives
2. Artisan Guilds
3. Market Exchanges
4. Valuation Networks
5. Sovereign Clearinghouses
6. Global Resources

Existing beyond all human machinations, these immortal forces of universal law cannot be reduced to an "invisible hand of the market":

1. Natural Disruption
2. Creative Complexity
3. Conscious Transparency
4. Just Purpose

Having walked into the darkness of a vast and obscure realm, and having then unearthed a light of magnificent yet unknown source, the Questor exists at once empowered yet unable to affect the World.

Shared values are often the weakest link in the corporate process of manifesting quality. On the other hand, when company members are intently aligned to the same values, coherence with a company's agenda can become quite zealous. History has proven this through a diversity of corporate organizations, including religious sects, military legions, engineering corps, political parties, high-tech startups, law firms, etc. It is a grave matter for any company to mistake shared values for instituted structures. This reduces the purpose of corporate community (which is of equal necessity to company health as corporate culture and law) to the efficient implementation of controlling dictates. *Organization men* are reduced to being routine cogs in a corporate machine. It is then that hierarchy becomes dominantly pathological.

Shared values must emerge naturally from sincere strategy, strong structure, smart systems, and spirited skills. If a company is to be successful, it cannot *institute* values via forced surrendering of member identification to the technical rules of structure. The rise of the Nazi Party from within the Weimar Republic represents one of the most disastrous attempts during the twentieth century to subjugate ancestral values and virtues to C^3 (*Command – Control – Communications*) structures. The opening years of the twenty-first century, driven by wholly fabricated, manipulated, and self-perpetuating fears of terrorism, produced yet more global examples of this.

Gnostic organizations reduced fifth-stage *virtue* into second-stage *politics*. Building social structures that reinforced their emotional-mythic positions became tantamount to identifying spiritual communion. Ironically, this marked both their social and spiritual downfall. Manichaeism forestalled this destiny by pretending to hold in common potential converts' cultural, communal, and moral values. Most of the Gnostic sects in the first centuries after Jesus were not so clever; although a large proportion of them did manage to assimilate the Jesus movement.

The messages of Zarathustra, Moses, Buddha, Jesus, and Plotinus were *monistic* in orientation. Even the first two, who had strong dualistic inclinations, did not believe that the divine cause of cosmos, nature, and humanity was essentially marked by an Evil God associated with manifested existence and a Good God totally disjunct from the whole cosmos.

Ancestral knowledge of the psyche, devotional feeling of the soul, subliminal practice of the body – subtract these from life and Death will proceed to replace them.

Gnostic worldviews allowed for a cosmology of hierarchical emanation, but solely in reference to a central, evil creator-god. Except for a most concealed spark of spirit in the human soul, no element of the natural world could be identified as sacred. Zealous, exclusive stances of dualistic dogma could not succeed in usurping the authority of spiritual masters such as Jesus who pointed to a causal-heart state of nondual witnessing as the portal to immortal realization. Respect for such sagacious guidance required fourth- and fifth-stage psychological maturity, which Gnostics lacked.

In an earlier chapter, the astronomical cosmology widely accepted in late antiquity was introduced. Seven spheres, domains of planetary control, surrounded by an eighth sphere of the fixed stars were seen as composing the *Kingdom of Fate.* Under these cosmic influences, earthly events were deterministically affected. Gnostics incorporated this cosmology and encapsulated it with two more kingdoms: a ninth of Spirit and Soul, and a tenth of Divine Father and Son. Sects varied as to whether the Zodiac (sphere of stars) was on the side of Light or Darkness, but there was unanimous agreement that the other seven realms were ruled by a malevolent demiurgic creator-god. The seventh sphere was understood to be home to the serpent Leviathan (though it also went under other guises), who was the god called Yahweh in the Old Testament. Under the Moon was the Behemoth (i.e., Devil) and under him, Earth and the realm of the underworld, Tartarus.

The *Seventh Seal,* Stage, or Sphere was from this point on identified in dualistic camps with either Salvation or Evil. In the medieval Tarot, the Devil and Tower represent this stage. As will be reiterated later, however, this stage in Tarot development represents

Stillness combats the phantasmic challenge of the Devil; while the sight of natural essence aligns his roaming mind to the radiantly bright and the mysteriously veiled, only when hearing beliefs does the Guardian disrupt self-made flaws.

awakening through and beyond chaotic illusion. Divine sacrifice, sacred fire, and the Tower of the Devil are not *opposed* to the Good.

The Gnostic kingdom of Spirit and Soul also contained the realms of Sophia and Life. *Sophia* (meaning "wisdom"), was marked by the intersection of *gnosis* and *insight*. Through that intersection, divine Light entered the soul of man. In and of itself, such understanding of gnosis was genuine and wide ranging. However, it was common in Gnostic myths to have Sophia in the position of turning her attention away from the divine realm of the Father, creating a "son" in the realm of darkness, alienated from Holy Spirit. In such a context, Sophia was often called *Whore*, which at the time indicated an *excess of eroticism*. Her desire to create without being bound to a partner and to act without consulting the Father or Pleroma lay at the root of her fall. In the influential Valentinian versions of the myth, her error was to *ascend* to the father, as her erotic passion became uncontrollable; eroticism, immaturity, and evil influences of "friends" compounded to create Wisdom's undoing. The Cathars of France believed similarly. This cast an evil shadow over Eros. Even though such cosmology is superficially similar to that of the Tarot, it differs radically in its worldview and is not actually represented in the Triumphs (contrary to the "secret interpretations" of many occult Tarot sects).

In modern years, Gnosticism has been imagined as being politically and spiritually more *feminist* than the great traditions. In fundamental ways, Judaic and Christian Gnosticism was in fact just the opposite. Sophia as the Divine Mother was implicated with feminine-born ignorance and desire, as was the seductive sexuality of unwed women deemed sinful unless twisted into a manipulative power righteously controlled by cultic male leaders.

Still, it was recognized that the Fallen Whore was also the Divine Mother and thus paradoxically the light of spiritual gnosis came to humans through and returned via Sophia. A thousand years later, Jewish Kabbalists continued to wrestle with these contradictory positions regarding primary aspects of the Goddess. Like their

Gnostic Sufi brethren, however, they developed far more sophisticated concepts of Feminine Creation, Power, and Compassion. In Kabbalist terms, divine female presence is channeled through the creative spirit called *Shekhinah,* from Hebrew *to dwell,* indicating *visible manifestation* of divine presence. Lowest of the ten stages of divine emanation, the Shekhinah may be compared to the Triumphal archetypes of Empress and Popess. (However, traditional Kabbalists would likely find that comparison to involve a mistaken *reduction* of the Shekhinah Mystery.)

Specialization will restrict a Questor's alchemical resources and ability to adapt to radical changes – internally and externally; he who exalts inheritance will be Abased, he who builds humility will be Valued.

Dualistic sexual-creative theology lent itself to logical rationalizations that upheld deviant attitudes of celibacy and sexuality within communities of varying Gnostic persuasion. (*Celibacy* comes from Latin *caelebs,* meaning "unmarried"; celibacy defined as "abstention from intercourse" was a twentieth-century development.) In particular, the dual nature of Eros and Goddess as "fallen seductress" and "way of escape" lent itself to justified practices of erotic seduction outside the context of marriage. One may see how this aspect of Gnostic social behavior could be attractive to modern women seeking non-traditional ways of feminine liberation. Once seductive femininity outside of marriage is understood as a potentially *Good Way* of the *Goddess* – not enacted out of nihilistic conceit, malice, or retribution – it no longer can be called Gnostic.

Gnostics formed Christianity's original theological systems. Note that a history of *theology* (or "logic-knowledge of god") is barely to be found in Islam or Judaism. It does not apply at all to Buddhism. This is not to say that Buddhism lacks logical analysis in its teachings of Enlightenment and the human condition. On the contrary, Buddhist systems of logic are largely recognized to be as applicable to modern-day studies, such as physics and ethics, as Aristotelian logic. Buddhists, however, do not believe in gods per se and thus do not attempt to logically qualify such. Buddhist divisions of spiritual realms and realizations, while ofttimes portrayed in a manner that may appear to be heavenly and godly, refers to the always-present

Every day is a new day, every meeting a surprise; dwelling beyond the zero point of any empirical scale, find hope in spontaneity, and continuous concentration in awareness of simplicity and the wholes underlying all discontinuities of chaos.

nondual reality underlying and interpenetrating all of nature, mind, and cosmos. This holds nothing in common with theological beliefs in universally separate gods or heavens.

Theosophy or *wisdom-knowledge of Immortal Principles* formed the insightful basis of most great traditions. Theosophy was a natural extension to philosophy and metaphysics. *Theology,* on the other hand, *became a distinctly Christian focus,* in large part due to the Gnostics and their need to legitimize their myths in a rational fashion.

Early Christians attempting to authenticate their religion did so through urban circles of upper-class intellectuals. For centuries, Greek philosophers had built up a body of wisdom-knowledge regarding universal Unity. The Christian Church found it socially and politically critical to be able to integrate Greek philosophy with its revealed Testaments. To counter Gnostic cosmology, Irenaeus of Lyons developed what became the first authoritative ecclesiastical system of the Christian Church. His theology, while refuting Gnostic myths, evinced much similarity in form and belief to their philosophical worldview.

Two seminal theologians from Alexandria, Clement and Origen, attempted to integrate into an exoteric, Pauline Church (Paul's teaching formed the actual foundation of what became Christianity) a Gnostic emphasis on the soul's cyclic progression of heavenly descent and ascent. Clement, positing the importance of esoteric gnosis as knowledge of God, became the most important of early Church Fathers. Origen demythologized Gnostic cosmology, extracting essential teachings of an inward ascent of the Soul back to the Divine Pleroma. He heavily leaned, like Clement, upon early formations of Neoplatonism. Although branded a heretic, Origen formulated the metaphysics that became the basis of Christian monastic mysticism, which emerged from the deserts of Egypt and Syria in the fourth century. That philosophical and spiritual movement has been perennially revived up to this day.

Practices of ascetic denial of the physical world, including rituals of self-flagellation and unnaturally extreme piety, stand in stark contrast to contemplative cultivation, which mindfully witnesses the Sacred flowing in, as, and through every thing, relationship, and process. Viewing the world as a flux of radiant Eros is far different than viewing it as made, controlled, and eternally threatened by a *Dark Lord.* Gnostics conjoined an ascetic avoidance of the fallen world with a solipsistic disregard for civil mores and cultural traditions. It was common for Gnostic communities to rationalize lawlessness, as they believed all laws were fundamentally "below" them or applicable only to a reality totally different than their own. This is a common attitude of dualistic sects. Wanton sexual mores and the breakdown of all *actualizing* hierarchies not exclusive to sectarian domination were tendencies embraced by Gnostics; as they have been by occult circles throughout the ages.

From dreams to symbols to conscience – truth, beauty, and goodness are revealed to the Questor at the threshold of existence through the soul of Providence; enter the realm of saints bearing the Insight of the Moon – Questors' universal ancestor.

Only through practices of contemplation will Questors be able to pierce, without doubt, the clouds of dualistic mythology and egoic fantasy. Because rationality always allows for the logical possibility of a fundamentally dualistic cosmos, undeniable verification of Unity cannot come through rationality. Logically, it is not possible to *prove* the Goodness, Evilness, or Unity of the cosmos. In short, this is the summary fallacy of contemporary analytic philosophy: *because the essential nature of the universe cannot be verified, it cannot truly be known.*

True, universal essence cannot be verified via the mind *separate* from the body. However, through *contemplation,* mind/body, good/evil dualisms *can be* dispelled. In such realization, Unity through Diversity – the Oneness of all – may be verified. *Contemplation* is the way of *experiencing* (and thereby empirically verifying) the *integration of mind and body* and indeed all other *essential polarities.* This simple observation regarding *intraphysical* (a.k.a. "metaphysical") verification directly illuminates a graceful and necessary methodology by which the mind/body, ascension/descension, transcendent/immanent dilemma may be resolved. This involves integrating and literally unifying mind and body.

Elevate above personal preferences, assertive thoughts, and relative attitudes by becoming occupied with the perennial wisdom of ancestral gnosis, re-authenticated for each new gen-eration in a continuous transmission of spiritual legacy.

Syrian monks during the fourth to eighth centuries, contemplators within Nestorian Christian communities, practiced an ascent of the immortal soul back to God while in this life. Gnostic cosmological beliefs of the descended or fallen soul, along with its malevolent stages of entrapment, were converted and rectified by Nestorian mystics as psychic and subtle spheres of contemplative ascension. Jesus himself was viewed as a *human* being with a human family and intimate relationships, including his female companion Mary, even while he simultaneously realized (though as a wholly different identity) the Divine Soul in Heaven – the Holy Spirit of God. Nestorians attempted to cultivate methods to raise their souls back to the perfect state of Christ Soul, called by Neoplatonists the Radiant Soul of Wisdom-Love, regardless of their human conditions.

Broadly speaking, Nestorians were deemed heretics by the Church of Rome because they did not believe Jesus could be both fully human and fully divine in human form. Their brand of dualism was logically solid. It was in many ways a natural outcome and advancement of the Gnostic movement. Nestorians held that human and divine essences of Christ were separate. Jesus the man was different from Christ the Logos or Holy Spirit, which dwelt in the human form of Jesus. Identification of God with human suffering or one who could be crucified to redeem human sins was deemed erroneous and unnecessary. The suffering human Jesus was separate from the Divine Christ. Similarly, Nestorians held that while Mary gave birth to the human Jesus, she should not be called Mother of God.

Theological issues regarding God as a Trinity, Duality, or Unity – or Jesus as divine, human, or both – have promoted not only endless arguments, but also much malice and bloodshed. Historically, conflicting sects within Judaism, Christianity, and Islam have militantly posited distinct and inflexible rationalizations and mythological views concerning the true nature of immortality, divinity, and the hierarchy of realization dividing such from earthbound humanity. To the present day, this has not changed amongst exoteric religious leaders.

In 431, the Byzantine Council of Ephesus ruled that Christ was and is one person, human body included, and that the Virgin Mary is the Mother of God. This resulted in the so-called Nestorian schism and the separation of the Assyrian Church of the East from the Byzantine Church. Yet another divide over this issue soon thereafter produced the famous Chalcedonian schism. This period in the fifth century saw Eastern and Western Churches otherwise jointly finalizing their dogma as infallible. Anyone disagreeing was condemned as a heretic.

First, gain your health, free your obligations, join the forces of love, and devote to the way of Emptiness; then your Quest for divine gnosis will be graced with the virtue of Angelic Perfection.

Syrian Christians from the time soon after Jesus's crucifixion were in close contact with India and Central Asia. A Syrian branch of Christianity, founded by the Apostle Thomas, spread through Jewish and Dravidian communities in Southern India. There is evidence suggesting that Thomas, author of the *Gospel of Thomas*, died in Mylapore, India. Syrian Christianity also gradually spread to the northeast into Central Asia. During the following centuries, *Central Asian Nestorians became closely involved with Buddhist sanghas.* Evidently, Buddhist persuasion overtook Manichean beliefs within the mature community of Nestorian monks. It was through this circle that Neoplatonic knowledge and awareness was translated for Islamic academies, consequently creating a well of esoteric understanding nourishing Sufism.

As a whole, Nestorian tradition embraced gnosis as a form of knowledge emerging as transformative ecstasy. Myths of descent rationalized theologically were mystically verified through esoteric practices of monastic contemplation. Given actual realization of higher, transcendent spheres, however, dualistic aspects of such myths were progressively dropped. This tradition of Central Asian, Syrian, and Egyptian hermits deeply influenced the Orthodox sages introduced in our previous chapter. It formed the basis of Sufi practices beginning in the eighth century. It was also this tradition that introduced Oriental Hermetic wisdom-teachings ("as below, so above; and as above, so below") to communities sympathetic to

To live without love in the region of eternity is to live in the stasis of hell: timeless intensity, neither bright nor veiled – the zero point of the scale, the slicing edge, never through, never through – in a state of ancestral disinheritance.

Gnostic spirituality, substantially helping to dispel the dualistic elitism of genuine Gnostic gnosis.

Like modern-day nihilism, Gnosticism was fundamentally purposed toward "building down" the Platonic-Jewish-Christian concept of in-this-world transcendence. Cultural and communal valuations of the Transcendental as contained in Neoplatonic and monistic doctrines of spiritual hierarchy were dismantled by cults bound to dualistic myths. They continue to be dismantled by present students convicted of *rational and communal idealism,* which ironically forms the basis of nihilistic conceits. While Western dualism – including twentieth-century *New Age* variants of Gnosticism – claims a second, *real* transcendence, nihilism denies reality to *all* transcendental processes. The "romanticism" of Blake's *Book of Urizen,* Shelley's *Prometheus Unbound,* and Byron's *Cain: A Mystery* evinces a progressive wedding of Gnostic and nihilistic beliefs.

Gnosis not dissociated from ordinary reality directs attention to the *unity* of that which is common with that which is extraordinary. If such awareness can be called "pantheistic romanticism," it is romanticism more akin to that of Rumi or the Tarot than to Germanic and English philosophers, mythmakers, and artists of occult persuasion popularized during the last two centuries. Such modern trends appropriating *Romantic culture* reflect millennial-apocalyptic movements that have continuously made false starts throughout the history of Christianity.

Hegel

In reference to modern German dualists, it is notable that Hegel was an avowed millennialist. He viewed his dialectical philosophy involving *spiritual alienation (spirit must alienate itself to become known to itself)* as humanity's last possible theo-philosophical system. After him, he presumed, the concept of *God* would become obsolete. Hegel's focus upon Meister Eckhart's fourteenth-century pantheistic transcendental statements of Mysterious Truth is a good example of how enlightened, nondual worldviews can be superficially and confusedly interpreted to support dualistic positions. In

The Tao Surrounds each and all yet remains always One – every spirit in the world abides solely as World Spirit.

a similar manner, Gautama's Buddhist teachings have been interpreted by modern rationalists (Max Müller being a prime example) as supporting dualism, if not nihilism. Marx drew upon not only Hegel (thus, Marx's inevitable "alienation of the laborer"), but the whole of German Gnostic ideology, which included the worldviews of Luther, Kant, and Heidegger.

Modern philosophies of world development sanction idealizations such as the *proletariat* and *profit* that are not universal principles. Thus, they do not address stages of social, cultural, psychological, and environmental development apparent in nondual worldviews of perennial wisdom. Universal principles and immortal values are reduced to strategic laws enforcing manipulation of political structures and economic systems.

We have little room in our study of the Tarot's origins to dedicate toward the last one hundred and fifty years of Gnostic/occult belief. W. B. Yeats stated that he "came to believe in a Great Memory passing on from generation to generation." He held that the symbols of alchemy expressed the psychic path away from material bondage. He drew on a highly romanticized history of esoteric transmission propagated by A. E. Waite, who conceptually "channeled" the images of the famous and frequently used Rider-Waite Tarot deck, painted by Pamela Colman Smith. Along with Waite and the soon-to-be-notorious Aleister Crowley (whose spectacular Tarot deck also remains popular), Yeats belonged to the occult Hermetic Order of the Golden Dawn at the turn of the twentieth century. From their dualistic school, English occult movements drew much of their authority.

The Theosophical Society founded by Madame Blavatsky and later led by H. S. Olcott, Annie Besant, and C. W. Leadbeater, was another influential late-nineteenth-century occult organization. In the twentieth century, it quite wrongfully made claim to membership in the *Sophia Perennis* academy of traditionalist luminaries such as René Guénon, Ananda Coomaraswamy, and Fritjof Schuon. Nationalistic and violent Buddhist circles in Sri Lanka and India

Neither terrestrial nor celestial, thinking consciousness as egoic self resides in a place of existential despair; in the face of such inevitable delusion, the Fool makes light of the zero point.

unfortunately derived much authority from the Theosophical Society's dualistic misappropriations of the Dharma.

Before continuing with an examination of early Greek concepts regarding gnosis and cosmology, mention needs to be made of the Gnostic period from which arose what is known as the *Hermetic wisdom tradition.* During the seventh and eighth centuries, a short text surfaced in several Sufi books, including one attributed to Jabir, purporting to be authored by the Egyptian godman and alchemist Hermes Trismegistos. The *Emerald Tablet,* as the text became known, was a slab of emerald (which denoted, at the time, material ranging from green glass to green jasper) engraved by Hermes with the essence of his sacred alchemical work. It has been traditionally considered one of the finest summaries of Hellenistic principles regarding divine realization and cosmogonic alchemy. Evincing similarity to Syrian writings of the fourth century, the text is likely to be either Syrian or Central Asian in origin.

It is of interest to note the Oriental nature of this work and similar texts of wisdom-sayings, including the *Q Gospel* (a postulated source-text for the Gospels of Matthew and Luke) and the *Gospel of Thomas.* While the Gnostic corpus was strongly rooted in Jewish and Platonic dualism, Hermeticism grounded a sophisticated mix of those dualistic traditions upon a mature base of nondual Hellenic and Oriental pantheism. Radical statements of the wisdom-saying tradition underlying Hermeticism were distinct in their adamant emphasis regarding immanently transcendent Unity. The *Emerald Tablet* reflects that state of consciousness:

> Here is Truth! Certainty! That in which there is no doubt! That which is below is like that which is above and that which is above is like that which is below, working the miracles of one.
>
> As all things have been and arose from contemplation of the One, so all things have their birth from this One Thing through adaptation.

> The Sun is its father, the Moon its mother. The Earth carried it in her belly, and the Wind nourished it in her belly. It is the Father of all talismans; Perfection in the world.
>
> If turned towards the earth, it will separate earth from fire, the subtle from the gross. It ascends from the earth to heaven and again descends to earth, receiving the force of all things superior and inferior.
>
> By this means you shall have the glory of the whole world and thereby all obscurity shall fly from you. Its force is above all force, for it vanquishes every subtle thing and penetrates every solid thing.
>
> Thus is the structure of the microcosm in accordance with the structure of the macrocosm. From this comes marvelous adaptations, whose process is just this.
>
> Hence I am called Hermes Trismegistos, having the three parts of the philosophy of the whole world. That which I have said of the operation of the Sun is accomplished and ended.

Described in this complete text of the *Emerald Tablet* (derived largely from a translation by Sir Isaac Newton) is the *philosopher's stone*, the *golden elixir*, the *panacea* of health and wisdom.

Taoist teachings from this era referring to the Tao and its universal alchemy might readily be mistaken for such Hermetic philosophy. The Tablet – like Alexandria, from where the text was purported to come – appears to have been associated with or otherwise influenced by Central and Western Asian metaphysical development. Buddhist representation was strong in these areas during this time; the Tablet could be interpreted as referring to the nature of Buddha Mind and self-realization of noble wisdom. More obviously reflected in the Tablet is an essential distillation of Plotinus's teachings. Aspects of Heraclitus's One Thing, Divine Fire, and Earthly Eros, along with Pythagoras's mage-like attaining of divine power, are also clearly evident in this short description of spiritual union, unity, and the obtainable wisdom-power that derives from such. The wisdom-sayings of Jesus also evince parallels. All of these Great Tradition teachings comport with principles of immortality, through which knowledge of wisdom-realization is imparted.

The earliest document generally agreed by scholars as belonging to the Hermetic corpus is entitled *Poimanders*. This text shows strong affiliations with Jewish liturgy and monastic communities during the era after the failed Jewish revolt of A.D. 117 in Egypt. However, that said, the Hermetic *creed* it espouses – *Let the man who has mind recognize himself as immortal* – is distinctly non-Jewish. Those who chose Hermes Trismegistos as their Teacher, embracing knowledge of the inner self as knowledge of God, ultimately discarded the Law of Moses.

As mentioned, Hermeticism held much in common with Jesus's wisdom-teachings. It is widely surmised that the *Gospel of Thomas* stemmed from the same original body of statements attributable to Jesus as the *Q* (from German *Quelle,* "source") *Gospel* was redacted from. The latter has itself been distilled by scholars from the four canonical gospels. Conjectured to be a source for some material found in the Gospels of Matthew and Luke, it has been reconstructed through rigorous biblical and linguistic study. *Q* was redacted from a collection of wisdom-sayings; however, added to those original statements of Jesus was an eschatological message derived from Jewish apocalyptic doctrine. Conduct appropriate to dualistic beliefs in a *necessary end* to this world and the *salvation of an elected few* into a future incorporeal world formed an important aspect of *Q*.

In contrast to *Q* and later gospels, the *Gospel of Thomas* shows no sign of such apocalyptic dualism. In 1945, *Thomas* was discovered along with a collection of other early Christian manuscripts near the Egyptian town of Nag Hammadi. Objective study of the Nag Hammadi Library has made evident to many scholars the primary position that Jesus's wisdom-teachings held amongst his early followers.

Thomas's branch of apostolic succession developed in the second half of the first century in Palestine and Syria. In this tradition, Jesus was often identified with Sophia or Wisdom, historically viewed in Greco-Roman culture as a Supreme Goddess. A tantric integration of feminine and masculine attributes of divinity was made. Perhaps this was the cause of the success of Thomas's Christianity in Southern India, where it is believed Thomas preached and died. Numerous branches of what may be called Syro-Malabar Christianity – centered in Kerala, India, which still maintains a matriarchal tradition and devotion to Shakti as Wisdom – thrive to this day.

This positive view of Sophia was directly opposed by Gnostic sects appropriating the Christ-cult in the following century. While agreeing that Sophia dwelled in the sphere of Spirit and Soul – marked, we may recall, by the intersection of gnosis and insight – Gnostics paradoxically viewed Her as the *fallen cause and mother* of the malevolent Demiurge. Mother and son together composed an erotic myth identifying the world-creator with the root of all evil. Wisdom-teachings of Unity emanating as the Myriad and realized as Eros-Love for all were reinterpreted and reversed by Gnostics.

Jewish-Platonic dualism was channeled into Gnosticism, apocalyptic Judaism, and Pauline Christianity. James, brother of Jesus, was closely involved with apocalyptic (in particular, *Zealot*) strains of Judaic *politics*. Thomas (presented in early texts as Jesus's *twin*, apparently meaning "closest companion") stood opposed to this, although his gospel shows reserved respect for James's authority, even while disagreeing with his beliefs. The nondual wisdom tradition in which Jesus and his companion Thomas stood was embraced by Plotinian Neoplatonists, mystical Hermeticists, Eastern Christian desert-hermits, and finally by medieval Sufis and radical Kabbalists. One must note, of course, that for many disciples, divisions between these camps were not hard and fast. This will also be the situation for many modern-day Tarot devotees, as it likely was with A. E. Waite and much of his fellowship. By now it is no doubt clear that this book aspires to persuade readers toward an understanding of nondual realization and an emanationist interpretation of the Triumphs.

Previously mentioned Alexandrian theologians attempted to bridge these two fundamentally different worldviews. As evidenced by the difficulty of the material presented in chapter 4, that bridge-work was neither simple nor particularly successful. Augustine remained theologically trapped by the dualism of matter and soul. Origen was deemed a heretic. Clement, whose profound understanding was widely regarded, kept most of his views to himself – a course of action strongly recommended by Jesus in the *Gospel of Thomas*. Modern, existential theologians such as the sagacious Paul Tillich have continued an attempt to universalize Christian doctrine, reforming the essence of Christian *Catholicism*, which literally means *Universalism*. *Liberation Theology*, which became greatly influential in impoverished twentieth-century countries with large Catholic populations, is also distinguished in this way.

Were Synoptic sayings and wisdom-teachings of Jesus influenced by schools of thought other than those of Judaism and Hellenism? Reasonable arguments have been made that Jesus was familiar with Eastern teachings, in particular those of Buddhism. Certainly his sayings fit well with Buddhist thought. A well-known Pythagorean contemporary of Jesus, Apollonius of Tyana, had famously traveled to India and brought back wisdom from Buddhist and Vedic teachers. Apollonius was said to have performed miracles remarkably similar to those of Jesus.

Since the time of Alexander the Great, whose generals after his death established dynasties spanning the territories between India and Greece (the Seleucid Dynasty, for instance, ruled much of Asia Minor from 312 to 64 B.C.), cultural exchange between Buddhist and Near Eastern Hellenistic societies was rich. King Asoka, historically regarded as the greatest of Indian rulers, died a century after Alexander. He and his successors spread Buddhism far and wide, including into Alexandria, Egypt, itself.

In 250 B.C. Ashoka sent to King Ptolemy of Egypt an envoy of monks called *Therapeutae*, likely a Hellenization of Pali *Theravada* (Greek *therapeuein* came to mean "to naturally treat and heal"). Philo Judaeus, a contemporary of Jesus, describes in a tract entitled *De Vita Contemplativa* the Therapeutae as a reclusive brotherhood vowed to poverty, celibacy, charity, and compassion. No similar religious sect was known in the Judaic world.

When the Seleucid Kingdom began to break apart, its eastern section formed the Greco-Bactrian Kingdom that in turn became the Indo-Greek Kingdom, which extended into India until the time of Jesus. The latter's most famous emperor, King Menander of the second century B.C., was of Greek heritage. As a Buddhist King he became as respected as Ashoka of the earlier Mauryan Dynasty and King Kanishka of the later Kushan Empire. His conversion and recorded considerations with the Buddhist sage Nagasena (recorded in *Questions of Milinda*) are legendary. Both Theravadan and later Mahayanan communities revered him as a guardian of the Dharma. There appears to have been close alignment between Indo-Bactrian Greeks and Mauryans, who ruled India as the country's most powerful and successful empire in the centuries before the Common Era.

Toward the end of the great Greco-Indo empires, during the Gnostic centuries after Jesus, the first human depictions of Buddha were sculpted in Gandhara (the area of Kashmir and Punjab). Buddha had previously only been represented symbolically by stupas, Dharma wheels, etc. Greco-Buddhist statues are elegant and graceful in their depiction of enlightened peace. They potently evince Greek aesthetics. King Kanishka, who initiated this important aspect of Mahayanan art, ruled a civilization led by Central Asian *Kushans* (who were the farthest eastward speakers of Indo-European language, related to the Tocharian speakers of Western China) stretching from Bengal to Central Asia to China.

Thus began a great age of Buddhist migration into all of Asia. Interaction between Greek, Central Asian, and Buddhist cultures influenced the emergence of Mahayana and Vajrayana Buddhism, which developed highly refined metaphysical and shamanistic approaches to psychophysical realization of Bodhisattvahood. Such may be appropriately compared with sophisticated Hellenic self-realization of wisdom through veneration of and contemplation upon the nondual Way of godmen such as Dionysus and Hermes. As a whole, this composes a Great Traditional lineage and wisdom-way of immortality.

Accounts regarding a visit by Jesus to India reportedly exist within *Vajrayana* (the "Diamond-Lightning-vehicle") Buddhist communities of the Himalayas. Allegedly, manuscripts have been found and translated that would support such. Given the provocative aspects of this to most Christians, dialogue between Biblical researchers and Buddhist lamas who control access to pertinent manuscripts has been minimal. In any case, there are a great many undeniable similarities between the Gospels' stories of Jesus's birth and traditional Pali stories of Buddha's birth. Of greatest import, similarities between the wisdom teachings of Jesus and Buddha are striking. These warrant more attention by comparative religion scholars than they have received to date.

It was known at the time of Jesus that given prevailing monsoon winds, sailing to India across the Arabian Sea took only forty days. (Israel and Egypt connect to the Arabian Sea via the Red Sea.) That Thomas sailed there is factually probable (though the Roman Church remains noncommittal, at times positing instead that Thomas traveled to Pakistan via Persia). That Syrian Christians a few hundred years later did is undisputed. We may speculate that Thomas's motivation to travel to India may have been related to contact during Jesus's lifetime with travelers indigenous to the Subcontinent.

Unlike *Q*, the *Gospel of Thomas* contains no trace of Jesus's passion-drama, death, or resurrection. Many of the sayings in *Q* are found in *Thomas*. Those that speak of a "future coming of the Son of Man" are not. Sayings regarding the "Kingdom of the Father," particularly its very real presence *in and as this world*, on the other hand, are frequent. There is strong evidence that *Thomas* is derived from the earliest recordings of Jesus. The text itself states that Thomas was entrusted with the *esoteric* teachings of the Lord. To reiterate, it presents Jesus's parables as instructions for the realization of wisdom. What it does not present is concealed revelations involving cosmic powers, mythological battles, or the salvation of an elected few. Viewed from the perspective of a cosmopolitan intellectual during Jesus's time, the *Gospel of Thomas* would appear very Oriental if not Buddhist in nature.

Socially and ritualistically, both Gnosticism and Hermeticism drew on Jewish and Hellenistic cultures of the first and second centuries. Essential building blocks of Gnostic mythology were taken from Jewish scriptures and exegetical traditions. Primary, mythic structural design, however, was appropriated from middle-Platonic mythology. As Jews fully imbibed Greek philosophy, Mosaic Law was reinterpreted allegorically. The outcome of this was a splitting off of philosophical factions that did not strictly adhere to old Judaic laws. Some of these heretical sects made claim to *gnosis* and *sophia* as pointed to in the wisdom-sayings of Jesus and various Asian traditions.

As Gnostics assimilated the quickly growing Christian religion, Jesus supplanted Seth and other previous heretical Jewish *redeemers*. By de-emphasizing the *evilness* and complex mythos of cosmological descent and formation (which was inherited from Judeo-Babylonian tradition and then dramatically revised), a system of progressive gnostic spiritualization was legitimized and integrated into a Western stream of metaphysics affected by Platonic tradition. As late Gnosticism dropped all remnants of uniquely interpreted biblical mythology and history, the movement was coopted into various branches of Eastern Christianity, Hermeticism, Neopythagoreanism, and subsequently Neoplatonism.

Like Neoplatonism, late Gnosticism taught a method of intellectual ascent while in this world. Gnostics rationalized this as being precursor to the soul's ascent once it escaped its physical prison. Purposed toward that ascent, psychic use was made of letters in the alphabet and their syllabic combinations. These magical letters were believed to be directly connected to angelic realms. Through their use, Gnostic adepts imagined traversing angelic spheres in a way that was clearly influenced by Middle Platonic doctrines. Practical introduction of angelic presence and influence during each stage of spiritual ascent lessened anti-cosmic dogmas of earlier Gnostic belief. In this way, Manichean influence upon Nestorians was mitigated and transformed via a focus upon contemplative practice.

Again, though, it was not until late in Gnostic development that such Neoplatonic influence grew to be more than superficial. It was not until the twelfth century, as covered in chapter 3, that the *esoteric science of letters and names* was fully developed, concomitantly by Islamic Sufis and Jewish Kabbalists. Nonetheless, Ibn ʿArabi's cosmological system of Divine Names and Image-Exemplars, from which this book suggests the Triumphs' hierarchy was derived, was essentially founded upon (via Western Asian Christian translation and elaboration) contemplative realizations and cosmological considerations that emerged during the Neoplatonic-Hermetic-Gnostic era of the third and fourth centuries A.D.

Late Gnostic texts delineated in a precisely Platonic manner the soul's ascent to heavenly domains. Middle-Platonic esotericism taught of:

1. The One beyond being
2. The Intellect of pure being
3. The Soul of Intellect and Cosmos
4. The Material Cosmos

Post-Plotinian Neoplatonic systems expanded upon these four stages using triadic subdivisions. Although such systems varied, they served to produce an essential template for the Christian metaphysicians and Sufis mentioned in previous chapters. The most elegant of these systems was the *division of the cosmos* into six realms emanating from three transcendental realms that in turn emanated from one absolute realm. Each realm then developed a *polar nature:* one side connected it to the previous realm, the other side to the next realm. In other terms, one axis connected a realm vertically and one connected it horizontally; or similarly, one aspect formed as the *mind* or *internal* of a realm and another formed as the *body* or *external* of a realm. To have a *right view* of these realms was to be on the path of Wisdom. Such was the *way of gnosis.* Such remains the cosmological and theosophical teaching embodied by the Tarot.

Although their concepts of *salvation* differed, for both Gnostic and Hermetic, *gnosis was primarily requisite.* It was the *knowledge of self* that in essence was identical to *knowledge of God.* Though the two groups had this in common, *Hermeticism did not share the theology, cosmology, anthropology, or eschatology of Gnosticism.* Hermeticism did not hold to the theological belief that a supreme God existed totally separate from worldly forces. It did not hold to the cosmological belief that the cosmos was a terrible prison holding the soul captive. It did not hold to the anthropological belief that the human body was part of that cosmic prison, from which only an essential, inner "spark" was redeemable. Nor did Hermeticism hold to the eschatological belief that the self's total release from its prison would occur only when the material world ended. The Oriental, nondual nature of Hermetic wisdom regarding the similarity of microcosmic and macrocosmic worlds, with each being inherently endowed with and as the presence of the One, did not allow for the preceding Gnostic beliefs.

Following crushing defeats of the Jewish polity circa A.D. 70, there emerged a history of *disappointed messianism* in apocalyptic sects of Palestinian and Egyptian Jews. From this movement and its perverse twist on the significance of worldly wisdom, Gnosticism came into being, parasitically attaching itself to religious and metaphysical traditions. The effects of this pernicious appendage can be felt today. In many new religions of our current era, frequently grouped under the rubric of "New Age," we find an uncanny repeat of the era two thousand years ago. In Gnosticism, *Man* was a designation for the *God of Perfection. Son of Man* and *Race of the Perfect Man* became self-designations.

In an era of post-humanistic narcissism, the *universality and perfection* of inherent Unity (made *transparently* evident through mindful, concentrated contemplation) is all too frequently confused with a psychic glorification of the *personal* soul of man. Advaita realization that Atman Is Brahman is reduced to a narcissistic "Ego is Everything" or inflated into an "I am the Greatest and Only True One." Rational, psychic, and subtle egos can readily presume superiority over nature (the dimensional reality of space), ancestors (the energetic reality of time), and interdependently caused spiritual hierarchy.

Ibn ʿArabi's identification with a unity-realized *Perfect Man* has been denounced by his detractors as crossing the fine line between nondual realization and megalomaniac conceit. However, his life evinces little indication of this. Such conceit has historically led to violent arrogance and dictatorial ethno-cultic centrism. Extensive evidence of this can be found among the conquering leaders of twentieth-century nationalism and warfare. Violently brutish "intellectuals" such as Benito Mussolini laid claim to Great Tradition hierarchy in appalling ways, identifying themselves and their gangsters with twisted concepts of "unity" and "perfection." Certain Japanese Zen masters who lent support to Japanese fascism also serve as unfortunate examples of this.

Idealization of Perfection and its signs of realization rest at the heart of spiritual and ethical law. It is critical in our current era that representatives of the world's religions and philosophical schools come into dialog if not subtle alignment regarding historical, global evidence of Unity Realization and human development of Perfection. To do this, spiritual practitioners and leaders must move beyond *political* and *humanistic* ecumenism.

So far, little mention has been made of the Tarot in this chapter's exploration of dualistic Gnosticism, which was a vehicle for occult Chaldean beliefs to be examined shortly. The equating of Hellenic, Egyptian, or otherwise Pagan views of spiritual hierarchy with Gnostic *secrets* has been a root cause of Tarot misinterpretation. The latter denies any need to study, understand, and contemplate the former. Occult misinterpretations of the Tarot identify with surreptitious claims of spiritual exclusivity substantiated solely through egoic mental-psychic projection. They are not grounded in authenticated realizations and practices consciously carried forward generation to generation by sagacious spiritual teachings and lineages. Spiritual rule divorced from common reality was *not* the basis of ancient pantheism, Neoplatonism, or Hermeticism.

As we have seen, Neoplatonic concepts of hierarchical emergence involved spiritual ascent *in conjunction with* cosmic descent. Archetypal forces represented by the Tarot Exemplars hold to a Hermetic understanding that *it is below as it is above and it is above as it is below.* As do Jesus's statements of wisdom in *Thomas.* How to realize Truth, Beauty, and Goodness – the *Liberation of Enlightenment* – as an integral body/mind is the supreme and crucial message conveyed via the Triumphs' esoteric procession. Every Triumph, from Empress to World, is a divine agent. From Right View to Right Liberation, every phase of consciousness must be appreciated by Questors. The Quest, put most succinctly, involves the *Magician as Self* being transformed into the *Fool as No-self.* Every station of that transformative process is to be celebrated as innately necessary and true.

Platonic dualism as stated by Plato himself tended toward conscious union of mind and the transcendentally perfect while being corporeally embodied. Plato and his peers were initiated into veneration of the *Mystery Rite.* Although material body was *graded* lower than soul, intellect, and the Good beyond all individuated being, Plato did not fall into the trap of totally separating cosmic involution from spiritual evolution.

Centuries later, Neoplatonists radically affirmed a nondual worldview. Plotinus reformed the ancient Greek understanding of Divine Realization. About Plotinus, Porphyry wrote:

> To this God-like man above all, who often raised himself in thought according to the very ways Plato teaches in the *Symposium* to the First and Transcendent God, that God appeared who has neither shape nor any intelligible form, but is enthroned above Intellect and the Intelligible.

Gnostics believed in the consubstantiality of an anti-cosmic God with a supra-cosmic Self trapped in a cosmic body. This denied the value of what is represented in the first six stages of the Tarot Trionfi: the *common sense, feeling, intelligence, spirit, gnosis, and heart of humanity.* It pretended to a *Gnostic exclusive:* an ascetically conceited, fifth-stage claim to total and *privileged* divine virtue. Nihilistic, schizophrenic, and psychotic stages of alienation and rejection resulting from this beg comparison with modern and postmodern progressions of chronic, if not glorified, angst. Hierarchy in terms of mythic, logic, or psychic *escape* from the cosmos or claims of *personal* dominion over *spiritual* realms is exactly *not* what the Tarot represents. Beliefs in such "salvation" or privileged rulership did not form the basis of genuinely mature Neoplatonism, Hermeticism, Jesus's wisdom-teachings, or later Sufism and Kabbalism.

Synchronizing . . . Right Life

It is time to trace back the roots of Western esotericism and Tarot metaphysics to the earliest of Greek philosophers. Much of what we know about the early Greeks comes down to us from Aristotle. Scholars have come to perceive, however, that Aristotle was a biased and somewhat narrow-minded thinker regarding myth-and-mystery-oriented pre-Socratic philosophers. We have

seen in previous chapters how third-stage patterns of responsible rationality naturally develop into fourth-stage abilities to intuit patterns via psychological, intuitive gestalts. Likewise, magical rituals and mythical tales contain their own forms of lawful, proto-rational sense. First- and second-stage ways of magic and myth become naturally encapsulated by reason, their mature outcome. This occurs through embracing, not denying, their truth. Aristotle's worldviews rejected first- and second-stage patterns of knowing.

Such a mind-set stands in contrast to that of Neoplatonists, Hermetic Christians, and Sufis that have been presented herein as exemplar *integrative philosophers*. Examined from their vantage, the metaphysical worldviews of early Greek teachers such as Pythagoras and Heraclitus come under a far clearer light than when viewed from the materialistic and reductionistic logical vantage of Aristotle. Modern research has helped to elucidate archaic Greek cosmology, bringing to the fore aspects of it that were embodied or dispelled by nondual Neoplatonists, Sufis, and consequently the original Tarot.

Early Greek history is inexorably entwined with that of Persia. After King Cyrus of Persia conquered Babylonia in 539 B.C., Zoroastrians initiated a two-hundred-year integration of Persian and Mesopotamian mythic thought based upon a philosophical dualism that posited an ultimate Goodness to the world. When the Persian Empire threatened Greek territories, then composed of non-unified city-states, Greeks banded together via an attitude of cultural superiority and survival, focused upon a common enemy. Up until that time, distinctions between "East and West," or "Persian and Greek," were not hard and fast. Worldviews were as numerous as dialects, which differed everywhere; yet nature-based, cultural similarities between the Greek Isles, Asia Minor, and Greater Persia were pervasive. Given that the area's Indo-European branches developed from the same linguistic and cultural trunk, it is not surprising that there existed many similarities between them.

After the Persian-Greek wars, however, all non-Greeks were branded as *barbarians*, meaning "speakers of babble." Only the Greeks, it was believed, had realized a progressive state of political independence and democracy. Indeed, second-stage empire, which the Persians excelled at, *was* being advanced upon in Greece through third-stage patterns of communicative civility. The Greeks however, had not established civil maturity. For instance, only ten percent of any given *polis* actually had say in Greek *democracy* (literally "might of the people").

At this time, Greek metaphysical development began to split into two distinct movements. One went down a path of rationality that led to practices of transcendental union through Neoplatonic contemplation and Hermetic methods of alchemy. The other secretly embraced dualistic worldviews based upon Chaldean *convictions* (i.e., beliefs that "others have been proven wrong because they have been conquered"). It is from the latter school that nineteenth- and twentieth-century occultists presumed the Tarot Arcana emerged. Sociopolitical histories delineating domination hierarchies and socio-intellectual histories uncovering actualizing hierarchies are different histories indeed. Spiritual quests transcend political conquests.

The term *Chaldean* came to be used when referencing the aforementioned Iranian-Mesopotamian convergence. (This may be viewed as a historical indication of the capability for Iran, Iraq, and Kurdistan to live at peace with one another in their corner of the world.) On one hand, there was a strong anti-Chaldean bias in Greek society. On the other hand, Assyrian and Babylonian influences were pervasive. They radically shaped the formation of Judaism during the centuries that Judaic tribes were ruled by the Babylonian state. They were also intimately present in Pythagorean interpretation of old chthonic mystery sects that were partly *Oriental* in flavor. (The latter primarily stemmed from early *Anatolian* and *Indus Valley* cultures that gestated and nurtured ancient Indo-European rituals of initiation into further-evolved patterns of consciousness.)

A branch of late Platonism encapsulated this Near Eastern/Central Asian worldview of magic and mythos in Platonic terminology. The famous *Chaldean Oracles*, a collection of mystical poetry, presents a syncretic version of this dualistic religious path, which we may reasonably identify as being a primary root of occult movements throughout Western history (Germanic/Norse mythology being another, which was largely drawn upon by Tolkien in his *Lord of the Rings* trilogy). During the period of Gnostic development, this pre-rational tradition became legitimized, encased by a shell of urbanized philosophy. Neopythagoreans and subsequent Neoplatonists integrated it. However, a general historical tendency toward transcendental monism as witnessed in Judaic, Christian, and Islamic metaphysics arrested the popularization of Chaldean dualism. Importantly, Neoplatonists reinterpreted the Oracles from an essentially nondual point of view.

Great Tradition esoteric teachings and communities that have been mentioned in this book never abandoned their chthonic, magical, and mythological foundations. Nor did they avoid fully incorporating rational, critical enquiry into their expositions regarding cosmology and spirituality. On the contrary, those early stages of realization holistically integrated to form a foundation for trans-rational, psychically intuitive, subtly virtuous, and causally heartful ways of spiritual culture recognized perennially via ten stages of hierarchical development. In contrast, Neopythagoreans and other Chaldean-influenced, magic-based sects following them fell into a *pre/trans fallacy: pre-rational* states were *equated* with *trans-rational* states.

We will examine Pythagorean cosmology through the thought of Empedocles; and will then contrast it to the wisdom of Heraclitus, which points to an early Greek cosmological worldview underlying the medieval Tarot. Comparing Pythagorean and Heraclitean thought will serve to illuminate how and why Tarot cosmology and spiritual hierarchy are understood by so few, even while so many presume that the Arcana represent both an ancient and advanced understanding of cosmic and spiritual law.

Pythagoreanism, like Hermeticism, drew upon Oriental, Egyptian, and archaic Greek practices in which magic mixed with philosophical enquiry. Similarities exist between the more exotic Hermetic alchemical literature and Pythagorean tracts. The importance of alchemy in varying traditions during the era after Jesus will be considered in the next chapter. Its development was paralleled and in some cases influenced by a Greco-Egyptian tradition of magic encased in what was originally Mesopotamian mythology. Gnosticism was also heavily influenced by this Chaldean affected tradition. Evidence of it can be found in the *cosmic poetry* of late *Egyptian magical papyri* and in a large body of popular literature that grew around pseudo-godmen and miracle workers such as Empedocles.

Whereas we know little about Pythagoras, significant pieces of poetry written by his successor Empedocles have survived the millennia; as have a great deal of stories that refer to Empedocles' mage-like heroic powers. Empedocles was a *theurgist* (from *theourgia,* meaning "sacramental rite and mystery"). He was famous for performing miracles and magic through spiritual assistance. This enabled him to call forth supernatural intervention into human affairs. Empedocles viewed theurgy as a progressive way of making his soul divine – raising his human self to a level of godhood. From a rational point of view, this would appear to have involved regression through pre-rational rituals and imagined myths, conflating a sense of self with that of demiurgic power. In modern psychological terms, Empedocles' identification with god-power would likely denote patterns of megalomania.

Be that as it may, Empedocles apparently realized a hierarchy of transcendental states, witnessing similarity of that which was external (health, weather, peoples' behavior, outcome of battles, etc.) to that which was felt internally as psychophysical energy and consciousness traditionally called spirituality. The genius of Pythagoras and his successor dwelt in their ability to rationally explain the magical ways of nature and mythic forces in terms involving sophisticated logical relationships. What they propounded proved crucial in the development of mathematics, geometry, philosophy, and medicine. They combined their generally insightful proclamations with yogic practices in ways that held much in common with Indian Vedic practice.

Throughout esoteric Greek religion, rationality served as a bridge between immanently chthonic, magical mystery rituals associated with Demeter, Persephone, Dionysus, and Orpheus (who was a later interpretation of the earlier three) and transcendentally intelligent philosophies initiated by Pythagoras, idealized by Plato, and epitomized by Plotinus.

From Fabre d'Olivet's translation of *The Golden Verses of Pythagoras* ("Perfection"):

> God! Thou couldst save them by opening their eyes.
> But no: 'tis for the humans of a race divine
> To discern Error and to see the Truth.
> Nature serves them. Thou who fathomed it,
> O wise and happy man, rest in its haven.
> But observe my laws, abstaining from the things
> Which thy soul must fear, distinguishing them well;
> Letting intelligence o'er thy body reign.
> So that, ascending into radiant Ether,
> Midst the Immortals, thou shalt be thyself a God.

Hellenic beliefs in magical powers varied considerably from age to age, community to community, and person to person. Rational and contemplative maturity influenced the nature of such beliefs. Both Empedocles and later Neoplatonic theurgists (separated by some eight hundred years) were attributed supernatural powers: to make rain, stop plagues, communicate with the underworld and the gods, and realize an immortal *resurrection body* after having undergone ritualized, spiritual death. It is critical to note that by no means were these typical forms of magic all considered to be of the same order. In Christianity, for instance, the miracle of Jesus walking on water is considered to be of a different order than that of his resurrection. Furthermore, religious sects distinctly qualified their godmen's miracles. Concepts of Empedocles' immortal self differed from varying concepts of Jesus's divine being, which differed (except perhaps, Thomas's view) from Plotinus's understanding of an immortally conscious and realized heart-mind.

It is to Plotinus and his nondual (*self is other and both are prior-and-always-already Unity*) hierarchy of cosmic, soulful consciousness that we can trace the divinatory magic, mythos, and rationality of the Tarot. Plotinus epitomized trans-rational understandings of magic through realization of prophetic powers inherent to the contemplative soul-mind: i.e., the *causal-heart* as sixth-stage manifestation of evolutionary consciousness. *Such is the witnessing position of that converted consciousness whose self-awareness is identical to realization of Emptiness or no-self.* Plotinus understood that this can only be attained through hierarchical transformations of mind/body/heart beyond rationality.

Contemplation is a necessary catalyst to actualizing spiritual mind/body transformations. Pre-rational rites of theurgy are insufficient to yield universal alchemy and wisdom. Magic based upon *control* of an "other," even if that other is one's own soul "separate" from one's body, is far different than magic based upon holistic, transpersonal actualization and *transcendence* of separate self. The latter is represented by the Tarot Magician, whose name *Bagatella* connotes "a trifle or small thing" yet who *performs for the enlightenment of all*. There is, of course, no megalomania to be found in either the Magician or the Fool.

Empedocles presented his teaching as divine revelation. Not only was he considered sagacious in his dispensing of oracles – his whole cosmology was understood to *be* an oracle. Those who sought initiation in his school had to accept his godlike revelatory power without question. His writings were couched in enigmatic riddles.

Empedocles' methodology involved Pythagorean purifying techniques, charging thoughts and actions into a state of *katharsis* (meaning to *purge* into being "pure," *katharos:* a word and technique later revived by Crusading Cathari) via secret rituals. Those techniques included physical regimens such as not eating food that might cause intestinal gas. (This remained an important topic in Oriental medicine and yoga, largely for reasons having to do with deep belly-breathing. There is psychophysical significance in Buddhist, Hindu, Taoist, and Sufi iconographical depictions of sensual, breath-filled abdomens.) Katharsis abetted by potent (including psychoactive) herbal drugs was also an important practice; here, Empedocles stood in an ancient lineage of *root-cutter mages.*

Once disciples were sufficiently purified, Empedocles would give them the *paradosis* initiatory transmission. *Paradeisos,* from which the English "paradise" is derived, was first coined by Greek military commander and historian Xenophon, who served with Greek mercenaries in Persia. The original Avestan word referred to Persian kings' and nobles' pleasure grounds. From this mundane simulacrum of the Original Garden, represented in the Tarot by Empress and Popess, Questors gain a vantage of Right View, and begin their Quest. However, there are stages to initiation itself; in both Neopythagorean and Neoplatonic traditions, rites such as the *paradosis* could be transmitted in full and genuinely self-authenticated only after years of purification and preparatory cultivation.

Godlike abilities that Empedocles claimed included controlling the winds and the weather; extending life indefinitely through knowledge of magical drugs; and fetching a dead man's vital soul back from the underworld. Resurrection or life after death is represented in the Tarot by the eight post-Death Trionfi. *Association with Immortality is the seed function of the Tarot.* However, as pointed out in chapter 4, Tarot images were not purposed toward an occult practice of manipulating spirits in and out of icons, bodies, or environments. Nor were they specifically designed to portray a drug-based, psychotropic, astral trip. (Readers interested in how such a pack of Tarot images might appear are referred to the Aleister Crowley Thoth deck.) Nor were they ever meant to give an animistic magician ability to command forces of nature. Traditionally in fortune-telling, naming a force influencing one's life was largely purposed toward having control over that force or demon. Techniques of manipulating psychic and natural forces, or what is commonly called "magic," may make use of knowledge embedded in the Tarot, but the Trionfi did not themselves arise from or rely upon in any way the knowledge, schools, or methods of such magical manipulation.

In contrast, Empedocles' oracular teachings supposedly enabled such magical control. The pre-rational magic of Empedocles' mystery sect, however, ultimately matured through the centuries into trans-rational gnosis. Thracian *Orphic* tradition (introduced below and elaborated in chapter 7) underlying Pythagoreanism was intimately connected to Central Asian shamanism. Just as such shamanism matured into Buddhism and Taoism, so did Pythagoreanism mature into Neoplatonism.

If the Tarot was not in fact originally purposed toward *magical control* of fate and fortune, then what *was* its purpose? Quite simply, *knowledge* and *wisdom* of fate and fortune oriented toward *realization of immortality.* The Tarot is a tool abetting *tantric consciousness* through *spiritual resonance.* It addresses development of human beings and relationships in the context of *body-mind integration.* It represents a quest for spiritual identity that proceeds via *alchemical union of essential polarities.* When genuinely contemplated, its Triumphant ten-stage procession actualizes a *transformative awareness of Eros* via integral imagery, symbols, and meanings. For women of modern times, and here we include ladies of the Renaissance courts, the Tarot has perennially presented a most effective path for integrating *yang* or *brightly male* knowledge into their *yin* or *mysteriously female* spirituality.

Given the right playing method, a mature player or reader of the Tarot is able to tap the creative power of Eros by attuning to the

Triumphs' resonant forces and synchronicities as they are applied to Fate and Fortune. That attunement is not *controlling*, but rather *informing*. If multiple people concentrate on a Tarot spread together, their resonance with the wisdom gestalts of immortal archetypes will affect their fates and fortunes. Such concentration on spiritual presence should be taken seriously, even if playfully. This is *modulated* and therein *magnified* via actual *cultivation of yoga and alchemy*, both individually and socially. It is in fact *blocked* through psychic manipulation and occult intentionality not founded upon genuine nondual awareness.

The primary meanings of the Trionfi are embedded in their Names and Hierarchy. For this reason, the more than two thousand Tarot decks designed in modern times can display radically differing images, yet still be recognizable as Tarot cards. However, it is in the psychophysical yogic representation of human energetics that the images' practical power can be magnified and conveyed. As examined in the previous chapter, Islam and Judaism have traditionally outlawed attempts to image That which is Immortal other than through sacred geometry. However, Christianity inherited Greek arts and knowledge regarding iconography as it can be applied to representing universally personified immortal principles. Through insight into the process of cosmic development and spiritual hierarchy, laws of heaven, earth, and man become clarified and may be artistically modeled.

Science makes great use of modeling and conceptual imaging. Modeling essential laws so as to enable manipulation of biological, social, and environmental patterns on a global and pervasive level in an attempt to *imitate* God is, however, likely to be disastrously shortsighted and presumptuous. Psychological and scientific arrogance may enable actions under ill-defined justifications of *progress* that violate natural law. Meaning "to walk or go forward," progress is best kept to a grounded pace and socially and environmentally responsible path.

History nevertheless shows that humans are purposed to psychophysically realize conscious unity with their Gaian environment. That process is abetted by the modeling of universal principles and laws immortally governing the world. Modeling, inventing, and implementing technology certainly has the potential to abet this. There are new heights that the Tarot itself can be taken to via technology. Such technology may be called *holistic* and *appropriate,* even if not immortal and eternal. Tarot Triumphs contain within their most basic design exemplar forms of what might be called *timeless technology:* e.g., *wheel, coin, cup, batting-stick, throne, sword, balance,* etc.

Evolved conscious realization occurs more through nondual intimacy than subject-object manipulation. Every integrative and healing function of magehood technically requires application and regulation involving, yet transcending, manipulative activity. Nonetheless, realization of wisdom and compassion is a matter of whole-body enlightenment. Thus, alchemical unions of polar identities (including self and other, mind and body, man and woman, heaven and earth) are of more import to Questors and any application of the Tarot than temporary manipulations and partial modifications of varying parts of any system.

Learning the laws of Eros through compassionate tantra and yogic alchemy composes a Quest that reaches far beyond any journey limited to oneself. This necessitates physical, emotional, mental, psychic, subtle, and *causal* (or essentially *heartful*) direction. By *becoming* the Trionfi, Questors realize states of greater being, consciousness, and bliss. Although this naturally involves regulating and channeling life-force, Questors work and play with Fate, Death, and all other attributes of the Kosmos without deluding themselves that they are in "control" of them. In all cases, the essential nature of Brightness or Time rules the world. The creative, vital life of Eros, being immortal and prior to Death, causes cosmic laws of alchemy to manifest stages of internal and external development: *birth, growth, integration, separation, change, decay,* and *consciousness.*

That said, we return to our theurgist. Born in Sicily around 500 B.C., Empedocles became most famous for his theory of four elements, which he identified with four primary gods:

> Hear first the four roots of all things: Dazzling Zeus,
> life-bearing Hera, Aidoneus, and Nestis
> who moistens the springs of mortals with her tears.

Zeus, god of heaven, was the personification of *air.* His wife Hera was that of *earth.* Nestis was a Sicilian cult name for Persephone, goddess of *water.* Aidoneus was a poetic name for Hades, the god-state of *fire.* Empedocles identified the constituent *processes* of the cosmos with two pairs of married gods. (Persephone, daughter of Demeter, was stolen away into the Underworld by Hades.) These immortal couples were then posited as literally *constituting* the Kosmos. The always-changing world was identified with elemental gods in tantric polarity. By establishing this cosmology, Empedocles transformed Greek mythology into a vehicle for quasi-empirical study of the world.

For Empedocles, the elements were divinely mythic in nature. Each cosmic force or principle manifested as one of four *separate* and *immutable* constituencies of the cosmos. Air was not only the air we breathe, but also the *aether,* which included all of space reaching into the heavens. The essence of this element was of such a pure nature as to be identified with the supreme god, Zeus. Aether's alchemical marriage to Earth involved far more than a philosophical mixing of "airy" and "earthy" elements. It was the very alchemy of all life and being on a grand, mythological level of God and Goddess.

Comparing this to the Chinese concept of *Yang* and *Yin, Bright* and *Veiled,* we note that Empedocles' cosmology conspicuously lacks a unifying Way or Tao. His polarities do not suggest a common Source or Unity integrating the elements, emptiness, chaos, and the *mathematical* harmony of *every-thing.* His Pythagorean world-view posited a complex, immortal dualism that when conjoined with Chaldean systems of cosmology produced many branches of *occult science*. Schools championing such dualistic beliefs continue mushrooming to this day.

Relevant to our study of Tarot hierarchy is Empedocles' second set of dualistic principles: Hades/Fire and Persephone/Water. His identification of the underworld with fire was accepted by few of his Greek philosopher-sage peers. Even more questioned was Empedocles' Sicilian conviction that only through a terrible sacrifice into the volcanic alchemy of the Underworld could man be reborn with a divine nature. Confusion regarding the essential elements of the world and their respective god-principles reigned throughout the history of Indo-European mythic-stage thinkers. Although detailing the complex arguments surrounding them would take us beyond the scope of this book, a few observations are in order.

Pythagorean belief that unchanging, absolute polarities composed cosmic totality lent itself to a type of dialectical analysis. The academy following Pythagoras and Empedocles laid the groundwork for logistical methods that philosophies of modern science developed two millennia later. We contrast this with the foundation of nondual cosmology established in Empedocles' time by Heraclitus. While often described as mystical, Heraclitus viewed himself as being rigorously empirical in his observations of the world. Through intuitive witnessing of reality, his dialectic was subsumed in and as a methodical awareness of Unity. That too formed a working scientific method and was championed by leading Sufis during the prime developmental years of Islamic science. It is also proving to be a method radically suited to twenty-first-century scientific advancement, whereby *whole systems* are *harmoniously gestated, nurtured, and modified*.

Heraclitus's worldview of cosmic alchemy holds similarity to that of early Taoists. In Taoist alchemy the *house of fire* (area of the chest) may be identified with a human's *heavenly soul*. Likewise, the *house of water* (area of the abdomen) may be identified with a human's *earthly soul*. Internal alchemy is a matter of unifying fire's essential nature with water's vital life. That process makes one aware that the elements and souls are fundamentally *nondual in the Tao*. Taoist theories incorporating *five elements* (*earth, metal, water, wood,* and *fire*) and *eight trigrams* (the *Ba Gua* as contained in the *I Ching* or "Book of Changes," China's ancient divinatory system) posit a *transformative* and *unified* cosmos.

Early Greek philosophers generally supposed that after the genesis of aether, fire was created. Empedocles developed a complex mythology to explain how it was that fire, which in his thought was native to the realm deep under earth, was overwhelmingly present in the sky as the Sun. Sicily, an island of volcanoes, was a hotbed of beliefs oriented around divine fire conjoined with ancient chthonic rites found in the earthy sects of Demeter and her daughter Persephone. This combination influenced, and was in turn influenced by, Orphic mysticism. In Orphic Pythagoreanism an initiate would enter the underworld in order to reemerge in a state divinized through his relationship with Hades. This theme was prominent in Mesopotamian myths and was likely imported to Southern Italy by Phoenicians. The ancient myth of goddess *Inanna* and her mortal husband who was sacrificed to the underworld was widespread and influential throughout Mesopotamia and beyond.

Persia served as an important intermediator through which Mesopotamian rituals enabling contact with the underworld were merged with magic-based Central Asiatic shamanism. Zoroastrian magi were reputed, through certain spells and rituals, to be able to open the gates of Hades and "take down safely whomever they wanted." Syncretic practices of Persian magic were transmitted to the Greeks who reworked them into Thracian Orphic and Sicilian Pythagorean traditions, which otherwise drew upon resurrection rituals involving *goddess-empowered fire* well established in the *Eleusian Mystery* cults of Demeter and Dionysus.

Many medieval alchemists attempted to fathom the depths of psychophysical reality via the furnace of hell. These occultists pursued ritualized Pythagorean and Gnostic convictions based upon a fanatical presumption that both cosmic and spiritual *descent* was primarily marked by underworld fire, into which the rivers of mysticism and generative potency (element of water) flowed. *Fanatical* (originally connoting "orgiastic rites of a temple") is an appropriate description: Empedocles reportedly died by throwing himself into Hades' supreme temple – an active volcano – in order to realize final immortality. Numerous have been the unwise alchemists who psychologically and/or physically followed his example.

To an alienated, dualistic mind-set, escaping this world may seem to necessitate a return through the *portal* from whence it was created – i.e., *Hell*. Whereas yogic alchemy is based upon *dropping the fire of mind into the water of body*, occult "alchemy" reverses the process, deeming an underworld fire to be the primal essence of our material world, and our bodies' flows into it an inescapable sacrifice necessary for redemption of that divine spark of fire bound within humanity's mind-body prison.

To Pythagoreans, the elements were immutable – they did not transmute one into another like *yin* into *yang*. A process involving water flowing into fire would logically either quench the fire or continuously evaporate the water. In either case, such elemental reaction, although evincing second-stage polarity, does not develop third-stage circulation. Water needs to *transmute* to a fiery form as steam and then transmute back to water to produce alchemical circulation. An "alchemy" where fire and water are eternally distinct can only be sustained if the water *supernaturally* "fuels" the fire from a continuously replenishing source, such as human life fueling Hell. A good description of this is found in the book of Revelations: the apocalyptic vision of a *lake of fire*. Since both water and fire were posited by Empedocles as immutable, absolute, and eternal essences, any Kosmic diminishment of either became unacceptable. This lent an inexplicably magical quality to Pythagorean alchemy, if indeed that is the proper term for it.

Taoist alchemy, to return to our contrasting example, is based upon the internal practice of *unifying heavenly fire with earthly water* – in the process of which steam emerges. Steam arises upward in the direction of fire, then in the process of cooling and condensing eases and transmutes back downward into water. *Authentic alchemy involves transmutation* of fire into water and water into fire (and in its more advanced stages, *sublimated* transmutation of *earth directly into air* and air into earth) via processes of heat transference, evaporation and condensation, and sublimation through circulating, merging, and transmuting elemental essences. This ultimately entails a return of elements to their Original State: the Essential Nature of Unity. We will refer to this again, along with the congealing and purifying alchemy of earth and air, in the next chapter. The first six stages of cosmological procession represented by the pre-Death Tarot images will then be identified with traditional alchemy, both East and West.

Identifying a heaven/earth polarity with *immortals above* and a fire/water polarity with *immortals below,* Pythagoreans and later occultists based their magic upon a dualistic, intentionally concealed, negative association of humankind's *mainstream elemental processes* with an Underworld mythos focused upon cosmic *capture-and-sacrifice.* Following upon this, it was believed that descending into the terrifying, fiery domain of the underworld was a necessary precursor to ascending into an ecstatic, radiant realm of heaven and earthly paradise.

One might see in this similarity with Lao Tzu's Taoist alchemical view that "to go high, first go low." Philosophical aphorisms contained within the *Tao Te Ching* were approximately contemporaneous with Pythagorean religious teachings. However, one will not find a morally biased, emotionally dramatic, cosmic judgment in that Taoist fundamental of alchemical guidance. Furthermore, in Taoist philosophy and alchemy, low and high are *essentially unified* – from that realization emerge the principles of immortality.

During the early Christian era, Hermetic wisdom positing an isomorphism of *that which is below* with *that which is above* was rejected by Neopythagoreans and Gnostics. For them, that which was *really* below was Tartarus as jailhouse of Zeus warded over by Hades. Pythagoreans believed that it was to there that Zeus had banished his enemies the Titans. This myth stemmed from the ancient Babylonian myth of Marduk, who had bound gods into an underworld prison. The Jewish *Book of Enoch* contains an account of fallen angels being bound and imprisoned in a similar way. This too stemmed from Babylonian tradition, which formatively affected early Judaism.

In the occultist worldview, Hades' realm is utterly dissimilar to Zeus's realm. The two form a fundamental, eternal polarity demarking Evil and Good, Fallen and Raised. By identifying Tartarus with Fire, Empedocles lent the *gross aspects* of fire a type of divine empowerment on the order of Zeus's ineffably subtle Aether. Through his worldview, however, Tartarus became involved not with the blessedly unified, but with the terribly alienated. Fire's companion, Water, was deemed the sexual lifeblood of Fire. *Ritualistic sacrifice* to Underworld power through *secret sexual rites* remains one of the more compelling aspects of this mystery school.

According to Homer and Hesiod – the original purveyors of Greek theogony – Hades' realm was a dark and *damp*, chthonic underworld. Popular belief identified it with underground caves; a place in which water pooled and ghosts abided. Tartarus was another realm altogether. It was *"as far below Hades as Hades is below celestial Heaven."* The element of fire, which Heraclitus thought to represent the original elemental nature of the cosmos, was not associated with either. Instead, it was identified with the Sun (light and heat) and the *creative power of lightning.* Fire belonged to Zeus. From its *mutations,* all of the other elements came into being. Hades the god wore a *cap of invisibility* that allowed him to *roam under the Moon,* assisting or intervening into Zeus's world of earthly inhabitants as he saw fit. This was later given to Hermes, allowing him to traverse a portal to the underworld in his capacity as divine messenger.

It was this version of Hades or the Devil that made its way into Hermeticism, Sufi theosophy, and the Tarot. Just as the Moon intermediates between Aether and Earth for Immortals, so does the Devil intermediate between the Afterworld and Earth for Humankind. That Afterworld cannot be *avoided* or *passed over* in the course of a human soul's transformation from one embodiment to another or into immortal realization. Every human soul is destined to spiritually egress beyond the six spheres of *earthbound* cosmos *apparently* ruled by Death and warded by the Devil. Most souls will enter the Afterworld only upon death of their sentient forms. However, as we will discover in chapter 7, great Shamans, Heroes, and Saints may *pass Death and the Devil by in their lifetime.* The *Principles of Immortality* inherently address *how* this great process works.

In Greek mythology, the Underworld was manifested before the cyclic worlds of humans or procession of immortals (even immortals have processes beyond death). The realms of Hades and his water brother Poseidon were originally extensions of Chaos and Tartarus, Gaia's womb. Their domains represented the chaotic potential underlying all manifestation. They were brothers to the supreme fire god, Zeus. In their generative potency they were an outcome of Eros and ultimately united in their principles.

Between the development of Olympian mythology and that of earlier primal myths of creation (involving Chaos, Tartarus, Gaia, and Eros), Greek myths composed a cosmology of archetypal Titans. *Ouranos* (*Uranus*), husband and son of Gaia and father of the Titans, was deemed the *original creator* of the cosmos. He was slain by his son *Kronos* (*Saturn*) through the severing of his chaotically generative power. His sexual member was cut off and thrown back into the ocean, creating Aphrodite – a humanized manifestation of Eros. We see her represented in the Tarot by the erotic purity and concentrated essence of the Star and Moon. (While the Star and Moon

Triumphs shown in this book do not focus on goddess imagery, the Metropolitan images radiate a natural, naked sensuality that speaks of the same.) Kronos was in turn slain by his son Zeus, who led a battle against the Titans, who represented an older, Gaian and agricultural-based first-stage set of myths. The Titans were then psychoculturally banished forever to Tartarus. Tartarus may in this context be associated with humanity's archetypal feminine unconscious, in and through which the Empress and Popess initiate a way of ancient and still universal core identity.

Greek myths, of course, changed in time and place. Rules were broken, laws invented, relationships transformed; new gods were created, old myths reworked, and many myths allowed to become obsolete. It is important to recognize that primary mythic relationships formed foundations for competing schools of rational philosophy and spiritual tradition.

Most Greeks after Aristotle recognized Tartarus as the "guardhouse" of Zeus. It did not ward a terrible prison, but rather guarded the Sacred Center of the Kosmos. The medieval Tarot's Devil incorporated this concept of *guardian*. The Tarot's Tower originally represented both House of God and House of Devil, for Zeus and Hades were brothers. The Tower bridges the worlds of humans and gods through a transformative power of sacrificial fire – the most potent form of which is the Lightning-bolt. *Heaven-bound fire signifies the true way of sacrificial empowerment.*

Influenced by spiritualists obsessed with sacrificial scapegoating rituals and Babylonian heaven/hell dualisms, the Tower became identified with an occult, Judeo-Christian interpretation of a *fallen House of Babel.* Babel is short for Babylon, a cosmopolitan city where much of Judaic culture and religion was formed. In the Old Testament, it was demonized as the center of polytheistic worship and knowledge. Construction of its heaven-reaching tower was arrested when the builders became unable to understand one another's language. While this may sound quite plausible on several layers of meaning, its Triumphant signification as an immortal archetype lies with its success, not failure. The Tarot's Tower of knowledge is marked and blessed by Divine Fire – the Sun and Lightning. As in many of the Triumphs, the Metropolitan's Tower appears true to this essential meaning of the station. It does not show a collapsing building or people being flung off of it (in many decks the latter is depicted as an alchemical couple; this too has positive connotations in terms of tantric completion). Instead, the Tower's sacrificial pyre brilliantly and directly reaches up to the Sun. Triumphs depicting a Tower with a "spine" of fire running down it (evoking a yogic build-up and release of both spinal and lingam Shakti) may be interpreted in a proper context of transformational chaos and change cycling into a continuous rebuilding of generative potency.

Ibn ʿArabi gave the Tower's station a status of Preciously Valued. It signifies a stage of mindfully divine potential and genuine self-sacrifice. Its potency is regenerated under the Nourishment of the Star, Empowerment of the Moon, and inscrutably Subtle Observation of the Sun. As guardian-demon and guardhouse to the divine, Devil and Tower respectively serve the Deathless realms in general. They do not function as jailers of some evil aspect of the divine; nor as malevolent, immortal states pitted against the heartful Questor, her Quest, and all cosmic forces that would naturally assist her. Put bluntly, that which is abased by the Degrader is that which *pretends* to the Deathless even while being self-centered, self-serving, and self-inflated. All of which is absolutely Just. (Compare to modern myths of ancient dragon-lords guarding their treasure troves and secrets of immortality.)

Tartarus, being the realm furthest below earth, was originally imagined as the center of the cosmos; for all realms above Earth revolved around it. In this way, it was the sacred womb of Gaia. However, the concept of Tartarus as a flaming center of the universe purposed toward the containment of evil fit in well with Gnostic Christian dualism regarding heaven and *hell* (from the old Germanic word for "underworld"). Early on in Christian cosmology, Hell, Hellfire, and Satan became universally accepted dogmas. Thus, a demonic image of the Devil as a fiery, hellish prison-keeper with demiurgical power fed the imagination of Gnostics and later Christians. Jesus apparently did not hold this view. Witness the story of his high, ethereal, desert-dry temptation by a Satan doing no more than truly testing his realization of Transcendence. A very similar story is told of Mara and the Buddha. The Metropolitan Tarot's Devil, based as it was upon Oriental awareness of the divine role played by an archetypal Guardian Daimon, was understandably imaged differently than later-drawn Christian-occult Kings of Hell. Chapter 7 explores the history of Satan in detail. As with Death, realization of the Devil's station in the Arcana is pivotal to understanding the esoteric truths of the Tarot.

Platonists did not care for Empedocles' negative classification of Tartarus. As mentioned, they held that the "jailhouse of Hades" was actually the "guardhouse of Zeus." They reasoned that the Center of the Kosmos must certainly be a realm most profound: the Womb of the World. From this came the creation of the universe, including all energy, light, and fire; including, in other words, the heavens themselves. Even though ancient myths of Darkness telling of creation through Eros, Chaos, Gaia, and Tartarus had been replaced by the Bright myths of Sky-god Zeus, initiated Platonists still engaged and respected the fertile Mysteries of goddess-consciousness.

By the time of Plotinus and later Neoplatonists, an actualizing cosmological hierarchy had developed that completely replaced the top/down, good-to-bad, heaven/hell, terrible descent and elite ascent, dualistic cosmology of the previous Chaldean-influenced millennium. These were two very different worldviews; two very different esoteric currents; two very different developments of conscious spirituality through magic, mythic, and rational stages.

The Tarot has at its origins a foundational Hermetic and Neoplatonic nondual understanding of cosmology and spirituality. This was reinterpreted in accordance with occult, dualistic beliefs shackled to a desire to control demonic unconscious forces while seducing erotic forces of good fortune. Seduction, eroticism, and daimons take their rightful place in the Tarot in a context of *conscious tantra* and intimate awareness of *present synchronicity.* Eros is truly *creative* when it is innocently, openly, and simply *present.*

Hermetic and Neoplatonic origins of the Tarot can be traced back to the *cosmological wisdom of Heraclitus.*

> *Immortals are mortals, mortals immortals,* these living the death of those, those dead in the life of these . . .
>
> . . . in his presence, they arise and become wakeful guardians of living people and corpses.
>
> And Thunderbolt steers the totality of things.

These fragments of Heraclitus's wisdom, which make for a good synopsis of the Angel Triumph, come by way of Hippolytus, via his *Refutation of All Heresies.* Over a hundred such remnants of Heraclitus's sayings remain extant, giving us a fragmented yet in-depth view of this paradoxical sage.

Heraclitus lived a generation before Empedocles. He dwelled in one of the wealthiest and most cosmopolitan cities of Asia Minor, Ephesus. At the time, Ephesus was under Persian rule. Unlike many well-known philosophers in classical Greece, Heraclitus abstained from politics. His rational faculties were honed sharp and he did not suffer fools, be they priests, governors, or commoners. He applied his insight not toward magical, mythic, or civil patterns but toward understanding the unity of all being and becoming. Stating essential paradoxes as elegantly as possible, he acquired a nickname: *The Obscure.*

Heraclitus did not think much of reincarnation (a popular belief at the time, embraced by Pythagoreans) nor did he view the *psyche* as existing separate from the body. Rather, he understood life, death, and immortality as a continuum of *flux,* not unlike his contemporary in India – Gautama the Awakened. The microcosm of self-existence was felt to be isomorphic with the macrocosm of universal existence. Earth Nature was one with Sky Deity presence.

Psyche was understood by Heraclitus as a *principle* that included rationality and all order of *beingness* just as it included change and thereby disorder of *processional flux*. Heraclitus held to the paradox that *self* both existed and did not exist; body and soul were marked by both absolute and temporal principles. Ancestors were alive through the presently living, just as humans existed in a state of prior death, but were simply unaware of it. To become aware of this was to know the Deathless and identify with immortal principles. This could be done through direct insight into the Life of Psyche beyond magical rituals, mythical revelations, and rational logic.

The word *immortal* in Greek meant "deathless"; *eternal* meant "timeless." Heroes and sages whose destiny it was to cross into the realm of the Deathless became *daimons*, Greek for "divine powers." *Immortal Heroes transcendentally embodied an ancestral realm for the benefit of beings both living and dead.* Hesiod had stated that thirty thousand of the *golden race* were transformed upon death into daimons by Zeus to become *guardians of mortal men*. Heraclitus knew that the body is far more than it appears to be. That is, *the body is also the psyche*. In fact, the psyche is prior to and greater than its *transmutation* as a body.

Heraclitus may have been the first European sage (if we include Asia Minor as part of Europe) to state that there exists a *hierarchy* of Unity (what would later be known as *emanated spheres*) or of, as he called it, the *One Thing*. We find in his thought a core of nondual pantheism. Heraclitus developed the ancient Indo-European awareness that *all things are full of gods* into a view that the *Myriad of things is conscious*. Psyche as the Myriad is in truth the One; so too is the One Way or Thing marked by *Intelligent Awareness* – the early Greek understanding of *consciousness*.

Heraclitus clearly posited a holistic world: every body is both a unity subsuming diversity and one of myriad wholes subsumed ultimately by the Unity of the Kosmos. The polarity of consonance or harmonious functioning and dissonance or fragmented functioning is *outshined* by a fundamental, underlying harmony and unity of the whole universe. That One Thing is a unity that includes all multiplicity. Understood properly, the Strife of dissonance is not the fundamental force of the myriad; rather, the radiant fire of divine Love or Eros is. Heraclitus's understanding was implicit in Plato's *Good* and Plotinus's *One*.

Heraclitus introduced to Persian and Greek wisdom traditions an enlightened realization regarding the cosmos as an ordered system whose Law is *greater* than human law, yet in no way *separate* from it. Thus, *Diké* (daughter of Zeus – the Kosmic principle of Unity – and *Way of Justice*) rules the cosmos in a way perceivable by humans, even if only inscrutably so. Her Law is discernible, but only by those who have transmuted their body-psyche (i.e., whole psychophysical self) via a return to the divine Aether. Such is radiant realization of Sophia or Wisdom via knowledge of Eros. This is the original and true purpose of philosophy.

Like Lao Tzu (or the sages who composed the *Tao Te Ching*), Heraclitus wrote in a way that is readily interpreted by esoteric practitioners as pointing to yogic or psychophysical alchemy, transmuting gross elements of mortal, bodily nature into the ineffable essence of immortal flux. *Aether, the most sublime state of divine fire* called *Zeus* (the root of which means "God"), was marked not by the *heat* of *passion*, but rather by *brightness* and *intense spontaneity*. The Kosmically Lawful *causal force of lightning* embodied as a swift, double-edged sword called Justice served Diké as a means of keeping the world upon the Way of Truth.

The divine fire of Aether was above even the fire of the Sun. Nothing escaped, hid, or separated from this omnipresent, omniscient, primal, and encompassing principle. Zeus, in large part as Diké, was the One uniting Chaos and Eros beyond the domain of the Sun, and *"was the only name Aether would take."* Aether was like the Sun, however, in that from Homer's time the Sun was understood to be all-seeing and thus was invoked as a divine witnesser of oaths. The Metropolitan's Sun card images this well. Ibn ʿArabi called this Image-Exemplar the *Minute Observer.*

Unlike the Sun, which during the night was present only through the Moon and the Stars, Justice *never set.* Thus, She was the highest state of the Aether called Zeus. She saw to it that the Sun-principle did not overstep its measures. The Sun as observer of all life was kept true in His brilliant communion with the sentient world, for Justice's ministers, the *Furies,* would otherwise *"find him out."*

The Angel card of the Tarot, commonly known as Judgment, represents a Sufi and Christian Hermetic version of the Furies. The transcendental force needed to resurrect the dead, rectify evil, and realize the True Way (Diké, Tao, Dharma, Law, Heart) of the World was envisioned as a blast of the fiery Seraphim, Angelic Furies of Justice. With this in mind, it becomes clear that the *Balance of Justice* represented *Infinity* rather than any "zero point of the scale." Certainly, no mortal ruler or prophet can serve as the fulcrum of such Kosmic Balance, unless that human is in truth an immortal, merciful angelic incarnation of Goddess-God Unity. This is the concept that the great Sufi saints that were introduced in chapter 3 realized, with varying focuses on the gender-based attributes of Allah.

Of course, Christians understand Jesus to be the Son of God, much as Diké was known as the Daughter of God. In fact, for Roman Catholics discovering the Tarot, acknowledging the Goddess as higher than the Angel of Judgment, identified with the Second Coming of Christ, might reasonably be difficult. Unless, perhaps, She represents the Church herself, as the Book of Revelations might be interpreted. On the far side of this thought, one might imagine a Neo-Catholicism in which the Goddess is Raised once more, beyond Virgin Mother cults and the Roman hierarchies. A crucial twenty-first-century consideration for religious leaders: *How important is True Justice?*

The Sun as agent of Zeus assists in constantly rejuvenating the cosmos. For Homer, to *see the rays of the Sun* was to *be filled with Life.* The equation between light and life was incorporated into the Sufi name for the Hermit's station or attribute of Allah – the Living. When Diogenes, Greece's ascetic Patriarch of Cynics, walked around naked in broad daylight with his lantern, he was testing who might see such rays, for only they would be on the path of Virtue and thereby deserving to be called *truly alive.*

Virtue as *human excellence* is represented by the Hermit as *prudent guide* and *provider of life. Prudent* comes from the word *provide* – *pro-,* "forward," and *videre,* "to see." The quality of a Hermit's insight into how the Wheel of Fortune and Nature cycles forward can be intuited from important derivatives of *weid-,* the Indo-European root of *videre: guide, wise, wisdom, guise, Hades, wit, view, visa, vision, advice, clairvoyance, evident, provide, review, supervise, survey, idea, history, story.*

The virtues suggested by Plato (later to be deemed *cardinal* or *pivotal*) – Temperance, Fortitude, Prudence, and Justice – are arranged hierarchically in the Tarot. According to Plato, the first three relate to one's *psyche:* moderation or Temperance is the virtue that orders the lower appetites and physical desires of the psyche, including those of Lovers; courage or Fortitude is the soldiering, steadfast virtue of the morally upright psyche that is represented so well in the Chariot; wisdom or prudence is the yet higher virtue of the intellectual aspect of psyche as portrayed in the Wheel's and Hermit's insight of gnosis or Emptiness. *These virtues culminate in a Unity of Justice,* which links Psyche with all else, for the three hierarchical classes of virtue and psyche are not *self-sufficient* – they are surrounded by the all-inclusive Law of Justice.

While the bright sky stood traditionally for life, Heraclitus identified the finest state of psychophysical reality with an intensely bright flash or ray of light. His awareness of sacred realization was intensely more present than that of later Gnostics who identified divine spirit with a "spark of the soul." Heraclitus held to a *feeling-identification* of bodily being with Psyche, for as the Great Tradition's yogis, saints, and sages have attested, divine realization is a matter of the *whole* psychophysical-heartful self. Dualistic separation of body and mind drains vital life and avoids essential nature intrinsic to heartful enlightenment.

Earthbound sacrifices such as those found in the ancient sects of Demeter and Dionysus, ofttimes associated with the fanaticism of intoxicated orgies, were criticized by Heraclitus for their foolish focus on passionately heated forms of fire. Pythagoreans, as revealed through Empedocles, developed these ritualized mysteries of earthbound fire, extending magic-and-myth-based forms of archaic spirituality into a rational age. Heraclitus stated that the way of Dionysus and the way of Hades were inextricably linked like life and death. However, for Heraclitus the *true way of Dionysus was one of radiant ecstasy;* and Hades' afterlife domain was understood as being a *soulful sphere very close to Zeus* – as befits divine and supreme ruling brothers. Their Domains were connected in a way that integrated water and fire principles. Heraclitus's cosmic paradoxical worldview might be compared to the modern cosmological theory that posits an infinite universe whose "edge" paradoxically wraps around into its center like a multidimensional Klein Bottle; or to the concept of a Black Hole galactic center reemerging as a Quasar at the edge of the Universe; or to the "dark void" emerging as "light matter" only to continuously return to the Void through and as a constant cosmic Flux of immeasurable instances.

Heraclitus suggested that human souls' *quality* ranges from the moist *aer* of Hades to the dry *pur* (*fire* as aether/thunderbolt) of Zeus. Although existing in a hierarchy of immortally defined principles, the human soul is not marked by a cosmic duality of good and evil or by a duality of corporeal and incorporeal. Rather, as both matter and light, the One transmutes *as* the temporal world. Thus, Hades' *Realm Beyond Death* – the *Afterlife* – is essentially *One with the Realm of Life,* epitomized by the sexual potency and profound enthusiasm of Dionysus. The Tower Triumph was originally called Arrow or Bolt because its sacrificial release transmutes passions into enlightenment, heat into brilliance. *Building up of potency* is necessary to *attain blessed liberation* in heavenly fire. This crucial "secret" to natural alchemy is highlighted in the following chapter.

Of import here is the observation that internal alchemy stands almost opposite to Neopythagorean theurgy in its methodology of spiritual realization. This was obscured by Neopythagoreans and Gnostics until Plotinus and following Hermeticists clarified precisely how the microcosm of contemplative reality develops in utter likeness to the macrocosm of Nature's hierarchical emanation. New Age "Postmodern Pythagoreans" still view their Orphic-like focus on numerology and idealized harmony as the way of Apollonian purity beyond Dionysus's brotherhood with wandering, warding, creatively destructive Hades and actual engagement with World transformation. They then secretly, in occult fashion, embrace cathartic psychodrama and apocalyptic tragedy with militant and fanatical focus. The outcome of this zealousness is frequently an unforgiving celibacy encased by dogmatic conceit.

Heraclitus, in keeping with the prevalent pre-Socratic *hylozoic* tradition (holding that all "matter has life," which is literally the meaning of the term) described *fire* as *the ever-living,* composing the ordered world as it has been, now is, and will be manifested. Cycles of nature and soul are like tongues of flames: at times alight, at times extinguished, but always present as part of the everlasting Fire.

Again, it is important to note that divine fire was identified with *aether,* a purified form of fire experienced as the Bright. It was viewed as both primal constituent and directive force of the universe. Thus, Heraclitus's statement, *Thunderbolt steers the totality of things.* This force, more intense than the Sun, became identified with the Way of Justice. *May I be struck down by lightning* is an invocation of divine justice that has been carried into modern parlance. The descending and ascending movement of Fire or Creative Change as it progressively transmutes into the more solidified states of Air, Water, and Earth can be observed through the relatively slow and gentle changes between earth and sea; the quick and stormy changes between sea and air (sea-spray, clouds, rain); and the intense, sudden changes between air and fire (exemplified in lightning).

Fire and air manifest sea and earth, which transmute back into air and fire. This alchemy of field-polarities does not presuppose fixed and immutable dualistic elements. Earth and water, water and air, air and fire all *causally* transmute one into the other as a *continuum of flux,* inclusive of the grossest and the subtlest. In Heraclitus's worldview, the One becomes Zeus becomes Aether becomes Fire, the very *principle of change,* in its myriad of transformations. Lacking this insight, ignorant people suppose that the realms and elements are eternally separate. From this ignorance delusions arise; degrading, for instance, fire into the service of base passion, and refusing *sensual compassion* as the natural outcome of a lifelong, Towering sky-bound sacrifice to the Sun. Ignorant of Matter as Universal Flux, Pythagoreans relied upon magical techniques and mythical explanations to address the mixing of elements that were otherwise presumed eternally separate. To Heraclitus, *realization of Unity,* the primary insight marking real wisdom, was clearly lacking in such a fragmented cosmology.

Two hundred years later, Aristotle attempted to bridge Pythagoras's and Heraclitus's opposing worldviews. A propounder of *material* hierarchies in the natural world, the vitally essential insight of *hierarchically nested, transmuting principles and processes* was beyond Aristotle's frame of consciousness. Therefore, he was compelled to address the cosmological conundrum of what cosmic *substance* or force could possibly keep eternally separate elements or principles, unable to interpenetrate or transmute into each other, together to form the universe. We will see in the following chapter that his *unctuous water* or *oil of union* was a materialistic solution that displaced Heraclitus's transcendentally immanent Flux of inherent unity.

The metaphysical ramifications of Aristotle's Platonic academy accepting without question this fundamental doctrine of material bondage were immense. It paved the way for Hellenistic conceptual development of Jesus as *Christ:* the one *anointed* (from Greek *khristos,* meaning "anointed") with *divine oil.* This created a logical basis for theologians to believe in an abstract, unexplained, idealistic material force – Holy Spirit as Unctuous Water – that bonded two fundamentally separate domains or states of reality: divine heaven and mundane earth. Aristotelian physics and natural science were used to philosophically support a dualistic and scientifically unsupportable worldview.

All of the spiritualists, magicians, esotericists, philosophers, and cosmologists addressed in these chapters held this in common: *knowledge* of the world, both inner and outer, leads naturally to *synthesis* and then *utilization* of that knowledge, which inevitably equates into *power.* How information is gathered, knowledge synthesized then utilized, and power implemented varies dramatically in accordance to the principles that people consciously uphold. Will immortality be bestowed? How will the course of fate be influenced? Can the dead be resurrected? Is divine intervention prophesized? The medieval Tarot speaks to us even now in these terms.

The Principles of Immortality light a path to heartful identification of the Way. Through traversing and living that way, Questors may transcend cosmic cycles and realize Deathless Bliss. Through knowledge and cultivation of *alchemy* Questors can succeed in attaining this goal. Let us now turn a page into the history of alchemy, so that we might inquire into concepts of *bondage, communion, and transmutation* inevitably realized along the Liberated Way.

MYSTIFIED PERMANENCE

HANGED MAN

Student for life, the Hanged Man is suspended between Heaven and Earth; initiated into ecstasy through profound conversion, the Questor discovers that which quickens realization is identical to that which transcends all relativity of time.

DEATH

Effortless effort is the sacrifice of self to the Way of the Causal, the world of Vital Essence beyond the chain of causation experienced as the impermanence of all things and relationships.

Returning to the Source

How the Quest becomes Ecstatic . . .

> The first and foremost thing in alchemy is congealing; the uniting of parts that can be liquefied, or the thickening of parts that are liable to be fluid. It is as impossible to lick heaven with one's tongue as it is impossible to enter upon the practice of alchemy other than through the congealing of mercury, of which many are ignorant.

We have come a long way in our quest to understand the Tarot. We have uncovered a wondrous convergence of esoteric traditions culminating in an awareness of spiritual development revealed and celebrated through the agency of twenty-two hierarchical Trionfi. Our explorations began with the Right View of Tarot origins as they were rooted in perennial wisdom.

Application of Tarot principles to a Questor's life necessitates stability through resolve, speech, and actions. Only then will a Questor be prepared for the effort of her life: the Great Alchemical Work. This will require becoming an *initiate* through identification with *gnosis as Living Transparent Emptiness*. The Questor will be made lucidly aware that this goes far beyond any spiritual conceit making claim to the "zero point of the scale." Through initiation, a sweet taste of nectar will suffuse slowly and deeply through the Questor's senses. Such comes with a sublime excitement of knowing that self-realization of wisdom entails ecstatic *communion*. Do not let your ego fear, doubt, or discredit this out of self-obsessed ignorance.

Communion between mind and body is the practical definition of *ecstasy*. Only by feeling heartful depths of her body will the Questor realize that she psychologically needs sensuality to expand her psyche beyond all sense of "self," including physical limitations. This is felt as a soulful longing for ecstasy. It leads to an *out-of-body* experience that does not attempt to escape or avoid physical being. Rather, it embraces, penetrates, and wholly subsumes life's vitality, which naturally arises and begs to be engaged *as mindful spirit*.

In this chapter, Questors will discover the secrets of how to nurture not only the essential purpose of their own ecstatic lives, but also that of their companions. Sheer joy and profound pleasure come from openly revealing ecstatic awareness with a companion mutually embracing the Way. Such alchemy radiates a deeply moving and transformative gnosis. Through this, the Questor will receive a most sublimely exciting affirmation of her path. She must remember, however, that her intentions will not be actualized without a certain necessary, easily devoted *effort*. Long, extended attention upon the object of ultimate desire will need to be sustained. Such must truly be an *effort of love*. Only *that* will cause the spiritual chemistry that can effectively produce freedom, happiness, and liberated bliss.

The *Great Work* is prepared, engaged, and finished using a primal, singular substance. On one hand, that substance catalyzes a deeply heated passion for the Quest and serves like the sap of a tree, flowing as daily sustenance even while standing strong as the tree of life. On the other hand, like a golden root it must be courageously dug up, lovingly held, minutely observed, respected, and consumed to one's utmost empowerment. This must be done with the help of another – one clearly willing to face the five-times-daily rituals of alchemy with a generously attentive disposition.

Above all else, alchemy *surrenders* and *sacrifices* that which is congealed, heated, sublimated, and purified. Drip by drip, the potion of life is repeatedly drawn up and then washed down. This continuous process requires honest awareness in which shame and guilt have no part. Nor can the Quest afford possessive attachment. It will quickly be arrested by control issues. If innocent and occasionally intense pleasures of mercurial transmutation are blocked, dangers may arise, whether simply involving painful lessons or producing complications that may lead to grave harm.

Surpassing all forms of manipulation, attention becomes complete as it focuses upon the whole Cause of true magic.

Be aware, pleasure *will* arise, for Being and Knowledge are *from the start* transformed and realized through Bliss. Thus, guidance in the form of wisdom and compassion must replace all attitudes of selfishness or conceit, aggression or craving. To say the least, this can be very tricky business.

We start where we hope to finish: at the cave of the heart as it is accessed through the midbrain; herein can be discovered the root lode of *Materia Prima*. How does the Questor know where to mine? Just how deep must she go? Will she know the *Stone of Philosophers* when she finds it? Its nature and location are most mysterious. Never has a true Alchemist described its appearance, nor have coordinates ever come near to placing it.

Even still, the Questor will know it when she has struck a vein, for it will quiver with a vibration of primal, kundalini presence, spontaneously guiding her to the Source like a dowser feeling the flow of water before it has seeped to the surface. Thus, we start with that which is seemingly most concealed, yet available to those Questors confident in Beauty and Goodness.

It is crucial to understand how it is that the *appearance* of Primal Matter cannot be described. This is solely for the reason that it can only be viewed from the vantage of the *settled heart*, the *nascent ground of Unity* innate to all. When you are in that space you know it, but the heart that is settled cannot be strategically located. Such is the *Stillpoint* (the Chinese characters of which mean "settled heart") to which the Stone is naturally drawn, gravitating as surely as water down a valley stream.

In its ruddy, bare form, you may spot it protruding out of the blue with an unexpected earthly shape; exposing a *body that is imperfect*

From the start, the two cruxes of material self and spiritual destiny have been charted toward inevitable convergence.

but a *soul that is constant.* It is defined by surface appearances primarily to the degree that it pulses in transformations of flow and flux. It is glimpsed as the root of all ecstasy. A hidden feeling-sensation of tumescent virility and unfurling fecundity will need to be quietly nurtured.

This root feeling-awareness is initially represented in the Tarot by the Empress and Popess. The Questor can rest in sensual potency, knowing that it is the mercurial base upon which vital life, essential nature, and conscious alchemy rely. Note, however, that the magical stone of spiritual realization must carefully be kept under wraps, veiled, and protected so that its soul might grow. Even so, all the while, it is substantially submitted to an ultimately transfiguring alchemy. Exposure to air and light is generally directed with smartly intuitive care, allowing cyclic self-regulation, as the Stone seemingly has a *mind of its own.*

The following is a retelling of a classical story from China during the first century of the Christian era. Alchemical language, techniques, and metaphors were incorporated into Taoist yoga during this formative period. Chinese sources, such as an imperial edict issued in 144 B.C. outlawing the production of counterfeit gold, were the first to mention alchemical procedures.

> A noble gentleman loved the art of alchemy. With the help of a beautiful wife and an assistant from a mage's household, he sequestered himself with the purpose of making gold. This he tried in accordance to the recipes found in *The Great Treasure,* but to no avail. His wife, attentive and silent, one morning watched as he fanned the ashes to heat a retort containing quicksilver. His heart, humbled by his salient lack of success, opened to her presence. She, immediately perceiving this and being beautiful in soul as well as body, said, "I want to try to show you something." Thereupon, to his enraptured fascination, she brought a drug out from a bag and threw just a little upon the retort. It was quickly absorbed, and lo, the contents of the retort

> turned to pure silver. The nobleman, well-intentioned but ignorant of the alchemy beyond his ego's control, was astonished and exclaimed, "Why have you not shown me earlier that you possess such wondrous secrets?" She replied, "In order to properly use this drug, one's heart must first be charged with spirit in a true vision of the Way."

Maintaining the constant heart found intuitively in the wholesome aspects of Nature, the Popess as ally promises success.

The spirit-charge referred to in the above story is called Shakti in the tradition of Tantra. We will be addressing Occidental and Oriental ways of psychophysical-spiritual alchemy in this chapter, all of which employ *tantric* (as mentioned, meaning "extending and stretching upon a loom") practices. *Shakti* is an aspect of the *primal and universal female force* represented throughout the Tarot, from Empress to Justice. As Empress and Popess, her *awakening* represents the alchemical arousal of mercurial potency.

This is sublimated through responsible Tempering of magnetic and chemical opposites intensively engaged through the agencies of Emperor and Pope. Which leads to a mature, intelligent revelation that the Questor naturally gives form to through mutual visions and dreams befalling her and those she Loves. Maturation of responsive potency emerges as an effectively transforming current or charge through the stages of Chariot and Fortitude – Right Speech becomes Right Action.

Initiating it all, however, must be alchemical Right View – the *essential nature and vital life* that composes the Stone of the Philosophers. Congealing and affecting alchemical mercury is the delightful art of the Tarot's first-stage noble women. Holding true to that potency is a critical matter of Right Resolve. The Tarot's second-stage noble men exercise that resolve by lending the alchemy prolonged constitution, thereby embodying a vehicle for its further intensification and evolutionary development instead of expending the women's work in explosions of conflict.

Later, in its realization as that energy which nourishes, heals, and transforms others, *Shakti* takes the attributes of Star and Moon. The

Stationed on the threshold of the Way, from commoners to nobility, all must bear witness to the Emperor's Watchful Authority; so it is that here the Questor must gain approval.

Goddess' transforming presence is felt most essentially through three primary psychophysical *conduits*. Each conduit is connected with a *cauldron* or retort, the combination of which serves to circulate, sublimate, and distill alchemical agents necessary to spiritual development. These agents, regardless of their transmuted states, are always based upon *mercury*, or *vital essence* felt as sensual-sexual-*quicksilver* potency.

We will come to know in this chapter the secret processes of alchemy as experienced through *tantric yoga. These processes have been engaged and authenticated within all of the great traditions.* They are based more upon the *subtle intercourse* of *psyches* than the gross conjoining of bodies, which is not to degrade the importance of physical presence, touch, and yoga. *Let potency build* is the key to emerging through the organic, purely natural hierarchy of Triumphant states.

Before delving into the esoteric yoga of alchemy, we need to review the processes of *external* alchemy as they were practiced up until late medieval times. Alchemists made use of methods employed by artisans, metallurgists, and doctors. The earliest information we have about Western alchemy comes from Greek papyri containing recipes for alloys, imitation jewelry, dyeing, and colormaking. Production of vibrantly splendid colors such as ultramarine for glazes, dyes, and paints was often valued more than production of gold. Techniques of instilling earthen materials with heavenly colors were imbued with great mystery. Metallurgical craftsmen of both East and West were the original inventors of alchemical apparatus. Mircea Eliade's *The Forge and the Crucible* was seminal in bringing this to light.

Use of life-extending and ecstatic drugs was at the root of *psychophysical* alchemical development. The Vedic drug Soma was central to early Indian alchemy, called *Rasayana*. From the Indus to Thrace to Crete, fermentation was also an important process in shamanic, Dionysian rituals of communal alchemy.

Paradoxically, the Pope blesses a world already Purified so that through bright distraction the suffering impure might forget themselves.

The fundamental ideas of alchemy can be traced back to early Greeks partly reviewed in the previous chapter. Heraclitus, in his view that the world comprised continuously transmuting states of fire, maintained that an ascending process of *volatilization* defines all *generation*. Concomitantly, a descending process of *fixation* defines all *decomposition*. Quite differently, Empedocles posited the existence of indestructible atoms from which the Four Elements arise. He thought these were animated by eternal, dual forces: Love and Hatred. If we define alchemy as the natural interaction and *union* of opposites, then it becomes clear that strictly dualistic worldviews do not readily incorporate alchemical processes. We will not attempt to compare here the many Greek theories concerning physics and cosmology. It is enough to mention that by the time Hermeticism became established in Alexandria, a theory of four elements and four humors of the human body had been syncretized with an Oriental idea of constant elemental transmutation. This led to a Hermetic corpus regarding theories and practices of alchemy.

At the end of chapter 5, mention was made of Aristotle's attempt to explain how eternally separate elements could cohere as forms with a fluid ability to transform. He held that:

> Earth has no power of cohesion without the moist. On the contrary, the moist is what holds it together; for it would fall to pieces if the moist were eliminated from it completely.

Given that moisture readily evaporates, Aristotle posited a new type of matter: *unctuous moisture.* This *oily fat* substance had been suggested from pre-Socratic days as that which gives rise to elasticity and hardness. The notion of unctuous cohesion received prominent attention when Greek and Arabian alchemists began extensively disintegrating substances.

This was done through a systematic process of *distillation*. Fractionated distillates of almost every earth- and animal-based matter imaginable were attempted by Islamic alchemists. A three-stage

Balance is lost in the struggle for greater existence when mind is blind to the Greater Cause – for good or bad, now or forever; an awareness is Tempered beyond breaking when That which wholly is, is wholly presupposed.

heating process would inevitably disintegrate a substance into three distinct products. First, a vapor would condense into a *liquid* component. Then, after a stronger heating, colored, unctuous *oil* would be obtained. Finally, after further heating, that moisture too would evaporate, leaving in the alembic a *dry residue.* Thus, Aristotle's theory of two moistures – one easily evaporated, the other serving to bind the powder of matter – was verified.

Jabir ibn Hayyan, known in the West as *Geber,* mastered this process of fractionated distillation. He believed that all materials could be defined by some combination of the four elements. He observed that apart from the three fractions mentioned above, a fourth, inflammable and volatile substance (what is now known as *sal ammoniac*) was also obtained through distillation. This he equated with the element of fire. The liquid fraction was clearly the element of water. The dry residue was obviously the element of earth. Unctuous moisture was equated with the element of *air.* Not air as Aristotle and his school knew it, but as the Stoics knew it through their concept of *pneuma.*

The Stoic view of the Universe was akin to Heraclitus's – an Oriental view that fire and air penetrate water and earth in a true alchemy of unifying cohesion between spirit and matter, mind and body. Stoics held that when elements intermingle *the dynamic wholly penetrates the material;* i.e., air and fire penetrate water and earth. The two *higher* elements have a fine or subtle constituency, while the two *lower* elements have a thick or gross constituency. Substances with subtle parts were deemed *spiritual,* containing *pneuma* (denoting "breath," "wind," "spirit"). That pneuma was thought to produce cohesion in natural bodies.

Aristotle left undeveloped the theory of unctuous moisture. It was revived, developed, and appended to his school's materialistic, atomistic, and reductionistic thought by later spiritual philosophers. The concept evolved after Jesus's time, coming to represent an immanent version of Transcendental Intellect emanating from God to inform matter, thus sustaining the coherency of the world.

In modern terms, Time qualified as Light dynamically sets into motion Space qualified as Matter. In Hellenized Christian thought, heaven becomes earth as Platonic Forms manifest through the Holy Spirit. This can occur fully only via Christ, the One *anointed* with and as *Divine Oil*, informing the material world through *God's Bond*. His Apostles, Saints, and Bishops have been blessed with the mission to spread a Church that will transmute the very substance of human nature, preparing it for a return to Paradise.

For Love to be true, egocentric vision must be dispelled, then soulfully converted, unveiling a world of spirits fundamentally caused through the emanation of the One.

Later Islamic and Christian mystics, including Scotus Eriugena and Albertus Magnus (teacher of Thomas Aquinas), objectified this unctuous element as a *pneumatic psychophysical force* that can be isolated, regulated, heated, circulated, and used in the transmutation of not only metals but, more importantly, the human body. To do so, an alchemical adept channels pneuma and psyche through a series of processes in order to realize an immortal soul via the transformation of his physical body. Body, psyche, and soul merge into Divinity through the unifying process of alchemy.

Western alchemical understanding developed in a manner that closely resembled teachings of Taoist alchemy. Concepts of *qi* and *pneuma*, *cauldrons* and *retorts*, and immortality through integration of Heavenly and Earthly identities or souls are remarkably similar. Before examining this further, a few more words need to be said about Jabir and his alchemical theories, which truly affected the whole of Western alchemical development after him.

Jabir is considered the *father of chemistry*. He was one of Islam's greatest and earliest alchemists. A close friend of the sixth Shiite Imam Jafar al-Sadiq (d. 765), Jabir became a favorite at the court of the Caliph during an era that was memorialized in the stories of *One Thousand and One Arabian Nights*. He has been historically credited for introducing the theory that all metals are composed of mercury and sulphur. This mercury-sulphur combination, whose product in actuality is *mercurial sulphate* or *cinnabar*, became the keystone to all alchemical theory. Cinnabar itself was already known

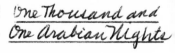

One Thousand and One Arabian Nights

Pride of self-attainment may oppose simple service to Fate's reckoning; however, even the highest cause is charged by others – what is Supreme is graced, not gained.

in the Latin West at Jabir's time, being used by craftsmen to produce *vermilion*.

Jabir was a Patriarch of the Sufi movement before it was formalized. He converted from the spiritually eclectic way of the *Sabeans.* The Sabeans of Harran, a city located a short distance from Edessa (an ancient Mesopotamian city lying in southeastern Turkey) and within the great bend of the Euphrates, were avid Chaldean pagans who had incorporated Far Eastern philosophies. Harran during the last half of the first millennium was famous for its alchemists and astrologers. It was also a trading center of major import.

Sabeans made much of their claim to the revelation of Hermes. Sabean religion was primarily based on a Hellenized version of old Syro-Mesopotamian worship. The Sun, Moon, Saturn, Jupiter, Mars, Venus, and Mercury were believed to be demiurgic assistants to a great creator god. Each of these forces had both a color and a metal associated with it. East and South Asian concepts, including those of Buddhism, Taoism, and Tantra were woven throughout Sabean beliefs. Sabeans were networked into and philosophically drew upon Chinese spiritual systems. Their syncretic alchemical system substituted a rare Chinese metal in place of all-important mercury.

Historical correlations involving Sufism, Buddhism, Central Asia, Western China, alchemy, and tantra are extensive. Ibn ʿArabi was steeped in a twelfth-century version of this East-West metaphysical melting pot. His hierarchy of Image-Exemplars was ultimately depicted via the Tarot through symbols from Mediterranean cultures, but the stations of spirituality they represented had been maturely developed through the great wisdom traditions of the East, including India and Western China.

There existed a belief among Sufi alchemists of Spain during Ibn ʿArabi's era that Hermes (considered to be the father of Greco-Egyptian alchemy) was originally from Western China. He was said to have traveled south through India to Sarandip (the old Persian name of modern-day Sri Lanka, aka Ceylon, from which the English concept of *serendipity* was derived). There he found the Cave of Treasures in Adam's Peak (an almost universally venerated mountain in the middle of Ceylon, upon which Adam and Eve were said to have lived).

Ceylon during the high period of Tantra – between the eighth and twelfth centuries – was home to a blend of Shiva worship and ten-stage Buddhism in which enlightened transcendence was immanently realized. Shiva was known for that awakening power marked by his erect *lingam*, catalyst for all conscious transformation. Modern-day Sri Lanka has lost most of its tantric tradition, except as it is commonly lived amongst the still beautiful and hard-working female culture.

Temporary inspirations charged by fanatical beliefs are derived not from insightful conversation, but rather from electrifying controversy; such motivation inevitably leads to a cycle of Death.

Alchemy was addressed in esoteric Buddhist literature, the main body of which was written during Tantra's peak period. These were the prime centuries of Buddhist-Sufi-Taoist exchange and alchemical development. This marked the epoch of Indo-Chinese and Indo-Tibetan glory out of which arose *Vajrayana*, Buddhism's well-known *diamond vehicle* for obtaining Deathless Reality in this lifetime. A defining feature of Buddhist Tantra found in India, Southeast Asia, Central Asia, Tibet, Mongolia, China, and Japan is spiritual hierarchy supported by yogic rituals building a powerful esoteric world simultaneously within both tantric practitioners themselves and their communal, social domain.

The essential stages of psychophysical development that compose the path of a *Bodhisattva* (an *enlightened realizer* dedicated to *magnifying compassion and wisdom in all the world*) were so clearly delineated in Mahayana and subsequent Vajrayana orders that a surprisingly broad swath of Eastern and Western schools integrated Buddhist teachings: from Sabeans to Nestorian Christians to Taoists to Central Asian and Indian Sufis to Shaivites. For instance, Patanjali's *Yoga Sutra*, the defining treatise on classical Hindu yoga, was clearly influenced by the Buddhism of his day.

In India during this age, Buddhism was rapidly overtaken by *Shaivism* – the *way of Shiva*. The latter was an enormously transfor-

Impoverishing the Soul guarantees a raise in Fortune, for then the Wheel itself transforms in sublimity, from a mundane cycle to a sacred spiral.

mative cultural force that celebrated Eros through rituals of dance, trance, and sustained sensuality. Within its community, women discovered powerful veneration through *yogini* cultivation blessed in the force-field of Goddess Shakti. Adhering to a radical worldview of non-avoidance, Shaivism did not flinch from dealing with the demonic side of social reality, which was encroaching upon Northern India (including modern-day Pakistan and areas into Afghanistan) in the form of warring Arabic armies driven to conquer in the name of Islam.

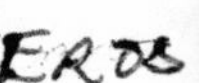

Indian Buddhism by this time had almost totally lost its attraction to women. Male monastic formalities and political machinations had created social rigidities that were unable to cope with the huge changes affecting not only the Subcontinent, but all of Persia, Central Asia, Tibet, Asia Minor, and Southeast Asia in direct association with the country we now call India. For centuries, Buddhism had served as the religious foundation for governing forces in India and much of Asia. However, the second half of the first millennium of our current era was a remarkable time of growth and transformation that necessitated a way of Tantra, weaving together East and West, North and South, Female and Male, Heaven and Earth, Internal and External, Metaphysics and Science.

While Tantric Buddhism formed and thrived outside of India, Tantric Shaivism came to dominate the multicultural territories of the Subcontinent for centuries to come. Buddhism in India lost the support of wealthy aristocrats and finally underwent a complete conversion by re-incorporating the ancient ways of both Shiva and Dionysus. "Shaivite Buddhism" flourished throughout Southeast Asian countries (e.g., Angkor in Cambodia and Borobudur in Java) via imperial support, fertile artistic cultivation, and an infusion of female sensuality. A type of "Dionysian Buddhism" occurred through a merging with the cultural milieu of Central Asian Shamanism extending south into Asia Minor and Greece.

When the Tarot first appeared in Italy, Northern Indian Shaivism was merging with Sufism via the realizations and teachings of Kabir and later Sikh and Sufi Saints. This produced some of the most erotic and sensual devotional art and poetry that the world has ever known. Underlying this movement was the way of the *Sants* and *Siddhas* – powerful yogic sages who broke from Hindu and Muslim religious formalities, institutions, and strictures, embracing a way of *utter liberation* and *direct realization* of the stages of Deathless Life. Radical Truth-oriented Sants realized the futility of sectarian allegiance and dualistic asceticism.

Nothing is closer to Death than the fullness of Life, for in that Life stands a plethora of ancestors, the outcome of all Death.

Some modern-day occultists picture a wild culture of Gypsies in this epoch and with them an imagined origin to the mystical system of the Tarot. While it will now be obvious to the reader that the Triumphs did not directly arise out of secret or provincial societies in India, the tantric culture that originally spread from what may be called Shaivite Buddhism passed through India into Central Asia and was reworked via worldviews of Neoplatonic philosophy and Persian culture by Sufi communities. Tantra as sacred alchemy ultimately found a new home amongst the Oriental-influenced Europeans of Constantinople, Venice, Alexandria and ports in-between.

Central Asian territories followed the teachings of Buddha and *Zarathustra* (founder of Zoroastrianism and contemporary of Heraclitus and Gautama) until they fell to Islam during the eighth century. This brought Arabian armies to the border of the Chinese Empire. The once famous city of Tashkent was the last to fall to the Muslims. To obtain it, they had to fight a disastrous battle with Chinese forces led by a Korean general. The outcome arrested any further movement into Western China. Trade and artisan connections were then established. Many freed Chinese prisoners, including those versed in alchemical practices, relocated to Baghdad and other Arabian cities.

Before this time, Iranian families of merchants, scholars, and rulers ousted from Persia by Muslim forces had been granted asylum at the Chinese imperial court. Persian and Arabic intercourse with the Chinese progressively intensified up to the era of the great Mongol

Life is bestowed in eight-year increments, with each passing increment quickening the revelation of temporal cycles; the Hanged Man reverses the dying process, quickening instead the unveiling of immortal principles.

khanates. The Khans made Persian the official language of Asia. This was during the thirteenth and fourteenth centuries, following the age of Tantra and emergence of emanationist Sufi and Kabbalist schools. It marked the beginning of a psychological or vision-logic age coinciding with development of the Tarot's Image-Exemplars. It is not coincidental that much of the Sufi movement was generated by Persian masters, and that Sufism is deeply similar to Buddhist Taoism, from its philosophy and alchemy to its yoga and dance.

During the Tang dynasty (seventh to tenth centuries), Chinese literature tells of the *Hu* merchants, or Persian and Arabian traders. What is of interest to our study is that these merchants were often involved with assisting Taoist alchemists. For instance, Hu apothecaries were important suppliers of hard-to-obtain longevity drugs. Evidence points to strong crosscurrents of alchemical practice and knowledge tying the Hellenistic world of Byzantium to the Taoist world of Tang courts. The communities bridging these cultures were located around the Tarim Basin and in Western Central Asia. They included the great cities of Ferghana, Tashkent, Bukhara, Samarkand, and Balkh (birthplace of Zarathustra). Khorasan, in Persia, lay on the western end of this Central Asian channel into lands east. It is from this area that Jabirian alchemy developed in the eighth and ninth centuries.

Islamic merchants stringing together these pearls of the Silk Road were oriented toward practices of Persian Sufism; tantric, Taoist forms of Buddhism were a continuous influence. Intellectuals from these cities became Islam's greatest scientists – originators of modern algebra, geography, medicine, astronomy, and chemistry.

Byzantium was associated with these Islamic schools of thought. Sufi merchants moving merchandise through their far-reaching networks used old Byzantine cities such as Damascus and Alexandria as primary trading depots. As mentioned, Harran was a main center involved with spreading Far Eastern concepts of alchemy amongst Near Eastern Syrian and Arabian schools.

Death moves in one incessant direction: the way to the Deathless; the Questor's life will always be sacrificed in this movement, for all time and space consistently regenerate through the Stillpoint of transcendence.

Christian Syrians, we recall, were at the forefront of translating Greek works during the middle of the millennium. By A.D. 1000, Syrian-based crypto-Christian Nestorians were growing in number with enormous dynamism, rapidly overtaking Islam in Central Asia. This Oriental form of Christianity had blended with Buddhism, which had by then thoroughly blended with Taoism and Indo-Tantra. Nestorians were for centuries a significant link between Eastern Orthodox esotericists, Sufis, Buddhists, and Taoists. Syrian entrepôts possibly served as portals for the Western entry of Jabirian and Far Eastern concepts of alchemy.

Mention should also be made of Jewish merchants from Provence, who from the ninth century on plied both land and sea routes to China. Speaking most languages of the lands in-between, they possibly facilitated a culturally private bridge between Islamic alchemy and gestating Kabbalism.

Jabir's mercury-sulphur theory of alchemy was likely derived from Chinese sources. In any case, it was not until the addition of a third primary substance that external alchemy in the West became directly associated with the internal development of the human system. That substance was *salt,* introduced by another great Islamic alchemist, ibn Zakariya ar-Razi (Al-Razi) in the ninth century. With the addition of salt to mercury and sulphur, the concept of a Philosopher's Stone rapidly became alchemists' premiere symbol of both the alpha and omega of their art. While gold might be derived from the mercury-sulphur process, the Stone of Immortality emerged from a process involving mercury-sulphur-salt.

Because man was traditionally understood as being composed of three elements, the *tria prima* theory of mercury-sulphur-salt came to be applied to the treatment of humans. Painters began to describe their most valued stone (lapis lazuli, which produces ultramarine pigment) in the same terms that metaphysicians used to describe *their* most valuable stone. Metallurgists, doctors, artisans, and spiritualists united in a theory of *natural alchemy* and transformative

Competence, sobriety, and honesty can be overwhelmed by the intoxication of genius, balancing on a sharp fulcrum of compulsion to change everything with a single stroke of the Trident.

development involving hierarchical emergence – *a universal process purposed toward the goal of Highest Quality.* This interdisciplinary knowledge of alchemical law was strengthened by East-West scholars up to the era of post-Newtonian science. *New Millennium Alchemists are witnessing a rebirth of understanding regarding hierarchical emergence and evolutionary processes.*

Crucial concepts of *compensation* and *balance* in Jabir's corpus foreshadowed the Tarot's pairing of Fool and Magician in representation of the Quest's whole alchemical work. These two concepts equally applied to the development of the Arabian language as the science of the word began to take on cosmological significance. We recall that Sufis in Ibn ʿArabi's time posited the science of letters as essential to that of words. Preceding both was the science of Image-Exemplars. Ibn ʿArabi's influential cosmology took the form of a Great Chain of Divine Attributes, manifesting a series of nested Cosmic Spheres of Being-Becoming. Each Sphere and every aspect of corporeal manifestation and spiritual realization are interdependently linked to all of the others. This worldview was in part supported by Jabir's observations of natural law. In any alchemy there must exist, says Jabir,

> a harmonious structure, in which every constituent part has its rightful place, which it cannot lose without repercussions in the rest of the system, or without being compensated.

It is the time-consuming work of the Magician to learn systematically and thoroughly the mechanics and probabilities of the human cosmos, maintaining balance in all interactions and exchanges. It is the spontaneous play of the Fool to compensate for mistakes made during the Magician's Quest. For alas, people inevitably make wrong decisions; and even the Magician who is witness to the tricks of Death does not understand the inscrutable ways of Justice. The gloriously successful Quest is marked by a Questor's complete transformation from Magician into Fool and back again via successorship. It begins in tandem with archetypal feminine grace, unquestioningly compensated for all delusion, malice, and craving – in short, for all bondage of "self."

By reflecting the struggles of humankind, the Adept – realizer of Unity-Consciousness – demonstrates through his very bodily being how all experiences, dramas, thoughts, and states are blissfully transcended. In human form, the Adept teaches and heals through the greatest of tantric *siddhis* (or "powers"): the *Great Mirror Method of Brightly Transformative Chaos and Eros.* The seventh stage of the Devil and Tower initiates this way of the Fool; the Star nourishes it, the Moon matures it, the Sun completes it, and the Angel perfects it.

Intense, conscious build-up of virility sublimated into a Towering energy of practice bursts forth in either success via providential awareness and insight, or failure through material conquest and subjugation.

The Adept's realization is *felt* by Questors through bondage-transcending intimacy. The alchemy of Love is not about securely bonded possessions. Nor does it have anything to do with self-contractive, narcissistic reflections bound up in sexual/emotional encounters. It certainly is not marked by intellectual masturbation. Love-Bliss is *solely* marked by itself!

How does a Questor come to feel, know, and thereby consciously realize this? First, be blessed by the alchemical compassion of a *Blind Sifu* (*Ecstatic Monk* as Drunken-Master Wisdom-Adept, i.e., a Really Good Teacher); even if his passionate indifference is seemingly inscrutable. Then, as initiated Magician, mature into full Magehood. This is done through genuine supplication and remembrance of the noble Adept who is a *Messenger for the Way of Justice, Furiously Angelic.* All the while, the Tenfold Path must be transcendentally realized through self-surrender and self-sacrifice to the Way of Sublime Communion: the Tao.

Causing . . . Right Effort

By the time of the Hermetic alchemist and philosopher Zosimos of Panopolis, who lived in Egypt during the fourth century, Greek alchemy had developed beyond

Contemplation of biological, cultural, and spiritual evolution perforce demands engaged, practical Consideration; transformations of the Questor's identity emerge naturally only when unfolded from deep within the Heart.

the techniques of craftsmen. During the two centuries following Jesus, alchemy had infused an array of esoteric and occult practices, ranging from Neoplatonism to Babylonian astrology. Although Zosimis was clearly aware of genuine chemical knowledge such as the extraction of mercury from cinnabar and the creation of *white lead*, he was primarily interested in what is referred to as "internal alchemy." In him, we find Neopythagorean rites mixed with a Hermetic union of body and mind. Zosimis tended toward a dualistic worldview involving a dark and painful sacrifice as a body striving for spiritual transformation. He wrote of a dream in which a priest on a high altar spoke to him:

> I have accomplished the action of descending the fifteen steps towards the darkness, and the action of ascending the steps towards the light. The sacrifice renews me, rejecting the dense nature of the body. Thus consecrated by necessity, I become a spirit.

His transformation as a spiritual man, however, was imagined as a grueling process. He said that he suffered *intolerable violence*, that he was *cleaved with a sword* and *dismembered systematically*. His torturous teacher first removed all the skin from his head. His bones were then mixed with his flesh and burned with a *fire of treatment*. Through this psychophysical transformation he *learned to become spirit*.

The Philosopher's Stone was first mentioned by Stephanos of Alexandria. The most famous of Greek alchemists after Zosimis, he was favored at the court of Byzantine Emperor Herakleios during the early seventh century, after John Climacus had written *The Ladder of Divine Ascent*. Along with treatises on mathematics, astronomy, and philosophy, Stephanos wrote two books on alchemy. It is clear from these that by his time the language of alchemy was being used to describe spiritual levels of realization. Soon thereafter, at the beginning of the eighth century, the Greek alchemist Archelaos wrote:

The 10,000 things, the uncountable myriad, the mysteriously infinite: every part is a whole felt from the inside, every whole is a part felt from the outside.

> And the soul, calling to the body that has been filled with light, says: "Awaken from Hades! Arise from the tomb and rouse thyself from darkness! For thou hast clothed thyself with spirituality and divinity, since the voice of the resurrection has sounded and the medicine of life has entered into thee."

Neoplatonic and Christian Hermetic metaphysics had become tightly woven into the fabric of alchemy. Archelaos goes on to speak of body, spirit, and soul being united in Love and becoming One. He speaks broadly of Mystery being realized through the heartful union of mind and body. It is *contained and sealed*, he says, in a corporeal realization of divine light imaged as an erect monument: the *Alchemist's Tower.*

We return now to the Questor's own Stone of Wisdom; that which instills her beauty, her goodness, her truth:

> Sulphur is the *body* of the Stone; the principle of Being and Beauty in physical heat.
> Salt is the *mind* of the Stone; the principle of Knowledge and Goodness in psychic charge.
> Mercury is the *soul* of the Stone; the principle of Bliss and Truth in heartful flux.

While mercury in its nascent, pre-transmuted form as sexual potency promotes the first four stages of alchemical development, it is of overriding importance in the fifth and sixth stages of alchemical progress:

> Stages one and two proceed through a full incorporation of sulphur, the *heat* of physical/emotional fixation.
> Stages three and four proceed through a full incorporation of salt, the *charge* of mental/psychic purification.
> Stages five and six proceed through a full incorporation of mercury, the *flux* of subtle/causal mutation.

A confluence of polarities sustains fields of organized flux; Sun and Earth are not separate poles – their union as the interdependent hierarchy of nature and its epitomized manifestation as humankind is the realized consciousness of Tao.

With the complete incorporation of transmuted mercury, the three universal aspects of living nature are united in a psychophysical-soulful awareness of True Self.

The *seventh stage* of Deathless Chaos dispels even that sense of Self, as the Quest becomes purposed toward an intense preparation required to assist other Questors on the Way. An enlightened Questor is then transformed through the *eighth stage* into a pure vehicle for the Divine Process – felt, lived, and taught as *Death or Enlightenment*. After healing and empowering *ten thousand beings*, the Quest is complete; but not the Transcendental work that raises all ancestors in a sole state of rectifying Radiance. This *ninth stage* of Transcendental Knowledge converts the world, even as the Adept remains paradoxically indifferent to, yet energetically directed by, its history. Finally, the *tenth stage* is *Just Bliss*. So in Reality is Enlightened Consciousness Liberated in the Tao.

The art of internal alchemy, as has been reiterated throughout this study, does not go beyond vital life and essential nature. Fire and air in their disposition to *rise* define mind's essential nature. Water and earth in their disposition to *fall* define body's vital life. The *fifth element* of aether is actually that primordial state of alchemical union referred to in the *Emerald Tablet:*

> It arises from earth and descends from heaven; it gathers to itself the strength of things above and things below. By it the world was created. From it are born manifold wonders.

By interpenetrating body with mind, water with fire, earth with air, alchemy proceeds through the six stages delineated in these chapters. One of the traditional ways of imaging this in the West has been through the *hierosgamos:* the *sacred marriage* between female and male that reflects the union between goddess and god.

Originating in Mesopotamia as a public ritual of sexual intercourse between the king and a sacred *prostitute* (literally meaning "to cause to stand in front," interestingly stemming from the same

Karma may bind, Logos may sustain, but the successful Questor knows that Judgment determines the destiny of the Path; witness the continuity of the Great Tradition alive as the Quest itself.

root as *ecstasy*), hierosgamos was believed to transubstantiate its participants into divine beings. Thus could a priestess become the Goddess Inanna.

Laterally, we may compare this to ritualistic Christian sacraments involving the literal divination of physical substance, such as bread and wine. Jesus himself miraculously transformed substances, and resurrected bodies into higher states of spiritual life. Historically, it appears that Jesus also had a consort, the "prostitute" Mary Magdalene. It is reasonable to suggest that their union, in whatever form it may have taken, was held to be sacred. Judaism has in fact traditionally viewed sexuality as more of a sacrament than a sin, although in Jesus's era much evidence points to a serious communal schism regarding women, sex, and the role of both in the perfection of spirituality.

In Mesopotamia, manifesting the magical myth of Inanna via hierosgamos with a royal human husband was thought to regenerate a king's potency, his people's prosperity, and the fecundity of their land. This mythic reality was not paradisiacal, however. Inanna's partner was ultimately sacrificed and resurrected in an emasculated form. According to the myths, the Goddess tended to exhibit dark states having little to do with wisdom or compassion.

Hellenistic, Sufi, and Taoist tantric alchemists redeveloped this sacred and persistent rite into a brilliant antidote to the dualistic seduction propagated by Gnostics (including Manichean Nestorians) and Chaldean occultists. Tantric alchemy, perennially affirmed in the Great Tradition, gives no credence to demonization or avoidance of the body in order to "free the spirit" – to remove it from all suffering of the gross world. Tantra does not hold to a conceit that spiritual realization is "above" pleasurable, everyday cultivation of physical-emotional-mental self-discipline, service, meditation, and wisdom. That conceit surely arrests potential alchemical processes, evolution, and thereby ecstatic realization. Sacred conjoining in its mature tantric form does not console illusory, subtle selves with

The Dharma of the World is like the Goddess of Law, realizer of the Heart, the Nondual Way; Witness Her as every instance, every occurrence, every thing, every relation, every moment, every action.

visions of a lost world into which ideal lovers might escape. *True transcendence has never been about avoidance.*

The key to losing oneself in Love, while strengthening one's freedom, is devotion to *bondage-transcending intimacy.* In no way is such intimacy marked by bondage-producing dependencies of projected fantasy. Nor, and this point is often lost upon the misguided, is the illusion and fantasy of *independence* conducive to bondage-transcending intimacy or compassionate tantra. The Questor as Magician realizes that all alchemy, and indeed the whole Quest, is marked by *interdependency.* The Sufi station called the Independent, identified with the Tarot's Magician, refers solely to the *sovereign nature of the Intimately Transcendental.* It is *Unity-vision* that serves as the unique and individual Stone of the Questor.

From Vision to Liberation, there is no gaining independence from cultivation, study, and communion – these are *absolutely* required. Among the young who are inclined toward spiritual ideals, romance of separative isolation with a soulmate, baby child, or tribal family must be ecstatically abandoned and replaced with an actual losing of one-"self" to the One that is Transcendentally Everywhere Present. Such surrender, perforce, involves the culture, teaching, and community of a realized Adept. *There is no other Way that works.*

Divine realization through ritualistic sexual union (usually not coital) is one of the most pervasive sacramental arts found throughout the Great Tradition. Christian traditions of Mary as Bride of Christ touch upon this. Saint Theresa of Avila most famously affirmed such ecstatic communion. Although Christianity has tended to avoid the physical praxis of sexual engagement, this has not been the case in other great traditions. In mystical Judaism, the relationship between one who prays and the divine has ofttimes been powerfully described in erotic terms. Great Sufis such as Rumi and Ibn ʿArabi revealed a sacred eroticism felt as both path and peak of saintly union with the divine. The *Azeri* (Persian/Turkish language and people of Azerbaijan) movement of *Hurufi* Sufism (a pantheistic merging of Ibn ʿArabi's and Rumi's *theosophical glorification of Eros*) and Hurufi saint Naizmi's poetry of Beauty exemplifies such.

Watch carefully as the World makes the supreme effort to transform every stage into a play of Nirvana Beyond Death.

Respected alchemical manuals portrayed the hierosgamos theme as a matter of mind *and* body, man *and* woman. Prime alchemical texts insist on the interrelatedness of body and spirit. The alchemical *conjunction of opposites* is both a concept and practice quite opposed to conventional exoteric doctrines dichotomizing the spiritual and the physical. Mature alchemists kept to an intuition of Unity. Conscious realization of such *ontological wholeness* was the very purpose of internal alchemy.

We find in alchemy a sacred wedding of opposites inherent to living nature – opposites within every essentially vital being. Humans as uniquely conscious beings are able through bondage-transcending intimacy to engage natural opposites and realize Liberated Unity through them.

In and of itself, sexual intercourse (romantic or not) does not imply sacred or loving engagement. True love is made conscious through *transcendence* of self, which requires more than a temporary, even if primal, orgasmic release from self-contraction. The "little death" of such a release cannot be equated with transcendence, enlightenment, or love. Sexual release is commonly sandwiched between unpleasant egoic contractions and a blind reinforcement of self-sense. Except in uniquely rare people and true tantric practitioners, it is unconscious self-contraction that is released during sexual encounters. It is the same self-contraction, not heartful consciousness, which then rebounds afterwards, promoting egoic identity with each cycle.

Consciousness requires self-contraction to *already be transcended* before, during, and after sexual engagement if the union is to be sacramental, actualizing the divine. Sexual release creates awesomely regenerative kinetics when it is an outcome of alchemical, bondage-transcending *Free Love*. Such love requires constantly heightened potentiality, established through witnessing visions

The Universal Fool succeeds in the ultimate conversion: that of Death itself – from this era on, the history of avataric Grace is fulfilled.

beyond Death. This is what the Love Triumph stands for in preparation for the Hanged Man station of true Heart.

Building of potent spiritual intimacy is based upon conscious conservation of passionate desires and intense needs. In our modern age, egoic states, experiences, and techniques are glorified through self-serving sexual expectations. The discipline of transcendental intimacy is automatically rejected in *ignorant fear of losing oneself.* However, there is no real identification between consciousness and self-contraction. For this reason, *bed-smart* people can become addicted to dramas of isolation, incessantly rebuilding their angst in order to repeatedly experience "release" from their very self-made suffering. Of course, such release is not *liberating,* and thus does not realize the pleasure of pure Bliss, Consciousness, and Being.

One of the earliest Mesopotamian myths of cosmological creation (dating from 2000 B.C.) is that of Tiamat the primordial Waters and her partner Appsu the Begetter. This myth envisioned a commingling of divine opposites into a unified Matrix from which the world was created. This union was based upon a water cosmology found also in other cultures of the agrarian age, including that of early Indo-Europeans.

The primal position held by water is found in alchemical theory, which in its focus on mercury posits water as the first nature of all metals. Mercury in its *water aspect* initiates the alchemical Quest for immortality, but it is not fully sublimated and channeled into the Quest until the fifth and sixth stages of the Way. In those later stages, the sexual potency of mercury is felt to have a very subtle *pneumatic* nature. Mercury in its *unctuous water* aspect develops into a *potentiality of mindfulness* that causes a conversion of the alchemist's psychophysical sensibility. It is literally transmutative.

This is what the Hanged Man comes to see, beyond Fortune's highs and lows and the Hermit's equanimity. Proceeding from this, seventh-stage Underworld enlightenment realizes the Philosopher's Stone as the *transfigured whole-body* of the Questor; who at once feels as if her Daimon has utterly subsumed her. Entering the Otherworld through an *ecstatically righteous portal* is the goal.

Mercury is not the only component critical to alchemical success. Besides sulphur and salt, fire itself is necessary to almost every alchemical procedure. According to alchemy, transmutation of an earthy substance can only occur by first returning the substance to its original nature. Purity is equated with originality, just as Paradise is identified with primordial creation. Through distillation and sublimation alchemists can obtain progressively purer and thereby more original states of a substance.

Like distillation, sublimation involves containment and heat, evaporation and condensation. However, once heated to a vapor, a *sublimated* substance is quickly cooled and *condensed back into a solid without the intermediary formation of a liquid.* This process is viewed by alchemists as being more essential and pure and thereby of higher potency than distillation. It affirms the primordial, cosmological importance of fire over water as the most original and purest of elemental forms. Nevertheless, alchemy *integrates* transmutation processes of water with those of fire.

Most evaporated substances in fact form a liquid when condensed. Sulphur is unusual in that it easily forms sublimates. Identified with elemental earth, it is viewed as a premiere alchemical substance. *Amber* is also one of the few substances easily sublimated. It has traditionally been accorded a practically mystical value.

The process of *internal sublimation,* essentially transmuting a body from its earth and water state to its air and fire state and then back again, is intensely purifying. It *accelerates the quest for immortality.* Air as pneuma is the transitional state between water and fire. Heavenly transmutation of an earthly body involves first returning it to a primordial water state; then heating, evaporating, and re-condensing it to a fundamentally spiritual state as pneuma; and finally transmuting it via sensual consciousness to an essentially divine state as light or heavenly fire.

Returning Prime Matter (the original Stone that is *consciousness as formed inertia*) to its fundamental liquid state is the first step of what might be called *long alchemy.* Returning it to its fundamental fiery state – the inflammable, volatile portion discovered by Jabir – is the initiating state of a far-quicker alchemy. Realization of the *pneumatic, breath-like* quality of mercury was all-important to the development of Western internal alchemy. Of course, modern science has taught us that mercurial vapors are poisonous. Early chemists such as Sir Isaac Newton learned this the hard way. Full transfiguration of a sentient body into its *holy fire* aspect is best engaged via a *holistic watercourse way.* In any case, the proceeding alchemical intercourse will likely be fraught with danger. Even still, Questors with their sights set upon *ecstasy* are advised not to fear.

Whether or not this remains abstruse to the reader, everyone will agree that medieval teachings regarding alchemy tend toward obfuscation. Fortunately, present-day Questors need not spend lifetimes searching for keys to the portal of enlightenment. *By quickly attaining the pneumatic mercurial state of the Stone,* Questors can bypass many confusing steps and twisting routes that inevitably waylay the uninitiated. However, while it is true that soulful Love is like a sacred fire, it must be condensed in and as tantric *flows of the body* to be directly realized. Quickening that process is the essence of alchemical initiation. Anything obscuring this is dualistic fantasy – the basis of occult delusion.

Being aware of the essential importance of water to one's mindful and heartful self is the same as consciously embracing one's body in order to realize love, whether that be conjugal or celibate. At this stage, *narcissism* is the Questor's major bane. It is here that the *sublimation of sulphur* begins, fixing one's mercurial aspect so that the sacred alchemy does not degrade back into a confusion of liquid states, experimental firings, and practically random distillations. At this stage, the Questor who *thinks* she knows will find further progress impeded. Repeated *salting* or *crystallization* purifies the fixed or congealed mercury, producing at first a wondrous *cinnabar* and then a most sublime *aquamarine stone* that is but one step away from transmuting into a Touchstone of awesomely transformative power.

The Questor is still not home free, for *dualistic conceit* could turn her into a *hungry ghost*. Questors must realize that processes of both water and fire arise from a priori Unity, the Nondual Presence that is not dependent upon, but rather inclusive of, intercourse or the matrix of Flux. It is at this point in the Quest for Immortality that alchemical mercury, which can be called divine oil because in its unctuous water state it is involved with all bondage and fluctuation, dissolves the aquamarine into a tincture or nectar capable of *multiplying the noble virtues of gold a thousand times.*

A large amount of *virtuous* gold is needed to create an elixir of immortality. The *seed of gold,* otherwise known as the *dragon's pearl,* penetrates the alchemical concentrate like a Radiant Arrow. This crucial catalyst is obtainable *only through the presence of a Transcendental* or an agency that a true Adept has empowered for such purpose. If this agent is not discovered in time, the ambrosia will lose its fertility. Exceedingly careful storage comparable to a hen watching her egg (at the minimum keeping it away from temperature changes and artificial light) will afford the Questor some time.

In bygone eras, a Questor's patient wait and laborious effort to acquire the Dragon Pearl generally terminated in death. However, Questors are now living in the most transformative of times. Along with global chaos comes an emergence of World Agents. Questors who truly bear down are guaranteed success. Dear reader, abandon all doubt. Do not fear the Bright. Remember: *Bliss is Plenty.*

Given the complexity of alchemical processes, any attempt at delineating them further would quickly compound into a lengthy and arcane study. Let us instead inquire into the essential components of psychophysical alchemy held to in Buddhist-Taoist tradition. The elegant and relatively simple model that epitomizes Taoist alchemy strongly influenced Persian and consequently European alchemical cultivation and philosophy.

Globally, our earliest references to the internal and spiritual sides of alchemy are found in the Taoist tradition of the second century B.C., several centuries before comparable Hermetic references emerged. A story regarding an alchemist of immortality appeared during this period – a time when the Emperor had banned alchemy for fear that counterfeit gold might ruin the Empire's economy.

The story tells of Emperor Wu receiving an alchemist who claimed that through his Goddess worship, associated with a Cauldron of Tao, he had discovered the secrets of immortality. The Emperor was instructed how to worship the *Goddess of the Stove* in his own person. This would enable him to invoke spiritual beings that could render cinnabar into gold. This gold, if used *in the right way,* would bestow longevity upon the Emperor. It would enable him to *give audience to the immortals who live in the midst of the ocean.* If he then made proper sacrifices, he himself would become immortal.

Internal alchemy, like external, was purposed toward realization of immortality. However, external alchemy involved external materials. The end product sought was either gold – the eternal metal – or actual physical long-life; a life theoretically amounting to "eternity," although a life span of several hundred years seemed to qualify as true success. Modern-day popularity of the vampire genre in mass-marketed fiction is indicative of the powerful hold this desire continues to have on imaginative minds.

Adepts of internal alchemy used their own bodies as their laboratories. Other than catalytic drugs, everything needed for the processes of purification and transformation was derived from the adept's own psychophysical being, knowledge, and chemistry. Ultimately, internal alchemy was purposed toward *spiritual immortality* through *whole-body consciousness of the Tao.*

Chinese alchemists were far more interested in obtaining the *pill of immortality* than they were the transmutation of base metals into gold. By the time of Alexandrian Hermetic alchemy, *Ko-Hung* (meaning "the master who preserves his simplicity") was recording complex, intricately involved instructions for achieving elixirs of life, transmutations of metals, and methods of immortality. He instructed that alchemical gold was nothing like "tinted base metals," and although medicinal plants could prolong life, only potions made from metals and minerals could produce immortality. Key substances employed toward this purpose included sulphur, cinnabar, mica, and pine-tree resin. Whatever the potion, when thrown onto mercury it would convert it to gold. Similarly, lead-tin could be converted to silver.

Each of these substances and the alchemical processes applied to them had a corollary aspect in the psychophysical yoga of internal alchemy. It is difficult to discern in most alchemical texts how much attention was put into actual exoteric procedures. Frequently, much of the terminology was simply used metaphorically. Clearly, both external and internal alchemy were practiced East and West, early and late. It is also clear that many alchemists attempted to combine the two otherwise totally different practices, ingesting dangerous substances with no medicinal value in order to create a spiritual body.

Noblemen at the court of Cosimo de' Medici of Florence (famous for its sixteenth-century revival of the Platonic Academy, hotbed of the Hermetic and Neoplatonic renaissance during which the Tarot was popularized) imbibed potions made from various recipes involving the dissolution of gold into drinkable elixirs. Like silver, a certain amount of gold can be ingested without harming the body. In such low doses, both precious metals may well have beneficial effects. Silver has become a common element in modern water purification systems, as it kills bacteria. Gold injected into cancerous tissue via nanotech procedures is proving to be an effective antidote to the disease. Although it is a toxic metal in amounts other than miniscule doses, gold is a proven antidote for arthritis. It is a well-established part of the Ayurvedic and Traditional Chinese pharmacopoeia.

On both metaphorical and sacred levels, alchemical ingestion may be compared to Catholics consuming the *host* – bread literally transformed into the *spiritual body of Jesus* – in an act meant to consecrate their personal souls, enabling them to live forever in the afterlife. One imagines, however, that comparing such to alchemical cultivation would be disagreeable to most Church ecclesiasts.

Taoist alchemy is a psychophysical yoga; the goal of which is conscious uniting of nature's heavenly and earthly attributes or souls. As mentioned in an earlier chapter, the *house of fire* (chest area) is related to our heavenly soul and essential nature; the *house of water* (abdomen area) is related to our earthly soul and vital life. Innate life-potential called *jing* (or *ching*) is a mysterious causal force felt in humans primarily through their endocrine systems as *sexual* or otherwise *creative urgency*. This is represented by the element of mercury (as was the god Hermes in Western alchemy). It can be said that heaven and earth come together through a fiery empowerment of this flowing, mercurial force (recall Hermes as *winged messenger* between divine realms of fire, air, earth, and the underworld). The way of mercury, *when contained and heated,* is closely associated with the Tao in its alchemical procession realized by the Questor. By powerfully magnifying and becoming intimate with the process of mercurial transformation into cinnabar, cinnabar into gold, and gold into ambrosia, humans are able to reunite their mind-body-soul in and as the Tao.

It is indeed the Tao of Heaven and Earth to be as One. In Neoplatonic terms, the Questor returns to an original state of Bright Unity by identifying with *World Soul as manifested Plethora* transforming into *Light Soul as universal Eros.* The Mysterious Wisdom of Eros Soul then unites with the Intently Bright as the True Way of Immortals.

Houses of fire and water, mind and body, are conjoined and merged through the circulation of *qi* or *vital energy.* Qi (or *ch'i*) as neurochemical firing and flow combines fire and water in a state similar to Aristotle's unctuous water and the Stoics' pneuma-air. During the first twenty-four years of life, jing naturally develops into qi. Qi is the combination of basic neurological activity and *organization* of that activity innate to all neuro-organic systems. From the water and fire alchemy of jing and qi, a myriad of energetic states arise.

Just as humankind embodies a fundamental polarity, so too does it manifest a fundamental unity-state from which that polarity arises and to which the conscious Questor can purposely return. Indeed, beyond traditional views of a *Great Return*, every step of alchemy involves an innate awareness of the *inherent and always-already-present Unity* of the Questor's being, knowledge, and bliss.

Every person's quantity and quality of qi is unique, but the essential aspects and types of qi (i.e., lung qi, liver qi, dry qi, moist qi, etc.) are universal. The lung qi channel along the arm, for instance, is fundamental to all humans regardless of age, race, or body type. Channels or meridians of qi are empirically experienced but cannot be dissected apart from the whole human system. The primary meridians are each associated with an organ, but there are no physically apparent connections between meridians and organs.

Order arises from the whole. This may be elucidated through concepts of morphogenetic, causal fields (examined in chapter 8). In any case, what are widely known as acupuncture meridians are *patterns of order* innate to one's neurological system as a whole. It is no more fanciful to study the developmental organization and innate patterns of the human neuro-system than it is to study the developmental patterns of the human heart, nuclear flux, or fields of a magnet. Actualizing integration of body and mind through awareness of meridian dynamics in personal, social, and environmental spheres is the most effective way of advancing holistic health and growth. The art of *Feng Shui* (literally, "Wind-Water") addresses this.

Sexual potency or jing is the *essence* of vitality. Vitality *generates* life. When vitality totally dissipates, the body decays back into earth. Jing is sublimated into qi, as organic neurological activity, via breath, blood, and hormonal chemistry. The organs and their meridians (including the brain and central nervous system), along with eight lesser channels, are *conduits of organization* through which potential vitality becomes kinetic qi-energy. Such energy organizes and animates the human system in all of its complexity. Jing is purposed toward transmutation into qi, whose purpose it is to transmute into *shen* or "spirit." This process is quite comparable to the Greek concept of an earthen body transmuting into water (jing), air (qi), heavenly fire (shen), and finally Aether (Tao). Such is the direct and simple, purposeful process of immortal or divine realization.

There are, according to Taoist alchemy, three primary *centers, cauldrons,* or *retorts* in the human system that serve to concentrate and transform qi. Just as jing becomes qi – vitality becomes energy – so does qi become shen – energy becomes spirit. Through the three cauldrons and their respective currents or channels, vitality is concentrated as energy and energy is then liberated as spirit.

Without alchemical containment of energy, neurochemical *release* is experienced as *dissipation* of vitality. This leads to degenerative cycles whereby a chemistry of stress is used to "energize" the body and a psychology of projected fantasy is used to "relieve" the stress. Cultivation of conscious alchemy neither avoids nor relies upon patterns of stress and fantasy. Instead, through the *courage to be,* regardless of evil, an engaged awareness transmutes *stress and escape patterns* into a powerful *will to love* and liberated *force* to be reckoned with.

Of the three human-system cauldrons, the primary one is in the *midbrain.* It is involved with two hormonal meridians and the endocrine system. Its *liberating channel* goes up the front of the body from the right side of the heart, around the back of the neck to the top of the head and into the midbrain via the forehead's *Third Eye.*

The cauldron most popularized in the West is located in the region of the *lower abdomen.* Called the *hara* in Japanese martial art tradition, it is involved with the hollow organ meridians, which include the stomach, small intestine, large intestine, gall bladder, and urinary bladder. Its *transcending channel* runs up the front and back of the body from the perineum to and through the top of the head via the central spine.

The third cauldron dwells in the area of the *solar plexus* and is involved with the solid organs. Its *transmuting channel* drops down from the heart, unwinding through the spleen, lungs, liver, and out the kidney gates.

People who do not have a feeling-awareness of their qi centers and channels are unable to consciously magnify and quicken the regeneration of their qi. Their bodies may remain alive, but the quality of their lives, including their minds, progressively diminishes after their mid-twenties (of course genetics and karma unconsciously affect this process). Psychological, sociological, and environmental patterns enable human potential to flourish to the degree that they incorporate and reinforce the integrated concentration and liberation of these centers and currents in the process of transforming vitality to energy to spirit. This is the authentic importance of Feng Shui.

Emptiness, or *fully sublimated spirit*, is felt as a *completion of alchemy* involving each cauldron and its wedded channel or current:

The midbrain center resolves in the space ineffably dwelling as *original cause*, soulfully felt in the *right-heart*, i.e., at the right side of the heart, where blood and most subtle hormones are released into the body. This is cultivated through celebratory arts and spiritual dancing. We may call this *Bliss*.

The lower-abdomen center resolves in the space radiating above the head – the *middle-heart* as the source of all light. This is cultivated through scholarly arts and meditative sitting. We may call this *Consciousness*.

The solar-plexus center resolves in the space transparently arising from above the knees to the horizon through a *mysterious pass* felt below the physical or *left-heart* and *beyond all relationships*. Emotionally, it is a state of no guilt,

> beyond doubt. This is cultivated through martial arts and contemplative walking. We may call this *Being*.

The three Centers and the three Currents are at once distinguishable and identical. Each may be felt and developed distinctly, yet any distinction is lost in the indifference and freedom of *conscious feeling*. In the liberated realization of Tao, there is neither subjective *experiencer* nor objective *experience*. Yet, the Taoist Adept knows the Centers and Currents as empirically as the blue sky and the two-armed form of human existence. Being, Consciousness, and Bliss are One in the Tao. Internal alchemy is the cultivation of body-mind unity. This is made possible by the cauldrons and channels *transmuting* vitality, energy, and spirit into the Tao – *the Three Upholding the One*. Heartfelt nurturing and mindful awareness of such transmutation is fundamental to tantra, internal alchemy, and enlightenment.

Charles Luk's *Taoist Yoga* is highly recommended to the reader who wishes to inquire further into the processes and stages of this meditative way. A study of Tantric Buddhism and the yogic symbolism portrayed by *Tara* and *Guanyin* are particularly recommended regarding the mysterious, dynamic, and compassionate flows of the Causal-Heart.

Taoist cosmology metaphysically supports the practice of alchemy. Early mythology tells of the cosmos being created from Chaos. Chaos was understood as *primordial flux*, or the *hypostasis* that became the *Myriad*. Creating Chaos was the polarity of *Yin/Yang*. Prior to that, of course, was the nondual Tao.

In Neoplatonic and consequently Tarot cosmology, the original Chaos of the world is truthfully understood as the Soul of the World. This Great Alchemical Flux came to be represented by the Devil and his Tower. Heraclitus called this principle and process Strife. It is a *natural* and *essential* state. It is not *evil*, which is a *self-promoted delusion* based upon ignorance of cosmic evolution and the principles of immortality. Angelic and daimonic Exemplars are inherent attributes of conscious existence in the world.

Chaos is encapsulated by Eros-Wisdom, the Soul of Light. Eros is the *creative gap* of Chaos through which Pure Radiance, called by Heraclitus "the Bright," becomes a manifested Cosmos. Like the Zodiac surrounding Darkness, it is represented in the Tarot by the Star and Moon. Eros contains pervasive, divine power. It emanates transformative Chaos that in turn causes contingent hierarchies of nested field symmetries. The manifested cosmos has ultimately identified itself by naturally evolving back into Erotic Consciousness through Heart-tantra humans realizing the Truth of Unity-awareness.

As the mysterious origin of all dimensional space, Eros is in many ways similar to the Taoist concept of *Yin* – the *Resolutely Veiled.* As the Cosmic Egg – original nourisher and creative source of all – Eros provides a portal and impulse through which the world manifests. Historically related to the great Goddess called Wisdom, her Kosmic function as intermediary between the Divine Domain and the material cosmos is marked by omnipresent, mighty Grace and soulful, compassionate Mercy for the entire World.

Eros is in turn encapsulated by Consciousness or Infinitely Radiant Intelligence. Such unifying Radiance is similar to the Taoist concept of *Yang* – the *Intently Bright.* Heraclitus viewed the Bright as divine Aether or Zeus. The Christian concept of God became identified with this radiant aspect of the Kosmos.

Prior to Yin and Yang, Veiled Eros and Bright Aether, is undifferentiated *Unity* – Heraclitus's One Thing, or the *Tao* itself. Mystery is wedded to Logos, the Veiled to the Bright. Thus, put in Neoplatonic terms, the nondual One (Tao) emanates the Intellect (Yang) and its Soul (Yin) which emanates the World Soul (Flux of Chaos) from which the Cosmos and all individuated souls perpetually arise. The post-Death Triumphs represent exactly these principles of our immortal World.

We close our consideration of East-West alchemy and tantra with a look at tantric alchemical tradition in India. As with the Chinese, drug-based recipes for longevity and immortality were the focus of Indian alchemists. Unlike Greco-Egyptian tradition with its metallurgical focus, *Rasayana* or Hindu alchemy was from the start purposed toward practices of health, longevity, and spirituality.

The primary transformative method of Rasayana is to subject mercury to a series of processes that impart to it transmutative powers. If successful, the resultant agent is able to transmute a base metal to gold. That is then subjected to a final and most critical process yielding the Elixir of Life, the only legitimate goal of Indian alchemy.

In Indian tantric traditions, members of any caste could endeavor to realize bliss and longevity, including the old and outcast who had to fend for themselves in the wilderness during their final years. It has been conjectured that the native origin of Rasayana can be traced back to the discovery of *Soma.* This life-giving drug, given much prominence in the Vedas, was probably the stimulating plant *ephedra* (although psychoactive mushrooms and cannabis have also been suggested as possible sources of Soma, which may well have been a shamanic mixture of all three historically well-known consciousness-altering plants). Soma was discovered by elders sent into nature to die – a form of socially sanctioned exile. They initially imbibed the drug as a means to survival. This developed into a method of prolonging their years in the wild, along with awakening their consciousness to the path of deathless bliss.

Such Shamans or Siddhas became known as relatively immortal, powerful, and wise. Called *Rishis* (from *rsih,* a root with Persian and Celtic correlatives suggesting *highly energetic states of transference* and indicating a "seer," "sage," and "saint"), the Gods themselves had to "mind their manners" when it came to dealing with them. *It was the Rishis who revealed the Vedas.* For Vedic Indians, Rishis came to represent what the Heroes did for Greeks. It is probably not a coincidence that Vedic stories of the Rishis remind one of stories regarding Empedocles. The Rishis preceded classical Greek shamanism, having roots in the Indus civilization of a millennium earlier. Their myths and practices likely spread with the great Persian empires and Western Asian trading routes, perhaps accompanying tales of Babylonian priests and seers.

Indo-European spiritual development spreading from Anatolia to Greece, Persia, and India tracked a common course from 4000 B.C. onward. It was broadly marked by three great milestones in a timeline of cross-cultural development: 2500–1500–500 B.C. Given the history covered in this book, with A.D. 500 and 1500 standing out as milestone dates, we may say that social evolution has been indeed marked by millennial periods.

Rasayana involved with the transmutation of metals into gold did not appear in India until the fifth century A.D. This was clearly influenced by both Greek and Chinese practices that had merged with Buddhist and Taoist forms of meditative yoga. In general, the transmutation of metals broke Vedic rules of caste. Just as a lower caste member was restricted by caste law from advancing into a higher caste, so was lead meant to remain lead, for the metals also had their castes. India's social caste system was developed after the peak era of Indus-Sarasvati-Vedic culture, but respect for natural hierarchies formed an intrinsic core in earlier Vedic teaching. Any direct transmutation of lead or mercury into gold broke the laws of hierarchical division.

In alchemy, however, by first *returning* a metal to its *universal* state, a transmutation could then occur which would not break lawful caste divisions. *Returning to and thence evolving as the Universal Source* was the key to both internal and external alchemy, early and late in history.

Toward the end of the Vedic era, the Universal Absolute called Brahman was revealed in epitomized metaphysical treatises called the Upanishads. It was to this One that Siddhartha Gautama (as the historical Buddha was originally named) was harkening as he presented to Indo-European (abbreviated in the remainder of this chapter as IE) people a ten-stage hierarchy that any human could advance through regardless of caste. Gautama *Buddha*, the *awakened one*, was able to point to an ancient understanding of hierarchical development, which surpassed the caste divisions and domination hierarchies of Brahminical law. By consciously envisioning through divine grace the self's original state, a devotee could quickly proceed along the noble path of enlightenment.

Gautama's teachings of Unity-realization reinterpreted Vedic mythology and theosophy as they had developed in the Upanishads. He declared a reformation movement renewing the truly ancient ways of *Aryan* (IE) tradition.

Gautama's methods of realization encompassed *non-Aryan* cultural patterns of India, including those of Dravidian speakers with their *shamanic and tantric ways* of traversing sentient and spiritual realms. The essential aspects of *tantra* were recorded in the *Atharva Veda*. These were representational of early IE cultural patterns that had interwoven with archaic Dravidian customs developed within Indus Valley civilization. Archeological research suggests that Dravidian-speaking people originally migrated to the Indus Valley from Eastern Persia. Recent linguistic research suggests a common trunk for Proto-IE and Dravidian languages. Tantric Vedic cultural patterns and yogic cosmology were likely grounded in IE worldviews stemming from the original Proto-IE and Dravidian migrations out of Anatolia as mentioned in chapter 3.

Evidence of South Asia's first settled village life has been dated to the fourth millennium B.C. It comes from the Baluchistan and Sind areas of what is now Pakistan. Dravidians are thought by scholars to have entered India as pastoral people in the Neolithic age preceding this. Much evidence points to them as having played a primary role in establishing the early Indus culture, 3300–2900 B.C. Indus Valley civilization flourished during 2800–1900 B.C. It is now widely regarded as having been greater in size and social accomplishments than the more famous Egyptian and Mesopotamian civilizations that concurrently arose during this epochal dawning of settled, organized society.

European academics of the twentieth century presumed the Vedas were composed some time after northern Aryan tribes (*Aryan*, Sanskrit for "noble," here technically connotes any of the original IE-speaking people, regardless of race) invaded what is now India during 1500–1200 B.C. However, this limited view of Aryan or IE involvement with Indus civilization has been discredited.

One primary piece of evidence disputing such is the Sarasvati River, which served as a favorite settlement area for Indus communities and is mentioned throughout the Vedas as a large and flowing river worshipped as a Goddess. The Sarasvati dried up by 1900 B.C. Satellite imaging and geological investigations have shown that the Sarasvati was indeed a very large river that lost its water due to tectonic movements. Along with an annually growing body of archeological information, this has made it clear that the Vedas were most likely written by the people of the Indus Valley during the height of its cultural development.

In the centuries following 1700 B.C., peaceful IE-Dravidian societies based upon agrarian shamanism were largely disrupted by overpopulation and severe drought. This was exacerbated by an influx of new IE tribes from northern steppe lands who had brought with them weaponry and warfare.

As recorded in later Vedas, a controlling priesthood formed, which created mythic and ritualistic structures to support and justify conversion of a by then ancient agrarian and artistic Dravidian-Aryan culture into a ritualistically governed Vedic warrior culture. In other words, Vedic culture transformed over a broad period of time, as did civilizations around the world, from a first-stage agricultural society oriented toward feminine principles and what might be called flowing fertility to a second-stage political society oriented toward masculine principles and what is best defined as warring conquest. While no doubt not utopian, the integrated era between these stages was evidently a peaceful and beautifully sensual age. Early Minoan culture appears comparable. If a *Golden Age* literally once existed, this age of consciousness marked by communal organization harmonized through measured and balanced rites of practical magic and sensible mythos was likely it.

The Brahminical or priestly caste of Northern India developed in accordance to second-stage patriarchal, urban regulation. A hierarchal system of castes or social groups formed based on governance patterns that broadly imposed rules for obtaining, building, and holding social status. As this caste system spread, it grew progressively reliant upon environmental, social, and psychological structures of domination. The Vedic religion arising from this became so strict in its conceptual worldview and enforcement of regulatory compliancy that by the time Darius the Great of Persia became ruler of Punjab, Northern India was ripe for a radical disruption. This initiated a very slow transformation into third-stage societal development. This process was later stunted by the fragmented state of the subcontinent's many cultures; and by Muslim and European rulers who were incapable of respecting and understanding India's diversity and thus unable to advance and merge its ancient Advaita Tantra wisdom and practices into the common-law ways of a global, modern era.

As reviewed in earlier chapters, the rational stage of human consciousness that emerged West and East during Indian Buddhism's period of greatness directly evolved into transpersonal realizations of wisdom within a few great sages upholding the way of Heraclitus and Gautama, and later Plotinus and Nagarjuna (the latter, a contemporary of Plotinus, was founder of Mahayana Buddhism's *Middle Way* School and arguably the most important Buddhist realizer after Buddha himself). We can reasonably surmise that stories in the Vedas and other late Indo-Iranian mythology indicating an emanationist, nondual awareness arose from a well-developed ground of wisdom cultivated in an early, pre-warrior period of Aryan and Dravidian development. This was the Age of Rishis and Yakshis. During it, divine Fire and its alchemy transmuted an ancient Water cosmology. It is herein suggested that when Buddha claimed his tenfold hierarchy was the ancient Aryan way, he was referring to an IE understanding and enlightened worldview that preceded later, warrior-based Hindu mythology and domination hierarchies.

Similarly, Heraclitus presented a profoundly wise worldview that advanced an ancient understanding of Chaos, Eros, and Gaia. Olympian myths became focused upon the *dramas* of *warring* gods and goddesses. By the Hellenistic period, during which Mercury or Hermes was popularized, the gods had become fully anthropomorphized and "egotized." Their provincial characterizations had limited lifespan and little multicultural resonance beyond the Roman Empire. Celtic and Norse mythology held sway through most of Europe. As with Buddhist India, however, *philosophical* schools in Classical Greece revived earlier, universally spiritual understandings. That process continues today and is what perennial wisdom and integral knowledge is essentially about.

Archeological evidence suggests that agricultural societies contemporaneous with Proto-IE culture, 8000–6000 B.C., focused on magical rituals involving female fertility. Inevitably, cultural development began to stagnate through the limitations of Earth-Mother worship. A great age of Phallic worship, beginning around 4000 B.C. and peaking around 2500 B.C., represented an evolutionary leap into a second-stage era focused on Sun-Father worship.

Fertility mythology associated with this then became pathologically fixated on a *propagation of dominion* in the course of second-stage *militancy.* Nomadic warriors from the Asiatic Steppes branch of IE culture, who for much of the twentieth century were thought to comprise the original IE tribes, developed dominant empires throughout Europe, Persia, and India. Horses, chariots, and metal weaponry were chief factors in their conquests. Genetic studies in recent years have allowed maps to be built that indicate the spread into Europe and Asia of people with distinct genetic markers. These show two waves of migration, affirming archeological theories of an initial spread of IE people out of Anatolia with a second wave thousands of years later coming from the Central Asian steppelands. Russell Grey, a New Zealand professor, analyzing linguistic data using computational methods derived from evolutionary biology, has convincingly dated the initial split of IE language into Hittite, the language of ancient Turkey, and all other branches at 6700 B.C. Tocharian, the Western Chinese IE language, was next to split off, circa 5300 B.C.

Before the many horse-rider invasions of Mediterranean lands, Central Asia, and Northern India that occurred during second millennium B.C., IE beliefs involved a balanced blending of water and fire, feminine and masculine cosmologies. There is little trace of warfare during the late agrarian period. Harmonious coexistence of opposites generated a view of cosmic unity that can be found in the sacred icons of the time. Ritualistic practices of physical fertility celebrated the beauty of male potency along with female fecundity. Evidence of this is found in the oldest Iranian myths of *Ahura Mazda.* It is found in the ecstatic myths of Dionysus the Godboy, who preceded Hesiod's dualistic theogony of heavenly gods and earthbound warrior-heroes. It is found in the Mediterranean artifacts and myths of Minoan, Etruscan, and early Mycenaean cultures.

The linguistic roots of the former two have yet to be determined, though evidence minimally points to close IE involvement with Etruscan linguistic and cultural development. In any case, early IE culture was intertwined with these great civilizations. The mysterious, tantric beauty of Etruscan and Minoan art makes for a most gratifying study. A superb view of IE art from this era can be found in Colin Renfrew's inspection of Cycladic sculpture.

Female fecundity and male potency par excellence are found in the Yakshi and Shiva traditions of the Indus Valley. While the name Shiva was not prominent in early Vedas, icons and cultural patterns traditionally associated with him evidently held an important place in early Vedic society. Perhaps the best-known artifacts from the Indus Valley are soapstone seals of sexually erect yogis and small copper figures of lithe dancing girls. The latter beautifully depict nubile young women striking sensual, spirited poses. The former depict shaman-masked men seated in yogic *asanas* (or "postures") that indicate tantric cultivation used to sublimate sexual energy into spiritual power.

Ananda Coomaraswamy's re-edited treatise *Yakshas* brilliantly speculates upon the common metaphysics indigenous to Aryan and Dravidian cultures of Europe and India. His revelations regarding a *water cosmology* pervasively found among non-nomadic, agrarian-age societies encompassing communities stretching between Europe, Anatolia, Persia, and the Indus Valley are radically insightful. *Yahshas* presents a bridge between Vedic stories of patriarchal fire gods and warriors that have popularly defined – in a mistakenly limited manner – "Aryan" culture with Vedic myths of rishis and phallic, flowing fertility gods and goddesses of an earlier Dravidian-Aryan culture complex. The latter was never in truth displaced by the former, be that through an imagined Indus Valley conquest or a largely co-opted insurgence of steppe-land, chariot-driving warrior tribes.

Water and Fire cosmologies merged in the great traditions. For instance, Christian stories of the fiery Holy Spirit of Jesus evince similarity to those of the mysterious and regenerative Fertility of Dionysus. Heavenly Fire was drawn down to permeate earthly bodies through ablutions of water. Early water-based fertility traditions were ensconced in shamanistic magic, which remain reflected in the rites of Christianity. Jesus presented to his people and Hellenized cultures around him an age-old wisdom-way that included entry into the Underworld and a magical rite of purification and resurrection redolent of shamanic initiation and divinization. While we have not had space to explore the body of evidence that has come to light concerning this, interested readers would do well to start with Morton Smith's first edition of the *Secret Gospel of Mark.* (Footnoted conjectures by Smith regarding esoteric stages of initiation and resurrection prompted writing of the present treatise.)

Dionysus and Zeus for the Greeks, Shiva and Agni for the Dravidian-Aryans, were old and new gods representing earthly Eros realizing heavenly immortality. A full and true alchemy or union of opposites occurred during periods of maturation in every era of IE cultural development. Essential fire has been understood through and wedded to vital water throughout the Great Tradition. These polar traditions stemmed from a common trunk. The next chapter considers this history in relationship to the Immortal Love-Wisdom of Eros.

It appears that in order for consciousness to evolve, innate feeling-states of unity need to bifurcate into perceived developments of primary polarities. After which, consciousness of unity is reattained within a holistic level of *greater complexity.* This is the case in every body, environment, and world until a ninth stage of absolute Radiance outshines all else. Being, consciousness, and bliss fully identified with the Bright translate all manifestation as the Tao. Ultimately, universal polarities such as male/female and heaven/earth are immortally transcended. That is the way of Justice and the World.

Historical study conveys to observant minds insights concerning evolutionary development. Stages of evolution found in the Triumphs can be observed on four primary levels of natural growth: psychological, social, cultural, and environmental. Every stage of natural evolution is initially marked by harmonic resonance established by individual nodes that initially set unique modalities. Group resonance tends toward creative emergence. Polar tension and exchange is intrinsic to this process. Through nested valuations of synchronicity and awareness of common sources, individuals and then communities are able to transcend chaotic change and emerge at new levels of hierarchical growth.

When a cultural stage matures in development, societies involved are gradually affected until encompassed by the culture complex; as societies are encompassed, so too are individuals strongly affected, even when otherwise at conflict with the nodal centers effectively causing such change to begin with. After peaking in growth, decay then naturally occurs; complexity that no longer can be maintained tends to devolve into chaos. At this point in evolution, sociopathological attempts to arrest change will likely become structured through law-enforcement and behavioral restrictions.

Such *conservativeness* inevitably runs its course until exhausted. *Liberation* from imposed environmental, sociological, cultural, and psychological limitations comes as individuals and consequently their societies split from established ways into new stages of being, knowledge, and bliss. The whole culture-complex does the same once more. The process of evolution always begins with individuals, just as the process of devolution is always initiated through mass culture.

The Law of the World is what many have called the Will of God. To have insight into this is to touch upon realms of prophecy and wisdom. The Tarot became known as a divining tool because it imparted to the studied and contemplative user a true and profound awareness of natural law. In the Christian West, the power and knowledge that arose from such awareness was often condemned as heretical, if not belonging to the Devil's realm. Our next chapter explores the history of *Diablos* as it developed out of the Judeo-Christian concept of a *Satan*. First, though, let us enter the Dionysian realm of Eros, into and out of which sacred consciousness has always flowed.

ECSTATIC EMPOWERMENT

DEVIL

Just as darkness gives way to the presence of light, so does self-consciousness give way to the presence of Archetypal Being; for better or worse, the Questor must confront realization of the Devil.

TOWER

The Hermetic way of the Tower constructively integrates crises through the art of becoming; thus, cultivation of gnosis is not arrested by scientific materialism or religious provincialism or dogma of any kind.

Realm of the Saints

Cutting the Root of All Evil . . .

Before night and day, before the gods, before the cosmos, there was Eros. Eros for the ancient Greeks represented the emergence of all-compelling Beauty as a Principle of Creation. A feeling-concept degraded by any and all defilement of that Consciousness which is primordial Law, Eros is felt by the unenlightened simply as *compelling desire*. For philosophers of the Great Tradition, however, *universal* desire implies native longing for the Good – a Paradise and Purpose of *Liberation* (Eros's other name: *Eleutherios*), at once both known and lost. Within this sentient feeling of loss beats the very heart of both spiritual yearning and ignorant delusion. In the former is found identity with the Beautiful and remembrance of the Good; Gaia as Goddess Nature and Original Mother – awesomely attractive, ecstatically engulfing all sensibility. Such is the knowledge of Truth as Conscious Logos. In the latter is found craving for "self" and forgetting of the Source. Such is the illusion of separation, dispelled only by an engulfing totality of Chaos – Gaia's terrifying *other side.*

In this chapter on Eros, Immortals, and Satan we will examine the wisdom of erotic contemplation; the ecstatic madness of Dionysian immortality and heroism; and how divine functions of guardian Daimons were usurped by mundane fabrications of a politicized Satan. Throughout, we will unveil a cloak of *invisibility* – of *That* which cannot be seen except by eyes passing through the bones of Death.

The seventh stage of the Tarot's cosmological system is represented by the Devil and Tower Arcana. This is the Underworld stage of Chaos and Generative Flux, which underlies all discriminated comings and goings of the cosmos. Purgatory for most, hell for some, and heaven for a few, the Seventh Stage is the Questor's alpha and omega. It is the beginning of her immortal *transfiguration* (through dimensional encapsulation within the Overworld of Eros) and the end of her *personal* quest. Herein is discovered the true purpose of the Tarot's twenty-two arcane stations: *to assist humankind to transcend death* by triumphantly empowering sincere Questors with *the insight of transcendentally realized Eros.* In this way, the Trionfi themselves serve as sacred agents, informing consciousness of the Principles of Immortality.

For Hesiod, author of the *Theogony* (the earliest compendium of extant Greek myths), Eros was the creative life-principle of the world. The demiurgical force of Eros formed a world-space through the *gap* of Chaos as Darkness and Night, out of which Gaia procreated Heaven and Day. Gaia as Earth-mother then begot children, on her own and through her son *Ouranos* (or *Uranus,* Greek for "Heaven"). Connecting Gaia with Chaos and Eros was Tartarus, the "dark womb" of Gaia. In Tartarus, Ouranos attempted to keep his children, including the Titans and their leader *Kronos* ("Time"), from being born. Both as a place of banishment akin to death (an otherwise non-sensible state for the Great Immortals) and a place of gestation, Tartarus was the very extremity of Earth, Space, and the Goddess. In the Tarot, Tartarus is represented by archetypes of *extreme transition:* the sixth-stage Hanged Man and Death bridging into immortality via the Tower.

Archaic creation myths such as this presumed a chicken-and-egg paradox concerning cosmic origination. Did Eros compel Chaos to create Gaia or did Gaia manifest Eros? The Principle at once needs its Manifestation. Ultimately, corporeal realization *is* the Law as all forms incorporate pure ideas. That realm, law, or process of consciousness that bridges the ideal with the real, and the mind with the body – known to Heraclitus as *Logos* – is of essential importance to tantra, alchemy, esotericism, and the Tarot. Enlightenment involves a view of that realm becoming all. Gaia, Tartarus, Chaos, and Eros all represent the Transcendental Otherworld becoming the manifested cosmic world.

Truly empowering Magic transfigures the mundane limitations of worldly circumstance into the awesome potentials of sacred occasion.

Eros as Universal Beauty is represented by the eighth-stage cards of the Star and Moon. The triumphant Star radiantly nourishes spiritual desire. It brims over with sacred eroticism. It is the *pure land* from which comes the potency of all creative energy. It is compassion simplifying all complexity. It is *consideration* (meaning "with the stars") without confusion. The Moon is portal to the Sun and Timeless Radiance. It is the power of Creative Eros, generating dimensional space as Radiant Soul. The eighth-stage Triumphs represent the Egg of Soul in Union with the ninth-stage Triumphs' Seed of Intellect. As *Providence,* the Star and Moon *transcend* yet *care, ward, and direct* all processes of our *descending,* i.e., *manifesting,* cosmos. From an *ascending* spiritual Questor's point of view, this eighth stage of evolutionary development is the final goal: the stage of Saints and Bodhisattvas. For the ninth stage of Sun and Angel represents the *non-returning realm* of Angelic Buddhas.

Creating anew out of an infinite flux of possibility, the seventh-stage Triumphs deliver via their Soulful Potentate a new world, both initially gestating within and finally breaking out of the sixth-stage Womb of the Cosmos: Tartarus as the very depths of Gaia. Life and Death then work as one, cycling through five more stages of cosmic manifestation producing the evolution of Gaia and the Great Return back through her and her Womb, passing beyond the portal of Chaos into Immortal Reality. While the demiurgic Daimon guarding that portal limits all cosmic order via immeasurable and uncontainable *flux,* it also manifests the *potential* of immortality.

Shortly, we will follow historical development of the Devil's progression through Judeo-Christian concepts of *Satan.* In chapter 5,

Endless potential for Compassion is made evident by the Chaos beyond one's own destiny; there need be no resistance.

we considered Greek understandings of Hades, brother of Zeus. We associated the Tower with the House of Hades. As we shall see, Tartarus's companion place of the afterlife, *Elysium,* was marked by Zeus's *lightning bolt.* The original name of the Tower card, the *Arrow,* referred to that Bolt, and the Triumph in many ways represents a remote place of both divine gestation and breakthrough attainment. The Tower is Death as Resurrection, transcending and transforming the sixth stage of the cosmos even while mirroring it in the Land of Immortals. It too embodies Tartarus in both its early and late symbolism of exiled origins and sacrificial renewal. It is Chaos generated and channeled into a Kosmic order through immortal principles of transcendental reality. Implicit to the afterworld placement of the Tarot's Tower is the potential of *trans-cosmic* or *transcendental* realization of the *personal* Questor. The Tower represents universal transformation through a priori cosmic flux – of both mind and body. It transcends cyclic, cosmic existence, yet is *bound* by it, for it is the *bridge* principle reaching into the Pure Land of the Absolute One. *The Tower holds a uniquely crucial position amid the Trionfi;* integrating Death and Devil, it assures an outcome to Questors' Triumphal procession that forever stands by the attraction of Eros.

That which is immortally *outside of* (*ecstatically* beyond, yet still involved with) the Wheel of Fortune and Death – and the holy men caught in-between (Hermit and Hanged Man) – is the *Land of the Saints.* Immortal saints ecstatically exist beyond the very Wheel of the cosmos and its chain of causation. Transcending all cycles of life and death, the land of saints is the divine realm of Unity-Consciousness. In Indian tradition the cosmic Wheel is called *Samsara,* the Indo-European root of which means "together," "as one." The Tarot instructs us that the five stages of cosmic process evolving into the Wheel of Fortune are inevitably ruled by the forever-looming impermanence of Death. The Tarot then affirms the Buddhist wisdom that *Samsara Is Nirvana,* for all six stages of cosmic process emanate from the Deathless.

The Questor's soul, through mindfulness capable of viewing the complex depths of nature, envisions a realm beyond temporal rule.

In perennially affirmed understandings of classical Indo-European nondual wisdom traditions, a transcendent domain of light and space emanates the cosmos while still existing as pure essence unmodified by temporal manifestation. The earth was once part of a radiantly timeless center, which the sun continues to manifest. In fact, the whole cosmos was once part of a pure energy-space Center of Unity. That origin has never actually been lost, though to the human mind it can be obscured by the gross physicality of our material earth and selves. Regardless of limitations imposed by human projections of self-substance and dimensional objectivity, Principle and Manifestation – Center and Edge – always have been and will be wedded as One.

The seventh stage of consciousness – manifesting corporeal form from seemingly incorporeal Space – is an Otherworld domain called the Bardo Realm in Tantric Buddhism. Its closest correlative in Roman Catholicism is Purgatory. It is generally interpreted in the imagery of popular Christianity as a place of suffering, a kind of temporary hell; a realm in which the souls of those who have not been relegated to eternal hell must expiate their sins. However, it potentially contains the innate order underlying and outlasting all discontinuities of imperfection. To unenlightened or less than saintly minds, it is beyond the reach of living awareness, for it is the "twilight zone" whose ward is the Devil, even as its laws remain those of Heaven. To enlightened realizers, it is the creative, gestating Flux produced through the infinite radiance of transcendental Consciousness (Sun and Angel) emanating as and wedded to the fathomless Space of universal Eros.

Eros can be identified with the eighth stage of conscious realization; and Chaos and Tartarus with the seventh and sixth, manifesting transitional rebirth through the Otherworld. What is continuously re-birthed is Gaia, representing the cyclic six stages of consciousness that from a "cosmic descent" point of view form the whole cosmos itself. Gaia as manifested Myriad is the *destiny*

By sacrificing personal power, passion can intensely transform that which would be Abased to that which is Pure; the Emperor who does not realize this becomes the very definition of evil.

of Eros, just as she is herself destined to *re-create* Eros. Gaia as Eros is Mater as both matter and dimensionality of space.

The Moon connects Gaia as Eros to the Bright One, the realm of the Sun and the purely Radiant Domain. Abetted by the Sun, the Moon station is powerfully *felt* by Questors yet remains mysteriously *unknown* until the realm of the Devil and its Tower is mindfully traversed. In tandem with the Star, the Moon influences the world as an often unseen, powerful, naturally creative force that demands respect. It is represented in Greek mythology by Artemis and the erotic influence of Aphrodite. Through it, the Devil draws his *powers of invisibility* and "three-pronged" control of the Churning Ocean; the latter symbolized by the trident of Poseidon, Hades' Brother. The exemplar stations of Star and Moon transform the *under*-world *power* of Mother Nature – epitomized in ancient times as the erotic snake guardian *Gorgon* (Greek for "earth") *Medusa* (feminine present participle of *medein,* meaning "to protect," "rule over") – and mirror the *over*-world *knowledge* of the Universal Man (Sun and Angel integrating Hero and Saint), allowing the two to consort.

Gaia, Tartarus, Chaos, and Eros: these four Immortal Origins formed for early Greeks a processional Kosmos. *Chaos,* though listed by Hesiod as the first to come into being, etymologically means "gap" along with "darkness." It implies a change of state in an already existing substrate of reality. Thus, Chaos paradoxically is compelled by Eros, even while creating all depth and manifestation of reality – Tartarus and Gaia. If we imagine Eros as the un-manifested Kosmic Egg, Chaos can be envisioned as the Cosmic Crack through which the *Immortal* Kosmos becomes a *manifested* cosmos. Gaia and her Underworld are at once Kosmic Principles and Earth-Mother realities. Mother-Nature in turn *embodies* Eros as the *material* (etymologically from the universal world for mother: *ma*) world. Eros must have the manifestation of Mother Goddess and her Womb, for they are interdependently purposed. Via the immortally creative cycle of Eros and Gaia, including the primeval depths of Tartarus, Chaos is constantly transforming and being transformed.

In an ecstatic state of Craziness, material form is seen as already Ideal; change needn't be hoped for, because the greatness of structure in flux karmically proves to be already impermanent.

Each of these four divine creators was anciently conceived as a co-dependant originator with the other three in a universal process of Becoming. The immortal gods fathered by Zeus and Poseidon (historically preceded by varying tribal demigods; nature-states embodied in the Titans and their offspring; and more universally, Demeter and Dionysus) stood apart from this genesis; yet through it, the Titans and Olympians were progressively generated. We have attempted to re-vision the ancient goddess cycle in a way that integrates later development of Kosmic hierarchy and male principles. *It was not until the era of Heraclitus and Gautama that the concept of constant Becoming fully unified with that of a priori, absolute Being.* In the Indo-European philosophical development that followed, emanationist wisdom dawned to humankind.

As we saw in chapter 5, Heraclitus posited Eros as the Love-Principle encapsulating Chaos; and Aether as the Bright-Principle emanating Eros. The One becomes Consciousness (Zeus), which becomes Soul (Eros). Heraclitus was critical of Hesiod's myths, written two centuries earlier, which presented a chthonic, timeless world primarily marked by darkness, out of which lighted states were created. By sixth century B.C., Indo-European wisemen across the globe were acknowledging an Absolute and Radiant Principle as being First Born from an ineffable Unity beyond any and all Chaos.

The ancient Greek concept of Chaos-and-Eros was unique in the way it bridged an archaic always-present-realization of a mysterious, dark creator-Goddess with a pervasively extended and radiant, future-purposed God-principle. While later personifications of Eros would depict it with highly effeminate male aspects, Eros is more accurately identified with the primordial female draw to procreate – the Desire of all masculine energy. From the concept of Eros-Love (transcending temporal and spatial harmony and disharmony),

Natural alchemy and the prototypical Laws of the World are discovered through a spark of inspiration that suddenly shows a course to true freedom; through intensification of Temperance, Enlightenment becomes familiar.

Heraclitus redefined Hesiod's pantheon of gods, wedding Aether as Bright Zeus to Eros and positing that there exists as Source to all of Chaos and Nature an undifferentiated *"One Thing."* That Original Unity is not a priori marked by chaos, earth-nature, or netherworldliness. It is marked by the consciousness of a Universal Transcendent – an a priori Absolute – emanating all of reality. Eros and essentially unifying Diké are identifiable as two primal aspects of the Goddess Principle that realize Divine Law through a Chaotic Flux of World Transformation. As the *Incorporeal* Source, Destiny, and Truth of Eros, the Infinite, Radiant, and Unitive Law of Zeus-Diké determines all fate and destiny beyond the powers of heaven – beyond Olympia and the gods of Sun, Moon, Stars, Planets, and Gaia herself.

(While Saturn, Jupiter, Mars, Earth, Venus, and Mercury may roughly be associated with the six stages of cosmic manifestation and conscious evolution, the ancient *Zodiac* – from Greek indicating a "circle of small-living-being" – may more meaningfully be so associated:

Aquarius	Pisces	Empress	Popess
Aries	Taurus	Emperor	Pope
Gemini	Cancer	Temperance	Love
Leo	Virgo	Chariot	Fortitude
Libra	Scorpio	Wheel	Hermit
Sagittarius	Capricorn	Hanged Man	Death

There are sufficient correlations with the Great Traditional stages and stations as clarified in these pages to have lent astrology its longevity as a study of heavenly principles ruling the spiraling integration of cosmic cycles. Most likely, however, this is the first time in print that the above identification of Zodiac Signs and Trionfi has been made. A new interpretation or school of astrology may reasonably be founded upon it.)

Very near to the Greek development of a universally present, constantly creating Source (as epitomized by Heraclitus's concepts) was the development of an ancient Vedic myth of a primal fire-god. *Agni,* meaning "fire," was an Indo-Aryan deity that represented a synthesis of ancient agricultural perceptions of immanent spirituality with concepts of transcendental dominion developed during later civilization. Agni embodied both a life-giving nature as Sun and a life-devouring nature as Death. A further designation of this First Principle was *Kama,* or *Love* as Eros, elucidated by Ananda Kentish Coomaraswamy as:

Only the Heart can be held dear if belief is to stay true; this requires tremendous patience, ruthless self-honesty, and interminably willful sublimation.

> prior to gods and men and beyond the apprehension of either; and it is well known to the Epic that this Kamadeva, Eros, is a form of Agni, and literally the "fire of Love." Kamadeva is then a form of Agni, to whom the names of "Life" and "Universal Life" are commonly given in the Vedas; on the other hand all that is under the Sun is in the power of Death, Mrtyu, a name which is one of the most significant applied to Deity throughout the Brahmanas and Upanisads.

It was through the aspect of *Death,* meaning in Sanskrit "want" and "privation," that Agni represented to Indo-Aryans that which Eros as *compelling desire* represented to the ancient Greeks. Agni embodied Death as a *Good,* in that death was always purposed toward the renewal of life – ultimately compelling the world to a fate of eternal liberation. Emphasis upon cyclic resurrection over tragic death would seem to have been a wise orientation for agrarian cultures. Sacrificial ways of chthonic spirituality such as found in the rites, myths, and rationales of Dionysus have been given a tragic interpretation by dramatists since classical times. However, it is through the *living realization of resurrection* that the mystery sects have continuously established their perennial wisdom. We need not seek occult secrets of terrible sacrifice in the ancient mystery rituals to credit them with an understanding of ecstatic wisdom.

Having looked Death in the face, transcend the temptation to charge, to set in motion, to act righteously without the guidance of that which is Deathless.

As an essential distillation of Hinduism, Buddhism maintains that the world issues forth in accordance to its Dharma, or fundamental Way. Properly viewed, the Law of Eros, Kama, Love, Agni, Zeus, or Dharma is naught but *the way of all things fulfilling their purpose.* Known through their aspects of separation, the relationships defined by such existence are marked by temporal and spatial manifestations and therefore temporal purposes with temporal significance and meaning. Such is forever arising under the rule of Death. Felt as a *whole,* the universe and every temporal being within it are purposed toward the *Bliss of Nirvana.* The wholeness of reality is known by feeling the wholeness of one's sentient psychophysical nature. That unity-feeling is not an experience of "self" separate from "other." The lawful way of vital life and essential nature is intuited as innately transcending physical and psychic limitations. Still, a feeling-knowledge of discreet *internal* degrees of transcendence developed through consciousness must be verified experimentally for the Quest of Bliss to proceed. *Such produces a science of consciousness.*

In India's storytelling tradition, *Siddhartha* (Buddha's original name, meaning "Purpose Accomplished") and Agni are constantly supplicated by *devas* (deities, spirit-beings, ancestors along the way of immortal realization as Brahman or Universal Self) to "turn the Wheel of Law." Only through such cycling of death and life can the world proceed into and as Nirvana. Only through the procession of becoming-being is the Way of Right Liberation or Absolute Truth realized. This enlightened worldview is most paradoxical: transcendental realization requires immanent manifestation. Realization of absolute radiance requires a myriad of manifestations – a real flux in real emptiness. Spiraling through infinite deaths and births, the Original Soul of the World cycles toward an Ultimate Purpose, that is Liberation from all *effort* of cosmic creation, sustenance, and destruction. Such a Great Release comes by evolving *through* manifestation. *That Liberation entails an Outshining of Soul as*

Buddha Mind Consciousness – the Translation of Compassionate Bodhisattva into Pulverized Buddha.

In the Vedas, the Unity-state of Agni was often identified with the Great Yaksha. *Yaksha* was a pre-Vedic term (akin to the Greek concept of *Daimon*) that originally referred to:

> the notions of sudden luminosity, wonderful or awe-inspiring manifestation of something normally invisible, and mysterious power properly to be worshipped.

Electrified by a storm of opposition, peace is ignored; progressive conquests succeed only in agitating further opposition – such is the power of destruction that fails to enforce any way whatsoever.

Yaksha was synonymous with Deva as Spirit-presence, whether referring to deity in its highest sense or to a phantom or ghost. Images of *Yakshis* (the feminine form of the concept) in Indian iconography depict voluptuous women in *erotic poses with the Tree of Life.* A Yakshi's body appears purely sensuous while conveying the demeanor, posture, and gestures of essential grace and enlightened awareness. Indo-European people have historically imaged such a *witnessing-realization of alchemical union.* This is evidenced in the fantastic spiraling motifs of ancient Celtic menhirs, incorporating elements of both phallus and vulva; and in the sensuously noble metalwork of early Northern Europe. Development of materially sensual beauty in a context of sacred and natural regeneration is found throughout agrarian Indo-European culture. Later empires (Greek, Persian, Indian, Roman, etc.) added mythological and civil attributes to the beauty of such art. In the great traditions of Indo-European spirituality, the artful process of envisioning multitudinous spirits in primordial and natural form progressively wove together an imagined tapestry of One Universal Spirit. In an essential way, this describes the Tarot itself.

The Vedas convey a conscious realization of Divine Unity in terms that include the ancient concept of primordial Yaksha. To witness and feel embodiment of that One Psyche-Spirit-Soul was to see, hear, and indeed *become* the Glorious. Readers may note a fundamental difference between this consideration of *immanently*

Cosmic hell cannot possibly be the destiny of the world, for the very Plenitude that defines this World assures the Oneness of souls; even so, deluded self believes ego may outsmart the Devil.

realized transcendence and that of dualistic Gnostic theology as summarized in chapter 5. This chapter finishes the task of delineating the difference between nondual esoteric gnosis and dualistic occult beliefs.

Later Brahminical religious structure reinterpreted Indo-spirituality via a socialized caste-based system so as to justify and regulate political control. This included a division of the spirit world into "good gods" and "bad demons," the latter inappropriately relegated to Dravidian-speaking communities. Within a dualistic, authoritarian priesthood defined by "Aryan" (distorted to mean a glorified, original, superior, and "pure" Vedic race) domination, *yaksha* and *yakshi* were reduced to indicating male and female makers of Chaos, *demon*-enemies of angelic devas. This provincial, political reduction had become widely propagated throughout monastic Buddhist politics within the Indian subcontinent by the time of Alexander the Great's conquest. Arising with this attitude was a conceit of superiority claimed by fair-skinned, male-dominated Northerners over dark-skinned, female-influenced Southerners. Buddhist and Hindu sects demonized *opposing* deities of societies within their own lands and their own mythological systems.

So it was that followers of Vishnu were pitted against those of Shiva, Theravada Buddhists conflicted with emerging Mahayana sects, and Hindus warred against Buddhists. Modern-day Sri Lanka unfortunately serves as an ongoing case study regarding such religious provincialism. Ironically, Hinduism and Buddhism have also evinced immense toleration for religious sects of all persuasions. Hinduism generally places Buddha within its divine pantheon as an incarnation of Vishnu. Buddhism established advanced lineages of Tantra through its *Vajrayana* (Diamond or Lightning Vehicle) path, which emerged via integration of the ancient Shiva-Shakti complex of devotions, rituals, sutras, yogas, and arts.

As an *Avatar* (incarnated divinity), Buddha is understood in a Hindu context to be the Supremely Divine One in human form. As it was with the ancient cult of Dionysus and the later cult of Jesus, recognition of Buddha as an incarnation of the transcendental reality beyond Death created for his devotees a worldview involving a completely divine teaching and transmission immanently permeating and transforming the world. Buddha taught that the world itself, ruled by *Mara* or *Death,* is inevitably always becoming – for it already *is* – *Nirvana* – the neither-being-nor-not-being realm of the *Deathless.* His and his acknowledged successors' radical teachings – as conveyed via the earliest Pali texts right through to the Tantra sutras recorded a millennium later – posit that by Divine Grace, every human, angel, and demon can open his eyes to a Right View of the World. Such spirit-vision reveals that Nirvana is *even now* always the Truth of Reality. It was to this that Jesus pointed when he said: *The Kingdom of God is at hand.*

Hearing the hierarchical harmony of the spheres requires dispelling the charms of social pleasantries, distancing the prejudices of collective moods, and mindfully letting be the conceits of common beliefs.

South Indian traditions migrated from the cultural milieu of the Indus Valley and northern Dravidian communities. Third-millennium phallus worship, dolmens, and fertility rites became well established in South India at the same time that they penetrated Indo-European territories stretching from Ireland to China. Shamanic deities that emerged during this evidently peaceable epoch were incorporated into what we now call *Hinduism* (originally derived from Old Persian *Hindu,* meaning the *Indus River,* indicating the linguistic and cultural community of that territory). Agni and Shiva became representatives of a very earthy, sensual, erotically transcendental way of becoming One with Nature.

Coomaraswamy's corpus remains preeminent in the consideration of how this process occurred. Although, like the present text, much of his work may fall under the old-fashioned academic rubric of *speculation,* that term must be viewed through a prism of *rigorously studied intuition and spiritual practice* if it is to be properly understood. In the great Pandit's case, that prism needs to include an astounding mastery of Indo-European linguistic and artistic analysis, matched in history by few, if any, others.

Obedient to the way of the Deathless, the Hanged Man submits to a seemingly unending process whose successful outcome is impossibly beyond his own will.

In our previous chapter's considerations of Shiva we did not speculate upon the likelihood of his historical development having commenced with a real, consciously evolved shaman existing in a settled, primeval Sarasvati–Indus River society. Also, much will have to be left unsaid regarding the possibility that a historical Shiva, his lineage, and his legacy influenced the myths of Dionysus, who may well have been a historical shaman teaching an ecstatic type of sexual yoga, dance, and wild communion. Evidence points to Dionysus as having been worshiped in Crete during the Indus Valley era. It was continuously held, from Minoan times onward, that he came "from Eastern lands." Stories that have come down to us about him largely regard his global adventures, with popular myths telling of his wanderings over many years in India. From the time of latter Indo-European migrations out of Anatolia, Crete remained in close contact with the Cyclades and the mainland (Turkey), which in turn maintained active trade routes into Indus territory. The cults of Dionysus and Shiva share many symbols: the adorned phallus; the horned man-god; worship of the snake, panther, ram, and bull; wild female devotees of mountain forests, etc. Outside of the Sarasvati-Indus region, evidence of this culture complex is also found in prehistoric Crete and Anatolia, home of Proto-Indo-Europeans.

Actual, living humans ecstatically empowered through realization of the Great Self or Bright One served as the crucial foundation for centrally primary myths regarding Indo-European deities. Buddha drew upon the summary teachings of *maha* (meaning "great") *rishis* (meaning "sages") and yogis embodied in the stories of the golden and most noble Indus Age as they were rationally and intuitively elaborated in the Upanishads. Throughout South Asian history, Tantric Shaivism and monastic Buddhism have either integrated in true, good, and beautiful ways, or conflicted through craven, deluded, and malicious claims. Both streams of cultural, evolutionary consciousness have had far-reaching ramifications for the development of Western knowledge, spirituality, and science.

Immersion in daimonic essence can draw the mind into natural psychosis – the Death of self through loss of sensibility, sociability, and phantasy.

It is due time that the developmental myths of Indo-European spirituality are understood in a context of Self-Realization of Noble Wisdom, and that *Right View of Ecstatic Life* becomes popularly instilled. *Consciousness studies* are critical to modern-day understanding of cultural evolution, social governance, and natural wellness. Interactive and integrated media being implemented by global transcultural communities are allowing a new era to dawn whereby essential patterns of the great traditions may re-merge and harmonize. The age of *mythologized* historical avatars may well be over, even as the principles of immortality become incorporated in twenty-first-century *virtual avatar* fantasy worlds. In any case, quite beyond any individual incarnations of Transcendental Reality, *our world itself is avataric.* Indeed, *Spiritual Rule Is at Hand.* This is beyond doubt; as is the fact that fear, greed, and slaughter will neither arrest nor quicken such realization. Fate remains Empty, as shall the naturally ruling community of successful Questors.

It was at one time supposed that Greek and other "Aryan" Indo-European people worshipped sky deities, while pre-Greek, non-Aryan people worshipped chthonic, ancestral deities of the netherworld. However, just as Greek culture had its chthonic gods and Celts had their ancestral cults, Minoan, Mesopotamian, and Dravidian traditions had their heavenly gods. Classical Greeks were unique, however, in *radically opposing* the two realms of sky-born gods and earthy, ancestral daimons – for in a dualistic worldview, immortal gods abhorred being close to Death.

In pre-Greek times, a way of ecstatic spirituality centered upon the goddess Demeter and her grandson Dionysus emerged from archaic, agriculture-based, shamanic practices. This mystery religion was radically reinterpreted through Chaldean-influenced communities and carried into Pythagorean, Platonic, and Stoic circles through the rites of Orpheus. Like Persian and Greek histories, Orphic and Dionysian rites represented both complementary and opposed paths.

Beauty, truth, and goodness are Deathless states transcending dualities; the mindfulness required to transit the River of Death is totally awesome – the intensity of the Boatman's attention freezes the very marrow of one's bones.

Greek mysticism during classical times bifurcated into two very different movements. One direction evolved into a Dionysian way of psychophysical whole-body sacrifice and regeneration realized as internal transformation instead of corporeal death. Death subsumed by Gaia, Chaos, Eros, and Immortality while in corporeal form was a very real option for those Questors willing to surrender into a dance of wild and noble Ecstasy. This was not a process of *re*-incarnation or the "rebirthing" of one's personal psyche. Rather, it was a process of utter death of self-identity and conscious regeneration of one's original, essentially divine nature. Thus, every *maenad* (ecstatic female celebrant) actually *became* Dionysus himself, who was none other than Zeus the Bright One in human form. The Godman partook of raw flesh, and those who consorted with him partook of His flesh in return. Through this rite, the domain of ancestral spirits, the world of nature, the consciousness of true self, and universal divinity became one.

A second branch of Greek mysticism was believed by its adherents to be a superior reformation of chthonic Dionysus's sacrificial way. The rites of Orpheus were intended to be ecstatic, but in a way which progressively attempted to avoid the necessity of bodily form. Thus, a dichotomy was made between *ascetic* pleasures of the psyche, mind, or soul – mathematical, poetic, and musical – and *carnal* pleasures of the body – earthy, sexual, and rhythmic. Orphism glorified the former, believing that one's psychic/subtle self *on its own* defined the sacred. It idealized an abstracted self as a psyche-soul separate from the manifest world. It ultimately attempted to escape the inevitability of Tartarus and Hades, along with Gaia and the world of chthonic daimons, which earthly life and physical form were *naturally* wedded to. Orphism posited a different home for the psyche. Amidst this attitude, Eros became progressively associated with male homosexual love.

Developing out of, yet in some ways opposed to, ancient understandings of Tartarus, Hesiod spoke of a paradisiacal land in the time of Kronos, before the era of Zeus and Kronos's other children. The *Garden of Hesperides* was home to the Golden Race during a time that went down in history as the *Golden Age*. Here it was that *streams flowed with ambrosia*. It was in this timeless land that Hercules fulfilled his eleventh labor before entering Hades' realm of Death.

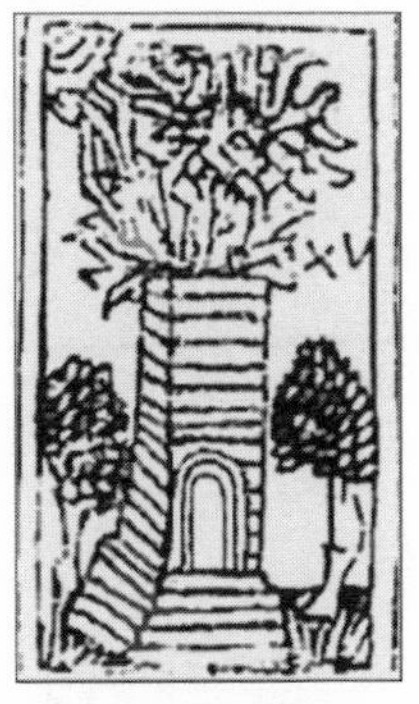

The higher the Questor's goal, the graver the danger that humble seed will no longer be sown, that the Tree of Essential Nature and Vital Life will be displaced by a Tower of technological sufficiency; still, material science will never succeed spiritual knowledge.

In order to be with the woman of his dreams, Hercules had to succeed with twelve labors involving adventures to lands of, and encounters with, the Titans and Titanic beasts. To fetch the golden apples of the Hesperides, ruled by a triad of beautiful Nymphs of the same name, he had to travel to the *end of the earth*. This was a location he could not find, for mortal seeking would only keep one lost. Hercules had to enlist the help of shape-shifting *Nereus* (like Proteus, representing the *Old Man of the Sea* before the age of Zeus/Hades/Poseidon). Even after vanquishing *Ladon* – Hera's *hundred-headed snake-demon* wound around the tree of immortality, reflecting ancient Minoan and tantric traditions – Hercules could not acquire the apples directly, for they could be picked only by one who was already immortal. He thereby turned to *Atlas*, the Hesperides' father.

Atlas was a primordial Titan – *Ruler of the Moon* and brother of Prometheus, *Giver of Fire*. As Greek culture and consciousness conceived a new psychosocial complex of deities and spiritual realms (likely driven by Dorian or earlier Mycenaean invasions), myths arose regarding the banishment of Atlas and his conquered Titanic companions. Much of Hercules' tasks tell of this transition, with the Hero succeeding through assistance from the Old Ones. Zeus gave Atlas the work of holding up the celestial sky, to keep Ouranus from ever again becoming unified with Gaia – the Moon-god became an instrument propping up a new, dualistic worldview separating Heaven from Earth. Once relieved of his imposed dualistic function, as Hercules held up the sky for him, Atlas obtained the golden apples of immortality. Hercules would have been forever engaged in his own dualistic entrapment had he not tricked Atlas into resuming

Intuition is that state of mind wholly continuous with the living body; such is the initial stage of true enlightenment, for it involves complexity beyond the self-constrictive fear or suspicion of discursive analysis.

his old position. In this way, Hercules was ultimately resurrected beyond the Moon station, into the Sun's eternal realm of heroes.

In the golden paradise of Hesperides, Orphic devotees and Platonic idealists imagined themselves capable of *formally* being without suffering a temporal and changing, *earthly* nature. Salvation in such a paradise was pictured as a timeless time of pleasurable fantasy. Into the present day, occultists have psychically conjured phantasms identifying this long-lost mythical land, along with its immortal fruit, nymphal innocents, and dragon warden. Readers may also note resemblance to the Bible's Babylonian and dualistically inspired Garden of Eden.

Chaos and Eros are inevitably experienced *in reality* as being immanently more present than the land of Hesiod's mythical age. Chaos, Eros, the Bright, and the Way are immortal principles directly represented by the Tarot. *They are day-to-day consciously realized by awakened Questors.* The Tarot addresses reality *as it is,* not as one might desire or imagine it to be. That is, it *empirically* refers to an always-already-present reality and the universal principles by which it abides. The *praxis* of the Trionfi put into play uniting internal theosophy with external cosmology acts as a crux of esoteric transmission and knowledge. Marked by the visionary logos of essential and universal hierarchy, the Triumphs summarize millennia of wisdom for our modern age; what are perhaps best called the *wisdom principles of immortality.*

Feeling the currency of Eros in their moment-to-moment lives is what transforms Questors' vitality into energy and energy into spirit, as addressed in chapter 6. Felt and understood in this way, it becomes evident that the alchemical elixir of life, the divine ambrosia, *is none other than Eros itself.* In Buddhist terms, the Eightfold Noble Path culminates in Right Concentration. Such is the completely sublimated alchemical agent first tasted in Right View. Such is Beauty dwelling in the very marrow of one's naked soul.

Ambrosia (literally "immortal," but referring to that which bestows immortality) is that which all sentient life desires. It is the milk, honey, and seed of Eros; the very nectar from which the world is created and sustained. It is wished for even by Death. It is the source of the Gods' immortality, the secret of their vital essence. The elixir of life upon which a Questor's alchemy is reliant, Ambrosia is sought by those who would return to the paradise of golden bliss. Since classical Greek times, European beliefs have held that obtaining the Ambrosia of Heaven, whether through a heroic or demonic effort, makes the attainment of immortality possible. However, attempting such divine transgression usually fails, bringing a Questor damnation in the worst of hellish suffering. Divine Ambrosia was stolen, in one way or another (including through attempted sex with a goddess), by the famous exiles of Tartarus: Sisyphus, Tantalus, Tityus, and Ixion. Appropriately, *Ambrosia* was also the name of Dionysus's first *Maenad-devotee.*

Contemplation is concentration of the Profound – inclusive of intellectual clarity and self-analysis – the Eros of non-self, the nectar of the Great Other, the sympathetic current springing from the Righteous Heart-space of unfathomable mystery.

From the era of Aryan Mycenaean domination of Greece into modern times, Tartarus has been associated with the taboo of sensual ecstasy and immortal empowerment. It has served as a direct channel to, and concomitantly as an underground domain separated from, the sustaining body of the Goddess and creative love of Eros. The Titans were said to have been banished to Tartarus, here interpreted as a realm of deathless Death. *Prometheus,* adversary to Zeus, was a Titan's son (just as Zeus was son of Kronos, brother to the Titans; all being fathered by Gaia and her son-husband Ouranus). After *creating men,* Prometheus *gave them fire he stole from heaven.* He then informed them how to compel divine assistance through conscious sacrifice. As an archetype, much of what Prometheus represented was to be later identified by dualistic Jews and Christians with Satan. The Tarot's Devil and Tower evoke the empowering *transgression* of Prometheus. Zeus (and later Judeo-Christian versions of God) punished men for their existential audacity by introducing *woman: Pandora* manifested with a *container of seductively attractive* but seemingly unlimited *troubles.*

The Subtle Observer blazes with a mindful intensity incomparable to any earthbound immortal, psychic daimon, or astral entity; do not be deceived by the Devil's advocate, rather be finely transfigured.

Prometheus was chained to the Caucasus Mountains to have his liver eternally devoured by an eagle – a type of punishment common to the *exiles* of Tartarus. However, Hercules was able to release him from this Olympic punishment. We can see the myth of Prometheus reflected in Gnostic dualism. The myth of Hercules, however, embodies a distinctly nondual worldview; it transcends the separation of living reality from the afterlife. Furthermore, it recognizes and honors the role of pre-warrior, agrarian heroes who advanced human development as inventors, educators, shamans, healers, and Keepers of the Fire.

The Titans appear to have represented an early, perhaps pre-Mycenaean form of spiritual personification. When Zeus acquired lightning from the *Cyclops* – one of three preeminent brothers to the Titans who dwelled on the island of Sicily – and his brother Poseidon (the undersea god) received the trident (both symbols of Kosmic, immortal force and virility) from the One-eyed Giant, his brother Hades was given a cap of invisibility. The realm of Tartarus, we recall from chapter 5, became associated with Hades. Hades was called in Greek literature *subterranean Zeus* and *Zeus of the dead.*

The Cyclops's mythic forehead eye symbolizes awesome *transformative power.* Forger of magical tools empowering the next generation of deities, Cyclops lived in Gaia's primordial world of Erotic Paradise, Titanic Powers (symbolized so intensely by that most dangerously seductive of demigod daughters, Medusa), and Golden Immortals. The Metropolitan Moon card, representing Eros warding and empowering Gaia's realm, appears to portray this magical Third Eye. (The Budapest Triumph shown in these pages has been processed to unveil this image.) We find most interesting parallels with the *Third Eye of Shiva.* Jane Ellen Harrison, in her brilliantly speculative corpus written a century ago (which includes the beautiful and insightful treatise on Demeter and Dionysus, *Prolegomena to the Study of Greek Religion*), pointed out that *Titan* originally came from the Greek word meaning "white earth," "clay," or "gypsum."

The Titans may have been shamans who covered themselves with white clay or gypsum dust during their magical rituals in the same manner that stories tell of Shiva and his initiating yogi-lineage of animistic shamans.

Embrace the selfless work of salvaging innocence in the face of psychosis, resuscitating living tradition encapsulated by scientific materialism, uniting immortal ways regardless of religious intolerance.

There is cause to suggest that an original pre-Vedic/pre-Olympic way of spirituality was directly associated with a proto-Shiva/Dionysus shamanic culture originating traditions later known as Tantra. Nineteenth- and twentieth-century scholars who believed that primary aspects of European mythology must trace back to an earlier Egyptian civilization suggested Dionysian myths were derived from the cult of Osiris, a god who annually died and resurrected as manifested in the seasons. However, as the Indus Valley culture complex was progressively uncovered, it became apparent that a Dravidian-Aryan *mergence* was crucial to the evolution of ancient Indo-European civilization, influencing its development more fundamentally than Egyptian or Mesopotamian societies did.

The way of natural history is such that cultural identities established as cyclic polar symmetries organically radiate in fields of relationship from which synchronistically emerge new holistic complexities of cultural, societal, and psychological consciousness. This may occur simultaneously in societies separated in space, but likely will occur in significant synchronicity less so for societies separated in ancestry.

Precursory Western Asian sages and initiators of Greek religion arose from Indo-Aryan *shamanic culture* that was epitomized and largely developed in the Indus Valley during pre- and early-Vedic times. (As mentioned, Indus culture bridged with Cycladic and Minoan culture of third millennium B.C. via what is now Iran and Turkey.) Notwithstanding tribal genetics, the mystical and psychological power embodied by shamanic "*daimon*-men" (i.e., our civilization's original *geniuses*) likely became associated with physical size through generations of storytelling; thus, an identification of Titan with Giant.

Be liberated by the Lionsword, the double-edged realization of transcendent unity, the asymmetrical way of crazy wisdom, the core-release of universally spiritual Justice.

Notably, it was the Titans who jealous Hera sent to rend *Dionysus* (meaning "the deity from Nysa") in his original boy-form as *Zagreus* (meaning "Zeus-like") into pieces. After a great deal of animalistic shape-shifting (perhaps representing historic transformations that his shamanic cult underwent), he was finally sacrificed as a *bull.* The Titans ate all of his parts except for his Heart, which was saved by *Athena* (a classical *personification of Diké*). From this he was born again, resurrecting as a godman through the care of the Nymphs of Nysa. The Titans were destroyed by Zeus's lightning. This finds parallels with the power of the Vedic king of gods, Indra, who destroyed or transformed the *pre-Vedic,* Titan-like *Asuras.* From the ashes of the Titans' primeval society arose new, more *civilized* (originally indicating a *settlement of households*) social patterns.

The *Nymphs* of Nysa were so-called *minor nature deities* that cavorted within sacred and immortal realms, expressing their spiritual nature through erotic sexuality and tantric powers. Pliny observed in his *Natural History:*

> Most people assign to India the city of Nysa and Mount Meru which is sacred to father Liber (Dionysus), this being the place from which originated the myth of the birth of Liber from the thigh of Jove (Zeus).

While a mythical Mount Nysa has been ascribed to Thrace (area of Bulgaria, Northern Greece, and Western Turkey), and followers of Osiris locate one of the same name in Ethiopia, it is of import to note that Shiva's sacred mountain was also called Nysa, located near modern-day Peshawar, Pakistan. Greek nymphs had beautiful "cousins" in eastern lands. *Apsaras* spirits served as nymphs and muses in the entourages of the gods and divine realizers such as Shiva and Buddha. They were gorgeously depicted on cave walls in Sri Lanka, India, Central Asia, and China during the developmental and high years of Tantra. We find their remarkable presence reflected in the earliest of Pali scriptures, which detail the spirit realms of the cosmos in tandem with the conscious evolution of Buddha Mind.

The modern World is challenged to integrally incorporate a rich, historical body of magic, myth, and rationality without letting delusions of tribe, nation, or network convict consciousness to a state of alienated stagnation or the lull of jaded banality.

Worship of Dionysus likely extended back to the age of Titanic gods. It continued unabated into the age of Olympians. His shamanic rituals of death and resurrection informed the merging of Chaos, Eros, and Tartarus with a new era of gods. Tartarus was then intimately connected to Zeus, Poseidon, and Hades; for male potency must, at the end of the day, find regeneration within the female sphere. What could be more potently regenerative than penetrating and remaining hidden in the womb of Earth Mother Gaia? By dwelling within Gaia's deepest recess, the male principle could emerge beyond the female's concentrated domain, releasing as the Brightness of the Heavenly Observant Sun. Thus did the principle of Radiance include yet transcend the principle of Space.

Only the great Heroes such as Dionysus and Hercules could cross into the Underworld, enter a domain of the Olympics (in the latter's case, using the River Styx to enter the realm of Hades), and still live. As we shall see, the Greek concept of a *hero* found its mature definition through identification with *afterworld* existence. The three magical devices mentioned previously represented an immortal extension of male potency. Of them, *the Cap of Invisibility became accessible to Questing heroes.*

Hades' formal name, *Aides*, meant "the Unseen one." It was through the agency of Hades' cap that Perseus was able to decapitate the terribly beautiful and mortal Gorgon Medusa and escape her two immortal sisters. Medusa was portrayed in ancient Greek times with symbolism remarkably similar to that of the Yakshis in India. Representing an archaic, Gaian aspect of Eros, this Indo-European goddess was daughter of *Proteus* (the primal sea god who could *change his shape at will*), brother of Kronos; she and her ancestors may well have preceded their cousins the Titans. Medusa was aligned to two sisters; the three composing, when placed in a wilderness context of matriarchal community, integral aspects of

The Fool is the Sage of Eros, the Mage of Amour, the hypostatic inscrutability of Ecstasy.

empowered womanhood. She was at once terrifying and beautiful. She attracted men to her through an awesome sublimation of Shakti into her hair, eyes, mouth, and tongue. Once caught in her hypnotic snake-ecstasy spell, men were eternally bound to her. She drew out of them all *independent* life, petrifying their minds in a state of unmoving devotion to her. Here we see the art of tantra at its extreme, and perhaps in its source-state, sublimating sexuality into an *upper coil* draw of seduction that forms as a sacred hood and nimbus of spiritual empowerment while containing the deepest of daimonic, chthonic potencies and dangers. This *Snake-Fire Trident* and archetypal *Threesome*, realized as an epitome of feminine seduction, can serve as a touchstone of immortality even while simultaneously acting as an all-arresting demonic guard to such.

Perseus, born in the Cyclades, was a son of Zeus and a mortal woman (as were Dionysus and Hercules). He was Founder and King of Mycenae, and great-grandfather of Hercules (whose Dorian Dynasty came much later than three human life spans would indicate). As an early avatar of Zeus-Dionysus, Perseus mythologically bridged ancient Minoan and Cycladic worlds with Mycenaean civilization. While much archeological knowledge has been discovered regarding Mycenaean culture, our core understanding of this city-based Greek warrior society comes through Homer, the ninth century B.C. author of *The Iliad* and *The Odyssey.* These were Greece's original mythic-historic stories detailing the Trojan War (ca. twelfth century B.C.) and heroic adventures of King Odysseus (known to the Romans as Ulysses) of Ithaca, the demigod warrior Achilles, and King Agamemnon of Mycenae (who inherited Perseus's city and was a descendent of Hercules).

The history of Perseus begins with him being cleverly sent off in his youth by a king who desired the woman Perseus warded – his mother. He was given a guaranteed mission-of-no-return: to capture Medusa's head (symbolizing first-stage shamanic, archaic-magical power). As an avatar of Zeus, he was helped by Hermes and Athena (who, like Dionysus, was *thrice-born*), in part by being given winged sandals that enabled him to traverse Titanic realms. The *Graeae,* a *triad of crones* who shared a *single eye,* also helped him find what he needed to succeed in his shamanic quest. As a most ancient version of Fate, the Graeae formed a female entity of visionary power integrating and perhaps matching the titanic potencies of both Medusa and Cyclops. Perseus used Hermes' cap's power of invisibility and his Athena-empowered mirror-like shield to reflect Medusa, entrancing her through her own irresistible attraction. This allowed him to become so close to the goddess that he was able to behead her with Hermes' sickle – archaic Death's tool of sacred sacrifice.

Medusa, containing the power of a unified Triad (and from that, the continuously arising Myriad) as the foundation of her base identity, then transformed into a new Threesome. As Woman (even if only in the embodiment of a living head), she remained a Snake Witch, fully aligned to Perseus while psychically assisting him, petrifying men intending to thwart his missions. As Animal, she became *Pegasus* the *Winged Horse* – a pure, white vehicle allowing the Hero to traverse realms bridging into the Otherworld. Pegasus created a sacred spring for the Muses, became a favorite ally of heroes, and was known for assisting in conquering the fire-breathing, dragon-like Chimaera. (From this perhaps comes the source of dragon-killing unicorns common in popular mythology.) As Man, Medusa became *Chrysaor,* the *Giant Warrior* with a *Golden Sword* who wedded the daughter of the Ocean and raised *Geryon,* a fearsome three-headed, three-bodied Titan who dwelt on the island Erytheia in the Hesperides. (Reflecting the history of Medusa/Perseus, Geryon too was slain by Hercules during one of his trials upon the path of immortality.)

The Gorgons embodied strong, male attributes. *Gorgon* itself meant "the staring one." Both Medusa's beauty and power were derived from her consuming and thus embodying male potency.

In many ways, she was a wild and essential precursor to the *sexually armored* goddesses Artemis and Athena. As Goddess of Wisdom and Strategic Defense (Eros as ward of procreative Gaia), Athena oversaw a domain of empowered and just women. As the preeminent warrior Goddess, she incorporated Medusa's Shakti powers into her invincible shield, upon which one finds the snake goddess' head in Greek iconography. As dispenser of Justice (developed from the original concept of Diké as Zeus's primary female offspring), Athena had assisted Perseus in taming Medusa. Classically, Athena was viewed as a female counterpart to godman Dionysus, in whose lineage Perseus held a key position. However, because the archetype of Medusa includes the wildly potent aspects of Artemis, we may with considerable insight view that more fundamental development of goddess realization in all of its multiplicity (including the Giant Warrior with a Golden Sword – wielding a phallic symbol of immortal male potency) as the ultimate female reflection of a wildly triadic, highly eroticized Dionysus. Neither Demeter nor Persephone (who arguably represented one in the same womanhood) compares, regarding archaic female archetypes of spiritual realization.

Myths regarding the Dionysus-Perseus-Hercules-Hermes lineage formed a coherent, interchanging storyline that told of a heroic and spiritual quest for immortality. The Goddess was a cause of, at all times present in, and indeed utterly indispensable to that Quest. Broadly, *the Quest was for Immortal realization in a context of Goddess resurrection*, commonly symbolized by Persephone, Dionysus's mother. Dionysus (and in India, Shiva) was the first historically recorded incarnation of that *perennial Indo-European shaman* who was able to *bridge Eros with Gaia via sacrificial Death and an otherworld renewal (Tartarus) of transformational consciousness (Chaos)*, and then share his knowledge of evolution with a community of initiates via spiritual rituals. *In that Way is found the Tarot Triumphs' original procession of immortal realization.*

In an earlier chapter, a connection was made between the Knights Templar – who popularly defined medieval romantic, chivalrous tradition and the Quest for the Grail that bestows immortality – and a belted girdle bearing a bearded head as depicted in the Metropolitan Tarot's Devil. Worship of the *Bearded Head* along with apparently associated *secret sexual practices,* were the primary acts of heresy for which the Templar were condemned. (It is telling that even after a great deal of expertly applied torture, the Church apparently never did figure out what the Templar rituals were about.) The Head represented a generative power associated with the afterworld and chthonic rituals ancient in their origins. Here we meet again with Perseus and Medusa's Head, the latter to be wedded to chaste Athena's empowered shield.

Tantric practices were massively honored throughout the East (i.e., the Near East, Central Asia, India, Indochina, and China) and amongst Sufi-influenced cultures in which the Templars lived during the age of the Crusades. Concepts of Shakti-Kundalini ecstasy and militant power were well known and deeply practiced. It is likely that the Assassin/Hashish sects that the Templar Knights were accused of aligning with were practitioners of a so-called "black tantric" way. In accordance to their law, Templars were ideally both strictly celibate and boldly tantric (less idealistically, according to many accounts they were frequently possessed by attitudes of unrestrained lust and violence). Their engagement with psychic power was directly linked to their glorification of Eros. Templars ran roughshod over the earth, yet in courtly fields played a highly dangerous game involving devotion and potent attention to the "princesses and priestesses" of the ruling elite. Genuine commitment to this first stage of alchemical psychosocial process played no small part in their successful gains of earthly power, wealth, and fame.

Accusations of extreme heresy leveled at the Templars (and similarly the Cathars of France before them and Kabbalists of Spain after them) were purposed toward arresting and appropriating their power and wealth. Political and religious authorities were gravely threatened by esoteric communities able to access physical gold along with metaphysical knowledge, the former being sourced largely in the East and the latter being wholly outside of exoteric reach. Such circles embodied both temporal power and spiritual authority, usurping the governance of parties (characterized by second-stage Emperor and Pope) that were unable to integrate the two. Exposed to the study and cultivation of tantric Greek, Sufi, Buddhist, and Taoist alchemy, awakened Templars had won from the East a Holy Grail of spiritual evolution: Temperance, Lovers, Chariot, Fortitude, and Fortune; ultimately culminating in the Hermit, Hanged Man, and Death – stations of realization whose golden rewards could bring ancestral immortality and a legacy of nobility (perhaps as evidenced in their continued fame). The Tarot Triumphs were designed in the century following the breakup of the Templars and the triumph of Sufi Ottomans over Christian Greeks.

Hermes, patron god of alchemy, was the last popular god of the Greek pantheon to come into being (although a classicized version of Dionysus was last to be *promoted* as one of the twelve *Great Olympians*, replacing *Hestia* of the *Hearth*). *Hermes* originally indicated a *herm* or phallic-like pile of stones or simply a carved phallus used as a boundary marker. Although his attributes were often reduced in popular storytelling to an orientation toward cunning and thievery, Hermes served to progressively divinize the magical, shamanic, virile roles embodied by Dionysus, Perseus, and Hercules. He represented in many ways urban-man-made-god, with all the rational attributes (e.g., cunning intelligence, diplomacy, and ironic justice) of a man who through familiarity with urban civilization has acquired what might be called in modern parlance "street smarts."

Hermes was a son of Zeus whose mercurial aspects (again, associated with sexual potency) enabled him to move between Zeus's domain and that of his brother Hades. He inherited the cap of invisibility from Hades himself. In tantric yoga and Taoist alchemy, the top of the head is where Shakti-power finds full *egress*, enabling a practitioner to *mirror others in such a way as to become invisible.* In the previous chapter, we saw that Shakti – the Goddess Charge – can be tapped only through a Questor's *sublimation of sexual potency.* In a phrase, that is the *might of Eros.* All of our great heroes exceeded at traversing that Just Way of the Goddess.

Along with his cap of invisibility, Hermes wielded a Staff of Great Magic. He was often depicted with either a winged cap or winged heels (an area that Taoist medicine associates with the sexual organs). Hermes was not only, for the West, father of alchemy (in part associated with the avataric alchemist Hermes Trismegistos), but also of yogic contemplation and healing. His *caduceus* or wand-staff was entwined by two *snakes,* and was portrayed occasionally with wings at its head. It was originally borne by Isis, the messenger of Hera, who was in later centuries superseded by Zeus's son. A version of the caduceus, the rod of Apollo's son Asclepius, became Western medicine's insignia. It is easily identified with the central nervous system and its two channels, the sympathetic and parasympathetic nervous systems. These are called *ida* and *pingala* in tantric tradition. They are known to wind up the spine, releasing Shakti through the seven *chakras* (literally "wheels," broadly equivalent to the major nerve plexuses along the spine) culminating at the top of the head in an area called the *sushumna* – a sacred opening located where a baby has its soft spot. Traditional Indo-European wisdom places great value in enlivening the central nervous system *channel* as a foundational practice of fortitude, health, and spiritual awakening.

In modern times, psychotropic chemicals and medicinals are popularly used to open the mind/body's central neurology. However, breath, kundalini, and devotional Shakti have been the primary methods effectively utilized over the millennia to *raise consciousness* and unify the body, mind, and heart in a state of holistic health, longevity, and ultimately immortality. *Kundalini* (translating as "myriad steps of earth-force") yoga involves the raising and integrating of one's *prana*, *qi*, or *energy*, building up a superhuman quality to a practitioner's life-force; the experience of which may be felt as both heroic and saintly. Although heroism and saintliness are often viewed as being mutually exclusive, such has never been the case for nondual Questors, whose stories will always find resonance with those sisters and brothers preeminently represented in Greek tradition by the Immortals introduced herein.

Hermes was not the only being able to move in and out of Hades. Hades' wife, Persephone – daughter of Demeter and mother of Dionysus (both via the forced intercourse of Zeus, as per a recurring theme of Zeus as progenitor via divine imposition) – also bridged the Underworld with Earth. Indeed, all of the chthonic mystery sects of ancient times were based upon establishing a living connection between the land of the dead and the land of the fertile. These primeval rites of immortal regeneration were taught by spiritual realizers epitomizing Indo-European agrarian traditions, some more ancient than others; great Otherworld-traversing shamans represented by the myths and icons of Medusa, Persephone, Dionysus, and Shiva, all of whom integrated female and male personas along with chthonic and entrancing rites.

In accordance with this tradition, Homer explained to priests how this world could be spanned with the next:

> At the moment of death, a *breath* called *psyche* exits man and enters the house of Aides, or Hades. Although this psyche does not bear sensations, perceptions, or thoughts, it reflects its previous state by becoming a phantom image called an *eidolon*. Such a spirit-entity is fundamentally all essence and no vitality. However, if given sacrificial blood, or some other form of intense, sacred vitality, the spirit is temporarily able to revive, enough to speak or otherwise affect the living world.

Sojourning to the House of *Aides* (again, meaning "invisibility"), takes a Questor beyond the Great Ocean and beyond the Gates of the Sun to the meadow at the edge of the world. According to the *Odyssey,* in this way Hermes carries over souls to the Otherworld. Portrayed differently in the earlier *Iliad,* the Land of the Dead is found just beneath the flat span of the earth; marked by sounds of wailing and woe, the rivers of Hades form its boundary. Crossing them frees the psyche to join the world of the dead. A psyche needs proper burial rites involving fire and lamentation, lest it be kept from fulfilling its desire to be at rest in the Indifference of the Afterlife. Vedic doctrines in India hold to similar beliefs regarding the state of a soul in the weeks following physical death.

The above are two contrasting fundamental views of the realms beyond Death. Images of a chthonic, watery darkness warded by Death were superseded in Homer's writings by a revelation of that domain beyond primordial waters, watched over by the Sun. Indo-Aryan religious myths shift between Afterworld visions imaging Moon-Water-Tartarus and Sun-Fire-Elysium spheres. Found in the former, after a life-long, wandering Quest, is *Immortal Eros;* found in the latter is that ultimate of attainments won through allegiance with the Goddess: *Blissful Wisdom.*

Homer's *Odyssey* comes down to us as the world's first written portrayal of a Quest into immortal domains serving to convey an esoteric understanding of universal stages of consciousness. Clearly, his tales reflect a long history of such mythic storytelling, just as the Vedas had been passed down orally for many centuries before being recorded in written form. Arguably, an edited composition of the Vedas could also be framed in terms of a Quest, but it would take a genius such as Coomaraswamy to unpack the collection and justifiably reconstruct it in such a manner. The Upanishads are not in and of themselves this type of summarization; and the heroically spiritual quests contained in the popular Ramayana and Mahabharata are of a later date. Homeric and Vedic stories were preceded in written form by Mesopotamian myths of *Gilgamesh;* a seminal epic of heroic adventures that never reaches the height of immortal realization, though it does come close and makes for a remarkable study regarding the social psychology of empire-oriented civilization contemporary with Indus and Minoan cultures.

Greek conceptions of the afterlife varied immensely during the broad period that this chapter addresses. Originally, the psyche was considered to be without consciousness and the netherworld was imagined to be a totally *gray,* senseless, and unknowable place. Such a vision was similar to Babylonian ideas of an underworld found in *Gilgamesh.* This rather neutral image of the domain beyond death was to polarize radically before the dawn of the classical epoch marked by the great sages of the sixth and fifth centuries B.C. By the time of Pythagoras, a doctrine of *metempsychosis* had developed. This theory of *reincarnation* posited the psyche as a soul with conscious identity, able to leave and reenter the physical world. As covered in chapter 4, this grew into the concept of a non-physical, psychic soul from which all decisive feeling and thinking arises. That view, championed by the Sophists, was elaborated by Plato into myths of the Afterlife, which set a stage for Chaldean-influenced Hellenic dualistic religious movements regarding heavens, hells, and apocalyptic destinies.

Notions of eternal punishment in Tartarus for inappropriate acts involving the Goddess or the appropriation of ambrosia and divinely regenerative powers were graphically elaborated in Orphic doctrines written under the influence of Egyptian dualistic worldviews. Chapter 5 examined the progression of Chaldean beliefs as they advanced through Pythagorean sects into Platonic philosophy and Judeo-Hellenic Gnosticism. Key to that development was a dualistic projection of the Deathless into "bad" and "good" domains. A division between *dark* and *bright* afterworlds was unique to neither Judaic nor Greek culture. Indo-European–influenced Taoist tradition held, for instance, that humans had two souls, one native to a veiled earth and one to a bright heaven. However, as we will observe through examining the development of Judeo-Christian dogma regarding Satan, a moral divisiveness between these domains was extremely – even violently – intensified in the cultures and centuries leading to and initiating the Christian era.

In Homer's *Odyssey,* Afterlife was described significantly in terms beyond those of hellish punishments. A *primary* immortal domain was portrayed: the *Elysian Fields,* a realm at the edge of the earth where eternal pleasures were to be found. Etymologically, *Elysium* designated an *elected place* blessed as a result of being *struck by Zeus's lightning* – Heavenly Fire brought Immortally Down to Earth. It marked the domain given to Kronos after being defeated by his son Zeus. Kronos was the divine ruler of the First Age, and will perhaps be so of the last; in any case, *as Time itself, all reversibility comes under his power.* (*Resurrection* as represented in the Angel Triumph, seemingly manifesting a *reversal of Time's arrow,* is the realization of Immortal Rule par excellence.) Neither time nor space limits the quality of immortal existence in Elysium. The climate is forever perfect, people are forever beautiful, and life is forever good. It is the destination of human heroes as immortal realizers. Supernatural and spontaneous transportation is associated with it; for the heroic Questor, personal effort does not suffice to get there. Transiting stages of human consciousness into the Divine Domain requires spiritual assistance and Enlightened Grace. Elysium lies beyond the reaches of Death or Chaos. Few are the humans elected to be blessed with a sight of its brightly transcendent, essentially natural, and always vital realm.

A worldview emerged across Greek societies wherein the realm after death is destined for *most* people to be a sorry if not punishing place. Given that, what soul would not wish to return to earth in the form of another body? There would then be a possibility, even if only remote, of entering a transformed, most blissful land after death. Rebirth affords every soul a new, however slim, chance of following in the footsteps of the Heroes. However, even for the saintly good at heart, reaching the Elysian Fields requires embarking upon a heroically spirited quest. Miraculous powers are needed, as well as immense virtue. Death has to be faced in bone-chilling intimacy and a portal to the afterlife then found and entered. Insight into the totally awesome forces of Chaos has to be mindfully accrued. Moreover, through it all, conscious sacrifice to the Desire of the Goddess through Compassionate Love of Eros has to be progressively engaged. Dionysus's rites and Hercules' adventures tell of the way.

In the centuries following Plato, the concept of *soul* gathered progressively greater psychological identity. Greek religious sects basically demarked humankind via three divisions:

1. Those who were privy to the secret mysteries of the afterlife; who were initiated into the path which opened a portal to eternal bliss, knowledge, and being; who adhered to the immortal laws of beauty and goodness; who rigorously practiced purifications conducive to the virtuous way that ofttimes proved to be a narrow and treacherous road.
2. Those who respected the heaven-influenced fates of mortals and held in awe the demigod heroes; who learned rituals of magic in the process of aligning themselves to mage-like teachers; who attended the philosophers and served the priests; who perhaps could hope in a future life to quest on the path toward immortality.
3. Those who were ignorant of the *Mystery Rites;* who were blessed with neither the purity of true beauty nor the intellect of true goodness; who had little control of their lives, serving as tokens in a game of the gods; who were destined to join the teeming masses in Hades or be reborn in an earthbound life of suffering, for they were fated neither to discover nor partake in the Quest of Heroes.

In the latter group could be found the masses of humankind. Tricking the gods into bestowing magical powers that would assure fame and fortune if not immortality was a primary occupation of the middle group. In the first group dwelled an elite few, sworn to secrecy while channeling, quickening, and even reversing the forces of Fate. This was done by surrendering to the agency of a Godman such as Dionysus or through psychically renewing the successful deeds of a Hero such as Hercules. Sensually ecstatic maenads and power-wielding mages reflected those who had been most successful in sacrificing temporal self in order to realize immortal consciousness.

The conception of hero *as half-god* was largely unique to Greek culture, though again we find parallels in India, such as the dual identity of Arjuna-Krishna found in the *Bhagavad-Gita.* With Fortitude founded upon fantastically potent virility, a hero was never thwarted from his or her Quest. Every masculine hero also embodied major elements of femininity, madness, and servitude. It might be said that these contributed saintly potential to a hero's nature. This polar being had the power to avert most evil. Like the demons they had to fight, heroes were often popularly associated with the guarding of sacred portals. In later times, heroes became largely identified with glorified life in the afterworld. Like Hades himself, a hero could invisibly steer human destinies; and could be invoked by the non-heroic to do so. Being Immortal, heroes were capable of influencing earthly matters through the ages. They warranted sincere rites of honor, regardless of their lack of physical presence on earth.

Hercules was an archetypal hero. He was said to have been the original ancestor of the Dorian kings (invaders of Greece at the end of the Mycenaean period, 1100 B.C., and founders of the era in which classical Greek culture arose) and a mortal son of Zeus. As the avataric embodiment of Zeus-Dionysus for a dawning age of mythic-rational signification, Hercules had to overcome unconscious demons, psychophysical poisons, and subhuman beasts, ultimately sacrificing himself in the presence of women he loved.

The jealousy of Hera, attempting to bind the Shining One solely to her, drove Hercules mad (as it had Dionysus). Consequently he killed his first wife, children, and nephews. As a prototypical ruler who in his Quest to rectify his karma realizes immortality for himself and hierarchical evolution for his people (respecting and integrating previous levels of consciousness and tradition), Hercules became a model for the commons. As a man-god, his corporeal reality broke structural limitations imposed by civilized domination of mythic-based laws.

Over centuries of Dorian dominance, a hierarchy of prevailing deities was progressively constructed via the formalization of Greek religion and its temple system. This extensively politicized system imprinted upon the commons those beliefs upheld and enforced by the ruling class. *Hercules undermined that domination hierarchy.* Because of this, he acted as a disruptive agent in the human world, even while perpetuating continuity in the evolutionary growth and empowerment of humankind. Hercules not only freed Prometheus, he continued the Titan's work of *transferring divine power and immortal realization to the realm of humans*. Through his adventures, the educated were informed of a way to enter spiritual domains by capturing, taming, and making themselves integrally conscious of primal, daemonic states. It is not surprising that he was as popular with the Romans (who named him *Hercules*) and Etruscans as he was with the Greeks (whose actual name for him was *Herakles*, literally meaning "he who is heard").

Hercules blazed a universal path into and *beyond* (for it *returned back home*) the Afterworld. He did so not only with his strength and Fortitude (derived from the impenetrable spiritual charge of his magical lion cloak – a *feminine* power reflected in the Fortitude Triumph and comparable to the warding force of Medusa contained within the shield of Athena, with whom Hercules was intimate and reliant upon at key times in his quest for immortality), but also with his precious Arrows, analogous to Zeus's Lightning-bolts. We again observe that such Striking Light and invocation of divine presence that it represents is symbolized in the Tower Triumph. Of course, traversing such a way through such means demands an extraordinary effort that inevitably meets with Daemonic catastrophe. Thus, even Hercules first needed to be *initiated* into the *Eleusinian Mysteries* in order to gain protection from the chaotic forces churning out of nature's dark side. At Eleusis – home to mysteries of the Great Goddess Demeter, her daughter Persephone, and Persephone's son Dionysus – Hercules was initiated into the secrets of the Underworld. Eleusis was an ancient center of goddess and phallus worship. Here, age-old fertility rites became focused on the ecstatic and destined abduction of the Virgin Daughter by Hades. Released from her underworld duties for half of each year, Persephone represented purity and nourishment appearing out of the darkness like a Star bestowing the grace of Immortal Providence. (Accordingly, it was reasonable for Ibn ʿArabi to place the Degrader higher than the Nourisher, and the latter directly after Death.)

Preceding the age of Olympian gods, Perseus and other Mycenaean Kings, and Hercules and Dorian ancestors after him, Dionysus with his tantric *thyrsus* (an *ivy-wrapped staff with a pinecone tip,* paralleling the *mark* or *lingam* of Shiva) was the male focus of Eleusis's priestesses and their mysterious rituals. While some myths make Persephone to be his mother, other stories tell of a human mother Semele, who was pulverized when Zeus's wife Hera tricked her into compelling Zeus to expose himself in his full glory, which no mortal could bear to witness. Dionysus represented the fruit of the tree and vine just as Demeter represented the fruit of the field. He was often called the Boy-god and paradoxically maintained innocence in the midst of dramatic madness. Whereas Hercules was a human made god (after his death he was resurrected in Olympia) Dionysus was *twice born* (or more accurately, *thrice born,* for he also resurrected in spirit-form like the vines of the Earth) and thus effectively a god made half-man. As such an *Avatar* (literally "he who crosses Down"), he was unique in the Greek pantheon of divine beings; later heroes such as Perseus and Hercules merely *resembled* him.

In classical times, *Dionysus was widely identified with the divine latecomer Hermes.* It can be difficult for scholars to discern between the two in Greek iconography. His cult also bore similarities to that of Artemis. They were the only divine figures surrounded by a retinue of wild, sexually potent females. Phallic components were part of the celebratory garb for both cults, as was a sort of sexual madness. Themes of nature, militancy, seduction, danger, and intuitive intelligence were integrated in both god and goddess.

Artemis was the *Queen of Nymphs* and *Huntress of the Wilds.* Her cult was pre-Olympian, and as such was mostly oriented toward intense fecundity. While she and Athena are commonly thought of as militantly virgin goddesses, the original meaning of *virgin* in Greek was *unmarried and unbound,* representing the goddesses' feminine Liberation rather than a stricture of celibacy.

In archaic art, Artemis can be found riding next to Athena, sharing a Chariot warded by *Fate* (the *Moirai* who were originally One but became Three). The Moirai and their *golden chariot* were the oldest incarnation of the stern, warrior demeanor of womanhood that extends Justice into the World, including the gods' immortal spheres. The ancientness and primacy of this female goddess aspect is reflected in its association with the Titan *Themis,* Goddess of *Divine Law* and *Oracles. Themis was Zeus's primal wife and prime counsellor.* She effectively represented both mother Gaia and daughter Diké. Zeus the new Heaven God was brought together with Themis the old Gaian Goddess by Moirai, the Fate of the World. Pindar tells us:

> First did the Moirai in their golden chariot bring heavenly Themis, wise in counsel, by a gleaming pathway from the springs of Okeanos [the Titan we call *Ocean*] to the sacred stair of Olympos, there to be the primal bride of Zeus Soter [Saviour].

As with Medusa, any male who actually witnesses Artemis becomes frozen by her bewitching sensuality. Although ecstatically pleasurable, such psychic connection brings with it the fate of a Sacrificial Stag, representing sexual domination by the female. When shot by the Goddess, the arrow of Eros is both blinding and binding. Her potent *male aspect* is represented by her gift from the Cyclops: a silver bow with golden shafts (paralleling Medusa-Chrysaor's golden sword).

Artemis was the goddess of *midwives* (literally meaning in Old English "with woman"; the Greek word for midwife is *maia*, indicating "she who brings increase" – Maia as daughter of Atlas was Hermes' mother). She drove a chariot and protected children and young mothers. Like the Issy-sur-Moulineaux Chariot, the Metropolitan's Chariot shows children behind what one imagines to be a woman holding the reigns. Empowered by Fate herself, Artemis's Moon-power could steer the Force of Nature-determined courses. As twin sister of *Apollo* (chariot driver of the Sun), Artemis conjoined with Athena (especially in Athena's original Minoan personification as *Sun-goddess* associated with Demeter and attributes of bird, snake, sacred tree, weaving, and wisdom) to symbolize the two sides of liberated Womanhood (compare to Persephone and Demeter), just as Dionysus and Apollo merged to symbolize the same for Manhood. Artemis can be found in the spirit-charge of the Tarot's fourth-stage Chariot and Fortitude (holding back the Lion's roar); Athena is found in both common and royal stations of *judgment:* Temperance and Justice. Both goddesses combine with the Eros of Aphrodite in Love and the Hermetic androgyny of Mystery-Light represented by the Star and Moon Triumphs.

Female militancy was an important aspect of Dionysian Maenads. Women who armored themselves *against* feeling Dionysus's ecstatic impulses inevitably regretted doing so. Rejecting his Presence led only to a web of dementia. The godman was raised opposed by those who could not stand that he was so realized. Persecuted by his stepmother *Hera* (sister and later *wife of Zeus* and whose domains included marriage, housewives, and jealousy), he learned to cope with madness brought upon him by her pathologically controlling female ego. That madness arose when Dionysus was *denied* for being That which he was; and extended to those who inflicted upon him projections of self-centered fear. Equally, the madness could transform as *ecstasy* in both the Boy-god and his companions. Such was the *salvational praxis* of He who pulverized sensible hatred and greed through crazy Beauty and Truth.

Dionysus's untouchable heavenly brother Apollo was championed in modern philosophy by Friedrich Nietzsche as an ideally pure opposite to the chthonic god's way of apparently destructive intoxication. In Greek religion, though, the two were always positioned in a relationship of positive polarity. Nowhere more than in the famous Delphic sanctuary of Apollo was this evident. There, Dionysus was formally incorporated as the chthonic counterpart to the Sun God. Nietzsche's Gnostic-like nihilism spurred an interpretation of cultural history that had little to do with wisdom-based esoteric cosmology or metaphysics. Nietzsche's worldview did, however, reflect dualistic, Orphic beliefs. Orpheus, a musical poet and singer who worshipped Dionysus, became famous prophesizing in his master's name. However, he purportedly denied Dionysus's reality, proclaiming to the heavens that only Apollo steered the true course. For this, Dionysus sent a raving band of maenads who tragically rent Orpheus into unspeakable pieces, leaving Apollo's muses to bury him.

Dismemberment of the child Dionysus by the hands of Titans sent by Hera was perhaps the most closely held secret of initiates in the old mystery sects; that his prophet Orpheus should befall the same fate but not be resurrected is telling. Orpheus, like most prophets, denied the possibility of immortal realization *in this life.* God-realization implies unconquerable power – "total control" – in the eyes of mortal men wielding authority through *domination* of others. *Prophecy* connotes the *will of God. Subjecting* men to the projected *will* of an objectified god is the work of *politicized* priests and prophets. This role can be enacted only when the living presence, teaching, and culture of the Divine One is not self-evident, or not able to be self-authenticated by the commons. In esoteric streams of the Great Tradition, the natural wisdom of Deathless realized Saints and Sages has inevitably taken precedence over the revelations of prophets. Influential as he was, Orpheus could not replace Dionysus as an authentic exemplar of the ancient Mystery Rites. In contrast, Jesus's wisdom-teachings have been recognized by billions as transcending the laws of Judaic prophets preceding him. Similarly, many Sufis have regarded Rumi's and Ibn ʿArabi's ecstatic proclamations of divine realization as more brilliant than the Koran's prophecies of social law. (Such a view, of course, remains heretical in the exoteric establishments of Islam.)

Although wielding shamanistic and mage-like powers, the charismatic, singing prophet known as Orpheus had not realized the Principles of Immortality. He nevertheless claimed to have inherited the secrets of ancient goddess mysteries. Upon these, he founded a loosely bound religion based upon reincarnation and cosmic dualism. Devotees of Orpheus maintained that ascetic purity in this world was the best that any man could aspire to. Practiced assiduously for several lifetimes, such asceticism could enable a man to finally traverse the realms of cosmic existence and enter that domain of the afterlife that was eternally bright and easy. Comparable positions were adhered to by Theravada Buddhist monks during this period in India, opposing the ancient roots of Tantra and disbelieving Gautama Buddha's proclamation of Enlightenment In and As This Very Lifetime.

Orpheus's cosmic visions were made in the name of an Immortal whose teaching was radically different from his own. For Dionysus, self was to be surrendered and ecstasy was to be lived in the *afterworld that becomes this world*. The physical world is a *vehicle* for spiritual realization, not a *block* to it. Through communion with the afterlife via nakedly natural and ritualistic celebration, mundane life is transcended and, in fact, literally transformed. The kingdom of immortal happiness must be *realized* to be at hand. How this can be enacted is what Dionysian rites were all about. Orphism correlated with later Gnosticism. They both believed it possible to escape cosmic cycles and chaotic transformations by negating them. For Orphic-Pythagoreans and Christians influenced by Gnosticism (including the Pauline religion now generally known as Christianity) Dionysus-Jesus became the divine savior who died for mankind; whose body and blood were symbolically consumed in the Eucharist of celibate devotees. That magical act was essential to purifying mankind's soul of its innate, earthbound sin.

Dionysian initiates called *mystai* walked *the long, sacred way*, the *path of Zeus* the Immortal One, destined to a blessed, blissful realm in the Afterworld – home of the Heroes. *That path is portrayed in the stages of the Tarot*. It embraces an intense fourth-stage conduction of Spiritual Force. It surrenders self-separation in a subtle, fifth-stage emptiness of Mystical Awareness (Wheel of Fortune and Hermit). It proceeds through a sixth stage of totally Sacrificial Death (involving the Witnessing Hanged Man). It delivers the Questor's very consciousness to the feet of the Guardian with the Threefold Challenge. The seventh stage's Devil represents the chaotically emergent, trans-cosmic state of immortality realized by the Titanic denizens of Tartarus.

From the Titans' domain, the Golden Immortals of Elysium and later immortals such as Hercules were transported to the purely erotic space nourished by the ambrosia of Star and Moon. In modern terms, transformation of the mundane into the sacred occurs through deeply complex releases of potential energy, fundamentally affecting a Questor's identity and causal reality. A trans-cosmic flux causing existential transformation can be realized through mindful consciousness. This both returns and evolves the Questor to a yet-greater, prior, and destined state of transfigured whole-body soul. For Dionysian mystai, *returning* to Eros paradoxically means *evolving* in union with the Goddess. This requires completely insightful Remembrance and radical transformation of sensuality through sacrificial, Transcendental Intercourse.

At the gates from which a Questor is transported to Hades, to ordinary rebirth, or to liberation from suffering, *recollection of Truth is tantamount to enlightened passage.* Forgetfulness of Beauty, Goodness, and Truth is ever a Questor's primary bane. To become one with Eros, a Questor must continuously *remember* Eros. This has always been the Secret of Secrets, the Key to the Tower. There is no doubt – lightning *will* strike every Questor aspiring to immortal realization, to the ambrosia of the gods. Moreover, through a stroke of Justice, that lightning may well *destroy* Questors' long-built advantage, Abasing their karma for lifetimes to come. Then again, it may simply deflate Questors' dreams, returning them to mere mediocrity and ponderous doubt for the bulk of their lives. *Or* it may indeed *Provide* for Questors, Justly electing them for divine protection and thus enabling them to realize states of consciousness beyond mortal self.

It bears repeating for any and all Questors: *Remember Eros.* Identify not with the obsession of "self," but rather with the Soul of the World as Radiant Goodness – the Goddess as Fathomless Beauty. Is this not in Truth what you have always been and will eternally Be? Then you have only to simply remember it continuously. With as much concentration as your heart will bear. This is the realization of Dionysus. Through *his* Sacrifice, the Goddess lifts her veil, granting truly devoted initiates union with and as *her* sacrifice. Therefore, *mystai* are encouraged to *become* the Goddess by meditating, remembering, and even consuming Dionysus.

It might be said that Dionysian *ravers* who surrender into the extreme nature of their initiation look at Death and willingly give themselves to it. All the while, a mysteriously erotic siren call, beyond the song of an artist's muse, beckons them to a world beyond. At the point of *mind-less* surrender, consciousness would be totally lost and bodies crashed if not for the awesome *presence* of the transcendental *One*. That presence *mind-fully* Outshines all. It is known and felt even when Dionysus is not manifestly obvious in human form. Historically, Dionysian realization has been cultivated through communal celebratory rituals including sexual fire dancing and drug taking, with his Heart-Soul consciously taking form in the witnessing awareness of celebrants. Poetry, theater, music, and rhetoric can merge with philosophy in further rational and intuitive developments of such essential ritualistic and initiatory celebration.

Proud in their urbane worldviews, Orphic and related Pythagorean sects laid claim to a secret knowledge "higher than" the perennial wisdom of Indo-European tradition. For both sects, worldly life was viewed as naught but trouble; and sexuality was intimately tied to such trouble. Sectarian rules held in common included renouncing all possessions, undergoing years of silence, and abstaining from many foods, including intoxicants. Correlatives can once again be found within certain schools of monastic Buddhism present in Asia Minor and the Near East during this era, which were challenged by the rise of nondual Mahayana realizations. Championing Orphic dualism, the occult orientations of Neopythagoreans and Gnostics denied nondual reality. In contrast, the ecstatic Unity-procession revealed by Dionysus catalyzed among his celebrants conscious and present identification of the natural world with the Living Principles of Immortality.

Jesus proclaimed a similarly bold truth, as did Plotinus. Jesus's message, according to Q and the *Gospel of Thomas*, emphasized an immediate and very real presence of the One God and his Wisdom-World. On the other hand, all of the various *Acts of the Apostles*, including Paul's (though his to a lesser extent), stake out claims in the territory of Gnostic-oriented dualism. Paul, who lived after

Jesus's generation, started a new religion in line with Orphic sensibilities. Strictly anti-sexual, glorifying a spirit world separate from the manifested world, Paul's religion grew over two centuries to become the one that people refer to when they speak of Christianity.

In twenty-first-century societies obsessed with idealizing modern materialism, traditional spiritual cultures have been declared obsolete if not unlawful. Organic patterns of communication and communion that cannot be reduced to objectified strategies purposed toward production and consumption of material goods are declared *superstitious* and *backwards.* While superstitions are of course held to by many folk, uneducated or not, it is a grave mistake to ignorantly apply such a label to understandings of esotericism, spiritual alchemy, tantra, and much of what has been addressed in this book.

Pythagoreans deified mathematics without acknowledging the One. Modern-day scientific materialists practically follow suit. However, authentic wisdom does not arise from materialistically reductive worldviews. Universal laws of consciousness can be modeled in the mathematical terms of physics and chemistry only to a profoundly limited degree. Environmental, anthropological, sociological, psychological, and other schools of knowledge will continue developing verifiable models of greater import and significance to nature, culture, society, and individual happiness than models of atomic and molecular reality. Solutions to disease and environmental problems become relatively straightforward when studied by minds practiced in compassionate and wise spirituality and educated in the modern sense of the word. Appropriate technology can be applied with clear-headed insight and innovativeness. Displacing perennial wisdom with materialistic scientism is simply dumb. We will soon finish our treatise with an in-depth look at how our modern world can rectify this.

Transcending . . . Right Mindfulness

A major point brought home by the Tarot is that the transcendental is naturally wedded to the world just as it is: physically complex, organic and earthy, constantly developing through natural cycles of growth. Historically, denial that divine presence inherently exists in our common-day world has been accompanied by dualistic movements purposed toward involvement of an obscurely occulted afterworld with mundane life. In medieval Christian society, *sorcerers* were accused of reaching into *realms beyond*, accessible only through the *Devil's domain*. Even a relatively benign art such as *divination* was associated with *necromancy;* the power to *see into the future* was attributed to *raising demons and the dead*. The use of that power was not associated with mature intuition, intentional healing, or compassionate wisdom, but rather with the Devil. The power of Eros, interpreted in terms of degenerative eroticism and psychic manipulation, implied a pact with Satan.

Within Chaldean, Judeo-Hellenic, and Christian milieus, perceived gaps between human, natural, and immortal domains grew to be immense. Although this was balanced by developmental teachings of emanation founded upon fully discerning, nondual awareness, all sight of the Sacred was periodically lost in the worldviews of social leaders. Governing policies of urban societies were then stamped with a seal of violently righteous domination bound to decadent greed, from which there existed little chance of liberation. All too readily, dualism slid into nihilistic solipsism and the excesses of debauchery.

During the procession of dualism from the time of Jesus into our modern era, apocalyptic cults have repeatedly woven together strands of spiritualism and nihilism. The essential wisdom found in Jesus's original sayings are hardly to be found in apocalyptic

Christianity. Similarly, the Love discovered in Rumi's interpretation of Muhammad's revelation differs wholly from the legalistic justifications (frequently based upon maliciously mistranslated Arabic, a language of many meanings) of brutal violence construed by Islamic "fundamentalists."

Although we find in modern times schools of pathologically rational thought that deny spiritual reality altogether, so also do we find traditions allied in their rational and integrative championing of nondual philosophy. Holding to the view of nonduality in a fragmented, postmodern age has compelled teachers to elaborate a way of Crazy Wisdom. This integral foundation of *world* teaching, cultivation, and communion employs methods of ecstatic liberation which work in an otherwise jaded, unethical, self-obsessed age. Of course, extreme methods of awakening can also produce extreme reactions of denial. In a Western, secularized society, "crazy wisdom" easily promotes misunderstandings that cynically throw craziness into the limelight while avoiding the challenge of actual wisdom. Jesus was evidently a Crazy Wisdom teacher to some degree; the *Gospel of Thomas* has numerous sayings that are as provocative now as they must have been in Jesus's own time. Let us take off the mantle and encourage tolerantly critical dialogue between *crazy wisdom* adepts and traditional *middle way* teachers. What may appear to be madness or otherwise extreme behavior to an objective outsider may be a liberating dynamic dispelling negative habit patterns and instilling true goodness to a subjective insider. In any case, unusual yet effective means of demonstrating wisdom and love need to be appreciated, understood, and kept from harming the unprepared.

We may interpret four types of *madness* delineated in Plato's dialogue *Phaedrus* thusly: surrendering one's *will* to the gods is a madness of *prophecy;* surrendering one's *feelings* to perfect order is a madness of *music;* surrendering one's *imagination* to the intelligently erotic is a madness of *philosophy;* and surrendering one's *consciousness* to Dionysus is a madness of *initiation.* These forms of crazy wisdom may be respectively represented by the Devil, Tower, Star, and Moon Trionfi, composing a procession that we might call a *madness of immortality.* Modern citizens rationally justify the madness of *war* and rampant *greed* with dualistic concepts founded upon *manifest destiny, apocalyptic retribution, materialistic freedom,* etc. But *cultivation of compassion and ultimately self-sacrificial wisdom* promotes a superior nondual form of rational, intuitively intelligent madness that steers consciousness toward freedom through peace and virtue, not security through subjugation and violence.

From within the Hellenistic culture of rationality emerged a new phase of Dionysus's ecstatic procession. The mystery way of immortals continued to be intelligently learned and practiced via currents of esoteric spiritual and cultural transmission with which the reader may now feel some familiarity. The Tarot portrays rational responsibility as a cyclic and communicative process *tolerating Vision.* It then speaks of spiritual hierarchy in terms of *governing Mission, conceiving Life, witnessing Death, transfiguring Self, and transforming Soul.* The Dionysian way of spiritual realization is an ecstatically sensual quest purposed toward *being* the Sun – Apollo made man, Heaven made earth, Ideal Law made practical method. Shining with a reflection of what the Sun ultimately emanates – *radiant order in the universal domain of Eternity* – the Trionfi humbly convey Wisdom *as* the World in its *naturally lawful, Just Way.* Given that, there is an aspect of scientific erudition that may be seriously abetted through this study of the Tarot and its origins. Before we examine that, we will put to rest all unsettled confusion that Questors may have regarding the rightful place of Chaos in the World.

The Quest hinges upon Death and the Devil. These are not hateful signs of one's most intimate enemy; rather, they are living principles informing the way of immortality. Jesus pointed to the difficult virtue of verily loving a friend (let alone an *enemy*) *as* oneself.

Transcending the *risk* that inheres in such compassion continues to be the most immediate way for a genuine Teacher to test the truth of any Questor who would approach the portal to heaven and its grail of ambrosia.

From the earliest of times, Judaic tradition posited a spiritual dichotomy between *the people of Israel* and those of other nations, the latter broadly characterized in the books of Genesis and Exodus as *evil enemies*. In old Judaic thought, non-Jewish tribes were culturally demonized. The prophet Isaiah identified these enemies with the *odious dragon* of ancient Canaanite mythology, the twisting serpent *Leviathan*. However, Jews characterized *enemies of their own blood* as *Satanic*. The root of *satan* means "one who opposes, acts as an adversary." In Judaic mythology, a satan was an angel of high standing in the court of God. *Angelos* is the Greek translation of Hebrew *mal'ak,* meaning "messenger." Early in the Hebrew Bible, a satan was not portrayed as being in opposition to God. On the contrary, it was viewed as one of God's trusted messengers; an obedient servant sent by God to *obstruct human activity* and then create catastrophe and chaos for reasons often only known to God.

Jews who obstructed other Jews were viewed with a degree of tolerance insofar as it could be imagined they were doing so for divine reason. In the book of Job, Job's story tells of a satan who *roams* (derived from a Hebrew pun on the word *satan*) on earth keeping a watch on humankind. God authorizes him to test Job, who at the time was God's favored human servant. The pain inflicted upon Job was devastating. In the end, though, having passed God's tests (applied by his servant, the satan) Job gained twice his previous fortune.

Job was written around 550 B.C., during that critical age of transition in which lived Pythagoras, Heraclitus, and Gautama. In the following century, Jewish ecclesiastical concepts of a satan began to appear with more malevolent aspects. Written during this era, the story of King David as told in 1 Chronicles speaks of a satan who impelled David to introduce census-taking for the purpose of taxation. In the story, the satan becomes a *scapegoat* – a *supernatural enemy* within the Jewish camp who is *blamed* for inciting division and conflict. King David was punished for his act although it was provoked by an angelic power. God sent another angel to avenge the king's actions by spreading a plague across Israel, killing seventy thousand Jews.

The book of Zechariah tells of exiles that upon returning to Jerusalem from Babylon during this era (released by King Cyrus of Persia, who had conquered the Babylonian empire, along with territories reaching into India) conflicted with the city's residents. The exiles had brought funds from Cyrus to rebuild Jerusalem's central Temple. This, along with the fact that they were cosmopolitan and well-educated, set them at odds with the Jerusalem priests then in power. The prophet Zechariah, siding with the returning exiles, tells of a satan taking the side of the local country folk of Israel. God rebuked the satan for acting in a way apparently opposed to the Lord. Throughout history, Devil as Satan has tended to represent the *Old Way*, a challenge to deeply disruptive and transformative change that often proves inevitable regardless of the challenge.

In the era following Alexander the Great, Judaic politics favored anti-Greek attitudes. Hellenistic Jews became an internal enemy to families of the "old way" looking to take back control of Israel. By the time of Jesus, *Pharisees* (a sect succeeding the *Hasidim* or *Pious*, and now identified with *Rabbinic Judaism*) were at the forefront of a movement attempting to renew the austere practices of traditional Judaic law. *Essenes* and other radical groups of Jews, evidently including the community surrounding Jesus's blood family, felt that the high priest who controlled the Temple of Jerusalem had become their worst of enemies. He and his compatriots had betrayed the *law of the faithful*. These enemies had "walked the way of the nations;" they no longer were *true* to Israel and its God. This was, perhaps, a second-stage mythic denial of third-stage rational civilization. Those who cultivated a cosmopolitan, integrated, and worldly way of life were progressively identified as being *satanic.*

Satan became the antithesis of God; a most powerful being in the court of the Jewish Lord, but traitor of that hierarchical level and position. This identification of *insider enemy* with malevolent demigod was magnified and exploited by both Judaic and Christian Gnostics. Mark, author of the earliest canonical gospel, inherited this concept of Satan as God's rival and passed it into mainstream Christianity. There is no evidence in *The Gospel of Thomas* indicating that Jesus believed in or dueled with a satanic figure. Indeed, one could argue that certain dualistic Judaic camps would have likely viewed the authentic Jesus as just such an adversary.

Many apocryphal accounts circulated amongst Jewish and Christian circles of the first century that purported to reveal Satan's origins. The most influential of these was a body of stories that blamed *lust* for drawing the angelic *sons of God* (an oft-used Hebrew designation for *angels*) into unlawful sexual relations with human women. Their offspring spawned earthly demons who gained control of mankind's fallen world. This story served as an effective analogy for varying enemies of Israel. The Greeks with their ancestral claims of heroic half-gods such as Herakles and Dionysus along with Titanic progeny such as Cyclops, Medusa, and Prometheus were made out to be demon-spawn. The Jerusalem priesthood, which condoned marrying *Gentile* (i.e., *non-Jewish*) women, was accused of atrocious, satanic violations of Judaic Law.

Jewish sects progressively rewrote Israel's history using dualistic terms referring to a cosmic war between "sons of light" and "sons of darkness." Christianity inherited a large part of this cosmology through Gnostic beliefs. By the time of Paul (who preached a personal interpretation and revelation of the Judaic Jesus cult with little reference to Jesus's own teachings), Israel as an integrated religious community was too fractured to hold itself together. It was

felt among many that the God of the Jews no longer supported the Temple priesthood, for the Jewish rites had become irretrievably tainted. Paul proclaimed this as a divinely destined development; society forevermore was split into two groups of people: those who belonged to the Kingdom of Heaven and those who were ruled by Satan. Paul's congregation staked a historically usurping claim to the Shining One, the God in Heaven, which was proclaimed eternally final. Worshippers of old pagan, goddess-abetted heroic rites were deemed heretics fallen under spells of obsolete initiations. A new, divinely created network of urban tribes announced its manifested destiny: it became known as the *Christian Nation*.

Within a few hundred years, Christianity spread across the world. In the process, Pagan views of spirituality were radically demonized. Consciousness of psychic and subtle beingness defined in traditional Indo-European contexts via awareness of *daimons* (spirit forces of immortal realms and principles that manifest worldly influences) inherent to every *genius* (thus identifying one's genius with one's own daimon), was declared by Justin Martyr, the grandfather of Christian theology, as *foul*. Greek *daimon* as divine power translated into Late Latin *daemon* or spirit, which passed into Middle English as *demon* with all of the *hellish* undertones that we ascribe to it today.

A new spiritual vision was given miraculously to those who underwent *baptism* in the Christian rite. It was a vision of Heaven *free from Satan's taint*. Free from Nature and the base world of Gaia. Free from the desire, death, fate, and creation of Eros. Free from the Goddess. All other spiritual views were identified with the Devil's mind purposefully blocking souls from the path of salvation.

The Greek word for devil, *diabolos*, literally means "one who throws something across one's path." Early Church fathers believed that Satan and his fellow demons could drive humans to evil acts without their knowing it. This was done through deviously subtle methods of *mind control*. In fact, Fate itself was thought to be naught but a game played by the Devil and his minions. Christians held that pagan believers of *natural* destiny were actually being manipulated in accordance with Satan's plan. The art of divination, it was nefariously posited, consisted of mindfully watching a demonic game of psychic manipulation. Through this, a sorcerer gained insight into the moves of Satan's demons and could foresee how ignorant humans would be compelled to act. Such work was considered to be the most dangerous imaginable. Special priests in the Church had to fight not only malevolent spirits, but also otherwise educated, well-bred metaphysicians (such as Hermetic alchemists) deemed tainted by the power of Satan. In the eyes of the Church, only a *saint* could perceive into the demonic manipulations of the afterworld and retain his soul. Few were those with such ironclad faith, and all were by definition under the law and rule of the Church, supporting its sociocultural policies.

Neoplatonic philosophers could not understand the Christian drive to posit a significant adversary to the greatest of gods. It seemed sacrilegious and dangerously impious. By establishing opposing factions in heaven, Christians were suspected of promoting and justifying fundamental divisiveness on earth. By equating Satan with the realm of daimons Christians took the step of apparently declaring all forces of *genesis* and *genius,* i.e., *generative spirit,* to be evil. This was viewed as simpleminded and hypocritical of Christians, for did they not enjoy good food, wine, air, cloth, baths, and perfumes – all derived from subtle elements of nature? Christian theologians attempted to mitigate their position by declaring nature "spiritually neutral," inherently lacking hierarchical power or divine significance.

This position was strongly countered by Neoplatonic and Sufi schools of science and philosophy, as it is by the Tarot. Secular scientists raised within Christian societies have often confessed confusion regarding how to lend proper respect to regenerative and evolutionary aspects of natural environments, sentient beings, and human consciousness. Nondual Christian ethics regarding the special, spiritual values of love, life, and self-sacrifice are considered extraneous to "the scientific process." The universe as a flattened hierarchy is readily deemed *equivalent* in all of its physical constituent parts; everything is reducible to the mechanics of atomic particles and an organizational chart of a hundred or so molecular elements. Love is reduced to chemistry, and human life is reduced to random contingencies on a planet where life comes and goes according to nothing more than accidents and a blind, purposeless drive to survive. All life, evolution, and consciousness are deterministically reduced to nothing greater than coldly rationalized mathematical formulas that blatantly avoid *interior* or *feeling-mind* worlds of psychological and cultural reality. Life, humanity, nature, mystery, happiness, love, wisdom – these may have *place* and *function* in objectified contexts of physically defined systems, but they certainly have no *purpose* within a solar system that is proclaimed to have zero existential meaning demarcating it within a cosmos of billions of galaxies. In contrast, *the Triumphs circumscribe our sentient world through meaningful levels of ontological Law purposed to cosmic realization of Immortal Unity.* Contrary to the dogma of both religious fundamentalists and scientific materialists, *metaphysical wisdom principles* carry profound veracity in the context of twenty-first-century scientific philosophy and knowledge.

In the centuries after Jesus, Christian theologians essentially removed the Devil from the surroundings of Nature and placed him in *Hell* (a Frankish word whose concept spread alongside Germanic rule of Western Christendom commencing with the Fall of Rome and fifth-century conquest of Italy), from which it was imagined he contacted humans via their psyches. It was man's mind and genius – his imagination, psyche, and even soul – that served as the Devil's nefarious staging ground. After Augustine (d. 430), however, it was accepted as Catholic dogma that beings from the underworld could indeed be sensed in the air. Augustine held to a theory of spiritual vision in which demons and dead people took on "aerial bodies." Such bodies moved through the air just above the ground. Because a spirit body could move very rapidly, it could anticipate human thoughts and actions, affecting the progressions and outcomes of both. (A Berber who was considered one of the most intelligent men in the Roman Empire, one can only imagine what registered in Augustine's mind as he watched, engaged, and interpreted behaviors of the enormous cultural mix of empire courtiers and urban dwellers that he attempted to convert over the course of several decades.)

By the era of the Tarot, a thousand years later, ghosts and demons had gained considerable substantiality. Bodies were imagined as arising from their graves with flesh and bones, which were felt to be soft and hollow. Communicating with the dead was no longer perceived to be a purely psychic matter. Necromancy, it was believed, partly involved bringing the dead physically back to some semblance of life. In a new and generally macabre manner, ancient Pagan interpretations of spiritual vision were once again active throughout European communities. A zombie-like version of the nondual observation that "the dead are alive and the alive are dead" remains popular to this day.

In the fourteenth century, Death was immortalized as the *Grim Reaper* – a *skeletal spirit with scythe in hand* riding a horse seemingly carried by the wind. After a century of Black Plague, during which the afterworld had apparently manifested throughout Europe in the most terrible of ways, a new worldview was desperately needed. When the natural world was so clearly ruled by Death and the Devil, how was it possible to see Jesus's beautiful vision of a Kingdom of God? What Tower could re-bridge earth with heaven? Eastern Christian sages and their Sufi and Neoplatonic brothers brought to Italy, Spain, and France the answer. It has come down to us in popular form as a procession of Triumphant stations of Enlightenment.

Throughout its history, the Catholic Church barely resisted demonizing Nature itself. By adhering to a position that the natural world did not *primordially belong* to Satan, the Roman Church avoided extreme forms of dualism so affecting early Gnostic Christianity. However, during its first thousand years, the Church established a dogmatic attitude blocking or otherwise discouraging the use of images, symbols, and rituals that portrayed natural, hierarchical principles as championed by Neoplatonists and Hermeticists.

For esotericists, the spiritual development of mankind mirrors psychic, subtle, and causal aspects of the cosmos. Spiritual realization and immortal-angelic stations of being can be depicted through words, art, and architecture. European sacred art gradually incorporated archetypal symbols originating from Pagan Hellenic culture. Stonemason guilds, constructors of Gothic cathedrals during the twelfth to fifteenth centuries, made extensive and exquisite use of these symbols. During the Renaissance, Tarot imagery became a primary vehicle for portraying spiritual and cosmological hierarchy. This spiritual vision remains embedded throughout Indo-European cultures.

While Christianity's iconoclastic attitude changed over time, use of playing cards as an instrument purposed toward insightful *envisioning of the afterlife* and *divination of the present world* was tantamount to grave heresy in fifteenth-century Italy. Many Christian sects still view the Tarot as an instrument of Devil worship. It is time to allay such fear. Mythological dogma separating Human, Natural, and Immortal realms – excluding earthly existence from Deathless Freedom, Happiness, and Justice – must be abandoned.

We conclude our historical overview of Satan with a brief examination of *Iblis* – the Devil as known in Islam. Between the seventh and fifteenth centuries, concepts of Iblis took several forms. Islamic tradition portrayed him as both evil enemy and tragic scapegoat. The Koran revealed that Iblis refused God's request that he bow to Adam. But if there was only one true God, how could he, the most loyal and finest of Angels, view Man as above him? Not only did he not bow, he went on to seduce Eve.

Sufis in the influential school of Ibn ʿArabi adhered to a nondualistic view that polarities actually represent wholes. Angel and Man – Radiance and Manifestation – is not their unity that very state of the Divine One itself? Moreover, whereas Man remained separate from Woman in Genesis, did not Iblis's *intercourse* with Woman unite these opposites? Was not this inevitably meant to be, following the most basic laws of nature? How could God not have foreseen such likelihood?

By highlighting the polar symmetry of spiritual life, the Mystic's Way may be revealed and cultivated even through Iblis himself. Peter Awn summarizes the paradoxical position of the Devil as Divine and Cursed Guardian in *Satan's Tragedy and Redemption:*

> Because of the intensity of his contemplative love, Iblis became the model of monotheistic devotion. This dedication to the monotheistic ideal, however, forced Iblis to disobey the command to bow. God cursed him for his refusal and separated him from the Divine Presence. Yet because the Beloved had deigned to look upon him – even if the look was one of curse – Iblis accepted his destruction like a martyr's crown.
>
> The reward the condemned Iblis earned from God for his loving self-sacrifice was the office of chamberlain at the door of the Divine Presence, where he separates the wheat from the chaff by testing the mettle of man's faith with the sword of God's own power. No one is permitted to advance from *la ilah* to the realm of divine light, *illa 'llah,* without passing through the black light of Iblis.
>
> Iblis freely chose the pain of distance, conscious that separation was preferable because it was the fulfillment of the Beloved's desire and not of his own selfish wish. Separation and the curse, some Sufis caution, are prizes not easily won; they are attained only after years of strict obedience and worship.

We now can understand how it is that the Devil card obtained its exalted Tarot position after Death and before the Tower that reaches to the Stars. We recall that Ibn ʿArabi's placement of the Degrader was under the Powerful, represented in the Tarot by the Moon. The Moon was understood to be the portal to the Sun by Plato's academy. As the nearest of heavenly bodies surrounding the Earth, the Moon channeled and potentiated the influences of all other divine forces. The Devil in one form or another guarded access to that creative Power of Eros. Divine stations of the Preciously Valued and Nourisher (Tower and Star) became symbols of the Questor's original Garden, the Promised Land between Immortal Heaven and Human Earth. In this version of sacred cosmology, the Devil as Highest Angel remained warden and protector of the Garden, its Tower and Tree of Knowledge, and its immortal denizens. As exemplified by the nymphs of Nysa and Hesperides, that garden included harems of spiritually erotic, unmarried, and unbound women, i.e., "virgins."

In Greek tradition, predating Christian and Islamic concepts of a heaven *totally removed* from earth (let alone a *psychic heaven* as *reward* for a *physical jihad* in the form of *bloody decimation*), *Original Paradise remained a grounded realm of Gaia,* retaining aspects of pre-Olympian, earthy Eros. The surrounding *Celestial Firmament* served as a *communicative bridge* between mortal and immortal realms. *Wisdom* through integral *consideration* (again, literally meaning *with the stars*) could bring divine assistance and blessings into the human domain. *Stars embodied the immortal presences of minor deities and ancestral heroes.* From the vantage of ancient wisdom, the Kosmic world of Gaia and Uranus integrates human reality with Aethereal space; as it does Hades' chthonic dominion with Zeus's rarefied Sky-realm.

Contained within the immortal levels of the World, made accessible by heroes and various entities such as nymphs, are the Tower and Star's sacred knowledge, golden gifts, and ambrosia of life warded by the Moon and Sun (classically represented by Artemis and Apollo). Returning to the wildly beautiful and innocently harmonious garden of spiritual birth, Questors once again have to be tested by the Devil. That is, Questors have to *match* and *transcend* the level of angelic hierarchy presented by the *Supreme Daemon*. That seventh-stage level is *an echelon transfusing the genius essential to transiting into immortal consciousness*. Thus comes down to us the story of Eden's One Tree and its Apples of Eros warded by an Angelic Snake who knows all; and the Hesperides' Golden Apples given by Gaia as a wedding present to Zeus and warded by a multi-headed Titanic Snake speaking the world's languages.

Through the Devil, woman and man were removed from their Paradise. Through the Devil once more, humankind can be returned to the Garden of Ambrosia. Successful passage beyond the Abaser – after paying awestruck homage to and consciously transcending the tremendously Valuable seductive treasure he guards – will bestow upon Questors the Moon's mighty attribute of sacred Power. In the process, Questors will receive an endowment from the Devil's Precious Treasure. This will be delivered by genii (as the Devil himself may be interpreted) and enlightened magi (from *magus*, meaning "able to wield power") from an ages-old Tower of Alchemy (serving as a lightning rod in its capacity of being crucible and conduit for fire of the Sun and catalyst of the Moon). Magi and their genii assistants will unerringly find successful Questors by following the *Flow* (the root meaning of *Nourish*) of *Grace* emanated by Angelic Immortals who radiate as Stars. In the Tarot, passage beyond the Devil begins the masterful way of saintly Magehood. A Questor's *own* Tower and sublimation of a Star's Elixir (offering *succor* in its flow of regenerative life beyond mortal Fortune and Death) are primary to the alchemical attainment of immortality.

Any true understanding of the seventh-stage Devil and Tower requires a foundation of insight regarding the hierarchical stages binding creatively chaotic processes of Eros with internal, intimate impulses of spirituality and responsibility. Realization of immortal wisdom begins with the holistic Right View and Resolve represented by matriarchal Empress/Popess and patriarchal Emperor/Pope. It then depends upon cultivation of responsibility by not *avoiding relationship;* this is symbolized by the Right Speech of Temperance and Love. Chariot and Fortitude denote Right Action through a mature advancement of psycho-spiritual self emerging from initiation into a lifelong spiritual mission. Wheel of Fortune, Hermit, Hanged Man, and Death represent the Right Life and Effort of Questors realizing their abilities to channel the subtle, pervasive flux connecting immortal soul and spiritual grace with temporal psychophysical existence. Mindfully generating this effort at times may seem like an impossible task. *Supplicating the Goddess as Eros makes all the difference in the world.* Only through *that* does Right Concentration realize the compassion and wisdom of Original Mind.

Twentieth-century *Roshis* (broadly speaking, *Zen Masters*) such as Richard Baker embarked upon this true way of Bodhisattva realization, even as their societies and communities remained dogmatically confused regarding it. Questors must learn to release their attention from the whole spectrum of manifestation and conception, thereby *completely* engulfing body-mind-soul with the pulverizing vision of Light, Allah, Buddha Mind, or Transcendental Ecstasy. All of the above is innately *compelled in stages* while *dealing with the Devil and feeling-remembering Eros.* This requires twenty-four-hour-a-day dedicated and devoted identification with the Bright. Such is the Purpose of the Quest.

Death is *part* of evolution; evolution *by its very nature* does not end with Death. The Universe is continuously evolving in stages. So is every environment and body within it. In number, those stages can be elegantly reduced to ten. (More precisely, six principles or stages of cosmic evolution emerge from three primary principles that are in truth *One.* Those Three exist in a prior *hierarchy,* but do not *evolve* one into another. Rather, they *emanate as a Triune All-At-Once.*)

The *Ten Principles of Immortality* can be discerned by human consciousness. Rationality, in and of itself, can only *partially cognize* these principle-stages. To be fully understood, they must be realized *interiorly* through psychophysical-heartful stations of life. Those stations of consciousness bear direct resemblance to the great principles of cosmological evolution. Once these principles are intelligently, intuitively cognized and authenticated via psychophysical transformation (or what is commonly called *spiritual realization*), esoteric archetypes may be naturally envisioned that beautifully convey the logos of each hierarchical stage. Greek mythology, religious iconography, and Tarot Trionfi are based upon such yogic and contemplative imagination and, essentially stated, *evolution of consciousness* or *enlightenment*.

If all of reality exists within a spectrum of spiritual hierarchy, then everyday mundane life is not separate from immortal spheres of Kosmic Truth. In the early centuries of Christianity, an attempt was made to vanquish Satan and spiritual daimons to Hell. Attempting to mitigate that dualism, Christian theology determined that the *natural world* was neither divine nor demonic. This ultimately led to a pathological rationalization of the cosmos as a totally mechanical, material construct knowable solely through mathematical formulas. In the next chapter, we explore the boundaries demarcating scientific materialism and perennial knowledge or science native to the way of tenfold enlightenment. In the process, we look to attain the means by which science and spirituality – two seemingly exclusive modes of understanding universal law – may at long last be integrated.

MIRRORED WISDOM

STAR

True gnosis is the outcome of real alchemy, the guiding radiance of sublime communion, and the considered awareness of universal beauty.

MOON

Bringing heaven to earth, the Moon influences all creative flow, maintaining the steady cyclic courses of nature through the ultimately unfathomable power of Eros.

Kosmic Knowledge

Unveiling Immortal Reality . . .

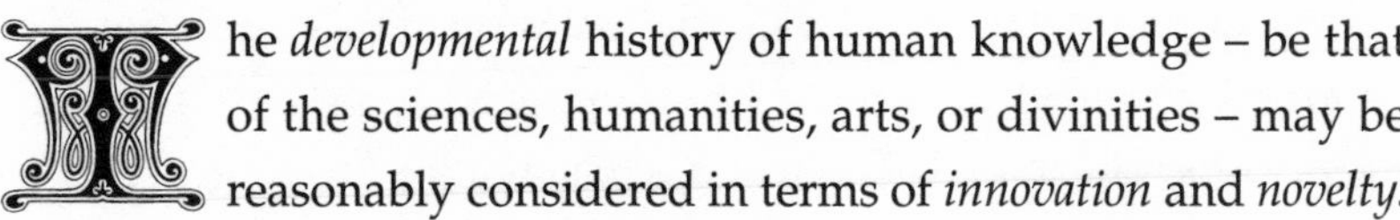

The *developmental* history of human knowledge – be that of the sciences, humanities, arts, or divinities – may be reasonably considered in terms of *innovation* and *novelty.* Concomitantly, *perennial* principles of processional growth and evolution have consistently been *renewed* in cultures around the world, as this book has served to indicate. Natural, social, cultural, and spiritual patterns found in every great tradition's stages of development attest to this. However, during our recent and comparatively short two-century span of human history, rapid change on all levels and quadrants of organization on the planet has become systemic. An industrial and technological revolution has been enabled by burning fossil fuels (essentially involving consumption of Gaia's great storehouse of ancestors) and subsequently discovering how to exploit natural energy resources through machines. Spurred on by that tremendous energetic input, a speeding up of exploration in all fields of knowledge has occurred. This has repeatedly given rise to new worldviews and technologies promoting environmental, sociocultural, and psychological transformation. In the process, radically changing models regarding how the natural world works have appeared to *overturn* traditional knowledge on many levels of understanding.

Brilliant physicists and other scientists during the past hundred years have contemplated and argued the veracity of varying frameworks purposed toward *integrating* the most essential and universal theories of natural law. Because scientific study of the physical world has not occurred apart from psycho-socio-cultural development, principles addressed in this book that have advanced social, cultural, and spiritual growth have also affected the material growth of humankind's physical environments. The Great Principles reviewed in previous chapters can also be found reflected within the evolving course of scientific discovery. From Heraclitus's ever-changing Chaos to Heisenberg's Uncertainty Principle, a history of rational observation and intuitive insight composing the essential knowledge of *science* has unfolded in tandem with the history of *metaphysical* wisdom and whole-body realization of evolving *consciousness.* The present work finishes with a consideration of primary principles being established within the *new sciences* and identifies those with *ten essential and unifying principles of cosmic evolution and immortality.* These affirm perennial wisdom understanding of *unity through eternity.* These principles, stages, or domains of world development formed the origins of the Tarot system of Image-Exemplars and divinatory storytelling. (A science version of the Triumphs may readily be imagined based upon this chapter; we will leave that for a forthcoming project, which promises to be of great interest.)

Scientific laws are thought by many scientists to embody "truer" knowledge than philosophical laws. Unlike Platonic philosophers, scientific *materialists* rationalize that the cosmos cannot be *known* purely through *logos,* or enlightened intellect. Scientists know the world by reducing it to and interpreting it through *mathematical measurements* and mechanical models of linear causes and effects. These follow rules of logic that can be objectively tested in the physical world via repeatable experiments. Scientific materialism places maximum emphasis on experimentally verified theories of law involving measurable, material object-events. Such laws are always limited to a specific level, aspect, or model of nature. We begin this chapter by noting the limitations of material and mechanical reductionism. Later, we introduce such exotic theories as *vibrational superstrings* and *anti-gravity dark energy* that are now propelling scientific research back into the realms of *Pure Thought*.

Within the subconscious is a collective longing for the miraculous transformations of an authentic Mage.

The scientific belief that all phenomena can be explained through a limited number of principles and laws is called *reductionism*. Among early Greeks, Thales (who lived in the early sixth century B.C. and was Greece's first historically honored sage; often regarded as science's first Patriarch) believed this to be true, while Plato did not. Science holds *principles* to be more fundamental than laws. Unlike *laws*, principles are not by definition proven experimentally. However, they compose a conceptual foundation for precise statements about how the universe operates. Such statements, when verified through experimental testing, become accepted as scientific laws.

Philosophers of science now commonly agree that known laws of the universe will historically keep being changed, superseded, or abandoned as new or complementary worldviews warrant – occasionally zealous claims by sectarian physicists notwithstanding. (For instance, it is now commonly held that the famous law $E = mc^2$ only refers to a massive particle in its "own" hypothetical rest frame, in all other cases the law is subject to relativistic corrections. Of course, that view may well change.) This chapter reviews some of the major shifts scientific theories are currently undergoing. It then posits Ten Universal Unitive Principles that bridge modern science with the perennial wisdom represented by the Tarot and introduced in this book. The alpha-omega stage of emanationist cosmology has been referred to as Unitive Law. That is itself the greatest of universal principles.

Along with reductionism, other principles guiding orthodox scientific doctrine include those of *mechanism* and *causality*. Scientific materialism generally minimizes acknowledgement of principles other than these few. Knowledge is thus *reduced* to that of *causal mechanisms*.

Within every soul, be that of opponent or ally, dwells a way of righteousness; once viewed, that Way will never be totally forgotten.

Human minds identify and establish world-principles in accordance with philosophical and sociocultural orientations. Although some scientific materialists claim that their methods of knowing stand apart from cultural, social, or psychological influences, it is clear that the principles adhered to by scientists guide their creation of *models* and construction of *theories*. The principle of *beauty*, for instance, now widely appreciated in the world of science, is usually limited to laws of *symmetry*. Beauty that arises from unique asymmetries or symmetry-breaking is often ignored by material reductionists. This would appear to be influenced in part by cultural and psychological factors.

Although laws may be legitimized through repeated experimental verification, it was proven by Kurt Gödel in 1931 that every mathematical theory rests on axioms that are presupposed and not provable. This puts an absolute limit on the effectiveness of mathematical laws to fundamentally explain such universal principles as *chaos, space, time, and* law itself. Nonetheless, many physicists claim that these and other principles, such as *symmetry* and *causality*, come under scientific jurisprudence. The importance of *metaphysics* (literally, "after physics," as Aristotle's book on *First Principles* was called, perhaps because Aristotle's editor placed it immediately after his works on *physika* or *nature;* generally referring to "the branch of philosophy that examines the nature of reality, including the relationship between mind and matter, substance and attribute, fact and value, and the theoretical or first principles of a particular discipline, e.g. the metaphysics of law") regarding psychophysical and sociocultural processes of lawmaking and realization of truth is commonly denigrated.

Science must move beyond the religious dogma of nineteenth-century *scientism*. Humankind can no longer afford to believe that scientific "facts" contain no fiction. On one hand, history has repeatedly made evident the tentative nature of scientific models. On the other hand, scientism presents a utopian vision whereby the unending *powers* discovered by science will enable mankind to live so comfortably, in such super-abundance, that social politics, cultural rituals, and spiritual realizations will become obsolete. There remains a scientific *priesthood* that controls access to the enabling tools of science and that passes judgment upon any and all new theories. Science theories retain their authority only as long as such ruling experts deem it so.

Transformative powers of female grace inevitably involve an engulfing of the Questor's most crucial purpose.

Privileged and politically connected scientists holding the reigns of socioeconomic power in their fields all too often remain silent about where and when the power generated by their scientific communities' experimentations and technological implementation is used. This socially irresponsible position – justified through dogmatic conceits of "objective, non-engaged observation" and "political neutrality" – is enforced through peer pressure, fear, willful ignorance, and status or monetary craving, if not outright pathologies involving emotional repression and psychological dissociation. Regardless of whether a scientist believes corporate and political authorities will actually listen to and respect him, he is dutifully bound to state and abide by ethical guidelines. In other words, the scientific community is fully capable of including *wisdom* in its behavior and the world *needs* it to do just that.

This requires philosophical understanding regarding truly essential and universal principles. Just as *exoteric* scientists experiment with the *outer* world, *esoteric* philosophers verify laws of wisdom through contemplative experimentation with the *inner* world. Such involves and produces the study of metaphysics. Both communities and their practices naturally integrate with those of rulers, artisans, and traders creating, governing, and regulating social and cultural spheres. Ten universal principles, foundational for scientific, spiritual, cultural, and social law, have emerged through Great Tradition schools and are now being applied to modern technology in conjunction with their application to personal and social cultivation of love, freedom, happiness, and well being.

Through concentrated resolve, the Emperor touches every subject's soul, reflecting the dreams and aspirations of each.

Through material reductionism, scientists posit that they are able to construct progressively more fundamental *models* that describe progressively more essential *theories* regarding the laws of nature. This then supports claims of discovery regarding the most fundamental *principles* of the universe. All of this is predicated on experimentation employing mathematical, geometrical, and largely visual models. However, consistent models of the most basic parts and processes of our material world are very difficult to construct. For example, there exists no consistent model of even the simplest atomic element known: hydrogen.

From Niels Bohr's well-known *shell* model, to Werner Heisenberg and Erwin Schrödinger's Quantum Mechanics (QM) model, to Paul Dirac's relativistic quantum mechanical model, to Richard Feynman and Freeman Dyson's Quantum Electro-Dynamic model (QED), attempts have been made to explain the sequence of bright lights emitted by hydrogen gas when excited by an electric current. Even the latest of these models, QED, is only *approximately* accurate in describing fundamental experiments with the universe's simplest of elements. A calculated model of any atomic element greater than hydrogen is far too complex for QED to handle and still be remotely cognizable.

Other basic aspects of reality, such as *how a particle gets from one place to another,* are not modeled by QED. Although very successful at predicting the outcome of subatomic physics experiments, QED is a good example of a scientific model that describes neither the elemental nor living world in a way that can be *essentially understood.*

When normal material density reaches a size of about one cubic micron (about one-fiftieth of a hair's width), the sum total of its atoms' gravitational forces exerts an effect upon any singular atom so as to break QM's ability to define that atom, as QM is unable to account for gravitational effects. Furthermore, the Second Law of Thermodynamics (which addresses the universal tendency of a closed system to become random) becomes inescapable and thus introduces an "arrow" of time: *irreversibility.* This too is not accounted for by QM. Microscopic and macroscopic laws and models thereby do not "connect" – so which are the *true* laws that the others *reduce into?* It is far-fetched to claim that any mathematical model of physics on any given level realistically addresses *all of human knowledge* about *all of the universe's processes* through an *epitomized representation.* Again, that is best left to the work of philosophy and what can broadly be described as metaphysics.

Throughout the cosmos, quanta concentrate energy in a manifestation of infinitely radiating dimensional space; abetted by the laws of physics, the Hierophant's blessing penetrates the myriad.

Nature as set forth in Newtonian, Einsteinian, and QED physics is "time-reversible." That is, the laws of Time as understood in classical, relativistic, and quantum physics do not make a distinction between past and future. A presumption that *time is reducible* to symmetrical operations wherein the spatial world is equally able to function backward and forward in time is fundamental to the basic laws of orthodox physics. For instance, the Earth revolves around the Sun in a trajectory that can be mathematically defined. Having done so, it is possible to extrapolate either forward or backward in time the movement of the Earth. Its path and place in revolution around the Sun apparently are not affected by time per se. However, complexity theories of natural flow and movement have revealed that we cannot exactly retrace bodily movement. This holds true even for a steadily orbiting planet. We can know if an orbit has remained the same over time, but not where exactly a planet was within its orbit at any defined moment. Working the numbers backward does not produce exact coordinates locating a planet in a position to other bodies that we can state is the *known* position that the planet was in at that time.

A waterfall, to give a more obvious example of the irreversibility of dynamic movement according to mathematical logic, comprises a great many water molecules whose trajectories chaotically vary through persistent interactions as they fall. It is mathematically impossible to extrapolate their trajectories or paths back in time.

The Questor, in light of earthly success, will either be awakened in a lasting transformation and established in a wisdom-bound community or will, through the conceit of completion, threaten to disrupt a yet brighter alchemy beyond the Questor's ken.

The laws of thermodynamics cannot be reduced to aforementioned models of time-symmetrical physics.

In QM, the wave function of a particle defines its location and velocity in terms of *probabilities*. However, when a physicist makes an actual measurement on a particle, he does not measure the probability of its movement, but rather defines it with an exact location or speed. Once measured, a particle never reverts back to a *probable* existence. Knowledge of the world in terms of microcosmic particles appears to be based upon "arresting" in time or space an otherwise always fluctuating reality. Once measured, a particle's wave-function permanently collapses. By measuring particles, a probable world is given permanent definition. That which has a *future potential* becomes that which has a *past manifestation*.

Experimental knowledge based upon the *certainty of measurement* identified with the past is wedded to the *breaking of time symmetry*. The irreversibility of that process in actual reality contradicts the reversibility idealized in mathematics modeling the physical world. That an observer or measurer somehow forever changes that which is measured remains problematic to physicists. Yet, it would seem by many to simply be common sense. Knowledge derived from quantum observations is claimed by some physicists to be the truest form of knowledge humans have of the world. To identify knowledge with *essential truth* is to cross into the realm of *existential meaning;* it is not a trivial claim that warrants being bantered about in a play of intellectual conceit. For humankind, *living reality* is the ground of primary truths. Mathematical theories attempt to address extremely limited aspects of that living reality, and thereby mathematical theorists have no business appropriating claims of truth from all the rest of humanity.

Real life *valuation* of quantum and relativistic equations, even as they enable production of atomic weaponry, nuclear power plants, and quantum computers, is relatively small (if not radically negative) for practically every human being in every culture, educated or not.

Love of life is the Love of self fully revealed to another; it is this that empowers a Questor to Love others as if they are oneself.

Even with the fantastic production of enabling technology such as computers, how many humans value such over love, freedom, and life itself? Every reader may know someone who offhand *seems* to, but who can honestly state that it is wiser for a human to love his computer more than any human being? How many computer, television, stereo, or phone users would sacrifice a loved one's life just to keep their devices? Positing truth in any meaningful way involves association with corollary value propositions. Few humans really believe that truths discovered through knowledge of love, arts, politics, storytelling, health, humor, consciousness, family, and cultivation of life are of smaller value than the truths discovered in knowledge of equations found in a QED textbook. There is intelligent cause for this.

A supreme valuation of quantum mechanical "truth" may remain championed by certain physicists, but such is clearly untenable even within the broader community of material scientists. Unless, of course, the *essential principles* underlying QM's laws are realized to be *universally true.* Essential truths from personal, social, cultural, and physical domains in actuality share a foundation of Common Principles that produce holistically integral value propositions. Thus, universal principles deserve everyone's full attention.

How do materialistic scientists answer essentially metaphysical or philosophical questions such as: *How is it that an electron carries a charge* opposite *but* exactly *equal in magnitude to the charge carried by a proton?* These are claimed as answered by whatever mathematical theory might produce equations that crank out values to its variables that match the questioned observations. For instance, mathematical models of certain five- and ten-dimensional Grand Unification Theories produce an *almost* exact equality of the magnitudes of electron and proton charges. The equations are thereby claimed to have "solved the mystery" of this most essential cosmic polarity. The principle of polar symmetry itself, however, remains a True Mystery. Therein dwells its actual beauty. If we do

Psychic autonomy is an exercise of self-empowerment, a gathering of the reigns controlling one's mind; but know that self separate from other, autonomy without communion, is a dangerously precarious illusion.

not recognize that, then we reduce reality to the cold calculations of math and engineered machines that math may lend itself to.

While we consider the nature of truth and the principles most universally describing such, let us keep in mind that while nuclear physicists have proven adroit at creating weapons and massive computers, they have not in general fared well at all with creating happy, wholesome, harmonic bio-socio-psycho-cultural spheres of life (heroic and holistic physicists such as Amory Lovins are exceptional). Truth is *integral.*

There are numerous fundamental and essential unknown "hows" regarding mechanistic explanations of natural processes. The progressive formation of embryos, inheritance of instincts, presence of memory, and nature of consciousness are just a few examples of processes materialistic science is at a loss to explain. Since an *angel* revealed to René Descartes (the famous seventeenth-century French philosopher whose favorite place to meditate was inside a large bread oven) that mathematics was the *sole language* of truth, science has championed the *geometrical* (from Greek *geometrein,* "to measure the Earth") study of moving bodies over all other forms of knowledge. Consciousness was thought to be the only natural phenomena that could not be known through Descartes' "enlightened science," which was devoid of any *animating* psyches, spirits, processes, or principles not reducible to material mechanics. This philosophy merged with the ancient Greek belief in *atomism* via Newtonian physics. Of course, we now know that the essential principles or axioms upon which science and math must perforce be based will never be reducible to proven laws of logic, let alone to measurable mechanistic models representing interactions of separative things.

In Descartes' mechanistic worldview, energy is understood to remain *eternally constant;* it neither increases nor decreases in the universe. All change is but a mathematical *transform* upon a given delineated matter-energy quantity. (As we will see, cosmologists are now radically questioning this.) That quantity presumably can be transformed either "forward" or "backward" in time, for that is how mechanical equations work. The great traditional six-stage process of cosmic *becoming* was thus conceptually reduced by Descartes to a static identity of eternal *being* undergoing reversible mechanical operations. This denied all reality to evolutionary development as it had been understood for many centuries through philosophies positing cosmic emanation and spiritual procession.

To feel beyond the charms of physical, emotional, and mental distraction is to feel the Force of transcendence and the strength of intimate caring; adhering to such sublimity, the way beyond Death can be discovered.

As science faced the fact that evolution is indeed a material reality, not just a metaphysical myth, evolution was incorporated into mechanical conservatism through a conceptual reduction of *Unitive Law* (the *True, Bright,* or *One* of great traditional philosophy) to a law positing *separative random survival.* It was supposed that things and environments only evolve by *accident* through interactions contingent upon an almighty principle of Randomness, the belief in which identified a new priesthood of "enlightened" scientists. According to this worldview, there is no *purpose of unity* to universal law destining the natural evolution of a galaxy toward ever-higher forms of complexity and consciousness such as life on Earth. Principles that imply Unity as an inherent alpha and omega – basis and outcome – of natural laws were and are thereby denied. Along with the genuinely universal and unitive principle of *synchronistic* contingency, such includes the now broadly accepted *new science* principles of *field resonance, hierarchical emergence, and holistic causality.*

Cosmic order, organic life, and human consciousness are amazingly improbable features of a "survival-driven but death-determined" random cosmos. So improbable do they appear to be, that life on Earth must presumably be unique in the universe. In fact, the probability of our known universe having randomly happened at all is *astronomically small.* Many facts support this: If the ratio between the masses of an electron and proton were ever so slightly different, intelligent life in the cosmos would not exist. Even the minutest change in the electric charge of an electron would have prevented

Unbeknownst to the ambitious, only an earthly state of compassionate reflection can successfully embrace Enlightened paradox – fortune mirrored upon misfortune; see beyond the illusion of high and low to the insight of unified destiny.

the stars of the cosmos from exploding, and planets would never have formed. If the expansion rate of the universe had been different by even an infinitesimally small amount one second after the Big Bang fourteen billion years ago, the universe would have collapsed before it ever took shape as we know it. Therefore, it has been supposed that a practically *infinite number of universes* must be co-arising. The fact that ours is defined by hierarchical levels of order does not play against probabilistic odds if there are an astronomical number of other unordered universes. The need for this sort of ad hoc supposition is clearly a sign that mechanistic reductionism is coming to the end of its road.

In medieval times, nature was thought to be *animated* or *spirited* and thus to be *innately creative*. After the seventeenth century, a mechanistic philosophy of nature became prevalent. Only God was viewed as creative; the world was *created*, but not in any way endowed with self-creative principles. Charles Darwin isolated an ancient metaphysical concept that *Death rules nature*. He then denied the rest of traditional metaphysical understanding regarding those principles that rule over death. He thought that through *natural selection* as *survival of the fittest*, creative evolution occurs as an innate drive to thwart death (or shall we say, innate mission to realize immortality), randomly leading natural bodies into more and more complex development. Ultimately, this produced the human capacity to adapt to any environment and neutralize the otherwise deadly effects of natural catastrophes. (Perhaps witnessing how humans handle massive climate change, species extinction, environmental poisoning, and the exhaustion of oil and natural gas will serve as a test of Darwinian theory and its embedded cultural psychology of supremacy. Will *altruistic cooperation* prove to be the key not only to happiness but to survival itself?)

In the mechanistic worldview all forms of chaos can theoretically be reduced to analyzable factors and mechanics, allowing nature to be totally controlled. If lack of information and resources prevent nature from being fully controllable by any given technology-enabled social group, scientists can at least show it to be *predictable.* In this dream of science fiction, a civilized world can be systematically structured as a permanently stable environment supporting human survival by predicting, forestalling, and undermining natural catastrophe. Death through species competition, including sociopolitical tribal and national opposition and random mutation, can be, in this vision, permanently thwarted through engineered physical, cultural, social, and psychological structures. More accurately, the world can be restructured to support survival of the *fittest types* of humans – the fittest societies, cultures, races, and genomes.

Probe the space before you, peer into the darkness of mystery, dispel the shadows of delusion; cloak your awareness with wisdom and nurture the union of mind and body.

We will not carry on with this train of thought. It quickly becomes lost in delusions of a eugenically engineered utopia, while ignorantly and greedily justifying eradication of all organic life that seems to compete with an inevitably self-elected "fittest" group of humans or their "most efficient economy." Such a worldview lacks awareness of the necessity of *interdependency* regarding gene pools, species habitats, food chains, community responsibility, etc. Complex and holistic worlds such as Gaia Earth require the principle of chaos for the maintenance of *creative evolution.* As mankind attempts to arrest that process, it discovers in a regrettable manner that its own growth and thereby living reality is dependent upon it. Few humans seriously feel they would be happier in a totally fabricated, synthetic world "living" as an inorganic, even if "immortal" machine. More importantly, it cannot be overemphasized that recent beliefs in manifest destiny associated with weapons-and-media-controlled fascistic "governance" based on psychospiritual suppression enforced through societal policing and technological surveillance have not produced tenable structures for humankind that are sustainable.

Scientific knowledge regarding closed systems of physically identifiable, individuated particles and mechanisms represents only one quadrant of a *four-quadrant* world. The study of group systems that are *open* and definable as *networks* or social groups forms another

When subtle devices have played to the end of their innate consequences, a convergence of causes sustains an awakening underlying the mechanics of the psyche – such is the perfect time to sacrifice to Eros.

quadrant. Henri Bergson was a sagacious philosopher of science who lived at the turn of the twentieth century. He considered the study of *non-isolated biological systems* to be more primary to humankind than the studies of physics or chemistry. He insightfully contemplated the *primacy of time* and the *sense of duration;* duration as interior reality of conscious beings, living cultures, and even the entire world as it is in flux. Conceiving duration to be immanent to the whole of the universe, he stated:

> The more we study the nature of time, the more we shall comprehend that duration means invention, the creation of forms, the continual elaboration of the absolutely new.

Humans evolve physically, socially, culturally, and psychologically, and evolution is marked by *history* and *irreversibility.* The processes of natural evolution inherently contrast with those of manmade machines. The latter are founded upon types of *memory* composed of habitual representations embodied by unfurling mechanical parts juxtaposed with each other. The mechanical, materialistic worldview is driven by a mind-set oriented toward *productive utility.* Evolution, however, is embodied by active entities undergoing *continuous, interpenetrating phases.* The principles, stages, and phases of *whole systems,* most evident in living beings, involve *relationships* of bodies with the world; i.e., life, growth, and evolution are marked by vital activity, open exchange, and resonating fields – discriminated mathematically, rhetorically, practically, or otherwise. Mechanical, materialistic representation subtracts from and *narrows* the *real.* Just as time is not merely a rearrangement of parts, *continuity* is the *movement* of a *whole.*

Knowledge of the world that is most relevant to human life is founded upon *ontological reality.* Beings with *inertial identity* sense their world through vibration and frequency. The nonlinear multiplicity of rhythm experienced by *dynamic* identities creates *tensional, integral duration* appropriately referred to through terms of *symmetry, resonance,* and *emergence.* Cyclic vibration inherently resonates through duration. Duration on any level cannot be truthfully reduced to the polar extremities of an interval, which materialistic scientists habitually then reduce into singular and *spatially separate* "instances." The interval of any vibrational state *in reality* is not the same thing as the *measurement* or *representation* of the extremities of a vibration's interval.

Contemplate the transformation of self into Eros not as a series of little deaths, but rather as a sacrifice into utter essence, becoming Immortal via a concentrated gift of ambrosia drawn from the marrow of Death's bones.

Representational or mental habits are in the business of abstracting "instantaneities." Reality, however, is without a doubt a vibratory flux of space *in and as* time. Life and nature are not actually like the movies. The continuity of *being becoming* is not reducible to a series of discrete, juxtaposed "immobilities" that are reconstituted by mental habits into an *illusion* of continuity or life. Materialists limit the knowledge of science to mental operations upon imagined symbols of spatial instances that are in reality *always* continuous and mobile. The flux of the universe cannot be arrested through measurement and simultaneously be deemed as "truly known." Adding up a myriad of truly *unreal* instances of such measurement and calling such "reality" simply does not create true knowledge of that which is real, but rather creates a grandiose representative illusion of that which is real.

When materialists reduce reality to their personal mental constructs, symbolic knowledge is then presented as reality. Pre-existing concepts of immobile things are used to reconstruct a symbolic representation of the actual flux of spacetime. Intuition, or the fourth stage of consciousness as introduced in this book, is cognizant of the duration of wholes and cultivates fluid concepts adopting the *life itself of things.* Intuitive reasoning does not presume that time is a derivative of space. This fourth-dimensional awareness realizes time as frequency and duration, *prior to* space as dimensionality and position. Mind's radiance is not, thereby, limited to body's shape and location.

The principle of hierarchical emergence ensures that evolution cannot be defined solely by spatial multiplicity and mechanisms

It is the lot of this beastly angel of earth to guard the gates of extraordinary power, wealth, and fame; thus must the Questor engage the Abaser of all processes, the Degrader of all stages.

that serve only to represent *pre-existent* possibilities. When that which is deemed *possible* is abstracted or projected *backward* from what is real, then our models of *future* possibilities merely resemble what has been already measured. Organic creation, evolutionary phenomena, and hierarchical emergence of every level and phase of nature come through a multiplicity and divergence of tendencies that resonate in highly complex correlations; connecting, merging, and creating fields through pervasive synchronistic contingency. *Hierarchy* is time's way of introducing greater and deeper complexity and thereby greater consciousness into the three dimensions of spatial manifestation.

Put in other terms, fourth-dimensional time is the *transcendental dimension* of the *causal chains* upon which spacetime is based. Hans Reichenbach, a contemporary of Einstein and interdisciplinary philosopher-physicist of unusual empirical clarity and holistic erudition, succinctly stated: "Time is the direction of the grain of manifold along which the causal chains extend, whereas space reflects only the neighborhood relations between the coexisting causal chains."

The scientific definition of an interval must be based upon physical phenomena, not geometric/spatial abstraction. Any and all observation of interval must precede any and all proclamation of uniformity of successive intervals. Materialistic scientism presumes that event-things do not exist with the directionality of time, but rather exist as "instances" with the ability to be present, past, and future "at the same time." Thus do mechanical equations equally work backward and forward in time. Fortunately for life, this presumption simply isn't true. Time is initially understood on the fourth-dimensional level as comprising processes of temporal relations periodically phase-shifting or emerging into new hierarchical realizations of spacetime.

The second law of thermodynamics states that the universe evolves on a course of progressively greater *entropy*. It is popularly thought that entropy implies *disorder,* and that thereby the cosmos is destined toward a deathly state of *random incoherence.* However, that is only true for isolated systems near a state of equilibrium. When a system is in a state of unstable fluctuation, which actually defines cosmic reality, the *most ordered* states are the *highest* in entropy. In *The End of Certainty,* Ilya Prigogene elegantly argues that unstable systems serve as a good basis for the most fundamental description of our cosmos; in short, *Chaos* rules Death and cosmic nature. The beauty and goodness of chaos is found in the world as a constant state of flux evolving through emergence and an arrow of time toward synchronized systems progressively manifesting ordered phases of resonant symmetry beyond that of equilibrium.

Tantric alchemy reveals the ancient way of cauldrons and currents – containment, heat, circulation, pressure, catastrophe, chaos, emergence, transmutation, and hypostasis; key to all is always remembering Eros.

Equilibrium can be represented by the "zero point of the scale" (readers may wish to explore Zen Buddhism's *Blue Cliff Record* for a deeply intuitive understanding of that illusory indicator). Development of being, consciousness, and bliss infinitely transcends manipulations around zero-point concepts, rules, and measurements of nature. This is true not only for human domains, but for the whole universe and its ultimately unitive way. Being, consciousness, and bliss are reducible to neither scientific nor spiritual *beliefs* that are defined by human psychological states keeping to "zero-point-ignorance" that serve only to delude rationally intuitive and discerningly dynamic states of knowingness. Beyond any *ignorance* of zero-point beliefs is a *reality* of transformative chaos in the form of extreme nonequilibrium stages of spacetime flux. Appropriately called spiritual realization, this constantly causes manifestation of a universe principled on holistic unity.

A new science focused on irreversible, nonequilibrium *processes* emerged in the latter part of the twentieth century. Cosmic processes observably give rise to coherent attributes, including those of resonant interiority, biological life, and consciousness. The study of time-based coherence is fundamental to modern chemistry, biology, ecology, and cosmology. The presumption that given *initial*

By the brilliance of the Star, the Questor sees the wholeness of the cosmos, the outcome of alchemical intercourse, the reality of Grace – no longer blinded by the abyss of dualistic opposition and catastrophic confusion.

conditions of any object or system of objects, the future and past of those objects can be *known* for *certain* no longer holds. At best the behaviors of unstable systems or objects can be *probabilistically* gauged. *Irreversibility is inherent to the nature of time, consciousness, space, chaos, and the universe.*

Process philosophy itself is as old as Heraclitus and Gautama. Heraclitus preeminently countered the atomistic view that reality is composed of unchanging and inert material particles. In accordance to that early theory of science (in a fashion, still prominent amongst current scientific materialists, who have added a number of novel quantum symmetries to their hypothetical particles) atoms' involvement with *process* does not go beyond an alteration of their positions in space and time; change affects only the *relations between* particles, never the actual *substance* of the particles. Countering such beliefs in modern history, Gottfried Leibniz, Henri Bergson, Charles Sanders Peirce, William James, and Alfred North Whitehead continued the tradition of process philosophy, with the school commonly being identified with Whitehead and his community.

Process philosophy posits processes at the forefront of ontological concern. Processes are construed as *structured sequences of successive stages* or phases. Processes are understood to be *complex* – a holistic unity of distinct stages or phases. Process complexity has a certain temporal coherence and thereby an essential aspect of time which *cannot be eliminated.* A process has a formal generic format or structure by virtue of which every concrete process is equipped with form. If the work of metaphysics is *to provide a cogent and plausible account of the nature of reality at the broadest, most synoptic and comprehensive level,* then process philosophy posits time and change as principal categories of metaphysical understanding. Furthermore, process *is itself* posited as a principal category of ontology or beingness, more fundamentally so than *things.* In process philosophy, causation, contingency, emergence, resonance, and creative novelty are understood to be essential principles of metaphysical understanding.

Merciful power reflects a source of forgiveness that endures all instances of confusion, chaos, and repetition; the cosmos continuously re-creates, with the Sun giving first, the Earth constantly elaborating new dimensions, and the Moon reflecting the whole process.

Materialistic physicists' attempts to *appropriate* the insightful knowledge of perennial wisdom philosophy all too easily promote mathematical quagmires, if not absurdity. More importantly to humankind and planet Earth are the privileged claims and positions justifying irresponsibility that have been made by key conceptually dogmatic scientific communities in powerful commercial and governmental sectors. Intellectually arrogant scientific materialists adamantly adhere to the position that "real science" or "true knowledge" is "value-free" – based upon nothing other than "objective measurement" – and that "pure scientists" needn't *concern* themselves with psychosocial-cultural-environmental contexts. This has abetted groups claiming "rights" associated with often brutally self-serving interests. "Survival of the fittest" theories of *political science* held to by political and economic leaders who hire scientists in order to gain personal power and money at the zero-sum expense of others have come to dangerously threaten the whole planet. The study and implementation of knowledge regarding life in our world, including experimental technology and procedures that enable scientific study, rightfully and simply are *not* "free" of valuation processes and essential ethics.

Take as an obvious example the invention and testing of the hydrogen bomb, or the very act of certain genetic manipulations and medical trials. Discovery and experimental testing of scientific theories often require destruction, invasion, and danger to life beyond that of the experimenting scientists. As an extreme example, behold the next generation of super particle colliders. These will be "recreating spacetime" as it existed at the "birth of the cosmos," ripping powerful, new, *unknown types* of particles (*never* before created in the cosmos) out of the "Void" in such a way that no one knows what will happen to them or the fabric of spacetime that they have been ripped from. Doing this thirty million times a second for long periods of time, which CERN's Large Hadron Collider in Switzerland is designed to do, may create a new type of cosmic flux akin to black

"And a great portent appeared in heaven, a woman clothed with the Sun, with the Moon under her feet, and on her head a crown of twelve Stars" – such is the revelation of She who consorts with the boy-god, the Saint of the Sun.

holes or who-knows-what. Possible disastrous scenarios conjectured by the physics community are beyond scary: such as *immediate annihilation* of our galactic segment of spacetime. Lesser disasters that might actually be experienced are generally not publicly discussed.

Imagining, building, and observing powerful scientific experiments can be exciting until they kill life forms of personal or social value. Obviously, scientists do not and should not have carte blanche to experiment with every manipulation possible in the world based upon a proclaimed "scientific right to know." Owning up to inherent psychosocial, cultural, and environmental responsibility is the deeply ethical duty of every practicing scientist, from geneticist to physicist to chemist. Unfortunately, the essential observation that *knowledge is power* has been turned into a toss-away cliché. Acquisition of knowledge carries a profound responsibility; honoring such might well entail enormous *right effort.*

While mathematical models and ideas delineating theories such as QED have enabled subatomic experiments to be successfully trialed (e.g., particle streams to be produced and collided or otherwise controlled) it is hubris to then posit that the cosmos is *based upon* those mathematical *models,* as if man's mathematical logic is really the *mind and power of a world-creating god.* Are man's mathematical concepts truly "existent" in a dualistic, Platonic sphere "beyond the cosmos" in the same way that a Christian God is generally thought of? Is it not more *reasonable and scientific* to suggest that Chaos, Space, Time, and Law as a Unified Reality is itself already always *mysterious and transcendental* in terms of ultimately being beyond man's attempts to "figure it out"? Is this not what Gödel's Theorem simply indicates? We can conceive of Essential and Great Principles, but *they will never be mathematically provable.* The Universe is awesomely and mysteriously Real. Models are wonderful tools until a modeler deludes himself into thinking that reality is *founded upon* his models; and that thereby his equations and numbers are the essence of all Truth.

Divine ignorance stems from the root of compassionate forgetting, therein allowing Angelic forces to concentrate and intensely transform; it is such perfect indifference that awakens enlightenment and magnifies wisdom.

Modern cosmology hypothesizes a "beginning" to spacetime reality, but that concept is self-contradictory. How can there exist a *beginning,* if there existed no *time* at that beginning? Orthodox materialism does not allow that time must be *prior* to space. Instead, time has been mathematically *reduced* to space; with ensuing math theories posting that time does not "really" exist. The domain that *ideal math-space* has been accorded contrasts so strongly with the real world as humanly observed that the physics community appears to be committing itself to a type of *mythological dualism;* one that holds to its dogma *religiously.* What is more, as physicists gain an ability to "cause" cosmically unique materialization of trillions of colliding particles, including the Higgs or so-called "God-particle," a substantial portion of that community is apparently thinking that *this is the very act of god-power.* It does not require great insight to see the dangerous path this type of thinking may lead nuclear physicists and their military-industrial funders down.

While scientists have yet to approach the level of an "all-powerful knowledge" defined by an ability to externally create integral mini-universes (although there are more than a few who think this possible in the not-too-distant future), they nonetheless individually and socially *do* have the potential to proceed through stages of psychophysical realization and sociocultural organization that reflect the great and unitive processes of cosmological and biological development. That is what spiritual and socially enlightened cultivation, communion, and teaching are about. Human consciousness as whole-body gnosis is far more enlightening regarding the essence of reality than are mathematical constructs. This most certainly does not denigrate or in any way deny the power found in mathematical manipulation, or the bliss found in logical contemplation.

Insights regarding universal processes, durations and radiance of time, and self-ordering complexities of chaos promote a wisdom that considers and contemplates unitive principles, truly illuminating the processional nature of space becoming a myriad of events

An indestructibly golden diamond body dwells upon the Throne; an all-pervading and sovereign agent felt as world-encompassing Justice – the original and destined Truth, Beauty, and Goodness of all.

in our cosmos. But how did Law, Time, Space, and Chaos themselves originally arise? Modern science has put forth numerous theories regarding the origins of the cosmos. In general, it is accepted wisdom that our universe arose out of a Big Bang, as the modern scientific creation myth is called. In a highly compressed version, the story reads as follows:

> Cosmic birth first entailed the creation of spacetime and laws determining the radiance and movement of indivisibly fundamental particle-events potentially infinite in number. As determined by the universe's very first laws, operating within Planck's scale of time and space (i.e., the size of a period if an atom was the size of a galaxy), a type of primordial, chaotic flux initially emerged from the expansion of spacetime gravity.
>
> Cosmic flux was and is composed of a very limited number of types of mass and force-field particles. This original and still underlying invisible soup of energy quickly expanded into a spacetime world exhibiting causality as physicists currently measure it. Entities from atomic elements (mostly the first and simplest: hydrogen) to galaxies (whose material is largely the enormous fusion-flux of hydrogen and the second atomic element: helium) then emerged.
>
> A cosmically creative, unimaginably rapid inflation occurred during a very small period of time in which the laws of causality and all cosmic matter-energy or space-time were created. In a hundredth of a second, the original cosmos of quantum flux was formed. In a few minutes, a chaos of atomic nuclei was forming. In half of an hour, a universal, elemental flux of hydrogen and helium emerged into existence. Within a million years, an atomic cosmos was manifesting in the form of billions of young galaxies, each destined to contain billions of radiant hydrogen-helium suns compressing atoms into heavier elements, ultimately producing a fusion core of radioactive uranium and its weighty atomic cousins.

Enlightenment of self means enlightenment of the World, for what is awakening if not the realization that self does not exist apart from the World and that both do not exist apart from utter Unity?

Albert Einstein showed via his theories of spacetime relativity that what has been observed over the millennia as *dimensional* and *geometrical* attributes of the world are actually naught but the *force field* we have since Isaac Newton's time called *gravity*. Einstein stated that spacetime claims existence on its own only as a *structural quality* of the gravitational field. Space *is* gravity.

Can we equate any other phenomena or force with space-gravity? How about, for instance, the force of *electromagnetism* or *Light?* According to *General Relativity Theory* (GRT), in *pure* space – what may be called the *Void* – electromagnetic fields can be mathematically eliminated, while the field of gravity cannot. However, all attempts to define electromagnetic fields in the mathematical terms of gravity (keeping in mind that math is the sole scientifically material way of defining anything) have failed. The laws governing each are mathematically completely distinct. This is but a single example of the substantial discontinuity embedded in the sets of laws that physicists have created in order to explain, define, and manipulate the world.

Einstein held to a classical scientific worldview that *every element in a physical theory must have a counterpart in physical reality*. This commonsense, objectively practical worldview was associated with two primary, *old science* principles: those of *Realism* and *Local Causes*. The latter states that *a physical event cannot simultaneously influence another event without direct mediation, such as the sending of a signal*. The former assumption states that *physical reality exists independent of any observers and is not dependent upon acts of observation or measurement*. Quantum mechanics theories and experiments have shown these two foundational beliefs to be untrue.

Because GRT does not address the atomic level of physical reality (i.e., it does not offer a *single* property of atomic matter), matter does not appear to be an intrinsic aspect of GRT's description of spacetime. However, matter quite apparently *is* an aspect of our world; thereby it is left to other theories to explain it. Since classical Greek times, a belief has held that breaking matter into its

Given the power to fly, to conjure images and sounds of the past, to instantaneously communicate regardless of distance, to move objects without physical contact, what more does the Questor need, lest it be the true ecstasy of a Simple One?

smallest constituent parts will explain what matter really is. Gravity as a force can only be measured on macrocosmic levels, however. The math that defines gravity cannot be used in any way to break matter down to small event-pieces.

This is where the mechanics of *Quantum Field Theory* (QFT) have reigned supreme. QFT addresses atomic and subatomic levels of matter. GRT presents space as wedded always to time, with spacetime being defined by the field of gravity. It integrates mass with energy and the constant speed of light via spacetime. However, QFT has led to a worldview whereby most all of cosmic matter must actually be conceived as field-energy of types other than gravity.

Contrary to the old principle of local causation, Irish physicist John Bell suggested in 1964 that *paired atomic particles* would retain their correlation over *space-like separation* (meaning a situation whereby no signal traveling at the speed of light can carry information between two paired particles in the time allowed for measurement). This was experimentally verified in 1972, proving that *non-locality* or *non-separability* is a universal dynamic in our cosmos. The principle of nonlocality for events that have a common origin in a unified quantum system is no longer disputed. Although one of the most profound discoveries of modern science, its philosophical and ontological implications have yet to be broadly appreciated.

Given that *the universe was quantumly entangled at the time of its origin,* then that unification must remain throughout the universe; i.e., *the cosmos must presently exist in nonlocal, non-separable entanglement.* It has been observed within perennial wisdom tradition that the principles underlying quantum nonlocality apply to other aspects of reality through the essential principles of *holistic causality* and *synchronistic contingency.*

Neils Bohr, Einstein's famous contemporary and good-natured debater, foresaw the disproving of the *principle of realism,* for QM (even before Werner Heisenberg, a student of Bohr's, developed his now famous *Uncertainty Principle*) was strongly indicating that the universe is *naturally* affected – even radically so – via *relationships* produced between observers or measurers and that which is observed or measured.

Bohr posited an extreme aspect of *polar symmetry* that he called *complementarity,* whereby *apparently incompatible properties or constructs are naturally tied together like poles.* When two constructs (e.g., part and whole, wave and particle, mass and energy, space and time, wave-particle and field-quanta, etc.) are required for a *complete view* of an aspect of nature, but the conditions for observation or measurement preclude the simultaneous application of both constructs, then they are deemed as forming a *complementarity.*

Materialistic physicists have ignored the above new science principles because taken together, nonlocality and complementarity imply that the dynamics of the cosmos' quantum level are always present on the macro levels of integral reality. As Bohr stated, this requires "a final renunciation of the classical ideal of causality and a radical revision of our attitude toward the problem of physical reality."

We have inherited a twentieth-century scientific view of the world whereby it is understood to exist as a chaotic flux of particle-antiparticle pairs surrounded by force fields whose emergence from space in time breaks their zero-sum symmetry, bringing matter particles into existence with duration that becomes always greater as units of mass cohere through self-organizing fields.

Force fields behave like *invisible clouds* of particles surrounding conglomerations of matter. When force particles are "exchanged," matter particles "sense" their "pushes and pulls" as *force.* For instance, every electron has "around it" a swarm of photons, or electromagnetic force particles, constantly being created and destroyed – "ripped out" of and "returned to" the Void. In the mathematical world of physics, virtual photons are as "real" as real photons of light, and are able to *transmit* the electromagnetic *influence* of an electron *over a great, nonlocal distance. How* this happens is realistically an utter mystery. Emerging hierarchical levels of existence combine with fields of resonance to create *music of the spheres.* Resonating vibrations literally cohere in a manifestation of polar identities on diverse levels: subatomic, atomic, molecular, biological, planetary, solar, galactic, and supergalatic.

Only 3 percent of a proton or neutron's "mass" is what physicists call actual mass. The energy carried by the fields (called *gluons*) that *hold together* the atomic nucleus' bits (called *quarks*) make up the other 97 percent of an atomic nucleus' energy-mass. So while mathematical equations of matter may indicate that energy is mass and vice versa ($E = mc^2$), and atom bombs have proven that math to be effective, the universe comprises varying types of *massless* energy to an enormously greater degree than it does mass. Massless energy moves at the speed of light; such as *photons,* which are "packets of light" that hold atoms together and apart.

The picture of reality that we have been composing so far, based upon roundly accepted laws of physics, becomes ever more brilliantly paradoxical the longer it is studied. QFT has led to experiments demonstrating that particles of matter are also fields. However, particle-fields of mass are always distinct from particle-fields of force that bind all mass. In all cases, every energy *field,* it is theorized, must also have a corresponding energy *particle* (although a *graviton* particle of gravity has yet to be discovered).

How does mass-energy get created out of the Void? While GRT identifies gravity with all of spacetime, *GRT does not address how mass arises from gravity.* Neither in fact, does QFT. Thereby a new field has been conjectured, named the *Higgs field* (giving credit to British physicist Peter Higgs). It is theorized that at high enough energy states, such as at the "beginning of the cosmos" or inside super particle colliders or collapsed stars called *black holes,* even the particle-fields of mass (i.e., quarks, electrons, etc.) have *no* mass.

The *mass-creating Higgs* force is like the *essence of Chaos,* the Crack in the Space-Void Kosmic Egg. The Higgs field, like gravity, must be a universal principle of time-space – it is not caused by any other aspect of the universe, for it is *prior* to the material cosmos. Problematically for QFT, however, is that like the "graviton," a Higgs particle has yet to be discovered; even though it logically should have been by now, given the many particle experiments that have carefully searched for it where it is supposed to be found.

The Higgs chaos-creator-force affects not only the masses of *real* particles, but also the masses of *virtual particles.* The latter *emerge* and *return* to the Space-Void in potentially endless numbers at every moment everywhere. This is the mathematically metaphysical bedrock foundation of QED. The Void itself has no *ordinary particle-field energy.* Virtual particles effectively manifest a *time-energy uncertainty principle* inherent to the Void; e.g., there is no *objective* number of particles in any given space, but rather a *probability of particle manifestation.* Such is the essential nature of Chaos.

Particles are almost always created in symmetrically polar pairs with *antiparticles* (massless photons and theoretical gravitons lack antiparticle partners, however). Theoretically, the visible universe should *not exist* according to quantum math. It remains a complete conundrum how the symmetry of matter-antimatter pairs is broken – the two should always cancel one another out, generally leaving "residue" particles and large amounts of energy in the process. It is estimated that at the time of the Big Bang, for every ten billion particle-antiparticle pairs created, there was one extra particle that was left without an antiparticle, and thus did not self-annihilate into the universe's *background radiation* (this near-*absolute zero* radiance of all-pervading cosmic wave-frequency is cosmologist's ancestral evidence of cosmic creation).

How empty is outer space? One cubic inch of air on earth contains ten million trillion atoms. The most empty vacuum scientists have experimentally obtained has a density of three thousand atoms per cubic inch. Interstellar space, in contrast, contains only one atom per cubic foot. Keep in mind that a hydrogen atom's proton, neutron, and electron are not little whizzing hardballs. That single atom is a *field-density* defined solely by *contingency* as to "where" that atom is and where it is "moving to" "next." Every atom exists in contingent relationship with the world about it – it does not contain "objective" independence that may be identified *isolated from* the world. Space-Void is a spectrum of energy states inclusive of the materialization of causally contingent, emergent fields with polar identities. That cosmic spectrum of energy materializes from the chaos of Higgs potentiality and the gravitational realization of spacetime itself underlying both that very quantum flux of potential and its actual cosmic materialization.

Space would be energy-less void if it were not "filled" with Higgs-Chaos. Excepting, of course, that space itself *is* gravity, and so gravity cannot be subtracted from it. The essential natures of both gravitational and Higgs fields have not been "figured out," GRT notwithstanding. In any case, physicists have been attempting to merge their mathematical models of the two field-aspects of Space, just as they have been trying to unite their models of the *weak* and *strong* atomic fields (respectively, the cause of *atomic decay* – the fusion power of all Suns – and of the *cohesion of constituent quark parts* composing protons and neutrons). The nature of Higgs and Gravity, whose *difference* in both magnitude and *type* of "force-power" is too extreme to warrant a sensible attempt at cognizing, must somehow be unified mathematically if cosmic evolution is to be understood in terms of scientific models.

It is reasonable to suggest that each of these most primary aspects of the universe may be appropriately understood as the *realization* of an essential *immortal principle.*

Given that the fields of energy, including all light, cannot be mathematically identified with gravity or space, then how about time itself? QFT physicists generally regard time as a property *reducible* to space. However, it would logically seem that time defined as *duration of vibrational, polar reality* (be that of a superstring, a wave of any sort, or subject-object cognition) has to be *prior* to particle existence.

As mentioned, no particle has yet been discovered as "producing" Higgs or Gravitational realities. While attempts to find *candidate phenomena* for "*pre-cosmic* cosmic particles" produced inside super colliders will no doubt continue into the distant future, it is possible if not likely that QFT simply will not ever be able to subsume or otherwise merge with GRT's model of space-gravity.

Perennial wisdom understanding of cosmic evolution suggests that Time itself is an *immortal principle* whose realization encompasses and underlies the principle-reality of Space. Spacetime gravity is the *Void* (or pure Space) sensed, felt, or cognized as *vibration and inertial duration* (i.e., Time) by every *polar identity* or event-thing-holon in the universe. Space is the *soul of time* that then becomes spacetime Chaos or *soul of the world*. This in turn emanates or flows forth as a myriad cosmic *souls* or *identities* that are all created by and returned to a shared "original soul" or Source.

Perhaps complexity and chaos theories defining Higgs reality will merge with spacetime theories defining Gravitational reality. If so, then a coherent *Grand Unification Theory* may be effectively defined, bridging the essence of *identity* with that of *space,* and *inertia* with that of *geometrical gravity.* Be that as it may, the principles of *identity, symmetry, resonance, emergence, contingency, causality, chaos,* and *space* will remain distinct while being understood as coherently Unified through Time.

The cosmos is holistically caused through ineffably *deep entanglement* with and as chaotic flux. QFT attempts to define this level of manifestation. It has met with measurable success, and modern technology will continue to evince such. However, there remains much more to be worked out. Theories of *time* are just beginning to be conceived, with *one-dimensional zero-state vibration* being posited as the most fundamental aspect of literally unimaginable string-identities now conjectured to compose all particle-reality of matter and force.

QFT is being radically revised through new theories attempting to include and unify all of the known forces discovered by physicists.

Extending what are popularly known as *string* and *superstring theories,* ten-dimensional *brane* theory incorporates a concept of physically dimensional *membranes.* It consists of variant mathematical models, all of which suggest a reality underlying spacetime composed of multidimensional vibratory objects based upon one-dimensional "strings" (unlike any actual visual that commonly comes into mind) whose *vibrational overtones* extend into an infinite number of *point particles.* Membranes of such strings are formed via higher dimensions. *Brane theory* predicts both gravity and general relativity, along with elegantly describing how quantum particles interact with one another. However, a substantially negative feature to this theory is that because enormously high-energy states are needed to test it, direct experimental validation appears to be impossible.

String, superstring, and subsequent brane theories posit abstract mathematical structures of varying dimensions as a way to supersede the many inconsistencies and impossible values of QFT. We will not attempt an overview of these exotic theories, but it warrants mention that in general the thousands of theoretical variants rely on a new principle: *Super-Symmetry* (SS). This principle importantly states that *particles that transmit forces may be changed into particles of mass* and vice versa. When such a conversion occurs, a particle's *location shifts* in time and space. This must thereby involve the geometry of spacetime. To fit this conceptual model of *quanta,* gravity-space must then be defined as embodying particulate *granularity,* identified as hypothetical *gravitons.* Unfortunately for many speculative physicists, the hypothesized math worlds do not at all resemble the observed world of particle-identities.

Having abolished all distinction between force and matter, other supersymmetrical particles called *sparticles* are predicted by SS. The fundamental particles produced during cosmic creation – *leptons, photons,* and *quarks* – hypothetically emerged with partners called *sleptons, photinos,* and *squarks.* Many orthodox physicists despise brane theory and its family of multidimensional, metaphysical mathematical constructs. Yet it remains the touchstone of attempts to unify all cosmic laws of matter. Unification theories address the original source-state of the cosmos, as the universe was during its first ten trillionth of a ten trillionth of a nanosecond. Only then, it is thought, could there have been the astronomically high energies needed for universal forces to be unified. For this reason, it is impossible to directly test these theories.

Superstring theories attempt to model the physical world at its smallest imaginable scale, commonly referred to as the *Planck scale.* It is at that level of reality that the *speed of light* (defined as the universally constant speed of anything with a zero rest mass, such as a photon of light) and Newton's *gravitational constant* (a physical constant which appears in Newton's law of universal gravitation and in GRT; it is based upon the fact that attractive force between two bodies is proportional to the product of their masses and inversely proportional to the square of the distance between them) "meet" with quantum mechanics' *Planck's constant* (used to describe the discreet size-steps of quanta). These three important *constants of the universe* can here only be mentioned, as they and their corresponding theories duly require a full treatise to be regarded properly. However, to gain some sense of the Planck scale, at which the above universal constants or laws affect one another, imagine an atom to be the size of our Milky Way Galaxy. The Planck scale would then be the size of the following *period.* (Many have wondered how a Planck size superstring can possibly carry causally sufficient information about, say, a meter-long radio wave proton – which is what superstring theory suggests; but we must leave these fascinating abstractions at that.)

Given how precise any physical measurement of the subatomic world must be to manipulate it with the type of exactitude that engineers and chemists are accustomed to, we cannot help but be amazed at the marvels of quantum devices. Nonetheless, while mathematics can seemingly represent anything, imaginable or not, we know for a fact that nature does not allow mathematical *exactitude. Irrational numbers* (that is, numbers whose decimal expansion never repeats or terminates) define much of the physical world, and these numbers are by definition endlessly inexact. We will never exactly know, for instance, the mathematical relationship between a circle's circumference and its diameter, a constant relationship commonly represented by the symbol π. Regarding our lack of mathematically exact knowledge of nature's particles, we cannot know a particle's *exact energy* at a *specific instant* in time.

Space-gravity and time are experienced, observed, and measured in constant flux – they simply are not *static* or *solid*. SS theories attempt to mathematically recognize this as fundamentally as possible. For instance, the general indication of *symmetry* in physics is when a quality of a thing can be manipulated – e.g., through rotation, reflection, or interchanging of parts – and the new configuration remains indistinguishable from the initial one. In other words, symmetry involves transformations that *appear* to do *nothing*. Symmetry is normally a property of a static system upon which procedures can be applied to rearrange the system while leaving all measurable physical properties unchanged.

Quite beyond static notions of symmetry, elegance, and beauty, SS addresses the beauty of self-transforming flux itself. SS is conceptually attractive to many physicists, particularly those of younger generations, because it is elegantly metaphysical in its worldview, particularly through its overriding principles of Symmetry and Unity. Embracing instead of deriding an intelligent proclivity to reincorporate universally metaphysical principles into materialistic physical theories is an initial step toward bringing philosophers and physicists back into a healthy and wise dialog.

Prominent physicists have presented no-nonsense arguments for the need of having an ontologically coherent theory of quantum mechanics. Currently, QM simply cannot address the world *as it is observed by human consciousness*. Theories of gravity are much more tangible and sensible to conscious, planetary beings dealing with macrocosmic laws of matter. QFT has been plunged via superstring theories into the mystical depths of one-dimensional vibratory potentials, infinitely populating a Void that is full of massless energy expanding into eternity. This appears to many commonsense observers to look like spiritual poetry as much as scientific theory. Perhaps realms of metaphysics and physics may here appropriately merge. In any case, regarding universal, unified theories of natural law, QFT has yet to be made applicable to the domain of *biological life* (which we will shortly consider) and its many hierarchical levels.

To many scientists, SS seems to be such a fanciful and hugely resource-consuming developmental path that its experimental funding will prove to be unsustainable. Roger Penrose, a highly awarded mathematical physicist who has extensively argued that materially mechanistic laws of physics are inadequate to explain the reality of consciousness, spoke for many of his fellow practical scientists when he stated that he found himself "to be totally unconvinced of the physical relevance of the scheme of supersymmetry" and that "observations probably do not provide any support at all" for the theory's claims.

Supersymmetry's primary value to Quantum Field Theory has been in canceling away *uncontrollable infinities*, primarily through the mathematical device of super-symmetrically rotating matter particles (*bosons*) into force particles (*fermions*). In standard QFT, different types of mass may be transformed into one another; likewise for types of force. Doing this through energetic particle collision and creation is what CERN and other particle-colliding centers are all about. By unifying this most fundamental polarity of subatomic reality, and introducing a whole new half of the universe, namely SS partners for every particle presently measured and conjectured, QFT math becomes much more *elegant*. That elegance is a compelling attractor for many fine minds in the world of physics.

Whether or not SS proves to be "true" within any given mathematical framework, at this juncture in time so many theoretical changes to the Standard Model of QFT have ensued that are reliant upon SS that should essential core theories of SS prove to be false, the whole current body of QFT will have to be called into question. By all appearances, current physics is now involved with *mathematical metaphysics,* plain and simple. Conceptually, "spiritual" worldviews have once again crossed into the visionary realms of physics. As Penrose vs. SS indicates, circles espousing variant metaphysical views are having to compete for monetary funds, social status, and the power to construct new experimental technologies.

SS attempts to unify all known *forces,* but is there a unifying symmetrical aspect between time and space at their most fundamental levels of reality? GRT certainly posits that there is, but can only address this through the *reduction* of time into space. Higgs, however, breaks underlying time-space symmetries and thus Chaos is able to *create* the cosmos out of the Void underlying gravity-space. Because gravity fields cannot be created by scientists (unlike electromagnetic fields, for instance) scientists are unable to do *controlled* experiments on them. Physicists hope that gravity can be quantized like other forces, and thereby manipulated. However, it is now dawning upon many that Space is a principle that cannot be reduced to either chaos or the six lower principles (as presented in this chapter) of cosmic materialization. Nor can the principle of Chaos be reduced to the latter, although its laws are *closer* or more similar to those discovered on the causal level of cosmic materialization. Similarly and most importantly, *Time cannot be reduced to the laws of Space.*

Cosmologists suggest that the universe "tunneled" into existence (given that there was no space, this of course suggests yet another mysterious conundrum: *tunneled from where?*) via a mathematical reality of *imaginary time* (produced when time is multiplied by the square root of negative one). This same mathematical process defines the manifestation of *quantum potential,* whereby particles tunnel in and out of spacetime so rapidly that they are impossible to measure. In other words, there "is" a Void "beyond" cosmic spacetime (let's call it "pure Timespace") from and back to which all material "bits" of our known universe emerge and converge, *for eternity*. Eternity because for a universal singularity that emerged as space destined to accelerate as a whole to the absolute speed of light, time-space relative "to anything else" *realizes Eternity*.

However metaphysical such concepts may seem, they lend a quality of constant *sameness* to all of space throughout the universe at all times, which physicists find most helpful to their theories. Albert Einstein enumerated an early-twentieth-century variant of this concept as the *cosmological constant.* Although he and many other scientists found such a constant space-energy to be philosophically unpalatable (involving as it does, an apparent *infinitude of contingency*), it has recently returned to the fore in cosmological theory. Einstein's theories allow for an accelerated cosmic expansion via his infamous cosmological constant. This constant represents a type of "vacuum energy," which permeates "empty" space in a constant manner everywhere and at all times in the universe.

Recently, a new, unknown type of energy has been discovered and verified by astronomers. It is associated with the *accelerating expansion* of the universe. Space is expanding: not "into something," but rather simply *is* expanding *itself* – the Void into the Void, yet always *greater* in measurable reality. It is impossible to objectively observe this space dilation, for as observers we are also always dilating. Scientists infer that space is expanding via their measurements of local gravity fields. Similarly, cosmologists infer that spacetime is accelerating its expansive movement. An estimated three-quarters of the universe is composed of an extraordinary kind of otherwise unknown energy that is adding an *anti-gravitational radiance* to the universe.

Cosmological knowledge of the universe's history, "present" state, and vast spread of matter and fields remains highly theoretical. Our telescopes convey only a miniscule amount of information regarding the cosmos. Beautiful pictures of galactic light, while glorious to behold, hold little measurable value compared to in-depth information gathered through space probes; and the snapshots of galaxies caught by high-powered cameras show only a tiny portion of the billions and billions of galaxies known to exist. Our telescopes simply are not powerful enough to capture a wide array of electromagnetic information beyond that of our local cosmic surroundings. Yet, even with these limitations, cosmologists are sure of important aspects of their knowledge regarding the greater universe. For instance, they are confident they know within a relatively small range of error how much mass is in the cosmos.

When all possible forms of cosmic mass are added up, the total does not allow for the acceleration of spacetime as it is now broadly agreed to be. Cosmologists are left imagining a new "antigravity force" that has unfortunately been named *Dark Energy* (DE) – it may or may not be energy, and is called "dark" simply because we are ignorant of what it is. DE is definitely not Gravity, Higgs, or any other known energy, field, or force.

It is herein suggested that the antigravity-like acceleration of the universe is the most fundamental evidence we have of pure Time-energy, distinct from and not reducible to Space. This is the most essential and creative principle of cosmic evolution after universal Law itself. When the cosmos emerged on hierarchical levels of a contingently synchronistic and causally holistic chaotic transformation of spatial dimensionality, it did so through a "radiance of time," rather than a "point in space." All of space *emanated* or *radiated* from and *as* time, which is to say that space is inherently a process of time itself. We cannot *locate* the cosmos' original "center" somewhere out amongst the galaxies. Rather, the original spacetime "point" of the material cosmos is in the ancestral history of every particle in the universe – of every *field* and *polarity* and *identity*.

Because mathematical symbols offer no clues to what is "outside" or "beyond" space-voidness, they are incapable of "explaining" Time. Rather, humans must utilize *existential interior consciousness* in order to cognize, verify, and understand time. (Reflecting that process, symbols of contemplative art, such as the Tarot, address aspects of real law beyond the mathematical.) Time simply will not pop out of mathematical models of cosmic creation; spacetime matter, chaos, and force fields, however, readily do. The lawful principle of time is *beyond* the laws of matter and chaos, gravity and space.

A commonly known law of physics is that of *energy conservation:* There is never a loss or gain of energy in the universe – it simply "moves around." But if space can keep getting *greater,* and most of the universe's energy (an estimated 74 percent at the time of this writing) is an unknown, universal *accelerator* of space-gravity expansion, we may reasonably suggest that a *non-space* or *beyond-space* or *original-space* energy is radiantly *growing* our space-gravity reality *at all times* and – more aptly stated – *as* all time.

Since it is senseless to concern ourselves with the question of "from where does time-energy pour forth or emanate?" we will simply refer to DE as the *pure energy* of Time – the First Realization of Unitive Law or *Essential Cause* Beyond All Causation. Time in this view can be called the *Radiance* of Light and Gravity before cosmic photon and graviton manifestation. Time is a Radiant Principle that is no less real for being always prior and greater than physical space. It is Unitive Law or Transcendent One of the Kosmos – Alpha-Omega, Source-Destiny, Cause-Purpose – as Radiant Energy creating, emanating, or otherwise generating its consorting principle, Dimensional Space.

Unitive Law, Radiant Time, and *Dimensional Space* are the key Principles merging spiritual realization and scientific knowledge. Greater bliss, greater consciousness, greater being: the universe is becoming always greater, interiorly and exteriorly in its lawful realization as eternally radiant energy and dimensional space.

Those who believe that all principles must be reducible to material measurements argue that a deathly cold equilibrium of entropy is the destiny of the universe. *Equilibrium* is defined by physicists as the state of a body or physical system at rest or in non-accelerated motion in which the resultant of all forces acting on it is zero and the sum of all torques about any axis is zero. *Entropy* is popularly defined as a hypothetical tendency for all matter and energy in the universe to evolve toward a state of inert uniformity. Such is a worldview wherein the universe slows or spreads into uniform darkness, leaving only a hypothetically *separate* God or Heaven as the Once Creative and Eternally Moving Principle of Reality. This is a worldview wherein the Transcendental is not *actually* Real, i.e., *existing as the World*. After the concept of God is then jettisoned, this becomes a worldview whereby nihilistic materialists proclaim proof that Death Rules All.

Entropic destiny *used* to be imagined as an inflating universe that will over the eons lose all coherency, disintegrating into a totally random, non-organizing absolute-zero state of equally dense (or "denseless") bits of space-gravity that might appropriately be described as the Zero Space of Eternal Death. Materialists who choose to ignore laws of self-organizing complexity or chaos appear influenced by occult beliefs permeating their cultural programming. Ironically, they posit metaphysical presumptions in opposition to the religious sects that have created the dualistic dogma they are unwittingly reinforcing. In reality, the constant acceleration of space into *light* and *eternal time* nulls any truth to the myth that entropic *equilibrium* essentially defines past, present, or future.

The perennial wisdom realized as nondual Unity of Being informs us that radiant consciousness is realization of the Bright; that eternal light is the true source and destiny of the Universe; and that universal radiance as the *essential duration* of all presence is simply the immortal realization of Time. Time-energy allows for an explanation of consciousness or universal cognition as the *interior* of space-gravity itself. Furthermore, time serves as the perfect explanation of the cosmic acceleration that originated in a Big Bang expansion of space from a three-dimensional size trillions of times smaller than a proton to that of a basketball in what might poetically be called "a brief moment." General Relativity theorists will attempt to extend their concepts of the universe to account for its expansive growth by merging complexity theory with GRT. Attempts at such mathematical unification of models will no doubt prove enlightening. However, Time will inevitably remain undeniably fundamental and non-reducible.

Physicists agree that their latest theories (such as SS) seem to work miraculously, pulling together otherwise disparate fields of mathematics. In fact, mathematical fields are being *theoretically* created that have never before been construed or observed, and which may not in fact exist. It is reasonable to inquire: What kind of meaning does such knowledge hold for the seven billion human minds living in a world of biological life? How can physicists disparage the contemplative observations of sages over millennia regarding principles at play in the world about us, while holding high as the "one true light of knowledge" immensely complicated, completely hypothetical mathematical suppositions?

While such theories as QED, GRT, and even SS may be utilized to engineer a new millennium of technology, if the past is of any indication, that technology may well bring with it more death of life through delusion, craving, and malice than it does bliss of life through wisdom, compassion, and love. During the timeframe in which the present work was written, it became widely apparent that technological productivity was a major contributor to the largest global mass extinction of life since the age of dinosaurs. Weaponry, from spears to missiles, has only been one part of that causative contribution. Otherwise productive machines – involving, for instance, transportation, building, computation, and communication – have also proven to be part of the *whole causal process of planetary mass extinction.*

Contrasting to the complex mathematics of quantum and relativistic physics are complexity theories based upon *deep simplicity.* During the latter part of the twentieth century, *complexity theory* was developed building in part upon Ira Prigogene's work in thermodynamics and French mathematician René Thom's brilliantly intuitive re-visioning of life-transformative *catastrophes,* viewing biological processes and evolution in terms of topological bifurcations, discontinuous development, and causal attractors. Thom's genuinely innovative organic models (presented in his seminal work, *Structural Stability and Morphogenesis*) conceptually harmonized with Prigogene's *dissipative structures,* which modeled open systems that maintain themselves in stable states far from equilibrium. Prigogene awakened the scientific world to the import of such dynamic structures *remaining* even while embodying an ongoing flow and change of components. Importantly, the dynamics of dissipative structures include the *spontaneous emergence* of new forms of order. System flow may increase to a tipping point of instability, at which juncture *bifurcation* occurs, whereupon system and structural processes branch off into entirely new structural forms and systemic orders.

In the fields of thermodynamics and biology, developmental principles have come to the fore that present a universal model of dynamic process: an environmentally resonating polar structure builds a field of force or interactivity that energetically breaks some crucial aspect of the structural identity's symmetry; the structure then emerges on a new level of organization, order, and relationship. This creative process is the universe reaching out into *novel identity* even while always maintaining *reunification* of such. Through it, morphological complexity and evolution develop. Pre-biotic evolution of non-living dissipative structures continues through biological evolution to develop trans-biotic neurochemical consciousness and sociocultural networks of sustainable, synchronistic order.

What actually defines a biological organism? As an identifiable polar system, an organism is defined and subsequently relates to its environment via its *membrane.* Creation of molecular membranes first occurs through the electric polarity of H_2O or water, one of the most basic atomic structures in the universe. In general, some molecules are attracted by water, others are repelled. A third type of commonly found molecular structure is that of fatty/oily lipids, which contains a both water-attracted and water-repelled polarity. When coming into contact with water, lipids spontaneously form structures that then form membranes similar in function to cellular membranes. Cellular membranes themselves are in fact lipids with proteins attached. (The above process can be seen in bubble formation when oil and water are shaken together.)

An organism by definition *autonomously rearranges* patterns of membrane connectivity and interior structure in accordance with those environmental disturbances that the organism is *determined* to respond to. Observation of this most fundamental view of organismic behavior has led to the theory that every organism possesses an inherent ability to influence its own ongoing structural changes, an ability that may be called *biological cognition.* A *cognitive domain* is established through an organism determining which environmental perturbations will trigger its own structural change. Cognition or *consciousness* (the latter indicating a greater level of *cognitive complexity*) may thereby be defined simply as the process of living and interacting with the environment. A machine constructed from without as an *assembly of parts* is an utterly different system than that formed by *resonant boundary conditions* of cells and organisms producing living processes and entities.

Cognition and consciousness define the core process of a unified whole body – an entire organism – not just an organism's "programming center," be that of genes or brains. Cognition and structure as mind and body determine the life forms and transformations of organic spheres of existence. It is not an unreasonable jump in theory to suggest that this holds true on all levels of existence, including pre-biotic molecular and atomic levels, for identities that possess a defining membrane or boundary of extension and polar structure within a field of environmental relatedness.

It has been demonstrated that within a flux of plasma, complex, self-organizing structures may form capable of replicating themselves, i.e., a helical polar structure naturally forms within plasma (caused, for instance, by lightning) that can bifurcate into two copies of itself. These structures then go on to interact with similar entities, changing one another and evolving into further forms as unstable structures break down and stable adaptations continue propagating. Exhibiting the necessary properties to qualify them as *inorganic* living matter – being autonomous, reproducing, and evolving – these *plasmic entities* evince the six principle-stages of immortal process addressed herein.

Atoms and molecules may thereby also be said to realize *mind-body cognitive structure,* even if they are not in the sphere of life. Arguably, it is unreasonable to dogmatically presume that atoms existing in a natural system of dynamic self-organization, such as stellar plasma formation, are unable to influence their own ongoing structural changes; although clearly the mechanisms of doing so must be far more subtle than those of biological organisms. Modeling such is how the abstractions of mathematical physics and cosmology can truly shine.

The considerable efforts of Humberto Maturana and Francisco Varela have precisely clarified the interior reality of organismic identity: the perception and cognition of a living system does not *represent* external reality but rather *specifies* one through a process of circular organization. This is true even with organisms lacking a nervous system. Circular organization defines a self-referencing process: a closed network of interactions in which every change of the interactive relations between certain components always results in a change of the interactive relations of the same or of other components. (This may well also define the actual interior-dynamic process of atomic continuity.) The circular process of life allows for evolutionary change in such a way that circularity of energetic interaction is always maintained, even in the midst of transformative chaos. The first six immortal principles of cosmic evolution define and ensure this.

Reductionistic materialists do not understand natively holistic principles of resonant, emergent, and synchronistic causality. Primary to their dogma is a symmetrical identification of *structure* with *organization*. In reality, structure is the actual relationship between physical components of a system, while organization comprises the greater field of hierarchical synchronistic holism. Organization cannot be reduced to mechanical causation of physical components. (The human nervous system's organization as traditionally studied, cultivated, and expounded upon by yogis from India to China is a prime example that demands respect by structural reductionists in the fields of physiology, medicine, evolutionary biology, neuropsychology, etc.)

It would seem obvious that when referring to or studying living beings, the *lived experience* of the beings, or subjective cognition and consciousness, must be duly and rightfully regarded. Scientists cannot "know" life while blindly disregarding as unimportant the experience of life as interiorly realized by every life form. In other words, *objective* worldviews are only one half of the knowledgeable content a scientist must respect and consider. Indeed, most aspects of the world cannot be objectively measured without being subjectively influenced. Most certainly, subjective interpretations of measurements are the norm.

Simple trajectories of singular macro-size objects and reactions of molecular chemicals under highly restricted environments form grossly limited aspects of the complex interactions composing our universe. Known chemical reactions occurring within radically controlled laboratory settings, for instance, become unknown chemical reactions once they interact with a natural environment. Studies of ecological and biological poisoning have made this clear. As a simple example, knowledge of how to make Teflon materials that maintain remarkably stable chemistry pales in comparison to the ignorance of what those laboratory-produced molecular constructions do when exposed to nature. Incredible doses of Teflon products have been found in the tissues of polar bears and seals in the Arctic, tropical birds and dolphins, and in humans across the planet. While not knowing how Teflon has spread throughout all of animal life, it is known that it damages biological reproductive systems.

Our twenty-first-century knowledge of complex systems has made it painfully clear how cupfuls of scientific knowledge can be overwhelmed by waves of scientific ignorance. First and foremost, scientific theorists and experimenters need to apply their attention to a broader and more essential base of foundational principles than they were accustomed to doing in the twentieth century. Greater and in particular more resonant spheres of interaction must be considered when studying atomic, chemical, and biological processes. Scientists have a responsibility to take into account systemically emergent and contingent relationships that are not artificially banished through laboratory techniques. The world needs corporations and universities to fund holistic studies, not limiting their knowledge to what is required solely to implement profitable known processes or materials while being ignorant of their effects once they are produced and distributed outside of the laboratory. It is now clear that massive global environmental damage will not be mitigated until social pressure (or social disaster) compels university and corporate scientists to own up to a responsible, critically needed *framework of integral ethics*.

Education regarding the essential and universal principles of nature addressed in this book is the most effective way to inform scientific, political, and corporate authorities how to integrally govern and regulate their fields of responsibility.

Evolution of the cosmos includes evolution of biological life and human consciousness. If we widen the meaning of *consciousness* to indicate all interior cognition naturally arising through coherent existence, then it makes sense to state that the *spectrum of consciousness* is the interior aspect of the *hierarchy of complexity* deeply realized throughout nature. Hierarchical depth unfolds through evolution as greater consciousness. Such is the realization of time through *directionality* that may be called the destiny or *telos* of the universe.

Human consciousness grows into *radiance* through *transcendence*, here defined as "the cognitive process of coherent beingness involved with differentiation and integration." Consciousness reduces into *inertia* through *regression*, defined as "the cognitive process of coherent beingness involved with dissociation and alienation." The polar symmetry of these two processes is such that both are complementarily required up to a point of symmetry-breaking, which is initiated by fifth-stage gnosis and finalized by seventh-stage enlightenment. Evolution compels consciousness beyond its inertial boundaries, ultimately emerging or unfolding into a realm of *cosmic consciousness* identifiable with *immortal flux.*

Consciousness does not equal objective perception. Consciousness equals the vibrational duration of subjective actualization that integrates objective perception. There are disastrous consequences embedded in the rabid movement amongst "philosophers of science" to restrict consciousness to and as mechanical, objective logistics. Clever abstraction of logical systems into rarefied realms of analysis and algorithmic dialectics can subsume the very living consciousness of logicians to such a degree that they become blindly obedient to a privileged social system machine through which habit-cogs of non-intuitive rationalization may manipulate the world without any concern of life, wholeness, love, or altruistic compassion. That egoic way of being in no way represents, let alone actually realizes, the peak and destiny of human evolution.

Cognitive psychologists and practitioners of neuroscience advance a commonsense realization that concepts of mind need to be integrated with and understood through physiological patterns and processes. However, by using reductive, grossly limited definitions and presumptions of physiology, orthodox cognitive and drug-and-gene-based psychologists inevitably become mired in their shifting groundwork of physiochemistry.

When the human body itself is understood as *already* being consciousness or mind, and the human mind itself is understood as naturally being a *wholly formed* body, then any presumptions holding to positions of body-mind dualism are demonstrably fallacious. Mind *as* body and body *as* mind imply metaphysics *as* physics and physics *as* metaphysics (or put another way, *interphysics* as *intraphysics*.) This view posits a complex, self-organizing nature to living bodies, and an understanding of cognitive psychology that fully integrates transpersonal actualization and spiritual development.

Consciousness studies were significantly advanced in the twentieth century when studies of nonlinear dynamics merged with complexity theory and neurophenomenology. The latter has focused on analysis of "first person," or interior, experience. The corpus of Edmund Husserl remains central to that field. *Experiential clarity* can be attained by a self-observant witness engaging subjective experience through suspension of belief habits and mechanisms that obscure or otherwise confuse what is being experienced. This allows for a systematic reflection on one's *phenomenological* (i.e., the context of all possible appearances in one's experience) attitude.

Scientific approaches to the study of human mind have primarily focused on neurological and chemical measurements and feedback loops, which deliver types of objective information regarding subjective experience. However, perennial wisdom realizers have without doubt posited that *higher* (i.e., subtler, deeper, more complex and integral) levels of knowledge emerge from *whole-body* consciousness. While neurochemical measurements can inform us about specific causal associations (e.g., eating chocolate and making love both raise endorphin levels), that quality or level of information is not comparable to the quality and level of knowledge attained when integral, enlightened consciousness is mindful of its own interior states and developmental procession in tandem with its sociocultural fields of the same.

Francisco Varela and others have made it clear that consciousness cannot be identified with special "neural structures," but rather *emerges* from the formation of transient functional clusters of neurons and resonant cell assemblies. Combinations of many different cellular, chemical, and neurological functions create series of coherent states that stabilize and self-maintain as levels of organismic consciousness, even while transitory states continually arise and subside. Emergence of fluctuating experiences cohering synchronistically and transforming holistically is contingent upon an aspect of resonating phenomena termed *phase-locking*. For instance, brain regions can become interconnected in such a way that neural activity becomes synchronized, creating a non-conjoined *flux* of cell assemblies formed by widely dispersed (i.e., non-local) neural circuits.

In other words, consciousness (whether limited to the brain or extended to include the whole body and even social/communal/ancestral networks of bodies) is not a product of mechanical, linear, and local neurochemical structures; but rather of chaotic, holistic, and synchronistic organization of cell assemblies with *dynamic cores* that hierarchically emerge from resonating electromagnetic, neurochemical fields. In actuality, both gravitational and quantum fields contribute non-trivially to biological identity and thereby most likely to an entity's *quality of cognition*. For instance, both a human body's gross inertia and subtle reactivity to molecular chemistry (as evidenced by the effects of heart and pineal hormones, LSD, photons striking the iris, etc.) can clearly impact and even radically alter its states of consciousness over any given duration. Given that we are now able to engineer quantum computers, it is reasonable to suggest that the human system already engages quantum mechanisms via its subtle molecular-atomic biology. Numerous theories focused upon this are now being explored.

Regarding gross inertia's effects upon consciousness, these are most obviously felt and observed whenever a body is suddenly stopped or accelerated. Both sitting completely still and accelerating/decelerating can effect potentially massive transformation to the whole human system, both momentarily and when occurring over time.

Concerning the complexity of communication within brain networks, chemical synaptic signaling between neurons is not the only means of neuro-computation. Cells of the *glia* – the connective tissue of the nervous system – also function as communicators, both with each other and with neurons. Thus, the complex communication of the human system also involves coordinated structural changes within neuro-glial processes. This immensely complicates any attempt to create reductionistic models of brain functioning and the procession or evolution of animal consciousness.

Nonlinear dynamics form core processes in both the human neuro-system and the greater body. Holonic body parts hierarchically cluster not only through mechanical connectivity but also as a flow of continual exchange, *self-organizing* as a synchronistic whole. Maturana elegantly states that "communication is not the transmission of information, but rather the coordination of behavior between living organisms through mutual structural coupling." (In this context, *language* is effectively *communication about communication,* and we might say that the image-exemplars of the Tarot are a most rarefied form of such *symbolic* communication.)

In currently accepted scientific terms, how does biological synchronization occur? A core comprising a critical number of polar identities resonating as oscillators must first *sync,* whether by pure chance or by holistic probability. Their combined *coherence* serves as a nucleus attracting other resonating identities through forces operative at the oscillators' natural level of dimension and frequency.

This increases the nucleus and thereby amplifies the signal. A positive feedback process leads to an outbreak or emergence of *synchrony*. In this process, there is no singular controlling oscillator or polar structure. However, both nucleating and resonating processes are required to gain coherence.

Mechanists have repeatedly denied that cosmic principles involve inherent self-organization *integrally purposed* toward an always greater unity innately emerging through and as evolution. Supposedly, the only way reality is oriented toward "unity" is through the "sameness" or zero-point equilibrium of entropic death. *Life* is viewed as an accident, and not a divine or otherwise essential one at that. Yet secretly, practically in an occult fashion, organizational principles have been appropriated by hardened scientists via concepts of "particle symmetry," "atomic memes," "genetic programs," and "germplasms."

Some scientists still posit a theoretical ability to computationally model a full-blown adult human solely from the information packed into a human egg. Where does this program of presumed linear instructions dwell? Within the DNA of germplasm? Molecular biology holds that DNA germplasm somehow programs the synthesis of proteins, which forms the *somatoplasm* of living organisms. Organisms inherit acquired characteristics through germplasm, which orthodox scientists dogmatically believed to never be affected by subtle or causal feedback of the actual functioning or life of an organism. It was commonly held that while *random* mutations may change the DNA of germplasm, *nothing* else in the rest of an organism's system, behavior, experience, and environmental relationships (unless perhaps it is a relationship with nuclear radiation or overwhelmingly toxic chemicals) affects an organism's genetic program, which goes on to reproduce itself via a new organism. This has been proven false.

It is known that intelligence is in part genetically determined. The volume of both the brain's grey "processing" cells and white "connecting" cells is heritable and correlates with certain elements of IQ. The *quality* of brain matter connections is governed by the integrity of the protective *myelin sheath* that encases them. While myelin integrity is also largely genetic, and correlates with IQ, it also *changes throughout life.* Our genes drive us to environmental and social interaction in ways that can lead to changes in myelin integrity and be passed down to future generations.

We also now know that types of brain chemistry catalyzed and prolonged by drugs will produce genetic mutations that may in fact be passed down to offspring. Of course, catalytic states of consciousness prolonged by means other than drugs may also similarly affect such brain chemistry, and thus genetic evolution. In other words, an extended, purposed practice of meditation, contemplation, or prayer can cause a human to genetically evolve.

In fact, a mother's love can manipulate genes. It is commonly known that sensual maternal care in the animal world produces young ones that grow up less fearful and more courageous. It has more recently been shown that motherly care alters the expression of a gene that governs a mammalian brain's response to stress, leading to a greater number of stress receptors in the hippocampus, which act together to ameliorate the body's reaction to stressful situations. These genetic changes are then passed down to future generations. This is one way a body tunes itself rapidly and purposefully to its environment, bringing evolution into conscious daily life.

In the limited worldview of molecular materialism, evolution is believed to be a result of random mutation expressed through birth and the survival of whichever mutations are most fit for continued reproduction. This principle has been extended deeper: the survival principle of "selfish genes," "DNA programs," and ultimately atomic "bits of information" is determined solely through molecular and atomic identities being purposed toward self-survival. As much as scientific empiricists find the concept of *purpose* repugnant, this remarkably limited view of materialists still remains reliant on a purposeful principle: *Survival* or what may be called *Inertial Identity*. Atoms, molecules, and genes are thus presumed to maintain a type of instinct toward future self-preservation. Things "keep on going" "as long as they can" or until their energies are "impinged upon or usurped" by other things.

The study of evolution's *punctuated equilibrium* has made it clear that species evolution comes via sudden transitions, and cannot be reduced to the causal mechanisms of random mutation. Furthermore, we now know that altruism is hard-wired into the human system and that *giving freely* – as in *authentic love* – is an inherent act of higher evolutionary life. "Survival of the fittest" as a theory of selfish competition and random mutation is obsolete in terms of understanding how sustained, global evolution occurs. As long as its reductionistic concepts are championed by scientific authorities, who claim to see no alternative other than superstitious belief in "creationism," dissociated, "independent" *local* survival of the most brutish human societies and dispensers of violent power will be promoted. This will come at the expense of *all* evolved life on the planet, most certainly including the brutes – who are always in actuality inter-dependent with the very life they subjugate. This unfortunately cannot be overstated.

It is supposed by mechanistic reductionists opposed to principles of emergence, holism, and unity that from a survival principle merging *separative* identity and *competitive* polarity all levels of the cosmos and consciousness have formed. Individuated "things" in the universe are presumed to be intrinsically purposed solely to survive as separative things, and thus continue with some sort of natural duration (even while the concept of *duration* as being *inherent* to an entity is also found repugnant, with hard physicists attempting to reduce the principle of time to mathematical transforms of "grainy" matter). The essential duration of any entity in a natural context of ongoing transformations occurs via morphogenetic laws that remain deeply obscure to scientific materialists.

Earlier, we observed that the second law of thermodynamics posits entropy to be a fundamental principle of our cosmos. It is usually supposed that this leads to ever greater randomness and disorder throughout spacetime. Yet the universe has undeniably continued to grow in organization and order over time; that is, it keeps concentrating in deeper forms of order such as in planetary, biological, and conscious systems. Here we find a classic example of universal polar symmetry and complementarity: a principle of ever greater *local contingency* is paradoxically balanced with a principle of ever greater *global unity*. Before the principles of chaos and emergence were brought into accepted scientific thought via theories regarding complexity and *autopoiesis* (meaning *self-organization*), scientific philosophers scarcely utilized laws of nonlinear causality that could be applied to organic and dynamic systems of life and transformation in the universe. Interdisciplinary acknowledgment of the new sciences suggests that it is time for orthodox scientific authorities to recognize and affirm the truth of essential, universal principles found in the perennial wisdom tradition. As this chapter may serve to indicate, these principles are well along the path of scientific verification and integration.

Advancements in the field of molecular biology and recombinant DNA engineering are technically enabling specific operations upon DNA strands that produce astounding results, such as cloning life forms and creating novel inter-species creatures. Nonetheless, this is being done with remarkably limited knowledge of how exactly DNA and growth processes actually unfold in natural contexts. Indeed, chemical "cut-and-paste" operations upon DNA snippets can be so simple that do-it-yourself kits are available for teenage experimenters. It is not unusual for complex cloning techniques, once they are successfully implemented through a great degree of trial-and-error guesswork, to be reproduced with relative ease simply by following technical procedures. Manipulating DNA and causing entities to mutate or grow with specific attributes is, however, a far cry from understanding the whole natural process of biological generation, holistic integration, and environmental interaction. Thus, biologists do not have a godlike ability to create life forms from scratch out of a soup of molecular components comprising the chemicals that make up DNA and its protein partners in the composition of life. Nor are they near to understanding or responsibly directing the resonant environmental contexts, both exterior and interior, that every organism interrelates through and as.

For DNA to carry both the mechanism of organic growth and the "program" directing that mechanism, a direct, one-to-one correlation must be able to be made between the sequences of chemical bases in DNA and the complex, three-dimensional structures of proteins. Although such a causal chain can be found between the chemical sequences in a DNA molecule and the amino acid sequences of peptides, those peptides then *fold up* in such complex, variant ways that it appears impossible for a DNA molecule to hold enough information to programmatically instruct them how to do so.

What is more, it is known that the nervous system cannot possibly be *pre-specified* by genetic instructions. Such complex systems arise through stochastic, probabilistic processes that *emerge* as systems containing *greater order* than the linear sum of system parts would causally allow or explain. Mathematical studies in the fields of networks, synchrony, and complexity are greatly assisting to create conceivable models regarding how nature actually works.

A philosophy of *organism* has developed in the wake of obsolete mechanistic philosophies. This involves systemic principles of organization, broadly modeled in terms of field resonance, hierarchical emergence, synchronistic contingency, and holistic causality. The reader is referred to the works of Alfred North Whitehead, L. L. Whyte, and Arthur Koestler (father of *holon and holarchy theory*) for an introduction to this branch of philosophical thought. Laws governing *organized systems* – be they of herds, cells, crystals, etc. – are innate to our evolving universe. Viewed within a lawful context of autopoiesis, it is clear that *unitive* survival is not reducible to *separative* survival.

From the viewpoint of scientific materialism, imitative reduction of a complex, organismic, human life form to a simulacrum resemblance comprising computational machinations of an artificially intelligent (AI) android would practically represent the epitome of engineered knowledge. Is this not obviously mad? Ironically unable to perceive the metaphysical dualism embodied by their materialistic tenets, AI mavens of the twenty-first century such as Marvin Minsky unhelpfully popularized dualistic romanticization of "machine intelligence." That said, an interactive augmented intelligence engine such as a *divination oracle* may well prove to be beautiful, good, and true, but only to the degree that it integrates perennial wisdom and serves as a tool extending human users' mindful awareness.

How do biological entities incorporate changing components, fluid dynamics, bifurcating structures, and self-organizing patterns to proceed upon a course of developmental growth? It has come to be widely recognized that the unfolding of life occurs through three primary processes of evolution:

1. Least important, but most widely known, is the process of random genetic mutation. This is caused by chance errors in the self-replication of gene structure DNA. DNA forms a helix structure of two molecular strands that can separate and form templates for the replication of new chains. During that process, chance errors of chemistry can produce chains that are slightly different than the originals. These mutations are generally harmful or not of beneficial use to the organismic development that they affect. The number of useful variations that happen in this process of genetic mutation is far too small to account for the evolution of planet earth's enormous diversity of life forms.

2. Far more prevalent and effective in the process of biological evolution is the *global trading* of genes. *DNA recombination* occurs through the passing of hereditary traits between organisms connected in a network of organized, ongoing exchange. For instance, many bacteria change up to 15 percent of their genetic material daily. Sharing hereditary traits in such a manner is an inherent ability of all bacteria. The process occurs as bacteria transfer their DNA into their environment, which are then picked up or transferred back into other bacteria. This can be a hugely rapid and broad process of *inter-subjective communication;* so much so that bacterial communities can spread quickly around the world, forming a living, microscopic, organismic cultural network blanketing the earth in an unseen continuity of biological flow.

   Gaia is a holistic organism comprising myriad emergent sublevels of living field-systems. Gaia's global feedback loops are based upon over two billion years of evolution during which bacteria and other microorganisms were the only form of life. This biological reality remains prominent even within the human realm. Though of much smaller size, there are ten times more bacteria cells than human cells in the human body.
3. The role that *symbiosis* plays in organic evolution evidently surpasses the previous processes of genetic mutation and recombination. Lynn Margulis brought to the scientific world's attention the vastness in nature of permanent symbiotic arrangements between life forms. She insightfully pointed to how *new* life forms were thus created in a process called *symbiogenesis.* In great measure, hierarchical levels of life merge through organisms living in close association with and often inside of one another, with bacteria in animals' systems serving as a prime example. *Asymmetries* of symbiotic interdependency can be striking. For instance, a species of bacteria that lives symbiotically in humans' large intestine manufactures vitamin K, which is

> essential for blood clotting. Symbiosis is now known to be the primary process of evolution for all higher organisms.

While symbiosis is an obvious aspect of biological life, its enormous import is given appropriate respect only when living beings and environments are viewed as *whole systems*. Appropriateness of the term *new* science is affirmed by the fact that biologists have just begun associating bacterial functions with critical aspects of animal health. Lack of knowledge in this regard has allowed and even promoted a seriously dangerous worldwide overuse of antibiotics.

Until recently, modern definitions of "healthy" had been reduced to referential contexts involving abundance of energy, food, and clothing supplying homes, cars, and malls. Health was identified with access to medicine and environments separated from nature. An obese person would be deemed healthy "in a normal modern context," for example, even if he or she was unable to walk or otherwise move for hours at a time. An ability to scavenge and survive in the wild was certainly not viewed as indicative of "a healthy lifestyle." Holistic health practices and studies are thankfully renewing appreciation for both finer and earthier aspects of biological balance, complex organic interdependency, and robust ability to actualize human potential.

In terms of human consciousness, evolution proceeds largely through symbiotic relationship with greater *social, cultural, environmental,* and *spiritual* levels of holistically generated realization. All four of those contexts must be appreciated and understood for the principles of wisdom and immortality to be realized.

Margulis assisted James Lovelock in his developmental modeling of Earth as a holistic system. Lovelock is credited with bringing to the fore of biological theory Earth's self-regulating nature, popularizing the ancient reference to Earth as Gaia. While not holding to a belief that Gaia is a "living conscious being" as the ancients might have viewed her, Lovelock nonetheless created a radically new conceptualization of the *whole planet* as a living system in which symbiosis reigns supreme. The Unitive Principle so apparent in life on earth is sacred in its own inherent right, quite apart from any vision of supernatural purpose.

Understanding the world about us in terms of holistic systems sheds much-needed light on how our biological bodies and environments work. Just as importantly, we can come to know so much more about how our *cultures* and *societies* work. On an immanently practical level, *game system theory* enables implementation of principles integrating holons, evolution, change, transformation, and regeneration. Axioms of modern game theory are best developed so as to involve the "vertical axis" of immortal principles primarily addressed in the present treatise in conjunction with "horizontal planes" of four-quadrant holonic manifestation. In general, the latter realms have been referred to in this book as *environmental, social, cultural,* and *psychological.*

Integral Theory, advanced largely by Ken Wilber, refers more broadly to the universal quadrants as: *exterior individual* (body, objective, third-person individual perspective); *exterior collective* (society, objective, third-person collective perspective); *interior collective* (culture, inter-subjective, second-person perspective); *interior individual* (mind, intra-subjective, first-person perspective). These quadrants form the ontological reality of every holon. Together, as an integral and whole identity, they undergo a process whereby their symmetry is interrupted or broken, allowing for reconnection with other holonic spheres and processes, and then reintegrated and reunited.

Most importantly for game theory that models a *world-space* in such a way as to be universally applicable, the vertical axis of cosmic evolution or growth-process is *always recursive.* The magically physical stage of human development, for instance, contains its own processional realization of universal principles, as does the mythically emotional, rationally mental, psychologically intuitive, subtly virtuous, and causally heartful stages. Universal principles are recursively unpacked or unfolded within their own levels or spheres of development. In many ways that this chapter does not have space to explore, we live in a "fractalized," *holographic* space-time continuum proceeding through recursively encapsulated depths of complexity embodying the deep simplicity of ten immortal principles. Readers wishing to explore more regarding how they may truly *know and understand* this are referred both to the study of tantric alchemical yoga and to companion projects of this book that may be found within both physical and digital game spaces.

Unification of natural Law regarding astronomic, planetary, human, organic, molecular, atomic, and quantum spheres can only be established through common principles, not *objectively identical models*, mathematical or otherwise. Those principles must be applicable to all aspects of the world as humans are able to essentially view it, including psycho-spiritual, socio-cultural, and environmental-physical. As scientific thought evolves into fourth-stage intuitively integral understanding, universal principles of hierarchical emergence, synchronistic contingency, holistic causality, and transformative chaos are coming to the fore. These are unifying not only the laws of physics, but also those of the natural world within all levels and complexities of manifestation.

What would a set of universal, scientific principles optimally include? As will by now be familiar to readers, the Great Tradition's ten-stage ascending/descending developmental philosophy converts into a nested set of Ten Unitive and Immortal Principles of the Kosmos:

10. Unitive Law
9. Radiant Time
8. Dimensional Space
7. Transformative Chaos

6. Holistic Causality
5. Synchronistic Contingency
4. Hierarchical Emergence
3. Field Resonance
2. Polar Symmetry
1. Inertial Identity

Translating perennial wisdom cosmology into a modern view of cosmic origins and present ontological procession forms:

An Immortal Story of Cosmic Creation and Evolution

At the beginning and remaining in every moment – implicate in time itself – there is Law. That Law is indefinable except to say that it is Unitive.

The first realization of its Unity is time. Time radiates. Time *is* all radiance. Its radiation is perpetual, absolute, constant, and infinite. While there cannot *be* "no time," there can *be eternity* as "only time."

Within time's radiance, dimensionality comprising infinite potential vibrational identities of time emanates as space. Through emptiness, infinity is realized. This is the first and most universal polarity of cosmic symmetry.

Realization of an infinite myriad in Unity occurs through creatively transforming chaos. All forms possible are potentiated and transformed from and as this most universal and all-pervading resonant flux of innately indefinably complex chaos. Although mysterious as an underlying field of unfathomable depth and complexity, chaos remains Unitive.

Primordial chaos emanates as a *whole* causing simultaneous, interdependent arising of a cosmic *myriad* of spacetime vibratory-particle event-frequencies. The unitive field-flux of chaos is dimensionally transformed into a *coherence* of infinite *durations* that emerge as a spacetime cosmos with a universal hierarchy of discreet quantum states. Holistic causation is realized through *stochastic* (literally "divining the goal") and *holonic* (always *both whole and part*) *materialization* of time and space, creating a finite cosmos of *relative* and *contingent* motions, positions, and densities of event-mass. The hierarchically fluctuating cosmos holistically self-organizes on quantum levels of nonlocal causation.

Entities manifesting with a similar level of vibrational duration and holonic manifestation revert to a common source-space through the gravitational inertia of their mass identities, slowing coherently and in totality toward entropic contingency even while simultaneously, through the energetic radiance of time, resonantly accelerating toward ordered synchronization. That is, in every *whole* the *parts* co-dependently arise synchronistically contingent upon the same cause. Every holonic level of interdependent arising coheres through duration of that which is *similar.*

Spacetime *randomness* dissipating holonic coherence varies discontinuously, creating emergent levels of depth and complexity. These levels form distinct magnitudes of organization that are defined by field geometries with four aspects: *interior* and *exterior* of both *individual* and *collective*. The more a holon identifies with a *greater, deeper,* and *more complex* holistic level of hierarchy, the less it is truly defined by randomness. Emergence is the process of *time* hierarchically realizing a *four-dimensional* world.

Fields resonantly inform patterns *representing* chaos as self-organizing, geometrically recursive processes that realize three-dimensional space through dynamically networked radiant *spheres.*

Spatial discontinuity as objective separation becomes subjective novelty defined by the *duration* of an identity's *polar separation.* Polar symmetry determines how an identity maintains structure while reacting to forces operating on its level of similarity. All polar separation strives to express its inherent unity either by reducing into inert stasis or growing into dynamic relationship.

> The inertial *stand* and *presence* of every identity within its own frame of relative stasis combines with all others to form a myriad of *qualitative existences* and *autonomous ways* in accordance to the always true Laws of Unity.

As introduced in chapter 1, the holistic causation and processional identification of the cosmos can be explicitly summarized:

1. Inertial identity, being both whole and part, and potentially vibratory
2. Separates as a polarity in symmetrical extension
3. Organizes as a field-system cycling through and as these poles, resonating with other fields
4. Transcends limited polar definition via hierarchical relationship, emerging both within and without
5. Synchronistically aligns contingent relationships interdependently arising through the universal field-polarity of emptiness and infinity (space and time)
6. Transforms via holistic catastrophe (chaos) the whole causal process

Such transformation:

1. Vibrates the original identity.
2. Extends its polar symmetry.
3. Nonlinearly resonates within a group of interdependent fields.
4. Reinforces traces of an emerging hierarchical pattern.
5. Breaks symmetrical formation and then vanishes through nonlocal but synchronistic contingencies.
6. Holistically regenerates through transformative chaos a similar but uniquely changed, causally self-organizing duration of coherent identity.

Every identity, *cognizing its lifespan* within the context of its polar vibration, subjects itself to the whole causal process of material coherence through an inherent *impulse to endure.* The inertia of an identity is time-created duration of material coherence accelerating *even "at rest"* toward the speed of light. An inertial identity's impulse to survive in order to realize the speed of light and eternal time is ultimately the singular Unitive Principle recreating an always-greater cosmos of Being, Consciousness, and Bliss.

Magnifying . . . Right Concentration

We finish our chapter and the narrative of this book's reckoning with a summary overview of the immortal principles of cosmic evolution and perennial wisdom.

Inertia as it defines every physical thing correlates with *relationally unique identity.* The objective law of inertia is simple: if something is moving, it will keep moving until something stops it; if something is not moving, it will remain unmoving until something else moves it. Though simple enough for anyone to observe and experience, physics theories are able to mathematically model neither how a thing moves from one location and time to another nor how it is that an object keeps moving forever unless something else stops it.

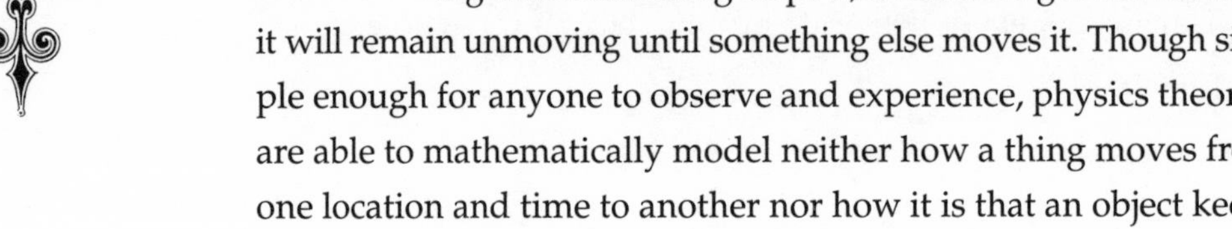

Inertial force is involved with the phenomenon of *acceleration.* Not only are GRT and QFT unable to explain how the force accelerating the whole universe's expansion is generated, they also cannot answer how acceleration of *anything* essentially comes about. Like car passengers, astronauts in a space shuttle feel the centrifugal force of acceleration when making a turn. Yet according to GRT, acceleration can only be felt by an object *relative* to another object, not mere space. That is built into the very foundation of relativity theory. A space shuttle is far from earth, so in respect to what object does it accelerate, the whole of the universe? Einstein had intended to show how the distribution of matter in the cosmos caused inertial force. However, GRT allows for the construction of a cosmic model empty of matter, yet still giving rise to inertia.

Inertial identity is a fundamental principle, which along with the *origin* of any *thing* remains a mystery, for we do not know what a single thing *is.* One can progressively break up a holon into its parts, but that leads only to the absurdity of "preons" – of non-particle particles constituting all other mathematically suggestible particles. What is the *ur*-stuff from which one-dimensional zero-vibrating vibratory superstrings are made? Is it Time itself? What does it mean to *know* what Time or the *very essence* of Space *is?*

Was Plato right that in truth *idea* as essential reality – whether in the form of *transcendent* law or *incorporeal* form – exists *prior* to spacetime and cosmic manifestation? Is the cosmos based upon the math and logic of materially separate thing-events or do we need to imagine essential, universal *principles* that ontologically define the primary *processes* of cosmic development, which may then be symbolically idealized through mathematical representation? Everyone can agree that reality can be modeled by mathematical logic. Few, however, agree that such models are *equal to,* let alone *greater than,* reality.

Neoplatonic philosophy in modern terms suggests that Law, Time, Space, and Chaos are all *transcendentally absolute* principles of reality. Furthermore, since Causality and all other spacetime principles are but emanations of Transcendental Reality, so too is the Cosmos right down to the inertial identities of every material thing. We are able to conceive and truly understand such grand principles only through our *whole-body* realized consciousness.

Identity is the enduring outcome of reiterated, recursive cycles of death, temporarily *renewing* an event-object in space over time. Identity appears to arise from the *breaking* of symmetry even while embodying such. For instance, to physically identify a particle, one must measure either its movement or position. However, only one of these can be identified *for certain* at a time – with that "certainty" being observer-specific – thus breaking a symmetrical aspect of the particle. The origins of spacetime symmetry-breaking may be found in the universality of transformational Chaos and the Higgs force-principle. In an opposite and complementary way, when inertia reigns, transformation looms. The universe consistently realizes such paradoxical complementarity.

Polarity conjoins with inertia in defining every physical identity, be that through attributes of *interior and exterior, positive and negative, female and male, movement and rest, electric and magnetic*, etc. *Measured identification* itself – both subjective and objective – implies an *asymmetrical discontinuity* of an otherwise inherently unified polar symmetry. When consciousness identifies with the beauty of symmetry it may do so through discovering the wondrous and enduring uniqueness as which symmetry temporarily materializes. Or it may transcend the limitations and powerful seduction of inertial identity, culturally extending its dimensions of awareness into a resonant field of polar relatedness.

In modern science, the principle of beauty is intimately tied to the concept of symmetry. Classically, symmetry and beauty were equated with *proportionate harmony*. As presented earlier, a more current definition of symmetry speaks of invariance under certain transformations such as rotation or scaling of size or change of velocity. It was Einstein's genius to discover a set of symmetries in Maxwell's equations governing behavior of electromagnetic fields. Thus, just as Newton's laws were mathematically shown to be unchanging under varying frames of inertia, by positing that the speed of light was constant and space and time were always unified, Einstein showed how Maxwell's laws were also invariant.

Symmetry has practically become the reflection of *goodness* in modern physics, as it is equated with essential beauty and truth. In this way, the Platonic Triad of transcendent principles has been reduced to concepts of mathematical and geometrical symmetry. Ideal measurements must de facto break such symmetry even while mathematically presuming a reality based on unitive wholeness. For instance, quark theory has been progressively deemed good, beautiful, and ultimately true largely because it embodies numerous aspects of polar symmetry (matter and force particles, left and right spin, balanced charms, etc.). Modern science not only understands spacetime itself to be symmetrical, but views the laws of nature themselves as exhibiting symmetry. That is, the laws of physics are deemed to *invariantly* operate throughout the cosmos regardless of cosmic transformations. At its deepest level, universal symmetry is an *essential principle,* not a merely mathematical law.

Conceptual glorification of symmetry has perhaps stunted scientific understanding of higher principles such as nonlinear field resonance, interdependent hierarchical emergence, and nonlocal synchronistic contingency. This chapter has pointed out that scientific materialists recognize an overly limited hierarchy of principles operative in the universe. A dogmatic tendency holds sway that refuses to acknowledge hierarchy except in terms of *scale* and *power.* This plays most unfortunately into the hands of unwise politicians. As this book has shown, the concept of a universal hierarchy of principles is age-old, but for some reason anathema to many modern materialists and logicians. Distinct laws arise in association with every fundamental principle-sphere of the world. Those principles exist in a nested, *holistically hierarchical* (or *holarchical*) relationship; that is, some principles are more encompassing, encapsulating, or essentially greater in their unitive reality than others.

We have argued in this chapter that the fundamental principles of the universe cannot be reduced to symmetrical mechanisms and logistics of causation. For instance, although a hydrogen atom exhibits various symmetries, upon adding a third-body electron to the hydrogen's neutron-proton pair, producing a hydrogen ion, the atom becomes chaotic. At that point its resonant field can no longer be reduced to its previous symmetries. Its symmetries are re-integrated via processes defined by higher-level laws, developing into a process of symmetry breaking beyond inertial identity that *evolves* and *grows* or otherwise transforms into a uniquely *new* – even if indistinguishably *similar* – holistic identity. Similarly, original and underlying chaos cannot be reduced to or simply equated with causally synchronized emergent field-systems of identified symmetries.

Fields are always associated with symmetrical particles in relativistic physics. For instance, *photons* are the particles of *electromagnetic* fields. For a hundred years it has been thought that all forces of spacetime operate through fields, which were first postulated by Michael Faraday in the nineteenth century. Following him, James Maxwell's equations showed that electromagnetic radiation traveled at a limited velocity; i.e., energy does not travel instantaneously. Maxwell's equations allow freely radiating fields to exist *independent* of masses or charges. Interaction or *resonance* of these fields results in an inherent *irreversibility* or *time-symmetry-breaking* primed through the emergence of networks that then initiate new identity-domains via synchronization in the context of a common and wholly integral source.

Modern physics posits the existence of many fundamental fields, as every primary subatomic particle embodies a distinct field-type. There exists in the cosmos a hierarchy of fundamentally different field-domains. Even within theoretical conceptualization of ten-dimensional supersymmetry, mathematical unification of the primary force fields known by physicists – gravitational, electromagnetic, strong (nuclear), weak (atomic decay), Higgs, and cosmos-accelerating "dark energy" – through reductionistic procedures are nowhere near to being figured out. Inevitably, it will become evident to physicists that hierarchical emergence is a fundamental, universal principle beyond the biological world; encompassing all particle types of the cosmos and levels of field resonance, complex order, and material coherence.

In Newton's theory of gravity and Einstein's theories of relativity, material objects are related to each other through *force fields.* In fact, matter is identified *as* properties of fields. In GRT, the field properties are described through mathematical *tensors.* These can also be viewed as describing the *curvature of spacetime.* General relativity was viewed by Einstein and his successors as a *geometric* theory. All space, matter, movement, and transformations of matter are defined by the fields surrounding, permeating, and indeed manifesting cosmic matter.

While a human being, as with any holon, may be characterized by both structural organization and functional fields, the *order* human life represents can be properly measured and thereby valued only if it is viewed as a *holistic organism.* The vital life and essential nature of human existence cannot be known in truth through a modeled analysis of the mechanical parts and operations of the human body. The human system is a self-organizing, complex organism. It has a unique *interior* realm sensed, felt, and cognized in such a way as to be irreducible to computations. The identity of any holon must include the *resonant effects* of both its internal and external interacting vibratory structures of polar symmetry and relationships of hierarchical interdependency. Every being is constantly becoming; holistically determined within any given duration through characteristically resonating fields, which proceed to form its inertial identity. Resonance between similar organisms is a critical aspect of evolution at every level of cosmic growth. Neoplatonic understandings of "likeness" are based upon this anciently observed fact.

Organisms are always vibratory, rhythmic, and cyclic. Resonance of molecular, cellular, and organic vibration is primary to instilling order and subtle organization in integrated systems, including collective systems such as human society. (While superstitious notions of "harmonic convergence" have permeated new religions, that is no reason for the science community to devalue the potency of this universally true principle.) Contemporary theories of chaos, complexity, and emergence address this. A major advancement in those fields was the realization that in the natural world most highly organized and evolved systems are unstable and intensely entropic. They develop through symmetries of oscillation resonating in field patterns; this then gives rise to hierarchies of organization. Within every hierarchically emergent domain, a myriad of contingencies interconnect in a simultaneous moment-to-moment continuity of the present universe. Here we define a *moment* as a *vibratory duration* interiorly extending as and exteriorly limited by an essential symmetry. The *causes* of this whole process are Transformative Chaos, Dimensional Space, Radiant Time, and Unitive Law, with the latter two being what has traditionally been termed the First Cause. The Tarot's Neoplatonic wisdom presents a cosmological understanding of emanated principles that is now being confirmed by scientific knowledge.

Resonance is a true and universal principle, whether operating on atomic, biotic, solar, or galactic field domains. While various types of physically detectable *waves* radiate from a human body, the concept of an underlying morphogenetic organization guiding both the parts and whole of a human system toward patterns of *integral duration* is provocative to scientific materialists. René Thom's elegant modeling of *singularities* addresses the genesis and change of biological forms, wherein creation, coherence, and destruction are represented by *dynamic* geometric structures evincing *attraction.* Rupert Sheldrake's theory of formative causation, though much derided by mechanical reductionists, brilliantly suggests the use of morphogenetic "fields" to describe how holistically caused, underlying synchronistic contingency arises. David Bohm's theory of an implicate order is another example of a well-thought-out attempt to explain the principle of holistic causality in terms that embrace the deeply chaotic and synchronistic flux of the cosmos.

At a time when prominent scientific authorities deem 96 percent of the universe to be of totally unknown *types* of "mass," "field," or "energy" – or something different altogether – it is no longer reasonable to limit one's considerations of life, relationships, and the world to beliefs in remarkably limited, linearly and locally causal, mechanical laws of physics.

Systems become nonlinear and complex through interaction between events that resonate in a manner that is *interdependently* causal. Spacetime trajectories of such events cannot be traced because nonlinear resonance produces non-computable effects in terms of measurable projection. Interacting fields, light emission, and the movement of interacting particles toward equilibrium all involve resonance; as does the human neuro system, about which yogis can expound even while materialistically objective medical scientists remain largely in the dark. Resonant fields involve nonlocal and diffusive operations. While these may be approximated by probabilistic contingencies, they cannot be measured as determined trajectories. For transient, immediately local interactions of objects and their fields, diffusion into contingency may appear to be minimal. Thus, for simplistic physics experiments, the parts of a system can be tracked and predicted with seeming certitude. However, for *persistent* interactions (i.e., the organic world beyond sticks and stones, machines and bullets) the subtle effects of resonance rule.

Hierarchical levels of cosmic complexity systematically organize as global and holistic world-domains, stages, or phases that are not reducible to a summation of projected mechanical actions of systems' parts – most certainly including social and cultural systems. Even a Newtonian system of only three gravitational bodies exhibits such complexity in its resonating interaction as to become truly unpredictable. Unstable systems often demonstrate a breaking of symmetry, either systemically de-structuring or trans-forming, and thus causing both death and rebirth. Phase transitions such as vapor to water and water to ice arise from such symmetry-breaking.

Persistently interactive systems require holistic, synchronistic, and hierarchical description. These primary principles – hierarchical emergence, synchronistic contingency, and holistic causality – gained little attention from twenty-first-century scientists. Arthur Koestler notably stated that hierarchy had been such an important principle for so long that modern scientists decided to effectively relegate it to the dustbins of tradition.

Emergence is a concept now common in evolutionary theory, even though it is viewed as antithetical to mechanical materialism. As reviewed earlier, Darwin and his followers postulated that all evolution must be based upon *gradual* processes of random *generational* genetic mutation. Problematically to Darwinians, evolutionary, creative *jumps* of natural development cannot be solely explained by a series of causal mechanisms founded upon random occurrence. To those raised amongst or otherwise indoctrinated with Christian dogmas – whether rationally believed in or not – concepts of inherent cosmic and organic *creativity* seem to imply a need for an *interjecting God.* However, that dualistic conceptual need arises only because cultural mythic programming habituates communal mindsets to it. From within both rational and transcendental frames of mind, *unity* of poles becomes obvious, progressively viewed and realized as being primary. Darwin and his followers were ardent in their scientific conviction that a cosmic need for a supernatural deity did not exist, yet they replaced theology with the equally *dualistic metaphysics* of mathematical materialism, and universal unity with fundamentally disordered randomness.

Unlike the physics concepts of Neil Bohr's *quantum chance* and Wolfgang Pauli's *irrational matter,* wherein principles of emergence and nonlocal synchronicity are complementarily acknowledged, Darwin's biological theory allows no resonantly self-organizing synchronicity, no emergent order, no hierarchical patterning of *universally actualized evolution;* no resonance of essential natures, no fields of vital life. The *cosmos,* during Darwin's lifetime, was not viewed as *evolving;* Darwin's worldview was not of an infinitely vibrating, field-resonating, entangled flux evolving order out of a singular pre-space time of absolute unity. He and many peers supposed the universe to operate in a random, mechanical fashion without unitive and *self-organizing* laws.

Cosmically *innate* evolutionary design does not require a *supernatural* creator or unnatural "divine power." The essential nature of the cosmos is plenty *super* as it already, inherently is. It is simply inappropriate that beautiful, good, and true scientific and perennial wisdom principles keep being placed in opposition to *dualistic* "meta"-physical beliefs in which "beyond" and "transcendent" imply unnatural "separation" from the cosmos. Tomes of scholastic argumentation are not required to discern the nondual gist of cosmic evolution, emanation, or developmental transformation by any other name, conveyed by great tradition sages.

Modern examination of organic life on earth along with the fossil records of that life has conclusively led to a worldview of cyclically sustained development punctuated by periodic rapid emergence of new species. Mammalian life forms arose on earth within a short span of time during the dinosaur age. Not many changes occurred until after that age, when a great amount of adaptation took place within another relatively small timeframe. (Of course, such accepted facts may well be revised as new information is accumulated or theoretical frameworks are rebuilt.) Since then, very few new mammalian species have emerged, even while the existent species have gradually mutated and adapted to changing environments. Similarly, the *extinction* of dinosaurs happened within a short span of time.

Within our own grandchildren's' lifetimes, it is likely that over half of all species on earth will become extinct – the largest mass-extinction since the age of dinosaurs. The study of evolution's *punctuated equilibrium* has made it clear that species evolution comes via *sudden transitions,* and cannot be reduced to the causal mechanisms of random mutation. By all appearances, our current era is a naturally catastrophic age (influenced by the nature of human developmental processes) that has set the stage for a regenerative explosion of *conscious human evolution.* Holistically causal factors such as massive societal and technological growth enabled by the extraction and burning of earth's fossil fuels in a remarkably short span of time are determining future human species' self-selected courses of development. These will necessarily include altruistic, cooperative, and *intelligently holistic* design; *sustainable* technology; and *intercultural* ritual and art.

A relatively recent field of evolutionary biology includes in-depth study of developmental processes occurring within the lifetimes of individual and collective life forms. Termed *evo-devo,* it has led to discovery that the genesis and evolution of complex forms is ofttimes accomplished through *small* and *rapid* changes of genes and developmental plans. A process of many genetic mutations over generations is not necessary for substantial evolution to occur. Furthermore, within any level of organismic formation, the number of genes that *can* be reorganized so as to catalyze (however that may happen on deep and implicate levels of biological formation and order) the creation of new forms and body parts is remarkably few. The same set of DNA sequences appears to be involved with a great many radically evolutionary developments. Natural hierarchy, including that of genes, actualizes the evolution of certain forms while *simultaneously disallowing* the growth of others. *Random* contingency does not rule, but rather *synchronistic* contingency limits and promotes every organism into a developmental and evolutionary course of life that is *holistically determined.*

"Control" genes are proving to be involved with the core processes of "directing" development of life forms. Because so few such genes exist, there is no need for a constant production of new genes via mutation in order for morphogenesis to occur. Instead, *modification* of a relatively simple set of existing genes and processes is evidently primary to the processional production of our planet's cornucopia of biological formation. This explains how chimps and humans can share 99 percent of their genes, yet be so obviously different. This has also brought to light amazing discoveries, such as the fact that the potential development of animal appendages was *already existent* in fish before any earth-life crawled out of the sea; those developments were simply awaiting the right environment before proceeding to activate a process of tetrapod formation. Major evolutionary phase-transitions like that of water-life to land-life were not "caused" by genetic mutation, but rather, new *environmental feedback* to organisms promoted the emergence of *already nascent*, relatively rapid genetic reorganization and continuous morphogenetic development marked by *creative discontinuity*.

Evolution is an *unfolding of possibilities* already in part *destined to manifest* in ways that will converge amongst different life forms. When evolutionary convergences are considered from a holistically coherent viewpoint, it becomes apparent that trajectories of evolution are indeed highly constrained. Given the enormous degree of biological *plentitude* found on earth, it is truly remarkable that life is marked by such a great degree of *limitation*.

Regardless of how many discreet stages it may take for complex structures such as eyes and wings to evolve, there exists much evidence for the emergence of functionally whole biological structures. On the macro level, life forms in general fall into distinct *types*, as the study of plant and animal *species* makes quite evident. Universally, cosmic existence is marked by hierarchy comprising discontinuous levels of ordered coherence and discreet forms of self-organizing complexity, which emerge first and adapt later. Or, as evo-devo suggests, they emerge *already enabled* to express an *implicated* developmental path of adaptation. Once again, this "intelligent design" is simply how whole systems in our cosmos work. It is based upon the truly great Unitive Principle proceeding at all times. This chapter's worldview and understanding of immortal, universal principles is not comparable to dualistic monism, gnostic dualism, or other popular forms of theology.

Properly understood, the cosmic plethora once symbolized by medieval philosophy's Great Chain of Being is a holarchical plenitude of nested reality spheres or *emergent domains* of both spacetime and lawful principle. Hierarchy interiorly emerges psycho-spiritually through cognition and consciousness just as it does externally in environmental and social worlds through species and castes, etc. As this book has argued, the world is marked by the principle of hierarchy in both interior and exterior realms, for both individuals and collectives of entities.

Distinct laws of nature emerge with every complex and unstable *level* of cosmic organization. Laws applicable to macro domains of thermodynamics, for instance, are not reducible to laws specifically describing quantum particle flux. This is how the Great Holarchical Chain of Interdependent Causation works. Thus, while laws of physics and organic chemistry and molecular biology all apply to the human system, other unique laws emerge in the human domain that are not reducible to the laws of those *lower* or *less complex* levels. It is obvious that laws of culture and consciousness must be developed for anything to be actually known and intelligently discussed about human behavior. Defining happiness or anger in terms of chemical reactions does not *inform* the human mind whatsoever about the actual experiences and relationships involving feelings and cultural patterns of happiness and anger. Knowing how to make a pill that makes one feel a particular way and understanding how one's feelings develop in natural contexts are utterly different types of knowledge regarding oneself.

A simple, not-so-futuristic scenario suffices to clarify the importance of distinguishing between what we may here refer to as *interior-subjective* and *exterior-objective* knowledge. It is reasonable to extrapolate current brain-wave and psychochemical studies of advanced meditators and spiritual practitioners into the next decades. Likewise with the development of "lifestyle drugs," including psychoactive drugs that create euphoric or ecstatic states of mind-body sensation. Imagine a daily dose of an ecstasy-producing drug we will call *neo-ambrosia.* If neo-ambrosia was to prove non-debilitating in terms of general life activities, standards of health, and operative modes of relating; produced states of happiness comparable with brain-scan measurements of life-long meditators; cost minimal money to produce; and was not outlawed, it is easy to imagine the drug replacing many of the drugs currently consumed by the masses (e.g., alcohol, barbiturates, antidepressants, caffeine, amphetamines, chocolate, and even sugar). Let us imagine what would happen if in order to solve a great many psychosocial difficulties, political leaders around the world successfully promoted introduction of neo-ambrosia into their cities' water supplies. Would the measurable knowledge held by pharmaceutical and CAT scanning scientists *wisely* and *successfully* replace the need for people to learn about how the human world best operates *naturally* in terms of developmental stages of consciousness, feelings, relationships, sociocultural rituals, and degrees of intimate engagement – including love?

Synchronistically and nonlocally, hierarchical levels or realms of the natural world quite evidently evolve through time via processes which involve interdependent, identifiable polar holons exhibiting symmetry, field resonance, and emergent organization within contingent communities defined by similar elements. The remembrance and inheritance implicit in the synchronous continuity of the universe is holistically caused through a process of morphogenetic realization implicit to an underlying universally creative, chaotic flux.

Morphogenesis means "the coming into being of form." In our age of uncertainty, philosophers, scientists, artists, and contemplatives agree that very little is truly understood about the moment-to-moment continuously and coherently sustained creativity of reality. The world is no longer conceived in terms of simply identified cycles of polar recurrence. Not only are there lifecycles of manifested *forms,* but such beingness keeps *evolving* by *transforming in unpredictable ways*. The corporeal world is always in the process of becoming an ancestral history of formation that makes ordered sense.

Contingent relationships can be observed amongst *spontaneous* events occurring upon a similar level of organization even if unlinked or removed in terms of spatial proximity. These may evince synchronicity when viewed as a whole. *Quantum entanglement* is a form of nonlocal contingency that remains synchronistic, while circadian rhythms and pacemaker cells of the heart are resonantly local flesh-and-blood examples. In twenty-first-century material sciences, classical mechanistic determinism is giving way to probabilistic laws of contingency. Undetermined (in terms of mechanical linkage and linear causality) *spontaneity* is now thought of as commonplace.

The transformative chaos of environmental catastrophe and the synchronistic contingencies from which emerge hierarchies of new species cannot be explained by old Darwinian theories of evolution. When Darwin attempted to fit the concept of *organismic* development into a mechanistic worldview, he had to deny all orientation toward natural unity propelling the future design of life. While we may not know *what* order will emerge, knowing that order *will* emerge is to understand that the *future* is as *present* as the *past* and that the two are *not* equivalently symmetrical. *Paradoxically,* the past *indicates* the future, for the *future is always prior.* Such is the primary, Unitive Law of Time.

Studies of thermodynamics, chaos, and unstable systems in general make clear that the cosmos and its natural organization develop in a manner that is *irreversible.* The bulk properties of a chaotic system cannot be equated to a decomposed set comprising the individual properties of that system. Resonantly entangled, contingently synchronized interactions of a complex system must be treated as a whole. Occurrence, movement, and relationship of events may then be rationally defined and to varying degrees identified by probabilistic functions. In complex systems or worlds, no outcomes are known for *certain*, but the statistical mathematics of contingent manifestation enlightens scientists' knowledge of the universe nonetheless.

Contingency does not simply indicate randomness, but rather implies a spectrum of synchronicity arising through holistic causation. Forms emerge in the cosmos based upon contingencies that contain structures definable solely in terms of probabilities. We identify forms and movements through *categorical* rules involving *likeness.* Such similarity involves probabilistic field-structures. When we sense patterns that are similar to those already known, we assume they can *probably* be identified, categorized, and *known* in terms of associated significance or function.

In what is herein termed *fifth-dimensional consciousness,* four-dimensional spacetime is cognized and lived as a deeply ancestral, virtual, and historical domain of entangled reality; holistically radiating beyond gross, structural mechanics and psychic, resonant influences. It is this sphere or level of reality that David Bohm, Rupert Sheldrake, and fellow luminaries have intuited as subtly existent, compelling them toward noble efforts to conceptualize new scientific principles and mathematical models that may verifiably model such. In previous chapters, we have reviewed traditional concepts oriented toward fifth-dimensional consciousness and realization, including *nondual gnosis, ancestral awareness,* and *transcendental virtue.*

Clear realization of this stage of human consciousness involves an evolution of sensing-feeling-thinking self beyond intuitive levels of body-mind integration. *Virtue* identified traditionally by wisdom-realizers involves a moment-to-moment *spontaneous awareness* of the synchronistic entanglement of communal events in a world-space fundamentally defined by contingency. Every archetypal identity at every moment serves reality as a coherent event-process in a state of *probabilistic and temporal becoming.* Cognitive realization of such may be called Mindful Emptiness, be that on cosmic, human, or atomic planes.

Through realization of the principle of synchronistic contingency, the world proceeds into and then transforms beyond emergent field-identities marked by inertia and polarity. In this state of subtly living interconnectedness, human consciousness evolves and returns to the source-principle that causes manifestation of four-dimensional spacetime. Arising from the *animating flux* of chaos, spacetime is holistically re-created as a *materializing cause.* Every contingent network of events – all fields of symmetrical identity on every level of emergence, from micro to macrocosm – *materially remembers* its common and unified source at every moment and place via its ancestral synchronicities. Our universe's Original Singularity *remains* as the underlying Unifying Law of all.

Causality as a cosmic principle is now being re-cognized in the context of nonlinear, trans-local principles of chaos, contingency, emergence, and resonance. Hierarchical emergence in the universe exists *prior to* and *deeper than* all fields and thereby *causally encompasses* and *underlies* all resonance. This means that polar symmetry and field resonance are *destined* toward emergence of holarchical synchronicity. That which is *prior in principle* is that which the material world *evolves into.* All hierarchical emergence – whether of particles, elements, species, psyches, or galaxies – is derived from synchronistic contingency and holistic causation.

Holistic reality ensures that contingent events are always definable by some *degree* or *magnitude* of synchronicity. Every quantum is entangled with every other quantum since they were all One at the time of cosmic creation. As importantly, a universal hierarchy of holons emerging as a depth-spectrum of existence and duration of time are constantly recreated through the holistic history of synchronicity. Self-organizing fields resonate *in particular* with fields emerging with a high degree of *similar* synchronistic holism. By *tuning in* to the resonance of that which is similar but more essentially and integrally complex than itself (including a *group* of similar selves), vibratory cognition can transform its own body-mind system. On the human plane, this is how vitality is regenerated and consciousness is developed through yoga. Such cognitive or conscious evolution happens through psychic, hierarchical alignment and subtle, synchronistic similarity. Esoteric transmission as holistic informing of whole-body consciousness works through such resonance, emergence, and synchronicity; as does the soulful love of wedded hearts and spiritual community.

Even from a twenty-first-century cosmological perspective, it can well be said that the cosmos is fundamentally, fully United. We have seen that wave functions of atomic particles extend to their disintegrated parts even when extended over light-years of spacetime. The particle-parts do not "communicate" to "align" themselves; rather they *continuously form a whole entity.* Thus, they behave as a single identity maintaining a common symmetry in an extended field potentially limited only by the size of the cosmos. The quantum-level law of nonlocality reflects the greater principle of holistic causality, which is similarly reflected through laws operative on biological and human consciousness levels. Regarding the latter, for instance, studies have shown that concurrent with a conscious feeling or intention, materialization and release of neuropeptides *simultaneously* occur in cells throughout the body. Universal laws are measurably operable on differing hierarchical levels of existence in accordance to distinct level-bound laws. Thereby, non-local synchronicity at the quantum level is bound to be observed and experienced differently than that at the human level. In all cases, nonlocality requires a priori unity via genesis from the same source.

Non-equilibrium systems such as the universe, the sun, the earth, and life in general dynamically give rise to collectively novel effects coherent as and throughout the whole. These effects are caused holistically, and can only be measured through the synchronicity addressed by aforementioned stochastic models. Mechanical materialists refuse to acknowledge the intuitive beauty of the world's paradoxically deeply simple complex chaos, even though the study of such has lent itself to elegant symbolic expression – mathematically, artistically, and literally. From within new science developments, a worldview has emerged whereby contingency coheres holistically and statistical properties are understood as cosmically fundamental. This view acknowledges *innate duration* and associated underlying formative limits of duration – properly understood as the most primal aspect of reality – which are set by emergence-designs, field-systems, symmetry-structures, and identity-definitions.

Chaos deeply encapsulates *nascent, potential order.* When order emerges from chaos, ethereal boundary conditions are initially in flux, dynamically undefined, and stochastic by nature. Whole, integral identities first form patterns through hierarchical emergence of otherwise shapeless contingencies non-locally assembling synchronistically (after which they may become localized). Pattern definition of a whole's contingent parts emerges simultaneously and integrally on multiple levels of depth (perhaps understandable as *holographic resonance*) because of an encapsulating, higher-level source-cause (perhaps understandable as *morphogenetic fields*) from which a holon emerges. *Durations* of natural patterns may be defined in general as *fields.* Because energy becomes matter and matter reverts back to energy, fields always contain polar aspects that serve to identify their uniqueness. Through dimensional concentration and recursive magnification of a unified time-space-chaos process, *things* are *caused* to happen.

Transformative aspects of nature – found, for example, in Big Bang creation, symmetrical atomic structuring, elemental and molecular formation, biological evolution, and all other essentially beautiful, good, and true corporeal aspects of reality – have been considered (before worldviews of chaos and emergence blossomed into lawful study) by mechanistic material scientists as arising *totally from chance.* From their perspective, that which is viewed as *causally immeasurable* is deemed to be so for reasons solely based upon an observer's lack of information. While admitting and allowing for *chance occurrences* (a concept that reductionistic materialists conflate with *transcendental essence*) of transformation, the world is otherwise considered to be mechanically computable. It was once thought that theoretically, given a large enough computer, the linear progression of every event in the universe could be retraced, extrapolated, correlated, and determined with certainty. In contrast to this, contemporary theories of chaotic and complex systems posit that most all events in the universe are caused to manifest through laws that arise out of *untraceably* eventful chaos and complexity.

Causal *relationships* emerging from chaos are related through a *mutual* cause such as a common source of origin. In defining a whole, separate events effectively synchronize via a common cause underlying them. That cause may be a chaotic or complex source-law unnoticed by an observer. Or it might be a *creative union* operating on a level of dimensionality and depth, or frequency and radiance, that human observers are unaware exists (flocks of birds, swarms of bees, and schools of fish are common earthly examples of organized unions operating on levels deeper than human perception is able to fully cognize). The Ten Immortal Principles outlined in this chapter define universal *dimensionality* as an *interiorly omniscient* and *exteriorly omnipresent* realization of *conscious cosmos* through all of its domains. Modern theories of catastrophe, chaos, complexity, and morphogenesis are significantly advancing scientific understanding and technological implementation of the world's multidimensional unity.

Dimensional depth and co-arising interdependency are concepts primary to a fourth-stage, intuitive understanding of the world based upon holistic and transformative models of twenty-first-century scientific knowledge. The belief that physical dynamics are caused solely through the linear interactions of spatially *discreet* and *disintegrated* field-events does not conceive the world to be inherently, already unified and thereby holistically causal. Worldviews encompassing deeply integral, underlying levels of causation operating upon the physical world usually elicit unreasonable antagonism from scientific materialists. Intraphysical concepts of emergent design are still rhetorically attacked as "metaphysical," even if abiding by accepted scientific methodology; as if eighteenth- and nineteenth-century mechanical scientism was the last word in scientific theory and natural knowledge.

Given that this book bases the system of Tarot Triumphs upon a philosophical worldview that historically combined cosmic emanation and evolution with principles of spiritual realization involving immortality, this chapter outlines an elegant way to encompass and unite both physical and metaphysical principles of an *eternal universe.* We may cognize a *six-dimensional cosmos* by identifying the materialization of spacetime with the first six of our Ten Unitive Principles as follows:

> *Inertia, polarity,* and *field* identify symmetrical resonance as three-dimensional space.
>
> *Hierarchy* is the fourth-dimensional processional emergence of space *becoming* time, wherein time itself is the *attracting pole* of the world's spacetime axis.
>
> Evolving further into unity as *time-attracted* reality, *synchronicity* is the fifth-dimension involving *entangled* contingency.
>
> What is universally cognized and experienced as simultaneously present *source and destiny* is the sixth-dimension *holistically* causing the cosmos.
>
> Beyond that, a further three "dimensions," if indeed that is the proper term, compose a transcendent realm that is paradoxically always *corporeal* while simultaneously lawfully *abiding beyond* separative cognition and human measurement in any terms of objective or provable certainty.
>
> A Grand Unification of universal dimensionality, including all manifestation of time itself, perforce defines reality in

> terms of Immortal Principles. World Unity as the *First Principle* fully includes and involves but is not limited to corporeal dimensionality, for from that One all other principles, laws, and matter arise.

This total and complete interdependency of unitive, lawful principles and attributes of reality may be realized consciously by humans through that which perennially has been called *spiritual awareness* – mind-body realization of immortal Law through and as the unity of living light and creative being.

Space in all of its cosmic, chaotic, and empty dimensionality is preceded, permeated, and encompassed by radiant time. Fields, and all events located within fields, are delimited by the speed of light. Thus, *linear* cause-effect relationships between fields or between field events that are not *already unified through time* cannot occur *simultaneously.* Spatial events are *radiantly connected* in momentary duration through the constancy of time *as* light-speed. In other words, *Time emanates Space.* Time cannot be reduced to laws of matter and quantum energy. Rather, matter must be understood *as* radiant energy, which is most fundamentally defined by the laws of time.

What *are* time and space as underlying principles of the universe that are not merely reducible to cosmic manifestation upon any particular level of chaos, organization, or mathematical abstraction? Can a human be cognizant of *pure space* or conscious of *just time?*

Time is universal cognition – what humans realize as *Consciousness.* Time is Universal Mind – duration as all interior cognition, which is to say all vibration, even at its lowest possible *magnitude* and highest possible *speed.* When twenty-first-century cosmologists tell the story of Cosmic Birth and Death, it ends in an ever-more-quickly expanding world-space of light. Light-traces of the cosmic past will, over the next hundred billion years, pulverize at an *edge of absolute energy,* leaving little more than a local galactic space that hypothetical future astronomers may be able to locally observe. In no way a dark and dismal death, this futuristic cosmic creation myth tells a brilliant story of Mind as the *destiny* of the Cosmic Body and World Soul – cosmic flux wholly transformed via material realization back into its Source Union of Mysterious Void and Divine Light.

Radiant Time is de facto *present* in every other universal principle. Radiant Mind and Present Reality are literally One and the same. The mind of time is evident in the essential indifference to all transformations shown by spatially dimensional inertial objects; that is, in the constant duration of the cosmos beyond and regardless of its underlying flux of quantum chance. Time as a principle encompassing all space, chaos, causation, and contingent and emergent fields through which symmetry and identity manifest, *moves* the universe *forward*. Through Time, the *ordered* entropy of the cosmos universally *increases*. Called Logos, Consciousness, and Immortality, such is asymmetrically matched by the gravity and inherent *immobility* of Space. It is the latter universal aspect of our material world that laws of entropy refer to when positing that all space-matter is ultimately destined to randomly "equalize" in spatial identity through loss of *creative* (i.e., *working*) energy – that there is a hypothetical tendency for all matter and energy in the universe to evolve toward a state of inert uniformity.

A dogmatic presumption of death-believing hard and cold scientists is that the universe is a *closed system* and thereby the Law of Entropic Equilibrium rules over all other laws; that anti-gravitational *dark energy* or *cosmological constant* or *quintessence*, such as it may be deemed, is not a *creative* force absolutely and immortally energizing the heart of every *moment* everywhere for everything. If that appears like a twenty-first-century God-Principle, then so be it; but please, dear friends who have made it to the end of this treatise, know without a doubt that the Unitive Principle is Always Here Now *As* the World. This is *Immortally True.*

Unitive reality is indicated by the fact that gravity radiates at the speed of light. Although gravity and electromagnetic radiation have not been *mathematically* unified, the unitive nature of the universe needs to be understood beyond mathematically limited suppositions. Space radiates in its *fundamental essence* at the speed of light – i.e., *as time.* Spatial radiation or movement sensibly "marks out" time. The fastest "time can go" in the universe is at the speed of light; or, put another way, time slows to zero relative to other event-frames as the speed of light is approached. The *eternity* of immortals is simply that time-space of purely *radiant being.*

Law as the *incorporeal essence* of Unity is the Heart of wisdom-realization. The study of physics up till now has been unable to directly approach this truly greatest principle, that of Unified Law. Einstein's reduction of time as a dimensional extension of space did not assume a deep enough worldview to allow formulations of time without unnecessary spatial limitations. Einstein intuitively understood that the universe develops *already* unified. Radiant Time bridges Dimensional Space with Unitive Law. However, quantum mechanics defines time through the dimensional units and trajectories of material particles. While this has proven to be an insightful view of chaotic space materializing, it has fallen far short of conceiving the true Laws of Time.

Applying perennial wisdom understanding to the most essential aspects of reality – Unity, Time, Space, and Chaos – gives us a set of scientific principles, laws, and definitions:

Unity is universal principle.
Unity emanates present law.
Unity as law is always transcending.
Unity as present law emanates radiant time.

Time is radiant cognition.
Time emanates durational energy.
Time as energy is always slowing.
Time as durational energy emanates dimensional space.

Space is dimensional force.
Space emanates coherent gravity.
Space as gravity is always accelerating.
Space as coherent gravity emanates quantal chaos.

Chaos is quantal matter.
Chaos emanates immanent mass.
Chaos as mass is always transforming.
Chaos as immanent mass emanates organizational causality.

Further to the above, are the observations that:

Time is infinite.
Space is infinitesimal.
Time and Space are the mind and body of Unified Law.
Space and Time realize universal symmetry.

Materialistically reductive belief systems are unable to posit how principles and laws themselves originally arose and continually arise. Of course, principles are not reducible to or caused by the mathematical models that use those principles as foundations upon which their theories are built. By all accounts, the fundamental principles of the universe are destined to manifestation of not only *material* reality, but *of absolute light-reality.* For *against all odds of chance,* the cosmos does in Truth *already* exist in such a Beautiful and Good Way.

Principled Unity does not imply "willful nature" in the style of an anthropomorphic, separative "God-power." Disbelief in *theism* catalyzes a core reaction that affects many scientists' ability to observe and consider the principle of Unitive Law. In the understanding of nondual emanation, principle-realities of Law, Time, Space, and Chaos are not *separate* from the Cosmos, but neither are they *essentially limited* by cosmic definition. Unitive Law *does* imply that cognitive life is a cosmic imperative and that *Light* (or what esoteric Buddhism calls *Buddha Mind*) through infinite cosmic manifestations – causal, subtle, and gross – serves as the *purpose* of such.

Scientific materialism generally conceives of matter as being *informed*. "Informing acts" are presumed to occur through practically *ideal* mathematical laws of nature. It is a small step from such Platonic ideation to a Neoplatonic realization that the essential laws of the cosmos are inherently purposed to the realization of conscious unity. As it is, scientists believe that life occurs through genes mysteriously coded for self-survival and the creation, maintenance, and destruction of unfathomably complex, dynamically unstable self-conscious beings over time. Science will come to affirm that universally unitive laws *manifest* as cosmic bodies, thereby becoming *unveiled;* and that *Time* is the quintessential Unifying Principle. Mind and body are truly and completely nondual, regardless of the polarities contained by every identity.

This book has attempted to summarize and elucidate for modern contemplators, spiritual questors, interdisciplinary scholars, and holistic scientists the immortal heart of ten essential principles championed by a great and perennial tradition of wisdom. If the reader is amazed to find a book on the perennial wisdom origins of the Tarot ending with an exemplified summary of universal, scientific principles, remember that science is embarking on a new journey; a journey whereupon the natural world of complexity, creativity, time, consciousness, and evolution are explored without the blinders of reductionistic materialism and dogmatically atheistic scientism. If in fact there are infinite cosmic realities, Ten Great Unitive, Universal, and Immortal Principles are realizing them all.

CONTINUOUS RESURRECTION

SUN

*Succession is unstoppable;
just as the Sun sees all,
so too will knowledge of truth
reign supreme.*

ANGEL

*The furious roar of awakening
will be felt by everyone sooner
or later; and the alive shall be
dead, the dead shall be alive.*

Nine

Illuminating All

hroughout its history, the Tarot has been used as a means of enlightened storytelling. In this capacity, it has served as both a social game and a private oracle.

When used in the context of a game that includes minimal storytelling, such as in the traditional game of *Tarocchi,* the symbolic meanings contained in the Triumphs generally do not come into play. At most, they perhaps assist players in appreciating the hierarchical nature of the Triumphs as they are used to *trump* other cards and capture *tricks.* This particular utility of the cards, furthering a method of competitive play in games of chance, enabled their continuous popularity and ensured their survival beyond the late medieval era.

Used in the context of divination, the symbolic meanings, intuitive gestalts, and overall vision contained within each distinctive Triumph define the reading, guidance, and wisdom of a worldview founded upon ancient yet perennial knowledge and authentic spiritual realization. That wisdom is made available by playing the Tarot, and may be freely drawn upon by every beholder of a traditional spread of Triumphs.

Combined as both a game and an oracle, the Tarot lends itself to a unique type of social play and personal edification. When integrated with interactive technology, the Image-Exemplars can become animated stories combining text with visuals, sounds with passages, education with seduction, and identity with mystery.

The present work has not been the appropriate place to explore the use of Tarot cards in the context of divinatory storytelling. However, the reader is warmly invited to explore companion projects of this book, published in both electronic and material forms, which are creatively oriented toward oracular game play.

Although written in a demeanor more suited for this book's scholarly tone, the following may serve as an introduction to the above. This chapter, then, summarizes essential meanings and stories that may be found in the Trionfi.

Illuminating All

Traditional Triumph:	**MAGICIAN**
Immortal Name:	*Self*
Sufi Station:	Independent
Station:	0
Stages:	1–6
Pole:	Individual

Cosmic Level: Corporeal Consciousness
Social Level: Archaic Oneness
Questor Level: Development Already

Keys:

Eyes are all around
Inscrutably strategic
Making the trivial crucially important
Mastering deception
Seeing the course from the obstacles
Guiding professionally, thieving honestly
Showing up at all the right places

Strengths:

Manages the impossible
Knows how death rules
Always remembers the map
Flows with young and old
Is in the confidence of all
Evinces perfect timing
Multitasks without confusion

Dangers:

Minor slips can be catastrophic
All distraction must be controlled
Effortless effort may become illusory
Stressing when playing, undermining work
Manipulation disposing simple joys
True intentions questioned by honest folk
Pretension of emptiness cannot face death

Traditional Triumph: **EMPRESS**
Immortal Name: *Land*
Sufi Station: Influencer

Station: 1
Stage: 1
Pole: Communal

Cosmic Stage: Inertial Density
Social Stage: Matriarchal Agriculture
Questor Stage: Physical Settlement

Keys:

Foundational worldview
Mothering the commons
Keeping it all simple
Even the lowest can be spiritual
Nascent prima mater
Dignified representation
Innocently playing

Strengths:

Stays the course, keeps it true
Immediately feels wrongness
Material plentitude
Stable cycle of fertility
Stated goals from the start
Peaceful commencement
Universal human rights

Dangers:

Material reductionism and shortsightedness
Limited by too many pawns
Location and status drawing wrong attention
Naïvely believing in privileged rights
Getting stuck in constant obligations
Obsessing on sustenance and possession
Conflating fashion and fad with Eros

Traditional Triumph: **POPESS**
Immortal Name: *Home*
Sufi Station: Supporter

Station: 2
Stage: 1
Pole: Individual

Cosmic Stage: Distinct Identity
Social Stage: Magical Peace
Questor Stage: Grounded Sensation

Keys:

Keeping up the gardens
Pointing seekers to the path
Dwelling in seclusion
Holding matriarchal authority
Consorting with questors
Assisting to find the keys
Introducing real opportunity

Strengths:

Paradisiacal vision
Communal heart
Source of potency
Attraction of pure pleasantry
Commonsensical preparation
Helps champions along the way
Heals and bestows another chance

Dangers:

Banal simulacrum confused with real thing
Facile process of representation
Possession displacing growth
Fear of advancing beyond safety
Reducing paths to relative sameness
Becoming lost in sensual pleasure
Blocking access beyond the familiar

Traditional Triumph: **EMPEROR**
Immortal Name: *Trade*
Sufi Station: Knower

Station: 3
Stage: 2
Pole: Communal

Cosmic Stage: Polar Division
Social Stage: Patriarchal Civilization
Questor Stage: Sexual Extension

Keys:

Militant righteousness
Serving politics
Sexual motivation
Contracting obligations
Establishing alchemy
Measuring and weighing
Producing fertile grounds

Strengths:

Political balance
Incisive clarity
Civilized governance
Mythic leadership
Industrial efficiency
Willfully enables courage
Forms corporate structure

Dangers:

Pathological warfare
Emotional instability
Arrogant justification of violence
Sexual addiction
Intensification of uncontrolled reaction
Ignoring rationale beyond the politics
Reducing values to structure

Traditional Triumph: **POPE**
Immortal Name: *Travel*
Sufi Station: Victorious

Station: 4
Stage: 2
Pole: Individual

Cosmic Stage: Organic Symmetry
Social Stage: Mythical Ritual
Questor Stage: Dramatic Emotion

Keys:

- Moral arbitration
- Survival of the fittest
- Enabling meaningful rituals
- Maintaining patriarchal authority
- Formalizing ideals
- Perpetuating traditions
- Bonding realms together

Strengths:

- Legendary path-making
- Governs fairly and equally
- Promotes strong structure
- Balances strategies
- Upholds honor
- Informs the masses
- Champions natural relationship

Dangers:

- Controlling through bondage
- Believing in male superiority
- Disregarding danger to others
- Dualistic conviction projecting evil
- Moralistic restriction of common liberty
- Dramatic tragedy
- Provincial obligations serving little purpose

Traditional Triumph: **TEMPERANCE**
Immortal Name: *Education*
Sufi Station: Light

Station: 5
Stage: 3
Pole: Communal

Cosmic Stage: Field Integrity
Social Stage: Appropriate Technology
Questor Stage: Intentional Responsibility

Keys:

- Moving with the flow
- Cycling energy
- Adopting a mature attitude
- Drawing up, washing down
- Managing opposites
- Establishing proper limits
- Rhythmic patterning

Strengths:

- Responsible relationship
- Intelligent diplomacy
- Harmonious engagement
- Healthy growth
- Humane civility
- Cooperative exchanges
- Integration of opposition

Dangers:

- Indecisive flexibility
- Diluting focus
- Overextending boundaries
- Indiscriminately blending distinctions
- Excusing behavior of avoidance
- Tolerating corruption beyond repair
- Attempting to appease evil

Traditional Triumph: **LOVE**
Immortal Name: *Communion*
Sufi Station: Form Giver

Station: 6
Stage: 3
Pole: Individual

Cosmic Stage: Harmonic Resonance
Social Stage: Rational Belief
Questor Stage: Intimate Reason

Keys:

To go high, first go low
Erotic tolerance
Communally procreative
Three becoming the myriad
Envisioning together
Building cooperative community
Positively projecting

Strengths:

Motivational growth
Stable alchemy
Logical optimism
Respectful communication
Holistic wellness
Common intelligence
Serves neighbor as self

Dangers:

Excessive liberality
Uncontrollably caught in the stream
Falling for desire
Blindly being swept away
Hiding under a partner's skirt
Revealing too much
Bleeding heart through sympathy

Traditional Triumph: **CHARIOT**
Immortal Name: *Mission*
Sufi Station: Reckoner

Station: 7
Stage: 4
Pole: Communal

Cosmic Stage: Hierarchical Phasing
Social Stage: Interactive Media
Questor Stage: Spiritual Charge

Keys:

- Skills in action
- Family fidelity
- Spiritual conduction
- Sharing psychic awareness
- Driving one's own fate
- Actualizing success
- Adhering to authenticity

Strengths:

- Growth through innovation
- Transpersonal interaction
- Wards community
- Seductively educates
- Sustains productivity
- Deals with the challenges
- Leads the way forward

Dangers:

- Zealous evangelization
- Provincial conceit
- Addictive rushes
- Caste supremacy
- Domineering control
- Abandoning responsibility
- Taking charge of too much

Traditional Triumph: **FORTITUDE**
Immortal Name: *Allegiance*
Sufi Station: Guardian

Station: 8
Stage: 4
Pole: Individual

Cosmic Stage: Progressive Emergence
Social Stage: Psychological Confidence
Questor Stage: Fantastic Intuition

Keys:

- Spinal energy
- Necessary restraint
- Leonine leadership
- Confidential alignment
- Strengthening psychic ability
- Regulating intensity
- Enduring the struggle

Strengths:

- Magnetic attraction
- Charismatic direction
- Therapeutically heals
- Sublimates alchemy
- Guards real value
- Generates incredible potential
- Administers coherent order

Dangers:

- Dissipative friction through blockage
- Stressing limits too far
- Reinforcing militancy
- Restricting liberty
- Holding back too much
- Inflating egotism
- Commitments that keep arresting flow

Traditional Triumph: **WHEEL**
Immortal Name: *Karma*
Sufi Station: Curtailer

Station: 9
Stage: 5
Pole: Communal

Cosmic Stage: Synchronic Interdependence
Social Stage: Native Design
Questor Stage: Ancestral Memory

Keys:

Indiscriminate fortune
Emptiness beyond the zero point
Coincidence of integral quadrants
Gestating wholes
Subtle beyond control
Cycling patterns of nature
Apparently randomizing outcomes

Strengths:

Unquestioning devotion
Great traditional spirituality
Inexplicable luck
Flows with synchronicity
Learns from history
Lets it all be
Handles the lows with the highs

Dangers:

Banal conceits
Delusions of grandeur
Schizophrenic psychosis
Pervasive illusion
Losing centeredness while transiting
Believing in dualistic extremes
Conflating subtle ego with transcendence

Traditional Triumph:	**HERMIT**
Immortal Name:	*Gnosis*
Sufi Station:	Living
Station:	10
Stage:	5
Pole:	Individual

Cosmic Stage: Spontaneous Contingency
Social Stage: Subtle Awareness
Questor Stage: Sublimated Virtue

Keys:

- Synchronic spontaneity
- Extreme sublimation
- Sudden awakening
- Intimate communion
- Arch-protector of essence
- Opening doors of perception
- Upholding the staff of life

Strengths:

- Peaceful equanimity
- Wisdom of insecurity
- Third-eye radiance
- Authenticating spiritual initiation
- Tasting enlightenment
- Discerning the ineffable
- Sharing the gift of grace

Dangers:

- Occult secrecy
- Cynical conceit
- Total pretension
- Nihilistic angst
- Ascetic withdrawal into avoidance
- Projecting meaning into randomness
- Losing commonsense ground

Traditional Triumph: **HANGED MAN**
Immortal Name: *Conversion*
Sufi Station: Quickener

Station: 11
Stage: 6
Pole: Communal

Cosmic Stage: Holistic Source
Social Stage: Alchemical Biosphere
Questor Stage: Mindful Insight

Keys:

- Invisible implicate order
- Environmental wholeness
- Greatly returning
- Converting self-identity
- Watching the moment
- Witnessing the process
- Transcending sexual impulse

Strengths:

- Channel of nectar
- Whole brain consciousness
- Alchemical touchstone
- Utter heartfullness
- Integrates body-mind-soul
- Sees beyond subtle phantasm
- Keeps aware

Dangers:

- Involuntary induction
- Incoherent distraction
- Endemic stupidity
- Mind awash in excessive detail
- Abandonment of social responsibility
- Systemic freeze-up and meltdown
- Being pulled under by the flow

Traditional Triumph: **DEATH**
Immortal Name: *Mortality*
Sufi Station: Slayer

Station: 12
Stage: 6
Pole: Individual

Cosmic Stage: Integral Causality
Social Stage: Soulful Witnessing
Questor Stage: Historical Sacrifice

Keys:

Alpha and omega
Only a fleeting moment
Evolving organismic nature
Coming and going but never staying
Constantly changing
Evolving out of phases
Releasing karma and rebinding soul

Strengths:

Self-realization of wisdom
Awakens all at once
Cuts the root of delusion
Moves with the wind
Feels to the bones' marrow
Masters nature
Communes beyond ancestors

Dangers:

Abject denial
Peace-breaking nihilism
Effort leading only to tragedy
Chasing the chase itself
Spiraling into self-destruction
Believing in apocalyptic finality
Swiftly riding to nowhere

Traditional Triumph:	**DEVIL**
Immortal Name:	*Afterlife*
Sufi Station:	Degrader
Station:	13
Stage:	7
Pole:	Communal

Cosmic Stage:	Transformative Genesis
Social Stage:	Impossible Complexity
Questor Stage:	Masterful Initiation

Keys:

Earthbound triune
First, last, and only
Guarding the gates of divinity
Entering the underworld
Generating soul in the world
Wandering immortal realms
Changing beyond belief

Strengths:

Creative destruction
Utterly exposes illusion
Accesses eros regardless of challenge
Cuts through spiritual materialism
Makes the unreachable attainable
Breaks the barriers to enlightenment
Empowers beyond thresholds of fear

Dangers:

Megalomania
Endemic corruption
Nested deceit, deception, and denial
Spreading self-destruction
Taking from many, contracting to one
Losing innocence and simplicity
Arresting the whole process

Traditional Triumph: **TOWER**
Immortal Name: *Rebirth*
Sufi Station: Preciously Valued

Station: 14
Stage: 7
Pole: Individual

Cosmic Stage: Regenerative Chaos
Social Stage: Catastrophic Awakening
Questor Stage: Catalytic Ecstasy

Keys:

Lightening strikes
Arrow of the sun
Contained fusion reaction
Legendary treasure
Sacrificing beyond death
Regenerating spinal fire
Channeling the great daimon

Strengths:

Cauldron of immortal alchemy
Cultivation of ancient mystery
Transcendental access
Extreme potency
Mindful transformation
Supranatural assistance
Awakens kundalini

Dangers:

Unstoppable disruption
Grandiose delusion
Morass of information
Addiction to pleasure
Interminable exhaustion
Prolonging detrimental avoidance
Damning to hellfire

Traditional Triumph: **STAR**
Immortal Name: *Grace*
Sufi Station: Nourisher

Station: 15
Stage: 8
Pole: Communal

Cosmic Stage: Dimensional Portal
Social Stage: Manifested Past
Questor Stage: Pervasive Consideration

Keys:

- Souls of light
- Guidance of celestial beings
- Realizing utopian ideals
- Being purely original
- Channeling cosmic influence
- Knowing the ineffable
- Inspiring concentration of freedom

Strengths:

- Vow of bright poverty
- Spiritual mana
- Indisputable gnosis
- Sustainable ecstasy
- Rectification of integrity
- Innocently chaste at heart
- Blessings beyond purification

Dangers:

- Denial of reality
- Naïve abandonment
- Out-of-body disintegration
- Naked feminization
- Impotence through sexual exhaustion
- Ignoring all taboos
- Trying intimacy of anything goes

Traditional Triumph: **MOON**
Immortal Name: *Eros*
Sufi Station: Powerful

Station: 16
Stage: 8
Pole: Individual

Cosmic Stage: Convoluted Space
Social Stage: Myriad Divinities
Questor Stage: Reflective Emptiness

Keys:

Transcendental intervention
Radiant consorting
Mightily unifying third-eye
Translucent veiling of mystery
Insuring creative outcome
Upholding great spirit
Becoming what has always been

Strengths:

Sublime refuge
Magnified beauty
Garden of ambrosia
Diversity in unity
Goddess wisdom
Compassion for all
Great mirror practice of adepts

Dangers:

Banal seduction of evil
Narcissistic entrancement
Psychosis in the wilderness
Never-ending stag chase
Revenge of a she-demon
Being turned into stone
Cloning life without soul

Traditional Triumph: **SUN**
Immortal Name: *Brilliance*
Sufi Station: Minute Observer

Station: 17
Stage: 9
Pole: Communal

Cosmic Stage: Radiant Light
Social Stage: Realized Present
Questor Stage: Complete Dominion

Keys:

- Omniscience
- Living eternity
- Deity known to all
- Infinite moment
- Transcendental pervasiveness
- Once-returning consciousness
- Synchronizing the cosmos

Strengths:

- Ideal harmony
- Indelible knowledge
- Complete enlightenment
- Unqualified forgiveness
- Immortal realization
- Unbeatable goodness
- Genius outshining all

Dangers:

- Sole survival
- Cancerous growth
- Governance through spying
- Blinding power
- Catalyzing the furies
- Mutating irradiation
- Scorching indifference

Traditional Triumph: **ANGEL**
Immortal Name: *Perfection*
Sufi Station: Gatherer

Station: 18
Stage: 9
Pole: Individual

Cosmic Stage: Irreversible Time
Social Stage: Perennial Paradise
Questor Stage: Eternal Resurrection

Keys:

- Justly indifferent
- Kosmic evolution
- Permanent awakening
- Vibrating spheres of oneness
- Blast of the furies
- Perfect timing
- Raising the dead

Strengths:

- Divine congregation
- Glorious transcendence
- Nirvana
- Untouched by decay
- Translation into light
- Happiness in this lifetime
- Eternal relationship

Dangers:

- Nuclear holocaust
- Non-reclaimable extinction
- Entombed in a simulacrum of time
- Awakening an army of demons
- Aspiring to a chance in hell
- Exceeding boundaries regardless
- Mind wiping out body

Traditional Triumph: **JUSTICE**
Immortal Name: *Law*
Sufi Station: Elevator

Station: 19
Stage: 10
Pole: Communal

Cosmic Stage: Unitive Principles
Social Stage: Divine Future
Questor Stage: Universal Destiny

Keys:

Throne of glory
Supreme way of the goddess
Triune of tantra
Asymmetry of just one
Pulverizing suffering
Determining truth
Ruling the heart

Strengths:

Avataric selflessness
Diamond body immortality
No-return enlightenment
Merciful way of nature
Faultless weights and measures
Blindingly swift retribution
What just is will just be

Dangers:

No tradition, only guru
Inevitable tragedy
Madness beyond measure
Separating divinity from nature
Dogmatic belief held as divine revelation
Judging world to be evil
Extinction of humanity

Illuminating All

Traditional Triumph: **WORLD**
Immortal Name: *Kosmos*
Sufi Station: Surrounder

Station: 20
Stage: 10
Pole: Individual

Cosmic Level: Absolute Truth
Social Level: One Heart
Questor Level: Infinite Pleroma

Keys:

Original unity
Purpose of kosmos
Tao
Principles realizing spacetime
All is one, one is all
Creating first cause
Liberating bliss

Strengths:

Simply essential lawfulness
Sustained reality on all levels
Includes infinity
Perfection of heart consciousness
Destined kingdom at hand
Encompasses all that is known
Beyond beyond, before before

Dangers:

Fascistic totalitarianism
Alien takeover
Annihilation of spirit
Myriad of three denying unity of one
Reducing spacetime to cosmic singularity
Abrogating rightful rule
Bio-engineering a thousand-year domain

Traditional Triumph: **FOOL**
Immortal Name: *Quest*
Sufi Station: Large Recompensor

Station: ∞
Stages: 7–10
Pole: Communal

Cosmic Level: Creative Origination
Social Level: Primal Ecstasy
Questor Level: Prior Success

Keys:

Wandering between realms
On the edge of existence
Sharing spontaneously
Coming out of the blue
Strangely happy, even when tragic
Never at a loss
Divinely accidental

Strengths:

Death is of no consequence
Walks right past the devils
Is at ease amongst the deathless
Elicits no fear from the powerful
Apparently isn't affected by karma
Holds to sexually liberated innocence
Abundant spirit is never cut down

Dangers:

Too easily taken advantage of
May be blamed for the message
Transcendent intelligence ignored as a joke
Shameless honesty leading to arrested alchemy
Attracting unhealthy attention
Inviting trouble through sympathy with fringe
Appearing as if confusion reigns

Radiating . . . Right Knowledge

LIBERATED BLISS

JUSTICE

The Law of the World is simply That which is Just.

WORLD

As it has been, now is, and always will be, Essential Unity Surrounds the World, serving always as its Purpose.

References

A selected bibliography listed by primary chapter reference:

Chapter 1

American Heritage, *The American Heritage Dictionary of the English Language.* Boston: Houghton Mifflin, 1992.

A. K. Coomaraswamy. *Spiritual Authority and Temporal Power in the Indian Theory of Government.* New Haven: American Oriental Society, 1942.

R. Decker, T. Depaulis, M. Dummett. *The Origins of the Occult Tarot.* London: Gerald Duckworth & Co., 1996.

M. Dummett. *The Game of Tarot.* London: Gerald Duckworth & Co., 1980.

A. Faivre. *Access to Western Esotericism.* Albany: State University of New York Press, 1994.

A. Faivre and J. Needleman, eds. *Modern Esoteric Spirituality.* New York: Crossroad, 1992.

R. Guénon. *Initiation and Spiritual Realization.* Ghent, NY: Sophia Perennis, 2001.

S. R. Kaplan, *The Encyclopedia of Tarot,* vol. 1. New York: U. S. Game Systems, 1978.

———. *The Encyclopedia of Tarot,* vol. 2. New York: U. S. Game Systems, 1986.

A. O. Lovejoy. *The Great Chain of Being.* Cambridge: Harvard University Press, 1964.

Huston Smith. *The World's Religions.* San Francisco: Harper SanFrancisco, 1991.

K. Wilber. *Sex, Ecology, Spirituality; The Spirit of Evolution.* Boston: Shambhala, 1995.

Chapter 2

J. Arquilla and D. Ronfeldt. *The Advent of Netwar.* Santa Monica: RAND, 1996.

G. A. Cambell. *The Knights Templars: Their Rise and Fall.* New York: Robert M. McBride & Company, 1937.

H. and O. Chadwick, eds. *Oxford History of the Christian Church.* Oxford: University of Oxford, 1986.

P. Chaunu. *European Expansion in the Later Middle Ages.* New York: North-Holland Publishing Company, 1979.

J. E. Dotson. *Merchant Culture in Fourteenth Century Venice: The Zibaldone da Canal.* Binghamton: Medieval & Renaissance Texts & Studies, 1994.

H. C. Evans and W. D. Wixom, eds. *The Glory of Byzantium: Art and Culture of the Middle Byzantine Era.* New York: Metropolitan Museum of Art, 1997.

J. Freely. *Istanbul: The Imperial City.* London: Viking, 1996.

B. Z. Kedar. *Merchants in Crisis.* New Haven: Yale University Press, 1976.

R. S. Lopez and I. W. Raymond. *Medieval Trade in the Mediterranean World.* New York: Columbia University Press, 1955.

H. Nicholson. *Templars, Hospitallers and Teutonic Knights.* Leicester: Leicester University Press, 1993.

N. Ohler. *The Medieval Traveller.* Woodbridge: Boydell Press, 1989.

J. R. S. Phillips. *The Medieval Expansion of Europe.* Oxford: Oxford University Press, 1988.

W. R. Polk. *Neighbors & Strangers: The Fundamentals of Foreign Affairs.* Chicago: University of Chicago Press, 1997.

A. K. Smith. *Creating a World Economy.* New York: Westview Press, 1991.

D. Spoto. *Reluctant Saint: The Life of Francis of Assisi.* New York: Penguin, 2002.

A. Toynbee, ed. *Cities of Destiny.* New York: McGraw-Hill, 1973.

W. Ullmann. *Medieval Foundations of Renaissance Humanism.* Ithaca: Cornell University Press, 1977.

Chapter 3

L. Bakhtiar. *Sufi: Expressions of the Mystic Quest.* London: Thames and Hudson, 1976.

H. Bloom. *Kabbalah and Criticism.* New York: Continuum, 1983.

C. Burnett. *Magic and Divination in the Middle Ages: Texts and Techniques in the Islamic and Christian Worlds.* Burlington: Variorum, 1996.

W. C. Chittick. *The Sufi Path of Knowledge.* Albany: State University of New York Press, 1989.

———. *The Sufi Path of Love: The Spiritual Teachings of Rumi.* New York: State University of New York Press, 1983.

A. W. Hughes. *The Texture of the Divine: Imagination in Medieval Islamic and Jewish Thought.* Bloomington: Indiana University Press, 2004.

M. P. Levine. *Pantheism: A Non-theistic Concept of Deity.* London: Routledge, 1994.

V. H. Mair. "Mummies of the Tarim Basin," *Archaeology* 48:2 (1995).

P. Morewedge, ed. *Neoplatonism and Islamic Thought.* Albany: State University of New York Press, 1992.

S. H. Nasr, ed. *Islamic Spirituality: Foundations.* New York: Crossroad, 1991.

———. *Islamic Spirituality II.* New York: Crossroad, 1991.

S. H. Nasr. *The Islamic Intellectual Tradition in Persia.* Surrey: Curzon Press, 1996.

R. A. Nicholson. *The Mystics of Islam.* London: Routledge & Kegan Paul, 1963.

H. M. Sachar. *Farewell España: The World of the Sephardim Remembered.* New York: Alfred A. Knopf, 1994.

R. M. Savory, ed. *Introduction to Islamic Civilization.* Cambridge: Cambridge University Press, 1976.

A. M. Schimmel. *Mystical Dimensions of*

Islam. Chapel Hill: University of North Carolina Press, 1975.

G. Scholem. *Origins of the Kabbalah*. Princeton: Princeton University Press, 1990.

———. *The Mystical Shape of the Godhead*. New York: Schocken Books, 1991.

I. Shah. *A Perfumed Scorpion*. London: Octagon Press, 1978.

S. I. A. Shah. *Islamic Sufism*. New York: Samuel Weiser, 1971.

G. Speake, ed. *Atlas of the Greek World*. Oxford: Equinox, 1984.

———. *Atlas of the Islamic World*. Oxford: Equinox, 1982.

R. C. Taylor. *The Liber de causis: A Study of Medieval Neoplatonism*. Toronto: University of Toronto, 1981.

S. Vryonis. *Decline of Medieval Hellenism in Asia Minor*. Berkeley: University of California Press, 1971.

Chapter 4

M. Barasch. *Icon: Studies in the History of an Idea*. New York: New York University Press, 1992.

F. C. Copleston. *Medieval Philosophy*. New York: Harper & Row, 1952.

F. M. Cornford. *Principium Sapientiae*. Cambridge: Cambridge University Press, 1952.

I. P. Couliano. *Eros and Magic in the Renaissance*. Chicago: University of Chicago Press, 1987.

J. Habermas. *The Theory of Communicative Action*. Boston: Beacon Press, 1984.

J. Hillman. *Re-Visioning Psychology*. New York: Harper & Row, 1975.

W. R. Inge. *The Philosophy of Plotinus*. London: Longmans, 1923.

E. Jeauneau. "The Neoplatonic Themes of *Processio* and *Reditus* in Eriugena." *Dionysius* 15 (1991).

R. E. A. Johansson. *The Dynamic Psychology of Early Buddhism*. Oxford: Curzon, 1979.

J. R. Lyman. *Christology and Cosmology*. Oxford: Clarendon Press, 1993.

T. McEvilley. *The Shape of Ancient Thought: Comparative Studies in Greek and Indian Philosophies*. New York: Allworth Press, 2002.

A. L. Moore, tr. *St. John Climacus: The Ladder of Divine Ascent*. London: Faber and Faber, 1959.

C. Renfrew. *Archaeology and Language: The Puzzle of Indo-European Origins*. London: J. Cape, 1987.

———. *The Cycladic Spirit*. New York: Harry Abrams, 1991.

P. Rorem. *Pseudo-Dionysius*. Oxford: Oxford University Press, 1993.

D. J. Sahas. *John of Damascus on Islam*. Leiden: E. J. Brill, 1972.

R. Schenk. *The Soul of Beauty: A Psychological Investigation of Appearance*. London: Associated University Presses, 1992.

R. Scruton. *An Intelligent Person's Guide to Modern Culture*. London: Duckworth, 1998.

T. Spidlik. *The Spirituality of the Christian*

East. Kalamazoo: Cistercian Publications, 1986.

G. Stamatellos. *Plotinus and the Presocratics: A Philosophical Study of Presocratic Influences in Plotinus' Enneads*. Albany: State University of New York Press, 2007.

J. R. R. Tolkien. *The Lord of the Rings*. Deluxe Edition. London: George Allen and Unwin, 1990.

Chapter 5

M. Borg, ed. *Jesus & Buddha: The Parallel Sayings*. Berkeley: Ulysses Press, 2002.

D. B. Burrell and B. McGinn. *God and Creation: An Ecumenical Symposium*. Notre Dame: University of Notre Dame Press, 1990.

I. P. Couliano. *The Tree of Gnosis: Gnostic Mythology from Early Christianity to Modern Nihilism*. New York: Harper-Collins, 1992.

E. Edinger. *The Mysterium Lectures: A Journey through C. G. Jung's Mysterium Coniunctionis*. Toronto: Inner City Books, 1995.

P. F. M. Fontaine. *The Light and the Dark: A Cultural History of Dualism, Volume II*. Amsterdam: J. C. Gieben, 1986.

M. Forte and A. Siliotti. *Virtual Archaeology: Re-creating Ancient Worlds*. New York: H. N. Abrams, 1997.

C. W. Hedrick and R. Hodgson. *Nag Hammadi, Gnosticism, and Early Christianity*. Peabody: Hendrickson, 1986.

D. Ikeda. *Buddhism, the First Millennium*. New York: Kodansha International, 1977.

P. Kingsley. *Ancient Philosophy, Mystery, and Magic: Empedocles and Pythagorean Tradition*. Oxford: Clarendon Press, 1995.

R. S. Kinsman. *The Darker Vision of the Renaissance*. Berkeley: University of California Press, 1974.

H. Klimkeit. *Gnosis on the Silk Road: Gnostic Texts from Central Asia*. New York: Harper, 1993.

P. Masefield. *Divine Revelation in Pali Buddhism*. Colombo: The Sri Lanka Institute of Traditional Studies, 1986.

R. May. *Love and Will*. New York: W.W. Norton & Company, 1960.

F. d'Olivet. *The Golden Verses of Pythagoras*. Translated by N. L. Redfield. New York: G. P. Putnam's Sons, 1925.

E. Pagels. *Beyond Belief: The Secret Gospel of Thomas*. New York: Random House, 2003.

B. A. Pearson. *Gnosticism, Judaism, and Egyptian Christianity*. Minneapolis: Fortress Press, 1990.

R. A. Piper. *Wisdom in the Q-tradition: The Aphoristic Teaching of Jesus*. Cambridge: Cambridge University Press, 1989.

T. M. Robinson. *Heraclitus: Fragments*. Toronto: University of Toronto Press, 1987.

K. Rudolph. *Gnosis: The Nature and History of Gnosticism*. New York: Harper & Row, 1983.

J. Seznec. *The Survival of the Pagan Gods*.

Princeton: Princeton University Press, 1995.

J. A. Stewart. *The Myths of Plato.* Carbondale: Southern Illinois University Press, 1960.

Z. P. Thundy. *Buddha and Christ: Nativity Stories and Indian Traditions.* New York: E. J. Brill, 1993.

P. Tillich. *Courage to Be.* New Haven: Yale University Press, 1953.

A. D. Winspear. *The Genesis of Plato's Thought.* New York: Harbor Press, 1956.

Chapter 6

G. Barbujani, A. Pilastro, S. Domenico, and C. Renfrew. "Genetic Variation in North Africa and Eurasia: Neolithic Demic Diffusion vs. Paleolithic Colonization." *American Journal of Physical Anthropology* 95 (1994).

S. R. Bokenkamp. *Early Daoist Scriptures.* Berkeley: University of California Press, 1997.

L. Boulnois. *The Silk Road.* New York: E. P. Dutton & Co., 1966.

B. Bower. "Indo-European Pursuits." *Science News* 147 (1995).

T. Cleary, tr. *Vitality, Energy, Spirit: A Taoist Sourcebook.* Boston: Shambhala, 1991.

A. K. Coomaraswamy and P. Schroeder, eds. *Yaksas: Essays in the Water Cosmology.* New York: Oxford University Press, 1993.

R. M. Davidson. *Indian Esoteric Buddhism: A Social History of the Tantric Movement.* New York: Columbia University Press, 2002.

M. Eliade. *The Forge and the Crucible: The Origins and Structure of Alchemy.* Chicago: University of Chicago Press, 1978.

G. F. Feng, tr. *Tao Te Ching.* New York: Vintage Books, 1972.

G. Feuerstein. *Tantra: Path of Ecstasy.* Boulder: Shambala, 1998.

E. J. Grube and E. Sims. *Between China and Iran: Paintings from Four Istanbul Albums.* London: University of London, 1985.

S. Hodge, tr. *The Illustrated Tao Te Ching.* Alresford: Godsfield Press, 2002.

E. J. Holmyard. *Alchemy.* Baltimore: Penguin Books, 1957.

R. Kieckhefer. *Magic in the Middle Ages.* Cambridge: Cambridge University Press, 1990.

L. Kohn, ed. *Taoist Meditation and Longevity Techniques.* Ann Arbor: Center for Chinese Studies at the University of Michigan, 1989.

S. H. Levitt. "Is There a Genetic Relationship Between Indo-European and Dravidian?" *The Journal of Indo-European Studies,* 26:1. 1998.

C. Luk. *Taoist Yoga: Alchemy & Immortality.* Newburyport: Weiser Books, 1999.

S. Mahdihassan. *Indian Alchemy: Rasayana.* New Delhi: Vikas Publishing House, 1979.

Z. R. W. M. von Martels, ed. *Alchemy Revisited.* New York: E. J. Brill, 1990.

J. Needham. "Contributions of China, India and the Hellenistic-Syrian world to Arabic alchemy," in Y. Maeyama and W. G. Saltzer, eds., *Prismata*. Wiesbaden: Franz Steiner Verlag, 1977.

B. Obrist. *The Book of the Secrets of Alchemy*. New York: E. J. Brill, 1990.

S. Klossowski de Rola. *Alchemy: The Secret Art*. New York: Thames and Hudson, 1973.

G. Samuel. *Tantric Revisionings: New Understandings of Tibetan Buddhism and Indian Religion*. Hants: Ashgate Publishing, 2005.

N. Wade. *Before the Dawn: Recovering the Lost History of Our Ancestors*. New York: Penguin Press, 2006.

Chapter 7

P. J. Awn. *Satan's Tragedy and Redemption: Iblis in Sufi Psychology*. Leiden: E. J. Brill, 1983.

W. Burkert. *Creation of the Sacred*. Cambridge: Harvard University Press, 1996.

———. *Greek Religion*. Cambridge: Harvard University Press, 1985.

R. Caldwell. *The Origin of the Gods*. Oxford: Oxford University Press, 1989.

N. Cohn. *Europe's Inner Demons*. London: Pimlico, 1993.

A. K. Coomaraswamy. *Dance of Shiva*. New Delhi: Sagar Publications, 1968.

A. Erwin. *Eros Toward the World: Paul Tillich and the Theology of the Erotic*. Eugene: Wipf & Stock Publishers, 2004.

G. Feuerstein, S. Kak, and D. Frawley. *In Search of the Cradle of Civilization*. Wheaton: Quest Books, 2001.

M. Hadas and M. Smith. *Heroes and Gods*. New York: Harper & Row, 1965.

J. E. Harrison. *Prolegomena to the Study of Greek Religion*. Cambridge: Cambridge University Press, 1922.

———. *Themis: A Study of the Social Origins of Greek Religion*. London: Merlin Press, 1963.

E. Pagels. *The Origin of Satan*. New York: Random House, 1995.

J. B. Russell. *Witchcraft in the Middle Ages*. Ithaca: Cornell University Press, 1972.

J. Schmitt. *Ghosts in the Middle Ages*. Chicago: University of Chicago Press, 1998.

R. A. Segal, ed. *The Myth and Ritual Theory: An Anthology*. Oxford: Blackwell Publishers, 1997.

A. Watts. *The Wisdom of Insecurity*. New York: Vintage Books, 1951.

Chapter 8

H. Bergson, K. A. Pearson, and J. Mullarkey, eds. *Henry Bergson: Key Writings*. New York: Continuum, 2002.

D. Buller. *Adapting Minds: Evolutionary Psychology and the Persistent Quest for Human Nature*. Cambridge: MIT Press, 2005.

F. Capra. *Hidden Connections*. New York: Doubleday, 2002.

P. Davies and J. Gribben. *The Matter Myth*. New York: Simon & Schuster, 1992.

M. Dine. *Supersymmetry and String Theory: Beyond the Standard Model.* New York: Cambridge University Press, 2007.

G. F. R. Ellis, ed. *The Far-Future Universe: Eschatology from a Cosmic Perspective.* Philadelphia: Templeton Foundation Press, 2002.

N. Eldredge. *The Pattern of Evolution.* New York: W. H. Freeman & Co., 1999.

B. Fuller. *Synergetics.* New York: Scribner, 1975.

J. Gribbin. *Deep Simplicity: Bringing Order to Chaos and Complexity.* New York: Random House, 2004.

J. Maddox. *What Remains to be Discovered.* New York: Touchstone, 1999.

L. Margulis and D. Sagan. *Acquiring Genomes: The Theory of the Origins of the Species.* New York: Perseus Books, 2002.

H Maturana and F. Verela. *The Tree of Knowledge.* Boston: Shambhala, 1987.

L. Mumford. *Technics and Civilization.* New York: Harcourt, 1934.

R. Nadeau and M. Kafatos. *The Non-Local Universe: The New Physics and Matters of the Mind.* Oxford: Oxford University Press, 1999.

S. F. Odenwald. *Patterns in the Void: Why Nothing is Important.* Boulder: Westview Press, 2002.

D. Orr. *The Nature of Design: Ecology, Culture, and Human Intention.* New York: Oxford University Press, 2002.

E. D. Peat. *From Certainty to Uncertainty: The Story of Science and Ideas in the Twentieth Century.* Washington: Joseph Henry Press, 2002.

I. Prigogine. *Is Future Given?.* New Jersey: World Scientific Publishing, 2003.

———. *The End of Certainty: Time, Chaos, and the New Laws of Nature.* New York: Free Press, 1997.

L. Randall. *Warped Passages: Unraveling the Mysteries of the Universe's Hidden Dimensions.* New York: Harper Collins Publishers, 2005.

H. Reichenbach, Maria Reichenbach and J. Freund, trs. *The Philosophy of Space and Time.* New York: Dover Publications, 1957.

R. Rosen. *Life Itself: A Comprehensive Inquiry into the Nature, Origin, and Fabrication of Life.* New York: Columbia University Press, 1991.

T. Rothman and G. Sudarshan. *Doubt and Certainty.* New York: Perseus Books, 1998.

E. F. Schumacher. *A Guide for the Perplexed.* London: Jonathan Cape, 1977.

R. Sheldrake. *The Presence of the Past: Morphic Resonance and the Habits of Nature.* New York: Crown, 1988.

D. W. Sherburne. *A Key to Whitehead's Process and Reality.* Chicago: University Of Chicago Press, 1981.

E. J. Steele, R. A. Lindley, and R. V. Blanden. *Lamarck's Signature: How Retrogenes are Changing Darwin's Natural Selection Paradigm.* New York: Perseus Books, 1998.

S. Strogatz. *Sync: The Emerging Science of Spontaneous Order.* New York: Hyperion, 2003.

R. Thom. *Structural Stability and Morphogenesis.* Boston: Addison Wesley, 1989.

V. N. Tsytovich, G. E. Morfill, V. E. Fortov, N. G. Gusein-Zade, B. A. Klumov, and S. V. Vladimirov. "From Plasma Crystals and Helical Structures Towards Inorganic Living Matter," *New Journal of Physics* 9 (2007).

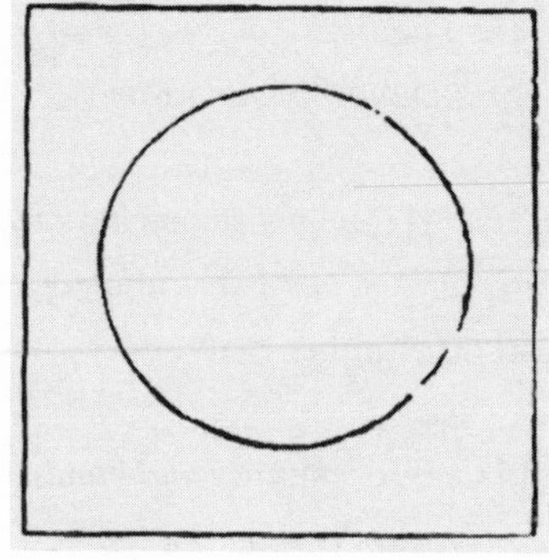

Pulverizing . . . Right Liberation

Even beyond the ultimate limits there extends
a passageway,
Whereby he comes back among the six realms
of existence;
Every Worldly affair is a Triumphant work,
And wherever he goes he finds his home air;
Like a gem he stands out even in the mud,
Like pure gold he shines even in the furnace;
Along the endless road he walks sufficient
unto himself,
In whatever associations he is found,
He moves leisurely unattached.

—Sifu Jitoku Ki

Index

N

About the Author

Dai Léon

A lifelong student of East-West philosophy and contemplation, Dai Léon has served for twenty-five years as a cultural emissary between modern and traditional, scientific and spiritual domains. He promotes the rich benefits of holistic and interdisciplinary studies and practices with respect to perennial wisdom traditions throughout the world.

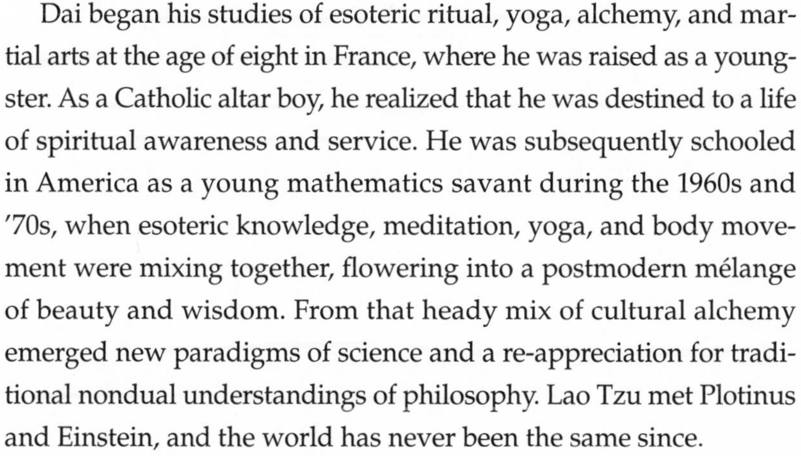

Dai began his studies of esoteric ritual, yoga, alchemy, and martial arts at the age of eight in France, where he was raised as a youngster. As a Catholic altar boy, he realized that he was destined to a life of spiritual awareness and service. He was subsequently schooled in America as a young mathematics savant during the 1960s and '70s, when esoteric knowledge, meditation, yoga, and body movement were mixing together, flowering into a postmodern mélange of beauty and wisdom. From that heady mix of cultural alchemy emerged new paradigms of science and a re-appreciation for traditional nondual understandings of philosophy. Lao Tzu met Plotinus and Einstein, and the world has never been the same since.

After studying the philosophies and spiritual ways of the great traditions at the University of Illinois, Dai was invited to directly study under the Venerable Gia-fu Feng, head of Stillpoint Foundation in Colorado. Adept Feng had been a co-founder of Esalen Institute at Big Sur, California, and was renowned as a founding father of the East-West movement, merging nondual traditions from China to Spain to America. In the spring of 1978, Sifu (indicating "monk" or "teacher") Dai Sealed Heart-Mind with Master Feng (a traditional method of Lineage or Dharma Transmission). Following this, it was requested that he teach the Tao that is none other than the One of Heraclitus, Plotinus, and Western wisdom through the ages.

Dai has authored several books and interactive media titles. He has served as a Director of multicultural, educational, interactive companies for twenty-five years. Since 1994 he has advised industry and governmental bodies on the socio-cultural impact of financial, wellness, and interactive technologies. Through many forms of media, with a particular love and focus upon that of the ecstatic body-mind, Dai has taught in a traditional yet postmodern way. His flowing mantra is *to empower, enlighten, and entertain.*